MENTAL HEALTH
IN
THE SCHOOLS

MENTAL HEALTH
IN
THE SCHOOLS

□

Thomas A. Ringness

The University of Wisconsin

RANDOM HOUSE □ NEW YORK

TO *John*

□

Preface

My interest in mental health in the school setting goes back to the time when I was a public-school teacher and later an administrator. This interest has continued through my subsequent experiences in teacher training, supervision of student-teachers, and training of school psychologists. At all these levels, I sensed strong interest among school personnel in mental-health issues. Questions were continually being raised about curricular practices, personality attributes of children, academic achievement, discipline, motivation, and other areas related to the affective (as opposed to the cognitive) aspects of development and learning. Many questions concerned pressures, stresses, conflicts, and anxieties of children, which fall as much into the preventive area of mental health as into the remedial area. Others involved what to do with children who showed obvious signs of maladjustment. Accordingly, I have attempted to bring together some of the material that has been found helpful to teachers in these problem areas.

This book is addressed primarily to teachers at all grade levels. Illustrations are drawn from both elementary- and secondary-school settings. The principles, of course, apply at all levels, and it is necessary only to adapt them to the age and grade of the child.

Much of the material included should also be of interest to school administrators, to guidance and counseling workers, and to others who work with teachers in their efforts to aid the child. The text presupposes a course in beginning psychology; the instructor can, however, build in necessary terminology and other omissions if students have not had such a course.

From the point of view of personality theory, I have tried to be eclectic in a "reasonable" way; there seems to be no one theory to which I can entirely subscribe, and I therefore follow the lead of Gordon Allport in daring to utilize what seems useful from various theories. I believe that reinforcement principles have perhaps the most value of any set of principles in helping the teacher to deal with classroom mental-health problems; however, I am not an out-and-out behaviorist and feel it necessary to give strong consideration to inner variables, as well as to those under environmental control. The prime emphasis is on things that the teacher can do to create a better mental-health climate for the learning process, but in choosing his approaches the teacher cannot neglect the individuality of the pupils with whom he is working.

Current psychological thought has placed considerable emphasis on the role of learning theory in helping us to understand development, especially the development of personality. Clinicians, furthermore, have had increasing success in applying principles of learning to the remediation of many kinds of mental-health problems. Because teachers are typically well grounded in learning principles, they should have relatively little difficulty in seeing the applications of these principles to mental-health problems.

A preventive point of view is stressed. Furthermore, emphasis is on classroom interaction, rather than upon individual work with the child. There is a deliberate attempt to show how typical teacher and school practices completely miss the point with many pupils. For example, teachers and schools tend to foster dependence and conformity, rather than responsibility and individuality; to place unnecessary stresses on pupils; to deal with motivation and discipline in ways precisely opposite to those that should be used; to fail to develop the "self-actualizing," creative, independent pupil; to short-change boys; and so on.

The content of this book is based upon research findings; however, illustrations are taken largely from the writer's own experiences. A few chapters are unique. For example, discussion of the influence of teachers as classroom leaders has rarely appeared in "mental health" books. I have never seen the relationships between school achievement and mental health spelled out in a book of this kind. Work with parents and with referral agencies is not usually touched upon. Guideposts to evaluating the school from a mental-health point of view are usually not presented.

Finally, although I have tried to include a reasonable survey of the literature in this field, the area is so broad that complete coverage of all aspects was nearly impossible. Accordingly, the reader is urged to pursue particular interests more deeply. In addition to the suggested readings given with each chapter, he may wish to consult such resources as *Psychological Abstracts* and *Education Index* for further information on any given topic.

Madison, 1967   THOMAS A. RINGNESS

□

Acknowledgments

The author is indebted to Dr. John Giebink, Director of the Psycho-Educational Clinic, University of Wisconsin, for his careful reading of the manuscript and for his valuable suggestions. He is also indebted to the publisher's advisers, Drs. James Bieri of the University of Texas and W. J. McGuire of Columbia University, for similar helpful services. Various writers have kindly given permission to quote and excerpt from their articles. Encouragement and suggestions from Philip D. Jones and Estelle Whelan of Random House were most welcome. A patient wife, who read for grammar and understanding, and several patient secretaries, student helpers, and members of several classes on whom ideas were evaluated should all be credited for whatever of value this book contains.

Contents

PREFACE   vii

ACKNOWLEDGMENTS   x

1 ▪ Mental Health and the Educational Enterprise   3
    The Extent of Present Concern   6
    The Nature of Mental Health   7
    Multiple Criteria for Defining Mental Health   11
    The Needs of Children   15
    School Roles in Mental Health   22
    REFERENCES   27
    SUGGESTIONS FOR FURTHER READING   28

2 ▪ The Teacher as a Person   29
    Studies of Personality Characteristics   32
    The Mental Health of the Teacher   38
    Improving Teacher Mental Health   50
    REFERENCES   60
    SUGGESTIONS FOR FURTHER READING   62

3 ▪ Teacher Leadership and Classroom Morale   63
    Leadership Style, Morale, and Achievement   67
    Teacher Personality Characteristics and
        Their Effects on Pupils   75

Interaction of Teacher and Pupil Personalities   77

Improving Group Morale   84

REFERENCES   91

SUGGESTIONS FOR FURTHER READING   92

4 ■ Classroom Control and Mental Health   94

Desirable School Discipline   96

Some Reasons Children Misbehave   101

Some Learning-Theory Principles   111

Methods of Classroom Control   114

REFERENCES   128

SUGGESTIONS FOR FURTHER READING   129

5 ■ School Achievement and Mental Health   131

Problems in Prediction of Achievement   132

Personality Factors and Academic Achievement   138

Dealing With Underachievement   145

REFERENCES   157

SUGGESTIONS FOR FURTHER READING   159

6 ■ Motivation and Emotions in the Classroom   160

Importance of Motivation to Behavior   160

The Relationships of Motives With Mental Health   163

The Nature of Motivation   168

Motivation and School Practices   174

The Role of Emotions   187

Emotions as Motivating Forces   189

Emotions in the Classroom   191

REFERENCES   193

SUGGESTIONS FOR FURTHER READING   194

7 ■ Frustration, Conflict, and Anxiety   195

Definitions and Effects   197

Results of Frustration, Conflict, and Anxiety   199

The Defense Mechanisms   207

Dealing with Frustration, Conflict, and Anxiety   213

A Further Report on Jimmy   219

REFERENCES   220

SUGGESTIONS FOR FURTHER READING   221

8 ■ Course Content and Teaching Method as Related
to Mental Health   222

Mental-Health Goals and School Subjects   223

Course Content and Mental Health 226

Extracurricular Activities and Mental Health 240

Learning Activities and Mental Health 240

REFERENCES 249

SUGGESTIONS FOR FURTHER READING 250

9 ▪ Common Sources of Stress in Schools 252

Common Curricular Stress-Producing Conditions 254

Stresses from Social-Class Influences 267

Peer-Group Influences 271

Sex-Role Stresses in the School 273

Academic Pressures on Pupils 275

Improving Ability to Handle Stress 277

REFERENCES 282

SUGGESTIONS FOR FURTHER READING 284

10 ▪ Studying Individual Children 285

Surface Impressions 287

Specific Characteristics 288

Criteria for the Study of the Child 291

An Illustrative Study of a Child by a Teacher 299

Interpretation of Data 311

REFERENCES 316

SUGGESTIONS FOR FURTHER READING 316

11 ▪ Working With Individual Pupils—Learning Principles 317

Assessment and Remediation 318

General Factors Required for Behavior Change 321

Reducing Inadequate Behavior 328

Introducing Adequate Behavior 333

REFERENCES 341

SUGGESTIONS FOR FURTHER READING 341

12 ▪ Working With Individual Pupils—The Self 342

The Self 343

The Self-Concept 344

Self-Concept and Mental Health 356

Changing Self-Attitudes 358

A Further Report on Mary 369

REFERENCES 370

SUGGESTIONS FOR FURTHER READING 371

13 ▪ Working With Parents 372
    Relationships Between the Child's Life
      at Home and at School 373
    Family Influences on the Child 375
    Home-School Conferences 382
    REFERENCES 402
    SUGGESTIONS FOR FURTHER READING 403

14 ▪ Recognizing and Referring Special Cases 404
    Needs for Referral 405
    Seeking Appropriate Kinds of Referral
      and Remediation 407
    Principles for Referral 413
    School Resources in Referral 425
    Community Resources for Referral 434
    Private Resources for Referral 435
    REFERENCES 436
    SUGGESTIONS FOR FURTHER READING 437

15 ▪ School and Community Mental-Health Programs 438
    School Mental-Health Programs 439
    Community Mental-Health Programs 451
    Limitations of School Mental-Health Practices 453
    Conclusion 456
    REFERENCES 457
    SUGGESTIONS FOR FURTHER READING 458

APPENDIX A ▪ Pupil-Teacher Rapport Scale 459

APPENDIX B ▪ Modification of Bales' Interaction
    Process Analysis for Teachers 463

APPENDIX C ▪ Dimensions of Teacher Leadership 465

APPENDIX D ▪ Outline for Child-Study Report 471

APPENDIX E ▪ Guiding Principles on Emotional and
    Mental Health 473

INDEX 483

☐

Tables

1 ▪ Sixteen PF Scores Having Significant Relationships
   With Motivational Orientations — 36

2 ▪ Rank Order for Choice of Teaching as a Profession
   by 63 Male and 37 Female Secondary Student-
   Teachers — 48

3 ▪ A Ranking Comparison of Teaching and 13 Other
   Vocations in Regard to Rewards Offered, as Viewed
   by 100 Secondary Student-Teachers — 49

4 ▪ Ratings on 5 Glueck Factors for Behavior
   and Location — 105

5 ▪ Eleventh-Grade Students' Opinion of Teacher
   Motivating Factors — 179

6 ▪ Eleventh-Grade Students' Opinion of Teacher
   Nonmotivating Factors — 180

7 ▪ Composite Total of Seniors' Opinion of Teacher
   Motivating Factors — 182

8 ▪ Composite Total of Seniors' Opinion of Teacher
   Nonmotivating Factors — 183

9 ▪ Ratings of 511 Teachers and 30 Mental
   Hygienists on Seriousness of Behavior Problems — 296

Figures

1 ▪ Is helpful supervision frequent?   56

2 ▪ Four patterns of child-to-child relationship   70

3 ▪ Four patterns of child-to-leader relationship   72

4 ▪ Relative achievement gains for different kinds of
teachers and different kinds of children   80

5 ▪ Schematic diagram of Dreikurs' concept
of deteriorating pupil behavior   110

6 ▪ Growth of emotion in a child   190

7 ▪ "My Family" by Karen   235

8 ▪ "Mommy, Dad, and Me" by Karen   236

9 ▪ "A Scene" by Bob   237

MENTAL HEALTH
IN
THE SCHOOLS

MENTAL HEALTH AND THE EDUCATIONAL ENTERPRISE

Health is complete physical and mental well-being, and not mere absence of disease.

WORLD HEALTH ORGANIZATION

In most classrooms there are certain children who pose problems with which the teacher cannot seem to cope. The usual teaching techniques do not suffice. The teacher's own innovations do not seem to help much either.

For example, most teachers have met children who behave in the following ways:

"Peter scores in the superior range on our intelligence test, but does very mediocre work in the classroom."

"Jan achieves well enough academically, but she seems unable to make friends and is left out of social doings. She looks unhappy most of the time."

"George gets into more fights than most of the other fourth-grade boys, and the fights seem more bitter. He is touchy and defensive, as a rule."

"Jeannie seems overmotivated. She works harder and longer than the others and wants her assignments to be done just perfectly. Although she is far from the brightest child in the room, she worries greatly if she fails to keep an A average."

"Bernie is shy and self-conscious. He cannot bring himself to recite in classes. Sometimes he hides his face in his arms when called upon to recite."

3

"Lou can usually be depended upon to be absent on test days. Once I called her mother and was told that Lou was actively sick to her stomach and had a severe headache."

Other children show a variety of unadaptive behaviors. Some are neurotic, some are delinquent, some have psychosomatic illnesses, and a few are psychotic. Almost the entire range of emotional disorders can be found in the pupil population of most school systems.

When confronted with behavior that does not seem "normal" and does not respond to familiar techniques, teachers tend to suspect the mental health of the child. This problem raises questions of how the teacher should proceed. Sometimes referrals are made to specialists. In other cases the teacher may simply become discouraged and try to shrug off the problem. Yet teachers can be helpful in many mental-health problems.

Concern for children like those described will form part of the subject matter of this book, for such children are not only unsuccessful and unhappy but also cause difficulties in the lives of others. Almost always they make the teaching situation difficult for the teacher and they interfere with the lives of their peers.

It has been suggested, however, that teachers may be *too* concerned with the pupil who has problems (Abramovitz and Burnham, 1959), that is, in psychopathology. There is another side to the coin. Most children function at least adequately, and many do much better in particular areas. For example, there are children like the following, who are a source of great enjoyment for most teachers:

"Mary is always thoughtful of others. When it became apparent that the school party would cost each child's family at least one dollar, Mary wondered how we might handle it so those from poor families might attend, and yet not feel that they needed charity from others."

"Averell is able to work for hours on problems which challenge him. Furthermore, he does not simply follow the leads of others. The experiment he developed in analyzing the pollution of the air from various types of fuel oils would have done credit to a graduate chemist."

"Alice is a leader from away back. She is the one they look to for suggestions on group projects. She manages to help everyone find a task he can do well, and the projects always seem to come out well. Everyone is pleased, and no one ever seems jealous of Alice, or to resent her directions.''

"Vaughn is quiet, but seems happy enough. He is independent and does his own thinking. This does not mean that he is unpopular or that he rejects others. He simply seems to direct his own life, for the most part.''

"Terry is making a great comeback from her long hospitalization. In spite of all the pain and her other problems, she grits her teeth and nothing gets her down. She's optimistic and won't let others make her dependent upon them. She doesn't trade on having been ill.''

Schools need to find ways to help such children remain adequate. It is necessary to find ways to run the schools so that children will not be harmed.

Finally, among the goals of workers in the mental-health professions (psychiatrists, clinical psychologists, psychiatric social workers, and others) are to learn how to prevent problems from occurring and to deal constructively with difficulties that are not yet severe enough to be characterized as poor "mental health.'' Many feel that the greatest strides in the mental-health field will be made in prevention areas, rather than in trying to remedy real emotional disturbances that have already developed. We shall therefore place considerable emphasis on helping pupils who are already in reasonable mental health to remain so and to attain even better states.

Our concepts will be aimed at application to *all* pupils rather than only to those who need special attention. This idea, although not new, has not always been well understood.

Nor is interest in mental health new to teachers and those who administer the schools, develop the curricula, or otherwise help to direct the academic lives of pupils. Good teachers have "always'' had concern for the emotions of their pupils and for their characters, attitudes, and values. They have tried to understand pupils' problems and to be friendly counselors to their charges. They have tried to help boys and girls understand themselves and their environments and to motivate them to make the most of their abilities. Understanding in such areas has progressed because of the efforts of teachers, as well as those of professional mental-health workers. There are literally hundreds of books and articles discussing personality and mental health that deal quite directly with children and the schools.

We shall attempt to bring together some of the recent findings, beliefs, and practices described in such publications, with as direct applications to school practice as possible.

The Extent of Present Concern

The National Association for Mental Health has provided figures on incidence of poor mental health in recent years. For example, during World War II, about 900,000 men between the ages of eighteen and thirty-seven were rejected for service in the armed forces for reasons related to mental health. Of those inducted, about 460,000 were later discharged for mental illness and another 250,000 for personality disturbances, mental deficiency, and epilepsy (National Association for Mental Health, 1952).

About one person in every ten, some 19 million people in all, is said to have some form of mental or emotional illness that requires psychiatric treatment. In 1966 about 770,000 people were admitted to mental hospitals and psychiatric services in general hospitals. At a conservative estimate, 300,000 children under the age of eighteen are served in psychiatric clinics each year for relatively less severe mental disorders, but there are an estimated additional 500,000 children who might be classified as showing psychotic or borderline behavior (National Association for Mental Health, 1966).

Physical diseases may have mental-health correlates. Some estimates suggest that perhaps 50 per cent of all patients seen by general practitioners have problems related to mental health (for example, psychosomatic illnesses). If we add to these figures those in which poor mental health has contributed to alcoholism, narcotics addiction, suicide, criminal behavior, divorces, and job failure, mental-health problems are seen to be staggering.

Such statistics are based only on serious problems. But what about such related problems as poor school achievement, school dropouts, delinquency, disciplinary problems, social isolation, or withdrawal? Problems of learning and social behavior are manifold. In addition to attempting to cope with such problems, schools are concerned with increasing pressures on children (and teachers) that may intensify the difficulties. For example, there is growing pressure on children to achieve college education, with concomitant pressures for high marks and attainment on college-entrance examinations. Homework has been increasing in amount, a matter of concern to many. There seems to be an increasing demand for special classrooms for children who, perhaps because of such pressures, do not seem to fit into regular classrooms. We shall discuss many areas of stress throughout this book.

The Nature of Mental Health

PROBLEMS IN DEFINING MENTAL HEALTH

We are unfortunately going to disappoint those who like precise definitions, for the concept of "mental health" is somewhat controversial, as we shall see. Misconceptions concerning the nature of mental health exist. In addition, there are differences of opinions among authorities. The "definition" to which we shall come thus represents a position, rather than a concept common to all who discuss the kinds of behavior characteristic of mental health. Ours is, however, a relatively widely accepted position.

If there are problems with the term "mental health," why not utilize terminology less conducive to controversy? One reason is that at the moment there seem to be no such terms. Another reason is that the term "mental health" has had wide historical usage and therefore provides a degree of meaning understood by many. Furthermore, such groups as the National Association for Mental Health and its subsidiaries and such governmental agencies as the National Institute of Mental Health (part of the U.S. Department of Health, Education and Welfare) have lent prestige to the term.

We shall begin by discussing what mental health *is not*. Having cleared away some of the misconceptions that many of us hold, we can hopefully come to a clearer understanding of what is meant by "mental health."

One is not mentally healthy or mentally ill. Mental health is not the opposite of mental illness. The latter term refers to a number of syndromes that have been found in many people and have been widely studied and treated. Among the mental illnesses are schizophrenia, paranoia, manic-depressive psychoses, and others. These are serious problems, and, when one is afflicted with such an illness, his ability to function adequately is usually greatly impaired.

But just as one may be tired, have minor aches and pains, or perhaps not be up to par in strength or endurance without considering himself ill, so may one fail to possess optimal mental health yet not be considered mentally ill. The absence of (serious) mental illness does not automatically imply that one is mentally healthy, for, as with physical health, many degrees of health may exist.

In many ways mental health is not analogous to physical health. Both terms describe the functioning of the individual, but in physical disease we are able to discover underlying tissue pathology. We can assess quite objectively muscular strength, pulse rate, and other physical characteristics. We are usually able to distinguish causes of poor physical health and to prescribe cures. Ordinarily it is quite clear whether a person is sick or well and, if well, to what extent he is in the best possible trim. There are commonly accepted criteria for determining these facts, and the symptoms of particular illnesses are quite similar from patient to patient. Definite disease entities exist.

With mental health and illness we are not on such firm ground. Aside from a few organically caused mental or emotional disturbances like those from brain injury, senility, drug poisoning, and the like, we cannot associate tissue pathology with poor mental health. Most of the symptoms of poor mental health or mental illness are simply problem behavior—behavior that is unadaptive and seriously interferes with the effective functioning of the patient. Indeed, Thomas Szasz (1960) suggests that we should really be talking about "problems in living" rather than about "mental health."

"Symptoms" vary from person to person in accordance with

individual personalities. What are called "mental illnesses" are in most cases simply descriptions of what the patient does—he hallucinates, he has ungrounded suspicions, he retreats from contact with others—rather than descriptions of basic pathological processes comparable to those of physical medicine. Terms for mental illness thus do not refer to *causes* of problem behavior, but rather to *constellations* of problem behaviors.

It is difficult to be certain when a person is mentally healthy or mentally ill, and court cases frequently bring contradictory expert evidence to bear. It is difficult to know when someone who has been diagnosed as mentally ill has been cured. Furthermore, even agreement that someone is mentally ill implies nothing about the reasons for the specific illness or about its clear-cut treatment.

Mental health is not definable by universal norms. Szasz states that illness implies deviation from some clearly defined norm.

. . . in the case of physical illness, the norm is the structural and functional integrity of the human body. Although the desirability of physical health, as such, is an ethical value, what health *is* can be stated in anatomical and physiological terms. What is the norm deviation from which is regarded mental illness? This question cannot be easily answered. But whatever this norm might be, we can be certain of only one thing: namely, that it is a norm that must be stated in terms of *psycho-social, ethical,* and *legal* concepts. (Szasz, 1960, p. 114)

State of Mind, a journal of the CIBA Pharmaceutical Company, offers an illustration of Szasz's point:

IS THIS MAN MAD?*

Imagine that the individual described in the following brief case history came to you for treatment. How would you diagnose his ailment and what therapy would you recommend? When you've come to a decision, check it against the "diagnosis" on the next page.

All through childhood, K. was extremely meditative, usually preferred to be alone. He often had mysterious dreams and fits, during which he sometimes fainted. In late puberty, K. experienced

* SOURCE: CIBA, *State of Mind* (January 1957).

elaborate auditory and visual hallucinations, uttered incoherent words, and had recurrent spells of sudden coma. He was frequently found running wildly through the countryside or eating the bark of trees and was known to throw himself with abandon into fire and water. On many occasions he wounded himself with knives or other weapons. K. believed he could "talk to spirits" and "chase ghosts." He was certain of his power over all sorts of supernatural forces.

Made up your mind? Read on, please.

The Actual Diagnosis. Believe it or not, K. was not found insane, nor was he committed to the nearest institution for the mentally ill. Instead, in due course, he became one of the leading and most respected members of his community. . . .

K., we should have told you, was a member of a primitive tribe of fishermen and reindeer herders that inhabits the arctic wilderness of Eastern Siberia. In this far-off culture the same kind of behavior that we regard as symptomatic of mental illness is considered evidence of an individual's fitness for an important social position—that of medicine man or shaman.

Quite clearly the cultural norms that define good or poor mental health vary from society to society. Let us pursue this point a bit further. H. J. Wegrocki mentions the "Dobuans, who exhibit an 'unnatural degree' of fear and suspicion; the Polynesians, who regard their chief as tabu to touch, allegedly because of a prevalent *'défense de toucher'* neurosis; the Plains Indians with their religiously colored visual and auditory hallucinations; the Yogis with their trance states"; and others (1964, p. 4). This sort of finding suggests that lists of behavioral symptoms alone are of little value in helping us to determine a state of mental health.

What can one say about the mental health of an entire society if it accepts coma, hallucinations, or other breaks with reality as desirable in its leaders? Such has been the case in regard to Joan of Arc, for example. Wegrocki suggests that one must examine the causes of such behavior in order to determine whether or not it is healthy.

Common terms may not be helpful. The concept of "normality" does not help us much in defining mental health, for it implies that what is common to the majority of a population is what is desirable. Yet aside from problems posed by the fact that a whole society may be aggressive, hostile, or fearful, there is also the question of who more closely emulates the ideals of a society than does the majority. We use the terms "subnormal" or "abnormal" to denote inadequate behavior, but rarely do we call a person "supernormal" even though "supernormality" might be most desirable.

Some thinkers have argued that the individual's subjective judgment might be a way of defining mental health. If he were in a state of "happiness" or "well-being" for example, he might be considered mentally healthy. Yet his environment must also be considered. People within the shelter of a mental hospital might feel quite happy but might be viewed by others as out of contact with reality or as exhibiting aberrant behavior. Conversely, it would not be possible to have a sense of well-being in a concentration camp, although many inmates of such camps have behaved in extremely healthy ways.

It is clear that mental health is not a simple, easily defined state. For this reason, many have suggested that multiple criteria must be employed in its definition.

Multiple Criteria for Defining Mental Health

Among those who suggest multiple criteria for defining (or rather, *characterizing*) mental health are Marie Jahoda, Barbara Biber, M. Brewster Smith, and Gordon W. Allport.

Jahoda (1958) has said that aspects of attitudes toward self, growth and development, self-actualization, integration of personality, autonomy, perception of reality, and mastery of the environment must be considered in judging whether a person is mentally healthy or not.[1]

Biber (1961) argues that goals for a healthy personality include positive feelings toward the self, realistic perception of self and others, relatedness to people, relatedness to environ-

---

[1] The term "self-actualization" will be discussed later in this chapter. "Personality integration" refers to adequate interrelationships among the various aspects of the personality. "Autonomy" refers to the self-determining qualities to be expected of the healthy mature individual.

ment, independence, curiosity and creativity, and recovery and coping strength in the face of trauma, frustration, and crisis.

Allport (1961) suggests that underlying life philosophy, a warm and deep relation to self and others, and compassionate regard for all living things are important aspects of the healthy personality.

Smith (1959) considers that social values and the nature of the culture are determining factors. The National Association for Mental Health describes some of the characteristics of people with good mental health: comfortable feelings about one's self, feeling "right" about other people, and being able to meet the demands of life.

On the basis of these and other comments, we offer the following definition of "mental health" for our purposes: *Mental health consists of being able to function successfully in terms of one's own goals, abilities, and opportunities within the context of one's social and physical environment.*

The mentally healthy person

1. is self-acceptant and has reasonably high self-esteem, feels generally adequate, but recognizes his own shortcomings and seeks to improve;
2. has a realistic evaluation of himself and sets his aspirations accordingly;
3. accepts responsibility for managing his own life and making his own decisions and does not vacillate or lean upon others;
4. is well-balanced, flexible, and consistent in his attitudes, goals, and ideals;
5. can withstand stress, tolerate some anxiety, and overcome the effects of trauma and frustration;
6. can relate well to others and has the good of society at heart;
7. seeks independence, autonomy, and self-direction and is neither completely conforming nor completely selfish;
8. attempts to solve his problems, rather than to escape them or to employ defense mechanisms excessively.

These criteria are quite obviously based on value judgments, and such judgments must be made in deciding whether or not a person is in good mental health. But note that the criteria seem to characterize the kind of person usually described in our society as mature, successful, and a good model for others. They describe the kind of person most of us would like to be.[2]

By these criteria, few people would be considered to have optimum mental health. (Indeed, K. A. Menninger [1965] suggests that at some time or another *all* of us have been mentally unhealthy.) But it must be recognized that the human personality is dynamic and forever changing and developing. The *direction* of change may be as important as is the actual state of being, and, although a person may not quite succeed in living up to all criteria specified, he may be progressing in a healthy direction.

Ernest Havemann (1960) believes that it is natural for us all to live with anxieties, to face problems, to feel frustration, and to endure conflict. He suggests that we need to learn to live with these realities and not to seek complete freedom from tensions. This idea is in full accord with our concept of mental health, for, although tensions may continue to exist, the healthy person will deal with them in healthy ways. He will attempt to improve not only himself but also social conditions that contribute to such tensions.

Allport (1955), Carl Rogers (1958), and others have fostered the concept of *becoming*, which suggests that it is the *progress* of the individual toward realizing his potentials, rather than the *actuality* of his achievement, that is important. No man may ever reach his ideal state, for his ideals grow with his progress toward them; he is continually discovering new potentials within himself and his environment that stimulate him to constant endeavor. The healthy personality is therefore involved in processes of self-improvement and expansion of horizons, as opposed to the constriction or regression associated with poor mental health. This point is especially important for the development of personalities of school children, for the school experience greatly influences the growth and development of all aspects of personality.

2 For the sake of variety, although at some sacrifice in precision, we shall employ the terms "emotional health" and "adjustment" (and "maladjustment") in this book; the reader will understand that the extended definition and criteria above are meant; they will be treated as synonymous with the term "mental health."

Perhaps the following illustrations will add further point to this discussion.

LEST WE JUDGE TOO HASTILY *

The difficulties in defining mental health and predicting future development can be seen from the following sketches. Keep in mind Menninger's argument that all of us may at some time have been in poor mental health. Also remember that poor mental health may not prevent adequate functioning. Finally, keep clearly in mind that "being different" or a nonconformist does not mean that one is in poor mental health.

> *Case 1.* Girl, age sixteen, orphaned, willed to custody of a grandmother by mother, who was separated from alcoholic husband, now deceased. Mother rejected the homely child, who has been proven to lie and to steal sweets. Swallowed penny to attract attention at five. Father was fond of child. Child lived in fantasy as the mistress of father's household for years. Four young uncles and aunts in household cannot be managed by the grandmother, who is widowed. Young uncle drinks; has left home without telling the grandmother his destination. Aunt, emotional over love affair, locks self in room. Grandmother resolves to be more strict with granddaughter since she fears she has failed with own children. Dresses granddaughter oddly. Refused to let her have playmates, put her in braces to keep back straight, did not send her to grade school. Aunt on paternal side of family crippled; uncle asthmatic.
>
> *Case 2.* Boy, senior year secondary school, has obtained certificate from physician stating that nervous breakdown makes it necessary for him to leave school for six months. Boy not a good all-around student; has no friends—teachers find him a problem—spoke late—father ashamed of son's lack of athletic ability—poor adjustment to school. Boy has odd mannerisms, makes up own religion, chants hymns to himself—parents regard him as "different."
>
> *Case 3.* Boy, age 6; head large at birth. Thought to have brain fever. Three siblings died before his birth. Mother does

---

* SOURCE: A. B. Abramovitz has drawn the case material from V. Goertzel and M. Goertzel, *Cradles of Eminence.* Boston: Little, Brown, 1962.

not agree with relatives and neighbors that child is probably abnormal. Child sent to school—diagnosed as mentally ill by teacher. Mother is angry—withdraws child from school, says she will teach him herself. (Abramovitz, 1965)

Case 1 is identified as Eleanor Roosevelt, Case 2 as Albert Einstein, and Case 3 as Thomas Edison! The importance of giving cautious consideration to human complexity is emphatically implied.

The Needs of Children

If children are to realize the mental-health goals we have suggested, attention must be given to their individual and collective needs. As school personnel, we must be reasonably clear about what children need if we are seriously to contribute to adequate personality development.

Almost any book on the psychology of personality, adjustment, or related topics provides one with an idea of the needs people strive to satisfy.[3]

Discussions range from rather general but encompassing statements like that of A. Combs and D. Snygg (1959), who believe that one strives to maintain or enhance his self and concept of self, through H. A. Murray's earlier list of twenty-two needs (1938), to lists of 100 needs or more. The number of needs listed seems to be guided primarily by the degree of magnification or detail one wishes to employ in describing human motivation.

Most statements of needs suggest that there are basic needs that must be satisfied in order for a person to exist as a reasonably happy, well-functioning individual and that there are also additional needs for self-expression, continued growth and development, and the use of one's talents and abilities. These two groups of needs may be identified as "maintenance-directed" and "growth-directed."

---

[3] The concept of "needs" is also a controversial one. Some psychologists argue that there are no needs as such, other than biological drives, and that what are called "needs" are really learned motives. For our purposes, we shall merely be concerned with what pupils strive for. "Needs" will be considered essentially as motives.

MAINTENANCE-DIRECTED NEEDS

Abraham Maslow (1954), of whom we shall say more in a later chapter on motivation, divides the maintenance-directed needs into physiological needs (or drives), safety needs, needs for belonging and affection, and esteem or status needs. This breakdown is useful for our discussion.

PHYSIOLOGICAL NEEDS. ■ Among the physiological needs or drives are those for food, oxygen, water, rest, and elimination, as well as others less directly concerned with the preservation of life like the desire for exercise and activity and the sexual urge. The biological drives are built in or instinctual, and unless they are satisfied the individual cannot function well. He may even fail to survive. By and large these needs seem basic to most, if not all, others. They do not usually diminish unless satisfied, and, although they are capable of modification, they cannot be ignored.

In our society and in our schools, the physiological needs ordinarily offer few problems, in contrast to other areas of the globe where food and water are insufficient, where privation is frequent, and where much human striving is devoted to obtaining the barest essentials for survival (although the War on Poverty has documented the fact that even in this country there are citizens who are physically deprived).

At school teachers see expression of the biological drives at times, as when a child becomes restless in class and seeks an excuse for physical activity, when a class becomes less attentive before lunch hour, or when a child is irritable because of fatigue. Particularly for smaller children, the school program is modified to include recesses, milk breaks, relaxation mats, and exercises. At the same time, many people would argue that American youth lacks the physical fitness and endurance found in certain other nations, because such health requirements as exercise, balanced diet, and abstinence from alcohol and to-bacco are not adequately met. Except for physically ill children or those from deprived areas, however, it is usually not difficult for children to satisfy biological needs, and they usually present few problems to schools.

SAFETY NEEDS. ▪ The safety needs involve preserving one-self in a dangerous environment. The presence of fear and the consequent desire for its removal, the avoidance of pain, and the wish for stability and a predictable or controlled environment are examples.

Safety needs are more noticeable than are the physiological needs. For example, "school phobia" may be basically the child's anxiety at leaving a comforting, overprotective home for the more fearsome environment of the teacher and peers; this fear, it should be remarked, may be a reflection of the mother's emotions at the thought of the child's leaving her for the broader school environment and may well be taught (quite unconsciously) to the child. Some children have physical fear of other children, which causes them to cling to the teacher and to withdraw from peers on the playground. Fear of a teacher or of gym activities can lead to such emotional reactions as nausea and even to psychosomatic illness.

There are real concerns for the child's safety built into the school program. Small children are given lessons in what to do in case of fires. Older children are taught to protect themselves in football, tumbling, and swimming. Warnings are given about experiments in chemistry class. Buildings are carefully constructed and supervised. On the whole, the safety needs are well met. There is little actual threat to safety in the school. Few children need fear pain or damage, and when they do it is necessary to investigate carefully to see whether or not the fear is based in reality.

AFFECTIONAL NEEDS. ▪ Needs for belonging and affection include those for security, for giving and receiving of friendship and affection, and for relationships with others in general. Rudolph Dreikurs (1957) considers these needs basic to human nature and shows, as we shall later see, that many of the behavior problems of children can be traced back to a feeling of not belonging.

The affectional needs are frequently less well met than are the physiological or safety needs. Some children suffer throughout their school careers because they are unable to attain feelings of belonging at school (or, for that matter, at home). Children from minority groups suffer in this way, as may those with inferior abilities, those from unaccepted social classes, or those with stigmas of other kinds. Some children, feeling lack of affection at home, cling desperately to the teacher or to peers. Older children may form cliques or join gangs in order to satisfy needs for belonging and friendship that they cannot otherwise fulfill. Those who feel rejected may withdraw completely or act in hostile ways toward others.

STATUS NEEDS. ■ Needs for status and self-esteem include needs to achieve, to master one's environment, to feel adequate, to accept oneself, to be independent and free, and to be recognized as capable and be appreciated by others.

The needs for esteem vitally concern the school, for there are myriad opportunities in school for their satisfaction or frustration. School is a place where self-esteem, achievement, status, reputation, and recognition are involved in almost every activity. Our society is competitive, and this attitude carries over into the schools. Unfortunately, some children are placed where they find it difficult to compete satisfactorily and thus fail to gain necessary need satisfaction through no fault of their own. If children lack necessary backgrounds, school assignments may be too difficult. For others, parental pressure to achieve may result in unrealistic aspirations. Marking systems may be too rigid, or grouping of pupils may be poorly done. The talents of some children may not be appreciated because those particular talents may not be in current vogue. The peer norms of athletic ability, "personality," and good looks almost automatically lead to certain degrees of frustration among many children.

Some children manage to remain in the favored 10 per cent in almost any school situation, and a halo of favorable evaluations surrounds them. Others are tagged as unsuccessful early in their school lives, and their reputations make it difficult for them to attain acceptance and self-esteem. Resulting feelings of inferiority, guilt, rejection, and anxiety contribute to sullenness, hostility, truancy, vandalism, and continued poor achievement. A vicious circle of lack of success, devaluation by others, and devaluation of self is thus perpetuated.

EFFECTS OF NOT SATISFYING NEEDS. ■ Lack of fulfillment of the maintenance-directed needs may lead to several kinds of behavior. The child may strive adaptively for a time, hoping to attain need satisfaction. Such behavior is healthy. It is also healthy to withstand a certain amount of deprivation or stress, but, when the tolerance threshold for stress is exceeded, the child may resort to unadaptive behavior. He may withdraw from the situation to seek his satisfactions elsewhere, or he may act in a hostile or defensive manner. He may seek to win the trappings of achievement by cheating or pretending achievement, denying inadequacy, or trying to win sympathy. When deprivation is extreme, he may become so seriously maladjusted that he cannot function in the typical school setting. If not given special attention, he may drop out of school or force others to change his environment.

GROWTH-DIRECTED NEEDS

Whether one thinks in terms of Combs and Snygg's concept of "enhancement of the self," Maslow's "self-actualization," Allport's "becoming," or some other formulation, he is saying that the healthiest person is one who continues to gain new competence and insight, who has developed the necessary freedoms and autonomy of self, and who has a value system that causes him to function in keeping with his potential.

We shall discuss here the concept of self-actualization. The term implies the need to live up to one's potentials, to become what one has in him to become, and to utilize one's energies to live life as fully as possible. Such people are self-dependent, and their satisfactions in living come from the realization of goals they set for themselves. There may even be a sort of compelling aura to their efforts, as when an artist feels that he *has* to paint or a composer gives up creature comforts to express himself in his music or a Curie is motivated to work with radium despite the financial cost, physical hardship, and danger.

In one study Maslow (1954) and others attempted to characterize as precisely as possible people whom they considered to be self-actualizing. In addition to studying certain college students, they examined public and historical figures, among whom were Eleanor Roosevelt, Spinoza, and Einstein.

Good mental health seems a prerequisite for self-actualization. That is, one cannot drink deeply of life if he is continually at the mercy of neuroses, self-doubt, insecurity, fear, anxiety, or guilt. But this statement does not mean that self-actualizing people never doubt themselves or feel inadequate; rather they do not permit such feelings to master them.

In brief summary (and one should read Maslow's work in the original for its full flavor), here is the description of self-actualizing people.

They had clear perception and acceptance of reality and ability to recognize their own shortcomings and those of others. They had desire to improve and eliminate the discrepancies between what is and what ought to be. They were spontaneous, natural, and without artificiality. They were able to center their attention upon problems outside themselves, having a sense of mission or task in life upon which most of their energies were expended. They had the ability to remain detached, reserved, calm, and dignified and possessed independence from the environment.[4] They found satisfactions within themselves rather than in dependence upon others. They experienced sometimes a sense of ecstasy, wonder, and awe, of limitless horizons opening up, a deeper appreciation of life's variety, and even somewhat mystical feelings. They had identification with human beings in general, sympathy and affection, and a desire to help the human race. They had deep and profound interpersonal relationships but fewer close relationships. In addition, they possessed democratic character structure; tendencies to concentrate upon ends rather than means; unhostile, philosophic humor; and creativity. They resisted conformity, conforming only for convenience or as a gesture to social living, and they were willing to be nonconforming when they felt it necessary or desirable.

Self-actualizing people

4 Some writers question the emphasis on independence from the environment. A. W. Staats and C. K. Staats (1963) argue that this approach emphasizes the genetic nature of man and the importance of actualizing this nature, thus tending to deny the importance of environmental variables in shaping behavior. But the concept of self-actualization does not deny environmental influence so much as it stresses the interactional nature of man's basic endowment and the environment; environmental influence helps to determine the degree of one's self-reliance and independence that can presumably be reinforced by others. It should also be noted that one's values are at least partially a product of learning from others at some stage of development, so that even self-actualizing people are not entirely independent but are essentially more self-directed than others.

Maslow and his associates did not find that self-actualizing people lack faults. He shows that they have their vanities, biases, tempers, and impatience. They are not free from anxiety, guilt, or conflict, and they sometimes antagonize others by their independence. But, in spite of their faults, they have found ways to release their energies productively and, not only to live life fully, but also to offer much to society. (This last statement furnishes additional justification for fostering self-actualization in people. For not only are such people in better mental health and living more satisfactorily from a personal perspective, but they also tend to help society to improve. Their love of humanity for the most part transcends personal gain. And, needless to say, society does need improvement, although there is much good to be preserved.)

The schools can do much to help people develop toward self-actualization. We can emphasize independent thinking, creativity, and the development of a personal sense of values. We can help pupils develop life philosophies that will stimulate them to try to solve social problems and help the human race. We can teach divergent thinking and can point out problems for them to tackle. We can de-emphasize blind conformity.

Yet schools frequently do little to foster self-actualization. Although there certainly are exceptions, on the whole we tend to emphasize conformity and dependence upon teachers', parents', and peer-group values; in many ways we interfere with the ability of the child to develop his individual approach to life. Perhaps the reason is that the schools, as instruments of society, tend to accept the value of preserving society over that of improving society. Furthermore, schools tend to inculcate the demands of society, doing less to help the individual pupil realize his own values. Not that strides are not being made in trying to make use of individual differences or that schools are not at all concerned with creativity and social problems; but traditional classroom techniques, marking systems, methods of grouping, and other curricular factors are geared much more toward conformity, regimentation, and group needs than toward encouraging pupil thought and activity. We shall pursue this topic further in a later chapter.

School Roles in Mental Health

A number of writers (Gray, 1963; Shaffer & Lazarus, 1952) have noted recent trends in the mental-health professions that suggest that school personnel do have professional roles in pupil mental health. Based upon the probability that there will never be enough mental-health specialists to handle the growing numbers of people needing diagnostic or therapeutic services, emphasis is being placed on attempts to prevent poor mental health by improving social conditions and by teaching people to deal more competently with their own problems. In these preventive and positive functions the schools have an important place. Furthermore, with the consultant help of specialists, schools are able to exercise screening and remedial functions. School personnel are increasingly welcome in the mental-health area.

SCHOOL GOALS AND MENTAL HEALTH

N. C. Kearney's statements (1957) of elementary-school objectives include fostering individual social and emotional development, fostering ethical behavior standards and values, fostering improved social relations and understanding of the physical and social world, and developing the child's ability to communicate. W. French's outline (1953) of general educational objectives in the secondary school includes self-realization, betterment of human relationships, and civic responsibility, among others. These lists are evidence of the concern for positive mental-health values among the associations of elementary- and secondary-school principals, who developed these objectives in conjunction with others.

In implementing mental-health goals, there are specific areas of concern. For example, the following roles are frequently accepted by schools, even where there are no formal mental-health programs:[5]

---

[5] W. Allinsmith and G. W. Goethals (1962) have written a monograph in which the roles of the schools in mental health are discussed and have included concepts similar to those listed here. Their discussion hinges on the concept of

1. elimination of unwholesome conditions over which the school has control;
2. helping pupils to become concerned with the betterment of society;
3. early recognition of mental-health problems among pupils (and staff) and referral to appropriate school specialists or agencies in the community for diagnosis and therapy when indicated;
4. coordination of the school's child-study and teaching efforts with those of the parents and appropriate community agencies;
5. remedial training, in either regular or special classrooms, for pupils who need special help;
6. study of the conditions of mental health prevailing in the schools and adoption of appropriate changes in curricula, administrative provisions, and other measures;
7. helping the school personnel to learn more about child development, learning, personality, and adjustment and to gain further insight into the needs of children and into their own personalities.

ADVANTAGES ENJOYED BY THE SCHOOL

The school has an immense potential mental-health influence for a number of reasons. To begin with, during school hours we assume many of the duties and responsibilities toward the child that the parents carry during nonschool hours. For any given child this care is exercised several hours per day for from 180 to 190 days a year; the care and training offered by the school is exceeded only by that provided by the home and is far beyond that offered by almost any other community agency.

During the time the child is under school control, he can be studied, both longitudinally and cross-sectionally; that is, comparisons can be made with his previous characteristics as shown by test scores, anecdotal records, and other data, and such data can also be compared with norms and with those of his peers.

---

prevention, which is used in a technical sense. There is "primary" prevention, which refers to prevention of occurrence of poor mental health; "secondary" prevention, which is essentially rehabilitation of those in poor mental health; and "tertiary" prevention, which is the prevention of further disability in cases where damage has occurred that cannot be completely repaired. In this sense, the roles we have listed for the schools could all be considered preventive. This monograph is recommended to the reader for amplification of what we have said about school roles.

Properly kept (and utilized) school records can provide hypotheses to explain the child's behavior and bases for prognosis far more accurately than can most other data obtainable on a child. Parents, for example, have only limited opportunities for comparing their child with others; specialists to whom a deviant child may be referred must lean on his current behavior for diagnosis unless they can turn to the schools for information concerning his earlier characteristics. (There is danger, however, that study of the child can result in his being permanently labeled in the minds of teachers or in certain value judgments' being placed upon him. The "self-fulfilling prophecy" may then cause teachers to "see" the child as they expect to see him, basing their perceptions on previous records. A common offense of this kind is expectation of achievement on the basis of intelligence-test scores. It is also important to refrain from invading the privacy of the child or his family. Such ethical problems will be considered in more detail in a later chapter.)

Schools have other advantages also. For example, they may have such specialists as guidance and counseling workers, school psychologists, speech therapists, nurses, social workers, remedial specialists, and consultant physicians and psychiatrists. In addition, schools frequently have close relationships with child-study clinics and other mental-health agencies. Psychological assessment and remedial help may thus be more easily and economically obtained for a child through a school connection than through other resources.

The school is in continuing contact with parents through reports and conferences and therefore has an advantage in furthering dual efforts to help a child who is in need.

Finally, the teaching-learning situation can be highly therapeutic. It is fortunate that what is good teaching practice is usually also good mental-health practice. In its concern for improvement of the child's academic performance, the school may thus not only help him to learn better but may also improve his mental health. This result is perhaps most likely when his mental health has suffered because of poor academic achievement and he has developed feelings of inferiority, guilt, and inadequacy. It is also quite likely that efforts to improve a child's adjustment will result in improved academic achieve-

"self-fulfilling prophecy" — expectancy theory

ment; problems of attention span, concentration, motivation, and perception may be caused by pupil fears, anxieties, conflicts, and frustrations, and the reduction of such tensions can result in better learning.

Let us illustrate this point briefly: It is known that most children with reading problems also have problems of mental health (Schubert, 1956). It is also known that some overachievers and many underachievers tend to have poor emotional health. Consider a first-grade child just learning to read. If he is less mature physically than required, he may have trouble with eye movements and may fail to learn to read at this time. He may even have continuing difficulty throughout his school years, which can result in feelings of inadequacy, with accompanying withdrawing, aggressive, or other maladaptive behavior. Or he may lack mental maturity, with similar problems as the result. On the other hand, J. E. Gardner (1964) has suggested that failure to learn to read can be the result of psychological problems like avoidance, in which the child may perceive the school as punishing or unrewarding and may actually become phobic or, less extremely, may develop a high absentee rate. Withdrawal, in which daydreams are more rewarding and less threatening than the external environment and in which the child therefore is less able to learn, perpetuates a vicious cycle of daydreaming and poor environmental coping. Psychological sabotage, in which the child plays parents against teacher or teacher against teacher; repression and denial, in which the child tends to develop habits of "not-think" as means of dealing with parental or school pressures or his own feelings of inadequacy; and passive aggression, in which the child copes with powerful authority figures by a "sit-down strike" against learning, may be causes of poor reading. These examples, of course, do not exhaust the psychological possibilities in reading problems but serve to illustrate the relationship between mental health and school achievement. If the school is sensitive to the pupil's mental health, both specialists and teachers can act to promote good learning and good mental health, frequently at the same time. Good mental health is an obvious concern of the school from an academic, as well as from a compassionate, point of view.

TEACHER ROLES AND PUPIL MENTAL HEALTH

It has been suggested that if teachers are concerned with the mental-health problems of pupils, the teaching-learning situation is altered and the teaching of subject matter may suffer. Some people argue that concern for pupil problems destroys the disciplinary and academic values of the schools. It has also been pointed out that teachers must be careful not to step out of their designated roles and must not attempt to become "amateur psychiatrists," for they might do harm to pupils. Others have argued that, as teachers must deal with groups of children, they cannot vary programs individually, even to benefit pupil personality development and adjustment. Finally, it has been pointed out that teachers lack the necessary time and energy to accept additional responsibilities.

All of these arguments have weight, but they reflect a lack of understanding of the role of the teacher in mental health. Psychologists, as well as educators, view the teacher as a referent of reality for the child. In school, children must learn to face life as it actually is and not as they wish it to be. They must learn to adapt to social mores and to consider the needs of others and not to expect unusual attention or deference. They must learn also to accept responsibility. Psychologists would not advise the teacher to be highly permissive, nor would they want him to attempt clinical diagnosis or therapy. The teacher is *not* required to step out of his role or to modify his behavior greatly. He *is* expected to examine his usual activities with mental-health principles in mind.

The teacher can examine his own attitudes and feelings and attempt to judge how he affects his charges. He can learn to observe children, interpret their behavior, and discover their problems. He can be concerned with the enhancement of self and the actualization of pupils. The entire teaching situation can be re-examined to see how it can be employed in preventive, positive, or remedial ways.

At the same time that the teacher studies mental health in relation to teaching, he will want to assume a position that is not unrealistically optimistic or unnecessarily pessimistic about what he can accomplish. Recognition of his own competences, genuine liking and respect for children, and attempts to understand them should make his efforts rewarding. That is what this book is about.

□

REFERENCES

Abramovitz, A. B. *Basic Prevention: Its Nature and Value.* Madison: Wisconsin State Board of Health, 1965.

Abramovitz, A. B., and E. Burnham. "Exploring Potentials for Mental Health in the Classroom," *Mental Hygiene,* 43 (1959) , 253–9.

Allinsmith, W., and G. W. Goethals. *The Role of the Schools in Mental Health.* New York: Basic Books, 1962.

Allport, G. W. *Becoming.* New Haven: Yale University Press, 1955.

———. *Pattern and Growth in Personality.* New York: Holt, Rinehart, Winston, 1961.

Biber, B. "Integration of Mental Health Principles in the School Setting," in G. Caplan (ed.) . *Prevention of Mental Disorders in Children,* 323–52. New York: Basic Books, 1961.

CIBA. "Is This Man Mad?" *State of Mind,* 1 (1957) , n.p.

Combs, A., and D. Snygg. *Individual Behavior.* New York: Harper, 1959.

Dreikurs, R. *Psychology in the Classroom.* New York: Harper, 1957.

French, W., *et al. Behavioral Goals of General Education in High Schools.* New York: Russell Sage Foundation, 1953.

Gardner, J. E. "The Teacher as an Observer: A Suggested Supplementary Approach to 'Problem' Students." Prepublication copy. Los Angeles: Children's Hospital, 1964.

Gray, S. W. *The Psychologist in the Schools.* New York: Holt, Rinehart, Winston, 1963.

Havemann, E. "Who's Normal? Nobody, But We All Keep on Trying," *Life,* 49 (1960) , 78–80.

Jahoda, M. (ed.) . *Current Concepts of Mental Health.* New York: Basic Books, 1958.

Kearney, N. C., *et al. Elementary School Objectives.* New York: Russell Sage Foundation, 1957.

Maslow, A. H. *Motivation and Personality.* New York: Harper, 1954.

Menninger, K. A. Address before the Dane County Mental Health Association, Madison, June 7, 1965.

Murray, H. A. *Explorations in Personality.* New York: Oxford, 1938.

National Association for Mental Health, Inc. *Facts About Mental Illness.* New York: National Association for Mental Health, 1966.

———. *Facts and Figures About Mental Illness and Other Personality Disturbances.* New York: National Association for Mental Health, 1952.

Rogers, C. R. *Becoming a Person.* Austin: Hogg Foundation, 1958.

Schubert, D. G. "Comparison Between Best and Poorest Readers," *Elementary English,* 33 (1956) , 161–2.

Shaffer, G. W., and R. S. Lazarus. *Fundamental Concepts in Clinical Psychology.* New York: McGraw-Hill, 1952.

Smith, M. B. "Research Strategies Toward a Conception of Positive Mental Health," *American Psychologist,* 14 (1959), 673–81.

Staats, A. W., and C. K. Staats. *Complex Human Behavior.* New York: Holt, Rinehart, Winston, 1963.

Szasz, T. S. "The Myth of Mental Illness," *American Psychologist,* 15 (1960), 113–8.

Wegrocki, H. J. "A Critique of Cultural and Statistical Concepts of Abnormality," in M. Zax and G. Stricker. *The Study of Abnormal Behavior: Selected Readings.* New York: Macmillan, 1964.

SUGGESTIONS FOR FURTHER READING

Allinsmith, W., and G. W. Goethals. *The Role of the Schools in Mental Health.* New York: Basic Books, 1962.
The entire book is worthy of careful consideration. Included are chapters on the curriculum, dealing with mental health in the schools, training of teachers, and a field study that is reported together with implications for mental health.

Crow, L., and A. Crow (eds.). *Mental Hygiene for Teachers: A Book of Readings,* Part I. New York: Macmillan, 1963.
Part I is entitled "Meaning and Importance of Mental Hygiene." Articles by R. H. Felix, I. F. Warren, W. C. Morse, A. B. Abramovitz and E. Burnham, W. Wattenberg, and B. Biber discuss such questions as how the public schools are related to mental health, resulting dilemmas, classroom potentials for mental health, and mental-health criteria. This section amplifies and extends discussion in our Chapter 1.

Maslow, A. H. *Motivation and Personality.* New York: Harper, 1954.
This book is one of the classics and easily read. Maslow treats the concept of self-actualization, his theory of a motivational hierarchy, a philosophy of psychology and science, and a host of other issues. We have referred to Maslow extensively in Chapter 1 and will discuss some of his ideas in later chapters.

THE TEACHER AS
A PERSON

Were we to ask a school administrator to name the qualities of an ideal teacher, he could probably provide an almost endless list. He would mention the need for adequate general and specialized knowledge, understanding of the principles of learning and child development, acquaintance with various techniques of teaching, desirable cultural background, and physical health, among other qualities. The ideal teacher must be a paragon of almost all virtues.

But here we are going to concern ourselves with the teacher's personality, for without the ability to stimulate learning, to form excellent teacher-pupil relationships, and to help children develop desirable attitudes and behavior, the knowledge he possesses may never be communicated to his pupils. The healthy, competent teacher approaches his life in the classroom differently from the unhealthy teacher and gains different satisfactions from his work. And, although mental illness cannot be "caught" as can the measles, the mental health of the teacher can affect the mental health of his pupils. The teacher with an inadequate personality can easily produce frustration, anxiety, or hostility in children.

To illustrate what is meant by an "adequate" personality, here are three thumb-nail sketches of elementary student teachers studied in a research project at a large university (Ringness & Larson, 1965). At the beginning of their student-teaching semester, they were interviewed by a psychologist and tested with the Thematic Apperception Test (Murray, 1943), a series of pictures of ambiguous nature about each of which the subject is asked to tell a story. The students were also tested with the Edwards Personal Preference Schedule (Edwards, 1953) and the California Psychological Inventory (Gough, 1964).

Miss H. was a friendly, outgoing young lady. Her test results showed that she was highly perceptive and creative and possessed a sense of humor. She was realistic and unanxious and could both sympathize and empathize with others. Miss H. scored high in desire to help others; she was found to be highly motivated, persevering, and adaptable. She was considered better than average in over-all emotional adjustment.

Based on these findings, we predicted that Miss H. would make an excellent teacher, able to relate well to pupils, colleagues, and parents. It was predicted that she would be creative in teaching, warm, understanding, and flexible. She seemed pupil-oriented but not to the neglect of course content.

In a subsequent interview Miss H.'s supervisor commented:

This girl has a great deal of insight into herself and knows exactly where she's going and why she's doing what she's doing. She can look at a situation afterward and tell you: "I was trying to do this, and this happened and that happened." Her self-evaluation was out of this world. I'm just amazed. I've seen very few students operate like that with this little experience, who know themselves that well, and who have such strong convictions of the kind of person they want to be.

The kids are free to challenge her, but there is respect, order, and control; they're taking a lot of responsibility, and there's a lot of communication between students and teacher. She knows them well and can use her information, right on the spot, which is unusual in a student teacher.

Miss B. was also an attractive girl but was a little "thrown" by the testing situation. Her Thematic Apperception Test stories revealed that she was threatened by the themes suggested by the pictures, and she resorted to such defenses as banality or relegating her stories to the realm of television plots. Miss B. seemed unable to display her real feelings and was considered inhibited. She liked situations structured and orderly. She had a need for suggestions and leadership from others and showed little need to affiliate with or to help others.

All in all, Miss B. was rather retiring, dependent, and constricted. Although sensitive, she was too inhibited to be fully responsive. We felt that she would be self-centered, hence unable to relate well to pupils. She seemed highly organized and hard working, but probably content-oriented and somewhat aloof and rigid.

Sadly enough, Miss B. confirmed these predictions and, as a result, was not certified for teaching. Her supervisor remarked:

She's very self-centered and will not take responsibility for her own actions; she is very dependent on other people, wants you to tell her what to do, and then tell her everything she does is wonderful. She's inflexible, and she's insecure. The cooperating teacher is terribly upset. The kids just don't like her. You can't help her. You just can't help her because she's so closed about everything. It's been a tremendous frustration for me.

The final illustration is that of Miss J. She was a sensitive, intelligent girl. But her TAT stories showed much guilt, conflict, self-doubt, indecision, and morbidity, with a suggestion of family troubles and difficulty with male relationships. Other test results revealed a strong need for support from others and for order but little need to affiliate with others, to achieve, or to persevere. She seemed to be holding herself in, in the face of inner conflict—an anxious person but under control. She was referred to the student counseling center but allowed to attempt student-teaching.

Miss J.'s supervisor remarked:

She had me extremely concerned about her on the last visit. She was kind of like a tiger with the kids. She was doing considerable screaming at them. It was very defensive behavior. She said: "I don't really feel it's my fault. It's their fault. I don't understand them, why they're this way, and they have not always been this way." And the next day there was improvement. It was almost schizo, really. You know, two people, here's one side of you and here's the other. Which was kind of scary to me, too, in a way, that somebody could be this different.

It should be noted that Miss J. continued to improve. Her counselor was asked if she could be certified for teaching because of this improvement, and he felt that the major problems had been cleared away.

These illustrations have shown some of the ways that personality characteristics may be translated into action in the classroom. Whether or not such characteristics can be changed, should it seem desirable, depends upon a number of factors. Important among them are a person's insight into his own characteristics and his desire to change.

There are clearly implications here for the selection of teacher-trainee candidates, for working with them at the college level, and for counseling, hiring, certification, and in-service supervision and training. Although the writer would not go so far as to suggest that all recruits be psychologically screened, he does suggest that the teacher's personality be more carefully considered by supervisors than is customary at present; in many instances counseling, rather than supervision, might produce desired changes in trainee behavior.

There are problems, however. As yet little has been done about teacher personality and mental health because of insufficient agreement in research findings on who will and will not make a good teacher. We do have some guidelines, but much more work needs to be done before it is possible to say that this person or that person will (or will not) be successful.

Studies of Personality Characteristics

DIFFICULTIES IN AGREEING ON TEACHING EXCELLENCE

One reason that it is difficult successfully to relate specific personality characteristics to teaching excellence is that there are problems in agreeing on what is good teaching and what is not. Different raters (supervisors, principals, others) may not have the same philosophies of teaching, and may therefore look at a teaching-learning situation differently. Furthermore, the moment such an observer enters the classroom, the climate of that room is changed; observers rarely see the "real" teacher or pupil behavior that is manifest when they are not present.

There are also problems in trying to assess the effect of teacher influence upon pupils. For example, if pupil achievement in subject content is a criterion of teacher excellence, can it be assumed that what pupils have learned represents what the teacher has taught? Many factors, some extraneous to the classroom, influence what pupils learn.

It is also true that what may be good teaching in one situation may be poor teaching in another. D. A. Worcester (1961) places much of the blame for inadequacies in characterizing good teaching—and subsequent failure to predict teaching success—on the erroneous assumption that teaching is a *general* ability. He believes that teaching must always be considered in the specific context in which it occurs. One teacher may succeed with certain objectives, a given group of pupils, a particular school subject, and in a specific school yet do poorly in a different situation. Ideally, therefore, one should strive to match the teacher to the community, school, classroom, and subject. As yet this kind of matching has not been very successfully achieved.

The foregoing discussion is not meant to suggest that *nothing* is known about personality traits and behavior of good teachers but rather to indicate some of the reasons that it has been difficult to predict who will be good teachers.

A number of researchers have been interested in teacher behavior and personality as related to school success. To illustrate the changes in thinking that are taking place, three representative studies will be briefly examined.

TEACHER BEHAVIOR AND PERSONALITY STUDIES

Among the more prolific writers on teacher excellence was A. S. Barr, who originally became interested in teacher characteristics as director of supervision for the City of Detroit. Barr later became a university professor and encouraged nearly 100 doctoral students to study ways of predicting successful teaching.

In one early study Barr (1929) was concerned with characteristic behaviors of good and poor social-studies teachers, basing his criteria on their general assessment by supervisors and administrators. Using time charts, stenographic records, and other observational techniques, he came up with a list of weaknesses of the poorer teachers. It included, in order of importance, inadequate provision for individual differences, too authoritarian a manner, formal textbook teaching, inability to stimulate pupil interest, weak discipline, inadequate daily preparation, lack of interest in the work, and inadequate knowledge of subject matter.

Notice that Barr was in reality characterizing poor teaching. Nothing in this early study attacked the problem of *why* these teachers behaved as they did. For this reason, although a supervisor might learn to judge good or poor teaching, he would have few clues as to why teacher weaknesses existed, nor would he obtain much information that would enable him to help such teachers improve.

Recent studies have tried to go beyond characterization of teachers or teaching practices; they have tried to examine underlying causes for such behaviors or at least to try to see relationships between teacher characteristics and teacher behaviors.

After thirty years of study, Barr decided that evaluation of the teacher should take into consideration both the products of the teacher's efforts and the teacher as a person and as a trained professional. Professional prerequisites for excellent teaching should include an adequate general cultural background; knowledge of the subject taught; knowledge of principles of learning and development; socially desirable attitudes and values; motivation for teaching; interest in subjects, pupils, and teaching activities; and skills in communication and teacher-pupil relations. Personal prerequisites included physical, mental, and emotional fitness. Teachers must be adequate both as individuals and as trained professionals (Barr, 1961). The teacher, as a person, thus became an important object of study to Barr and his students.

A recent classic study by David Ryans (1960) also examined teacher characteristics. The six-year research involved more than 6,000 teachers in 1,700 schools.

Three patterns of teacher behavior were identified:

Pattern X—friendly, understanding *versus* aloof, egocentric, restricted

Pattern Y—responsible, businesslike, systematic *versus* evading, unplanned, slipshod

Pattern Z—stimulating, imaginative, surgent *versus* dull, routine

After many kinds of data had been accumulated, teachers (both elementary and secondary) who rated high on all three patterns were compared by Ryans with teachers who were low. The group of elementary teachers rated high showed the following characteristics:

They manifest extreme generosity in appraisal of the behavior and motives of others; they express friendly feeling for others.

They indicate strong interest in reading and literary matters.

They indicate interest in music, painting, and arts in general.

They report participation in high-school and college social groups.

They manifest prominent social-service ideals.

They indicate preferences for activities that involve contact with people.

They indicate interest in science and scientific matters.

They report liking for outdoor activities.

They are young or middle-aged.

They are married.

Their parental homes provided above-average cultural advantages.

Highly rated secondary teachers manifested the first four characteristics above and also reported:

They judge themselves high in ambition and initiative.

They have been teaching four to nine years.

They have had teaching-type activities during childhood or adolescence.

They express preference for student-centered learning situations.

They display independence, though not aggressiveness.

There was evidence that both these elementary and secondary teachers find enjoyment in pupil relationships, prefer pupil-centered classroom procedures, are superior in verbal intelligence, and have more satisfactory emotional adjustment than do those who were rated low. In essence, the higher-rated teachers tend to be well-rounded, personally and socially adjusted, and genuinely interested in pupils. If one accepts as desirable the teacher behavior characterized by patterns "X," "Y," and "Z," there are some implications in Ryans' findings for recruitment of young people into the teaching profession, for there is the suggestion that the listed values, behavioral traits, and personality characteristics are relatively stable and are related to favorable experiences during developmental years.

One further illustration of some of the relationships between personality traits and teaching is offered in the work of J. V. Mitchell (1965). Table 1 shows correlations between scores attained on the Sixteen PF (Personality Factor) test and motivation for teaching by both elementary and secondary teachers.

TABLE 1. Sixteen PF Scores Having Significant Relationships
With Motivational Orientations

16 PF SCORES	MOTIVATIONAL ORIENTATION		
	Child Oriented	Practically Oriented	Subject Oriented
Elementary Group			
Intelligence	−.06	−.14	.30*
Dominance or ascendance	−.36*	.17	.14
Tendermindedness or sensitivity	.23	−.38†	.31*
Imagination and unconventionality	−.10	−.07	.30*
Self-sufficiency	.03	−.18	.30*
Secondary Group			
Sociability and warmheartedness	.30*	−.11	−.23
Dominance or ascendance	.30*	−.37*	.20
Adventurousness and social boldness	.31*	−.23	.01
Apprehension and guilt proneness	−.30*	.20*	−.05
Self-discipline and self-control	.18	−.18	.30*
Tenseness and excitability	−.39†	.44†	−.32*
Secondary-order anxiety score	−.33*	.32*	−.19

* p is less than or equal to .05.
† p is less than or equal to .01.
SOURCE: J. V. Mitchell, Jr., "Personality Characteristics Associated with Motives for Entering Teaching," Phi Delta Kappan, 46 (1965), 531.

The Sixteen PF test is a personality-assessment device that was developed to assess relatively stable personality factors (Cattell & Eber, 1963). In his study, Mitchell first tried to determine teachers' motivations for teaching, classifying according to whether they entered the profession primarily because of liking for and interest in children, enjoyment of subject content, or pursuit of economic advantages, good working conditions, and other related job satisfactions (practically oriented).

It is apparent that motivational orientations and personality factors are somewhat different for elementary than for secondary teachers (which may be related to differences in perceived roles). Taken as a whole, the practically oriented teachers seem to show less desirable personality traits than do the child-oriented or subject-oriented teachers. Child orientation for elementary teachers is related to low dominance or ascendance; subject orientation for elementary teachers is related to intelligence, tender-mindedness or sensitivity, imagination and unconventionality, and self-sufficiency. With regard to secondary teachers, child orientation is related to sociability and warmheartedness, dominance or ascendance, adventurousness and social boldness, a low degree of apprehension and guilt proneness, a low degree of tenseness and excitability, and a low degree of secondary-order anxiety. Subject orientation for this group is related to self-discipline and self-control and to low tenseness and excitability.

Practically oriented elementary teachers showed a lack of tender-mindedness or sensitivity. Practically oriented secondary teachers showed a lack of dominance or ascendance, as well as apprehension and guilt-proneness, tenseness and excitability, and secondary-order anxiety. Admittedly, there are many problems in interpreting these data and in trying to understand possible cause-and-effect relationships. Yet Mitchell's study seems to suggest that teachers' personality traits and motivations are related and that teachers who are not particularly interested in either their pupils or school subjects have less desirable personality characteristics than do those who are; in regard to some of the traits mentioned, the practically oriented teachers might even seem to have poorer mental health.

Although studies of teacher personality have failed to establish clear patterns of personality traits which would suggest personality-screening of teacher candidates, they have provided us with some suggestive leads. To the writer it seems well-established that in recruitment, training, placement, and supervision of the teacher, his personality as well as knowledge of subject, child development, and teaching methodology must be carefully considered.

The Mental Health of the Teacher

MENTAL HEALTH AND TEACHING BEHAVIOR

The teacher's mental health affects his work in a variety of ways. It affects his enjoyment of his work and the zest he brings to school. It affects his ability to communicate and to empathize with others. It may even affect his ability to improve, as poor mental health is not conducive to flexibility and change. Following is a discussion of factors in mental health and ways they may affect the teacher's ability.

THE ABILITY TO UNDERSTAND OTHERS. ■ When one is in good mental health, he may be better able to empathize with others, for his own anxieties and tensions are not so likely to get in his way (as in the examples of Miss B. and Miss J., for example). The person with poor mental health may be so immersed in his own problems that his point of view is biased.

The anxious teacher may misinterpret the feelings of others; he tends to project into any situation an interpretation too strongly based in his own feelings and too little centered in objective reality. For example, he may assume that each time a pupil whispers, it is with reference to him.

Or the insecure teacher may be easily embarrassed and take refuge in formality or overstrictness. He may talk too rapidly or too loudly, overcompensating in a desire to dominate relationships and thus protect himself. The compulsive teacher may not understand why some children are not neater or better organized than they are. The suspicious teacher cannot be sure that the speech of children does not contain hidden double meanings or that his charges are not cheating or misbehaving behind his back. The hostile teacher carries a chip on his shoulder and interprets every cough or dropped book as an attempt to defy him.

The healthy teacher, however, is interested in how children feel and what *their* needs are. He listens to children and tries to interpret the learning situation from their point of view. He tries to find ways to relate his subject to their interests and goals, and, when motivation flags, he looks first to his own methods and course content. He can accept the fact that children may have values that differ from his, and he evaluates them in relation to the pupils' cultural backgrounds, levels of development, and apparent needs. He is unthreatened and secure, so that he can tolerate the unexpected. He also believes that children may have legitimate emotions of their own and may have a right occasionally to be bored, angry, or tired.

COMMUNICATION. ■ In the typical class situation, the teacher frequently is at the center of the stage more often than he ought to be. He is therefore less likely to know the children than they are to know him—which has the effect of causing the children to adjust to the teacher more than the teacher to the children.

When this point is raised, teachers sometimes object, saying that, if they do not constantly raise questions or pour forth information, pupils remain silent; all too frequently they seem to lack ideas or the initiative to express them. But the desire of the teacher ought to be to help pupils express *their* thoughts, for that is one way in which children develop intellectually and emotionally. When pupils fail to initiate questions or ideas, it may be that the teacher has been too dominating or impatient and does not let pupils think and speak for themselves, or it may be that he is too interested in bringing forth the "right answers."

The healthy teacher wants to listen to pupils, and he therefore refrains from being too active in discussions. He can tolerate silence while a hesitant pupil marshals his thoughts. This teacher supports pupil ideas, even though some may not be as good as others. He reduces tension through humor or by changing the subject when necessary, but he avoids negative comments. He can tolerate emotional expression. One study (Ringness, 1965) showed that ninth-grade junior high-school pupils believe the stereotype that teachers want conforming, docile, and quiet pupils, rather than those who are active, creative, and challenging. This belief may be a reflection of the teacher's personality, for it can be threatening to the teacher's ego to come up against young and vigorous minds. To the secure teacher, however, this sort of interaction is a joy.

MODELS. ■ Because of their status within the classroom, because of prestige in the community, because of their adult stature, and because of their education, teachers are frequently used as models by pupils. The teacher demonstrates a value system; he is an example of how emotions are expressed, how interaction is handled, and how social problems are considered.

As emotional behavior in others is frequently initiated by one's own emotions, the teacher who shows anger may induce fear or anger in pupils. Similarly, the teacher who shows indecision may induce pupils to take advantage of him. The teacher who fails to control his own emotional expressions may find that he has a noisy, disruptive classroom. The writer remembers one of his own high-school teachers who frequently became angry and threw chalk, erasers, or other objects at pupils. This teacher was completely unable to maintain a friendly, working classroom. Another teacher used to cry when things did not go well, and pupils generally managed to find ways to bait her. As models, these teachers were examples of what not to do, and they failed to help their students learn positive emotional reactions.

EXPRESSIVE BEHAVIOR. ■ Fine actors convey meaning through gestures, facial expressions, or posture—usually to supplement dialogue. Not all expressive behavior (or nonverbal communication) takes place on the stage, however. It is as common in the classroom as anywhere else, but the difference is that it is frequently unplanned, unrecognized, or even in conflict with what one tries to express verbally.

Formal study of nonverbal communication shows that it is usually learned, and it varies somewhat from person to person so far as the ability to express one's feelings and to interpret others' expressions is concerned. Some expressive behavior is of social significance, as when one shows by a frown that he is angry or by a smile that he is approving, and others are able to govern their own reactions accordingly. But some expressive behavior is merely an expression of one's inner state, without particular social significance, as when one tugs at his ear, sucks his thumb, or blinks. A. T. Dittmann (1963) has stated that the study of nonverbal communication is of value in therapy. The supposition is that every external movement provides information about the psychophysical states people are in.

Of importance to teachers is the fact that expressive behavior may more truly reveal feelings than will verbal utterances. R. Stagner (1948) recognized early that it is not only what one does purposely, but also what one unconsciously communicates, that is important. He notes that parents tend to "civilize" the expression of emotions in children by encouraging verbal expression instead of overt bodily activity (like kicking or biting in anger) but that they also then tend to forbid even the verbal expression of strong feelings (as when a father does not permit children to shout at him) But even though both overt and verbal expressions of emotion are thus inhibited, there may well be an "unconscious, unrecognized gesture which reveals the emotional state to the observer" (1948, p. 225) .

In essence, what the teacher feels is not likely to be concealed, even though he might wish it were. He cannot pretend to like a pupil when in fact he dislikes him. He cannot conceal felt anger completely, for the falseness of his attempt will probably be discovered. The teacher who cannot accept some of his pupils emotionally conveys this failure, in spite of efforts to conceal it, and may be met with reactions of fear, anxiety, and antagonism.

In C. R. Rogers' concept of "congruence" (1958) , he says that one should try to reveal to others one's true feelings, in order to be seen as honest and trustworthy. The teacher therefore cannot afford to indulge in dislike of any child. Although some children are more likable than are others, each should be respected, and an attempt should be made to find some positive value in him as an individual. The alternative to displaying open dislike is either to display falseness or an impersonality that makes communication difficult. Should the teacher be genuinely unable to accept the *behavior* of some children, he should tell them what it is that he dislikes, for this communication permits them to change. (Clearly, this approach involves considerable tact and consideration for children's feelings. As we shall see, criticisms, especially those of a child's personal characteristics, should be framed in terms of recognition of his virtues but with a suggestion for enhancing them even further.)

From the point of view of the teacher's mental health and personality, frequent or considerable dissonance between what the teacher is attempting to express verbally and what comes through in nonverbal communication is a symptom of conflict. He is attempting to convey one impression but actually conveys two different ones. The teacher who is afraid of his classroom may try to put on a "tough front" and cover up his fear, but his expressive behavior gives him away. Such conflict, if it continues, can be traumatic, and should be resolved. In our chapter on conflict we shall explore this problem in greater detail.

INCIDENCE OF POOR TEACHER MENTAL HEALTH

There are teachers who are sadistic, masochistic, homosexual, alcoholic, or paranoid or who have other serious disturbances. One would think that the teacher who is highly disturbed would soon be weeded out of the schools or that treatment would be found for him. But some teachers with less obvious degrees of disturbance remain in the classroom, to influence pupils adversely. Early studies (Hicks, 1934; O'Malley, 1936) showed that teachers have about the same ratio of disturbance as does the general population, although one survey reported that as many as 20 per cent of the 600 women teachers studied were considered "unduly nervous," 11 per cent had had "nervous breakdowns," and between 20 and 35 per cent of the sample had adjustment difficulties. Quite obviously, such studies are subject to the problems of definition of mental health and its assessment, as are any studies in this area. Yet J. T. Shipley (1961) found enough information to write a book on teacher mental health, suggesting that many seriously disturbed teachers do in fact remain in the classroom. L. Kaplan (1959) compiled results of several studies that led him to believe that perhaps 3 million children are daily exposed to teachers so unbalanced that they should not be around children.

POSSIBLE SYMPTOMS. ■ Shipley, whose book offers cases of mentally disturbed teachers from forty-four school systems, offers illustrative sketches of teachers with serious problems; most seem to show psychotic or severely neurotic behavior, and the symptoms are quite obvious. Among the traits described are inability to control classes because of personality problems; use of corporal punishment in harsh, cruel, or unnecessary ways; excessive strictness; pupil abuse; and irritability. In many of Shipley's illustrations such problems as delusions and hallucinations, depression and manic depression, delusions of grandeur, psychopathic behavior, and sexual disorders are found.

Shipley refers to the following "danger signals," which suggest serious emotional problems. He makes the point that the signals are not "diagnostic" but that the presence of one or more of them should suggest referring the teacher for expert diagnosis and assistance.

SOME SIGNALS OF PROBLEMS

A person has serious emotional problems if

"He shows big changes in his behavior.

He has strange losses of memory, such as where he is or what day it is.

He thinks people are plotting against him, or has grand ideas about himself.

He talks to himself or hears voices.

He thinks people are watching him or talking about him.

He sees visions or smells strange odors or has peculiar tastes.

He has complaints of bodily ailments that are not possible.

He behaves in a way which is dangerous to himself or others."
(Matthews & Rowland, 1964)

These symptoms are likely to indicate severe disturbances. But poor mental health comes in many forms and it may not be particularly noticed by others or by oneself; it may be considered mere eccentricity or perhaps quite sensible reactions to one's situation. Yet small deviant behaviors may be the precursors of larger problems to come in the course of time.

The writer has met a number of teachers who gave evidence of being disturbed but who continued to teach. For example, there was Mrs. C., a divorced woman in her forties, who changed teaching positions almost every year, by request. She complained that she was always being put in embarrassing positions by a former colleague, who, discovering where Mrs. C. was currently teaching, would proceed to tell malicious things about her to her landlady, colleagues, parents, and principal. This malice always resulted in problems with the town; no charges were ever brought, and no real accusations were made, but her contracts were seldom renewed. It was clear to Mrs. C. that professional jealousy was at the bottom of it all. She thought it sad that her nemesis was able to remain anonymous, for school officials always claimed lack of knowledge of this woman.

According to Mrs. C., among the things said were that "she did not pay her bills; she was unable to keep discipline; she was in love with her high-school principal; she had been unkind to her mother; and she was no church-goer." In actuality, Mrs. C. lost her positions simply because of her inadequate teaching, which had often been mentioned to her in supervisory conferences. No one was gossiping about her or informing on her, although she could not be convinced of it.

Although Mrs. C. was urged to see a doctor for her headaches and to accept counseling, she declined to do so. She is still able to pick up a year's work, even with a record of ten years of inadequate teaching and a possible personality disturbance of a serious nature.

Again, there was Mr. M., a young man with a wife and two boys. Mr. M. lost his high-school teaching position, however, when it became known that he had made sexual advances to some of his male pupils. When the school authorities checked more deeply into Mr. M.'s university career, it was found that he had been asked to move out of two dormitories because of his homosexual behavior. This record had not, however, been known to student-teaching or placement officials, and Mr. M. did manage to teach successfully for nearly three years before coming to grief.

One final illustration may suffice to suggest the broad range of problems that beset teachers yet do not cause them to be removed from the teaching profession. On the contrary, many of them continue to teach inadequately for many years. A small-town principal was known to favor the classics, and in a four-year high school of eighty-seven pupils he taught four years of Latin, his favorite subject. Pupils had no recourse but to study this language, as otherwise they could not attain a full schedule of classes. Mr. L. opened school daily with a long reading from the Bible, followed by a patriotic reading or two from Revolutionary or Civil War writers. After listening to a short lecture on morality, pupils went to their classes.

Mr. L.'s concern for pupil morality may or may not have been admirable; extreme behavior is sometimes symptomatic of preoccupation of an unhealthy sort. In any event, his teachings were considerably biased, outdated, and unwanted by most pupils and their parents. When parents suggested a broader curriculum, Mr. L. became somewhat abusive. But, as he was nearing retirement and had served the community for a number of years—at a very low salary—he was permitted to continue. Mr. L.'s case will come up again in Chapter 4 in a discussion of school discipline.

Teachers with symptoms that appear serious to administrators, or to others who know how they deal with pupils, should be aided in seeking professional help. To persuade someone to seek help is easier said than done, however. To admit problems is threatening to many people; in addition, there may be a difference of opinion between the teacher and the administrator as to whether or not problems actually exist and, if so, whether or not they are mental-health problems. This book offers no pat solution. We do take the position that, when a teacher's behavior becomes such that it interferes with his work in any way, he should be faced with the fact and offered the alternatives of seeking help or finding other means of self-improvement, or of being relieved of his duties. Quite obviously, a conscientious administrator who is faced with this situation will move carefully; he will gather evidence that can be objectively evaluated by his superintendent and board of education before decisions are made. By most teachers, proffered help will be gratefully accepted, particularly if a good supervisory relationship exists. But, if necessary, for the good of the children (and probably for the teacher too), action should be taken.

Why are not such cases more frequently recognized and dealt

with before it is too late? Aside from the problems of teacher-administrator relationships and differences of opinion, it may be because of misguided kindness, because a little "queerness" is not viewed with alarm, or because the deterioration in the teacher's behavior has not actually been noticed.

Poor mental health develops gradually in most instances. R. F. Topp (1952), for example, suggests that problems may be firmly established before being noticed, so that the teacher can function passably for a time and can make a living at his job while being frustrated, unhappy, and comparatively inefficient.

Yet one can assess his own behavior from time to time, and others, if they have some idea of what to look for, can also be on the lookout for situations in which teacher mental health may deteriorate. For example, the teacher's appearance may reflect problems. Carelessness in shaving, in clothing, or in cleanliness and grooming may be symptoms of lack of consideration for others. Failure to make contacts with people outside the profession may result in an unrealistic one-sided point of view. Inability to carry on conversations with people not in the field should alert one to the fact that a teacher is becoming psychologically—if not socially—isolated.

Defense mechanisms employed by teachers may provide clues to their mental health. W. C. Menninger (1953) has suggested that some teachers unconsciously desire to escape their problems and that absences because of emotionally induced illnesses may result. Others employ rationalization; for example, they may excuse themselves for being too harsh with a child, for planning unwisely, or for putting things off. They may employ the mechanism of displacement by making others suffer for their own disappointments, as is the case when teachers who are criticized by a parent become unusually harsh with the child.

Other "symptoms" of poor mental health will occur to the reader. Some will be mentioned in Chapter 14 when signals for referral of the child for expert study will be discussed.

CAUSES OF POOR MENTAL HEALTH. ■ P. M. Symonds (1949) found that personal problems overshadowed all others in reasons for poor teacher mental health. Among them were problems in family relationships, love life, feelings of inferiority, physical health, finance, and inability to make social contacts.

His subjects did, in addition, mention problems in teaching and in dealing with superiors.

Working conditions contribute to poor mental health. J. Crescimbeni and R. J. Mammarella (1965) discuss some of the hidden hazards of teaching. For example, loss of courage may come about when the teacher has to adjust to being part of a large operation that functions as does big business—this situation seems to frustrate the teacher who wants to contribute to society as well as to seek self-actualization. School rules, restraints, and requirements are not conducive to individual enterprise and creativity. Loss of humor is always threatened, especially if teachers are too wrapped up in their work.

Amount of satisfaction gained from one's work is also vitally important, and this varies in accordance with the reasons one enters teaching. For example, the present writer (Ringness, 1952) found that excellent teachers were more likely than poor ones to enter the teaching profession to pursue a favorite subject matter, to serve society, or to seek variety in their work. Poorer teachers, on the other hand, were more likely to enter the profession because of its security against job loss or layoffs, its prestige, short hours and frequent vacations, financial reward, lack of physical strain, ease of obtaining education and a position, and interesting coworkers.

Table 2 shows the ranking of reasons for choice of teaching by sixty-three male and thirty-seven female secondary student-teachers. Items ranked 1, 2, and 3 were characteristic of teachers adjudged "good" in their first year of actual teaching. Lower ranked items were more common in "poor" teachers.

Ringness (1952) also compared student-teachers' views of the teaching profession's presumed rewards with those offered by thirteen other vocations, including medicine, law, business management, sales, journalism, the ministry, social work, engineering, advertising, research, accounting, farming, and the stage. Table 3 shows that, in general, student teachers feel that the rewards of teaching are those of interest in the activities and associations of the work itself, rather than in such "practical" matters as ease of obtaining an education or a position, monetary reward, or opportunity for professional advancement. With the exception of financial reward and ease of getting an educa-

TABLE 2. Rank Order for Choice of Teaching as a Profession by 63 Male and 37 Female Secondary Student-Teachers

Men	Women
1. Opportunity to pursue favorite (subject matter) interest	Opportunity to serve society
2. Opportunity to serve society	Opportunity to pursue favorite (subject matter) interest
3. Variety of activities, little monotony	Environment of interesting coworkers
4. Security against layoffs, job loss	Variety of activities, little monotony
5. Environment of interesting coworkers	Prestige and respect of the profession
6. Prestige and respect of the profession	Security against layoffs, job loss
7. Clean, attractive physical surroundings	Clean, attractive physical surroundings
8. Opportunity for professional advancement	Financial reward
9. Short hours, frequent vacations	Short hours, frequent vacations
10. Financial reward	Opportunity for professional advancement
11. Ease of getting necessary education	Ease of getting necessary education
12. Ease of obtaining position	Ease of obtaining position
13. Lack of physical strain	Lack of physical strain

SOURCE: Adapted from T. A. Ringness, "Relations Between Certain Attitudes Toward Teaching and Teaching Success," *The Journal of Educational Research*, 21 (1952), 35.

tion, however, teaching was ranked above the average of the other vocations studied in terms of rewards to be obtained.

Ryans (1960) found that teachers who entered the profession because of its intellectual nature, because they liked school, and because of its social-service character generally scored higher on the "X," "Y," and "Z" dimensions described earlier. Teachers who entered the profession because they were advised to do so, because of its prestige in the community, or because of possibilities for advancement scored lower.

As we saw earlier, Mitchell (1965) related teacher motives to certain personality characteristics and found that practically

TABLE 3. A Ranking Comparison of Teaching and 13 Other Vocations
in Regard to Rewards Offered, as Viewed by
100 Secondary Student-Teachers

	Men (N = 63)	Women (N = 37)
Financial reward	11	11
Ease of getting necessary education	8	8
Security against job loss or layoff	3	4
Attractive physical surroundings	1	1
Good working hours, frequent vacations	1	1
Opportunity for professional advancement	7	5
Opportunity to serve society	2	2
Prestige and respect of the profession	4	2
Ease of obtaining a position	7	6
Opportunity to pursue favorite interests	1	1
Variety of activities	1	1
Presence of interesting coworkers	1	2
Lack of physical strain	5	4

SOURCE: Adapted from T. A. Ringness, "Relationships Between Certain Attitudes Toward Teaching and Teaching Success," *The Journal of Educational Research*, 21 (1952), 43, 47.

oriented teachers appeared to lack certain attributes deemed essential for good teaching. They did not possess a self-disciplined, conscientious attitude toward their work but showed strong tension and anxiety. Those who were pupil-oriented or content-oriented fared better.

Teaching thus seems to be a profession one must enter with a sense of dedication rather than seeking for personal gain. A hypothesis may be made that people who go into teaching for primarily practical reasons fail to be motivated enough to spend the time and energy to teach excellently. Such people frequently are viewed as restricted, aloof, routine, and dull, and they have poor teacher-pupil relationships. Many of the satisfactions teaching can provide are thus denied these people. One who does not truly enjoy his work or who fails to do good work is a candidate for less than excellent mental health.

The reasons some teachers have poor mental health include pressures in both their personal and professional lives that may reinforce one another. These strains may be further aggravated if work fails to give satisfaction, thus contributing even more to poor teaching. We need now to consider what can be done to provide mentally healthy teachers for the schools and to re-habilitate those in poor mental health.

Improving Teacher Mental Health

TEACHER TRAINING AND SELECTION

Much emphasis is given by teacher-training institutions to the development of the teacher *as a person*. An effort is made to help student teachers better understand themselves and others, as well as course content.

F. T. Wilhelms (1960), writing about the program at San Francisco State College, considers the professional education period a time of self-discovery and personal development. In this program groups of students go through four years with a team of teachers. Unstructured, seminar-type classes are employed, allowing close counseling of the students by the faculty. Students interact with and help one another and get to know themselves. An atmosphere of freedom to explore and develop is provided, aided by the absence of grades for these classes. A part-time counselor serves each group of teachers. Among the advantages claimed for such professional education are that students gain greater understanding of teaching problems, child differences, and so on, when they are discussed in class from actual experience; students recognize for themselves the need for subject-matter background; students learn whether or not they really want to commit themselves to teaching; and students learn to teach in a reality-testing situation.

F. B. Stratemeyer and M. Lindsey of Columbia University (1958) address the following cautionary advice to supervisors of student teachers: Supervisors must themselves have a definite conception of what is an effective teacher; because students learn according to their perceptions of a situation, based in turn upon their attitudes, understanding, and past experiences, the supervisor must understand his student teachers as people; student teachers may not be quite adults and may have different developmental readiness for teaching; students should know their cooperating teachers, just as the latter know them. The writers also stress the importance of the cooperating teacher as an example or identifying figure for the student teacher.

B. Biber and V. S. Bernard (1958), in discussing the Bank Street College student-teacher program and theory of training, consider that a continuous supervisory-consultative relationship with the student should continue even after he has been placed in his first salaried teaching job. This idea is similar in intent to the internship programs fostered in many colleges and universities: While real, money-earning experience is being gained, the young teacher is not left to flounder through his first-year problems alone. For teacher training, they suggest that a number of questions have to be answered for and by the student teacher, including how he relates to children, how clear he is about the psychology of growth, how he views authority, what emotional strengths he possesses, and what motivates him to teach. Such self-exploration provides the opportunity to decide upon one's commitment to teaching or to leave it.

Other studies (Haines, 1960; Hatfield, 1961; Thompson, 1963) are also concerned with the attitudes, anxieties, self-concepts, and other personality variables of student teachers. These studies emphasize the need for training institutions to help students know themselves and to counsel them concerning professional and personal problems.

At the training level, emphasis has thus been placed not only on education in course content and teaching techniques but also upon the student-teacher as a person. Although excellence in teaching is difficult to assess, as was shown earlier, the acceptance of programs like those described has been excellent; student-teachers, training faculty, and the public schools that hire the graduates are generally convinced of the value of this approach.

We can illustrate some of the kinds of problems that arise in student teaching and some of the ways that supervisors have worked with them by excerpting dictated remarks from supervisors in the study (Ringness & Larson, 1965) discussed earlier.

SALLY

Sally felt that she never got any real evaluative statements from her cooperating teacher. When they *were* evaluative, they were statements dealing with "you wash a blackboard this way, then you don't get streaks," you know. There was a breakdown between them from the very beginning. . . . I must say that Mrs. J. does have insight into the students; Sally is somewhat defensive, a little lazy, and gives excuses, and that's just the wrong thing for Mrs. J. But instead of really trying to help the girl and trying to draw her out, she became almost negative and would look for faults, and didn't help her as she could have (and which she generally does with most girls). As you said [referring to the psychologist] this girl can become very directive. She was, but I don't think Mrs. J. realized how directive she, herself, is, so she kept criticizing Sally for things which are exactly like Mrs. J. She just didn't like *herself* teaching up there in front of her. That's the funny thing. I don't think that woman even realizes that Sally was an exact copy of her. Even the principal came in and said to Sally, "You don't have to be an exact copy of Mrs. J."

Well, then Sally did warm up a bit. There was one day that Mrs. J. wasn't there that they had a discussion and the children reflected their appreciation of Sally, and you could see this affected Sally. Almost as if it were the first time she got some positive reinforcement. This affected her. Then she became warmer.

She's a sensitive girl. I know that now. She presents a very poised and controlled picture for all to see, but this picture does not necessarily reflect security. She does need support and understanding in order to develop her potential. She is intelligent, but if discouraged, does not work up to her level.

So, I am trying to reinforce her feelings of needing to be autonomous, and to do things in her own way. I support her, and sometimes even defend her, though I don't tell her that. But it is surprising how she opens up and sees the need to be warm and friendly, and she is beginning to make progress. It is discussing things like this with her, and at least being open to being on her side, that seem to be making the difference.

JERI

Remember when we first talked about Jeri you said to me "I hope Mrs. M. doesn't become too overprotective." I didn't know Mrs. M. [cooperating teacher] at that time, but I can see it now, because I think Mrs. M. *does* tend to be protective and makes Jeri dependent. Mrs. M. almost takes the position of the "grand protector" and "I will shield you against the nasty old world." But Jeri is pretty good in self-analysis and we discussed things. She can see it and tries to improve. But she has discipline problems. When I last visited her room the kids were atrocious. They were noisy and she tried to talk above them and they wouldn't hear, and she wasn't following through with her threat to separate them and make them work individually. Then she rang her little bell and she said "Now what does this mean?" I felt like saying "Nothing!" because they were paying no attention to it. Later on I asked her how she felt about it and she wasn't very happy. I asked why she was frustrated. "Why didn't you follow through?" So we talked about it and she had excuses. She hated to penalize the whole group, but I told her she'd have to do something since they were being penalized anyway by not learning.

Well, we talked about this dependency business, and about how she would have to change and really strike out on her own and not lean on her cooperating teacher. My whole point was to face her with herself, and not the pretty picture of herself that the cooperating teacher had painted for her. Luckily, Jeri is honest, and she was able to finally face the need to be firm and to do things in her own way. I am looking now for some evidence of real improvement.

SANDY

Sandy has good rapport with the children, and she likes them and is comfortable with them. This permeates. But her teacher feels she spends too much time with the children. I don't think Sandy seeks them out, but she is young and pretty and has a nice way with them. I don't think Sandy pushes herself on the girls, but they come to her. In a way, this is good, but there are problems. She is giving of herself to the point where she never has any privacy or time to rest or prepare lessons. . . . And they take advantage of her. So I have tried to help Sandy see that she must reserve a little of her energies so she can do a really good job of teaching, and of home-making (for she is married). But I don't want her to lose her feeling for the kids or theirs for her. It's just that she hates to say "No." She sees this, and is trying to find tactful ways to do it. But she is suggestible, and does tend to give in, and also is flattered. So she'll have to work out for herself just how friendly she can be. There are possible discipline problems in this, too.

IN-SERVICE EDUCATION

Mental-health considerations would seem to make in-service education useful, as teachers may want help in learning how to help pupils who have problems of adjustment, learn poorly, or behave improperly. Whatever can be done to improve the teacher's professional competence is likely to bear fruit for pupils and also to enhance the efficiency and happiness of the teacher.

The improvement of teachers in service takes many forms. Sometimes schools provide subsidies or rewards for summer and extension college classes, workshops, or institutes. Sometimes teachers' study groups, aided by consultants, work on specific problems. Teachers may have individual conferences with specialists. Schools may undertake cooperative research with nearby colleges or universities, adding to the teachers' knowledge of their profession and their pupils. Provision of adequate supervision, a library of professional books and journals, released time for working on special problems, and encouragement of attendance at professional meetings are all likely to improve instruction and foster work satisfaction.

There are problems in determining the nature and amount of in-service education desired by teachers, compared to what is recommended or provided by administrators. For example, some teachers feel that they have too little voice in determining what in-service programs should focus on. They are not convinced of the values of certain kinds of programs, and they resent being required to attend certain meetings. Furthermore, they resent the extra time required if such meetings are after school hours. They believe that much of what is offered by such programs is "old stuff," unrealistic, or faddy; they believe that more specific help, directed to more selected groups, would be more valuable than what is usually presented to everybody. They believe that they have their own ways of self-improvement. They are not sure that meetings are sincere in purpose but sometimes suspect that they are mere formalities. They believe that a certain few tend to dominate in-service activities.

An earlier study by V. L. Replogle (1950) found that areas in which teachers wanted professional aid were

   1. improving teaching methods and techniques;
 * 2. utilizing principles of group dynamics;

* Mental-health concerns.

  3. locating community resources;
* 4. providing for individual differences;
* 5. handling pupil behavior and discipline cases;
* 6. meeting the needs of atypical pupils;
  7. enabling teachers to evaluate their own teaching competence;
* 8. caring for the needs of the emotionally maladjusted;
* 9. relating the ongoing class activities to the problems, concerns, and tensions of the pupils;
*10. using current teaching situations to make more understandable the contemporary social realities;
 11. making better use of visual aids;
 12. locating and making available expert resources and personnel, as special problems arise;
 13. identifying the possibilities of the current classroom activity to enable pupils better to understand democratic values, loyalties, and beliefs;
 14. constructing teaching units on problems and topics not found in basic textbooks.

Clearly, many of the problems of concern to teachers are related to mental health and human relationships. Those in charge of in-service programs may wish to consider these points further.

There is one other aspect of in-service training that bears mention: supervision by department heads, principals, or other designated personnel. Supervision of licensed teachers can be as helpful as that of student teachers, but all too frequently such supervision (and conferences resulting from supervisory visits) is meager. Figure 1 shows data collected by the NEA Research Division on the numbers of visits and conferences experienced by teachers replying to their questions. It can be seen that supervision, in this sense, is at a minimum. There are various reasons, of course. For example, strong teachers may seem to principals to require little supervision. There is also the problem of time to supervise, along with the principal's many other duties. Supervisory visits, however, might well be welcomed by strong as well as weak teachers, for they allow the good teacher not only to demonstrate his virtues but also to be reinforced in what he is doing. The principal may also gain, for he not only shows an interest in what his teachers are doing and affords

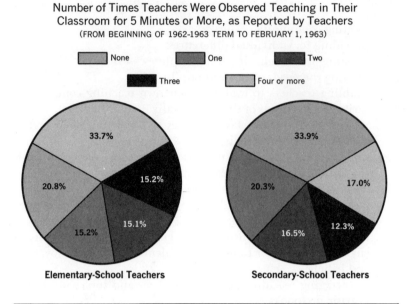

Number of Times Teachers Were Observed Teaching in Their
Classroom for 5 Minutes or More, as Reported by Teachers
(FROM BEGINNING OF 1962-1963 TERM TO FEBRUARY 1, 1963)

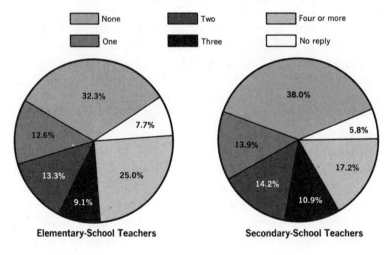

Number of Individual Conferences of 10 Minutes or More That
Teachers Had with Principal or Other School System Official,
as Reported by Teachers
(FROM BEGINNING OF 1962-1963 TERM TO FEBRUARY 1, 1963)

FIGURE 1.   Is helpful supervision frequent?

SOURCE: "Methods of Evaluating Teachers," *National Education Association Research Bulletin*, 43 (February 1965), 14, 17.

them recognition, but he is also able to discover creative teaching approaches that can be relayed to others. The weak teacher, of course, may be aided by suggestions and the supportive efforts of the supervisor.

IMPROVING WORKING CONDITIONS

Much possible improvement of working conditions requires administrative initiation or support. Classroom loads, salaries, grouping of pupils, handling of disciplinary cases, and similar problems require the coordination of the school system as a whole and the blessing of all concerned. Teachers as individuals and teacher groups may, however, frequently help improve working conditions by calling attention to needs, suggesting remedies, and enlisting support for changes that would better conditions.

The teacher may also improve his own working conditions up to a point. Some teachers may actually be quite inefficient and spend more time doing their work than is actually necessary. This inefficiency contributes to tiredness, boredom, and frustration. A few reminders may be helpful.

1. Work on time budgeting. Among the time-wasting activities are preparations of materials, paper grading, attendance taking, and other administrative routines that might be better handled by secretaries or clerks, pupil aides, cooperation among teachers, and purchase of ready-made materials.
2. Plan ahead so that relatively slack periods can be used for preparing final examinations, new units, or similar major tasks.
3. Refuse to accept too many extra jobs. Teachers sometimes take on responsibilities far in excess of their available time and energy because of desire to see something achieved, loyalty to others, or competitive or security needs.
4. Avoid competition with other staff members. Each person has his own interests and teaches in his own way. Competition merely tends to increase strain and frustration, and the conflicts and jealousies that may be engendered do not further mental health or interpersonal relationships.
5. Maintain a realistic level of aspiration. For example, all pupils cannot be brought to the grade level, all pupil adjustment problems cannot be solved, and every unit cannot be a masterpiece.

By adopting reasonable goals, a teacher can lessen his feelings of guilt and frustration.

6. Improve relationships with fellow staff members. Advice may be obtained through, and mutual support provided by, healthy interstaff relationships.

IMPROVING ONE'S PERSONAL LIFE

Trying to give "tips" on how to remain in good mental health may seem a bit patronizing. In spite of the fact that no one can guarantee ways to ward off mental illness or poor mental health, however, there are some guidelines for mental hygiene, just as there are some for physical fitness.

Teachers have two needs that are frequently not met: the need for the liking and respect of pupils and the need for a feeling of professional accomplishment. Pupils sometimes seem to regard teachers as superhuman (or perhaps not "human" at all) and fail to consider teachers' feelings. Attitudes toward teachers become stereotyped, and many different teachers can find themselves treated in the same way. Sometimes pupils take unfair advantage of teachers or treat them inconsiderately or disrespectfully. Or conditions may be such that teachers cannot feel professional accomplishment. For example, pupils may not be capable of being well motivated, materials may be old or scarce, the building may be poorly constructed and maintained, or classes may be crowded. Curriculum policies may be restrictive and school morale at an ebb—and extraneous community influences may militate against a good teaching situation.

A healthy teacher alters his expectations accordingly. When he finds that he does not enjoy his relationships with his pupils several practices can be helpful:

1. Make every effort to understand what individual children are like. When their backgrounds are better understood, many problem children can be tolerated, if not truly liked.
2. Tell pupils who are irritating what they do that is displeasing. This method offers them a chance to avoid irritating behavior.
3. Take an objective attitude about classroom happenings and avoid emotional involvement in unpleasant situations. Refuse to take things personally, thus avoiding feelings of guilt, anxiety, or hostility to some extent.

4. Keep in mind that a teacher cannot, nor is he expected to, succeed with all pupils and should not feel bad about an occasional failure to help one.
5. Recognize that some pupils are too badly damaged emotionally to be capable of giving or receiving friendship, and do not take their unfriendly behavior personally.
6. Remove or isolate troublesome children so that personality clashes do not occur.
7. Employ a sense of humor to ward off feelings of frustration or hostility.

It is also true that there are some suggestions that may be useful in the teacher's personal life. These aids to good mental hygiene are sometimes neglected:

1. Physical health should be cherished. Teachers sometimes come to school when ill, fail to get proper exercise, have poor eating or sleeping habits, or refuse to undergo physical examinations. Yet mental health is to some extent dependent upon physical health.
2. Social life should be adequate. Contacts other than with school staff should be fostered so that one does not live with professional problems twenty-four hours a day. (Some teachers live, eat, and plan recreation with one another, which is desirable to a point but can become highly confining in a psychological sense.)
3. New ideas should be cultivated. One can help oneself to enjoy life and become better rounded through reading, travel, sports, music, hobbies, taking courses, visiting galleries, enjoying plays, and other inspirational or recreational activities.
4. Cultivate self-acceptance. Although any person has areas of personality and behavior that can be improved, he should avoid harping on his weaknesses and failures and should concentrate upon his successes.
5. Attack problems promptly. Vacillation, retreat, and defenses are not conducive to the solution of problems, and in the long run anxieties, conflicts, and frustrations tend to continue and disrupt one's feelings of security and self-esteem.
6. Emotions should be controlled. One should not give in to impulsive activity. Hostility should not be directed against others, although sometimes it may be released in discussion, through physical activity, or in other harmless ways.

7. Spiritual values are important. Regardless of the form it may take, a life philosophy or religion is necessary to give point to life and to provide support when things go badly.

8. One may obtain the help of others—a therapist or friends, advisers, experienced teachers, administrators, and others who can help smooth difficult paths and provide actual or psychological support. (One problem faced by clinics is the reluctance of people to take advantage of the help that can be offered. Not only are some people fearful of discussing their problems with others—especially mental-health problems—but there is also frequent resistance to therapeutic counseling, almost as if the patient were afraid to come to grips with himself and his problems. Yet therapy can be highly beneficial, and much is to be gained by recognizing when one cannot cope with his problems and enlisting the aid of others.)

In substance, this chapter has been concerned with the relationship of teacher personality and mental health to success in teaching and to job satisfaction. The point has been made that much can be done to preserve the mental health of the teacher, as well as to improve it when necessary. Both the teacher himself and teacher-training and school officials can make inroads in this area. What is required is that needs should be recognized, that problems should not be side-stepped, and that preventive and remedial actions should be taken.

□

REFERENCES

Barr, A. S. *Characteristic Differences in the Teaching Performance of Good and Poor Teachers of the Social Studies.* Bloomington, Ill.: Public School Publishing Company, 1929.
———. "Personal Prerequisites to Teacher Effectiveness," in A. S. Barr (ed.). *Wisconsin Studies of the Measurement and Prediction of Teacher Effectiveness: A Summary of Investigations.* Madison: Dembar, 1961.
Biber, B., and V. S. Bernard. *Teacher Education in Mental Health,* reprinted from M. Krugman (ed.). *Orthopsychiatry and the School.* New York: Bank Street College, 1958.
Cattell, R. B., and H. W. Eber. *Sixteen Personality Factor Questionnaire.* (Rev. ed.) Champaign: Institute for Personality and Ability Testing, 1963.
Crescimbeni, J., and R. J. Mammarella. "Hidden Hazards in Teaching," *NEA Journal,* 55 (1965), 31.

Dittmann, A. T. "Kinesic Research and Therapeutic Processes: Further Discussion," in P. H. Knapp (ed.). *Expression of the Emotions in Man.* New York: International Universities Press, 1963.

Edwards, A. L. *Edwards Personal Preference Schedule.* New York: Psychological Corporation, 1953.

Gough, H. C. *California Psychological Inventory.* (Rev. ed.) Palo Alto: Consulting Psychologists Press, 1964.

Haines, A. C. *Guiding the Student Teaching Process in Elementary Education.* Chicago: Rand McNally, 1960.

Hatfield, A. B. "Experimental Study of the Self-Concept of Student Teachers," *Journal of Educational Research,* 55 (1961), 87–9.

Hicks, F. R. *The Mental Health of Teachers* (Contributions to Education 123). Nashville: George Peabody College, 1934.

Kaplan, L. *Mental Health and Human Relations in Education.* New York: Harper, 1959.

Matthews, R. A., and L. W. Rowland. *How to Recognize and Handle Abnormal People.* (Rev. ed.) New York: National Association for Mental Health, 1964.

Menninger, W. C. "Self Understanding for Teachers," *NEA Journal,* 42 (1953), 331–3.

Mitchell, J. V., Jr. "Personality Characteristics Associated with Motives for Entering Teaching," *Phi Delta Kappan,* 41 (1965), 529–32.

Murray, H. A. *Thematic Apperception Test.* Cambridge, Mass.: Harvard University Press, 1943.

O'Malley, K. E. *A Psychological Study of the Annoyances and Irritations of Teachers.* Doctoral dissertation, New York University, 1936.

Replogle, V. L. "What Help Do Teachers Want?" *Educational Leadership,* 7 (1950), 445–9.

Ringness, T. A. "Affective Differences Between Successful and Non-Successful Bright Ninth Grade Boys," *Personnel and Guidance Journal,* 43 (1965), 600–6.

———. "Relationships Between Certain Attitudes Toward Teaching and Teaching Success," *Journal of Experimental Education,* 21 (1952), 1–55.

Ringness, T. A., and E. A. Larson. *Effect of Clinical Evaluation on Supervision of Student Teachers* (Final Report, Cooperative Research Project S–343–64). Madison: University of Wisconsin, 1965.

Rogers, C. R. "Characteristics of a Helping Relationship," *Personnel and Guidance Journal,* 37 (1958), 6–15.

Ryans, D. C. *Characteristics of Teachers.* Washington, D.C.: American Council on Education, 1960.

Shipley, J. T. *The Mentally Disturbed Teacher.* Philadelphia: Chilton, 1961.

Stagner, R. *Psychology of Personality.* (2nd ed.) New York: McGraw-Hill, 1948.

Stratemeyer, F. B., and M. Lindsey. *Working With Student Teachers.* New York: Columbia University Teachers College, 1958.

Symonds, P. M. "Classroom Discipline," *Teachers College Record,* 51 (1949), 147–58.

Thompson, M. L. "Identifying Anxieties Experienced by Student Teachers," *Journal of Teacher Education,* 14 (1963), 435–49.

Topp, R. F. "Teachers Must Live Dangerously Whether They Know It or Not," *Illinois Education,* 41 (September 1952), 8–10.

Wilhelms, F. T. *The Professional Education Period as a Time of Self-Discovery and Personal Development* (Progress Report, Experimental Program of Teacher Education). San Francisco: San Francisco State College, 1960.

Worcester, D. A. "Some Assumptions, Explicitly and Implicitly Made, in the Investigations Here Summarized," in A. S. Barr (ed.). *Wisconsin Studies in the Measurement and Prediction of Teacher Effectiveness.* Madison: Dembar, 1961.

SUGGESTIONS FOR FURTHER READING

Gage, N. L. (ed.). *Handbook of Research on Teaching.* Chicago: Rand McNally, 1963.
For an extended technical summation of research on teacher personality, problems in assessing teaching effectiveness, and other research on teaching, D. M. Medley and H. E. Mitzel's "Measuring Classroom Behavior by Systematic Observation"; H. H. Remmers' "Rating Methods in Research on Teaching"; B. S. Bloom's "Testing Cognitive Ability and Achievement"; G. G. Stern's "Measuring Noncognitive Variables in Research on Teaching"; and J. W. Getzels and P. W. Jackson's "The Teacher's Personality and Characteristics" all supply additional data and commentaries on problems discussed in this chapter.

Kaplan, L. *Mental Health and Human Relations in Education.* New York: Harper, 1959.
This book contains chapters on incidence of poor mental health in the schools and on working conditions.

Ryans, D. G. *Characteristics of Teachers.* Washington, D.C.: American Council on Education, 1960.

Shipley, J. T. *The Mentally Disturbed Teacher.* Philadelphia: Chilton, 1961.
Ryans and Shipley have both been referred to in this chapter. Their original texts offer extended treatments of the problems of teacher personality and mental health as related to teaching success and mental health of pupils.

3

TEACHER LEADERSHIP
AND
CLASSROOM MORALE

The teacher sets the emotional tone for his classroom, both by
the attitudes he expresses and by the ways he handles classroom
activities. His leadership is closely related to pupil mental
health, as we shall see.

In Chapter 1 we referred to A. H. Maslow's hierarchy of
needs, and suggested that needs for belonging and affection, for
esteem and recognition, and for self-actualization may not be
met in many classrooms. When such needs are taken properly
into consideration, the teacher fosters good pupil mental health.
On the other hand, the teacher's manner of leadership may
cause pupils' mental health to deteriorate. Coincidentally, a
drop in classroom morale is likely.

There is a large body of literature dealing with teacher-pupil
interaction. We shall survey some of the studies in this area,
hoping to throw light on what may at times appear to be an
unsolved problem area. But before we enter upon such a
discussion, let us look at what some actual supervising teachers
have said about student teachers they have tried to help.

About Ann. She said to the boys and girls, "We have a visitor
in our room now, and we'll have *two* visitors this afternoon," and
they all said, "Who? Who?" you know, and she said, "Well, we'll

have Mrs. K. [the supervisor] and you'll also meet another person."
And they said, "Who is it?" and she said: "Oh, you'll meet him
this afternoon. He is the same age as you are, he looks like you, and
he has the same concerns and problems that you have." Well, of
course the children were dying to know who it was. This went on
all forenoon, and when the children came back after lunch they'd
look in the room to see who it was. Well, her discussion was centered around Sad Sammy and Happy Sammy, and Sad Sammy had
been in the lunch room, and Ann had made a chart of the cafeteria
and lunch room and brought them out, and she had made a very
clever big drawing of Sad Sammy. She introduced him and said,
"He is the same age as you are and he happened into the cafeteria
today, and do you know why he's sad?" And she led a very good
discussion about how things had been in the cafeteria—paper strewn
around, lots of noise, impolite children—most of it came from the
comments of the children, themselves—and then she brought out
Happy Sammy who looked so much different. The kids were very
thrilled, and she tried to summarize what they could do to make
Sammy like this all the time, especially in their first-grade room.
And she's got such a twinkle in her eye and everything the children
said, she says, "That's very good; that's very interesting," and things
like that.

She's very interested in painting and buys things in art for herself; she had a whole series of abstract and semi-abstract paintings
and she showed them to the boys and girls, and she got out of them
(for instance) how the colors made them feel, and "What does this
make you think of?" and she got answers from these first graders
like "rainbows," "sunset," and so on. I am very excited about her
work with the children because she includes so many in the discussions. And her teacher told me that she had done the most creative
dramatics in first grade. The kids are just crazy about her. They're
all right around her and want to help her. She can hardly send
them home at night.

About Janey. Janey is in the room with a group of very retarded
second graders. They are slow and deprived—real problems. I'm
amazed at her patience with these kids, and she's done such interesting things with them. She brought her uke, and she played some
songs. Then they all made up words for them. They did a very
creative bulletin board, and they made baskets that are all different.

And it's really an interesting thing; she's not threatened by the
fact that she cannot necessarily maintain control at all times.
Neither can the cooperating teacher, for these children are com-

pletely unpredictable. This doesn't throw her, by any means. She doesn't raise her voice, except to request attention. She's not up there saying, "This is the word, kids, and when I'm here you do it my way." She simply says, "In order to accomplish anything we have to have quiet." And she gets it, most of the time. But these children are hard to handle. They don't remember, and they lack self-control. But they are coming along.

About Sally. I wish I could say nice things about Sally. I saw one arithmetic class and the whole class got bad grades. She blamed the whole class for it. She said, "Well this was all fourth-grade arithmetic and it's all their fault," and so on. We discussed it. I said, "Well, did you think that everybody really failed and that it *was* all their fault?" Well, "It was review." There was a girl that was absent for a week. She didn't get a very good grade and Sally made some comment about "See what happens when you're not here?" that I thought was pretty sarcastic and wasn't needed. And I once heard her say when a child came up to her and wanted some help "Don't you know what a dictionary is for?" She could have said that in a nicer way.

These are actual examples of classroom interaction. They may serve to suggest some of the possibilities concerning how teachers foster good morale and, along with good morale, good mental health in their pupils. It is clear that the first student teacher, Ann, was warm and supportive. She was able to involve many children in discussions and obtained good thinking from them; she was free in her manner and able to accept differences in ideas of children. She handled the problem of manners and good behavior in an interesting, unthreatening way. Even the least secure child could feel "at home" in Ann's classes. Work went on and morale was high.

Janey, the second student teacher, had a difficult class. But in spite of the children's being hard to control, she exercised patience and was even able to get creative efforts from these deprived and retarded children. They were not badgered, and were not encouraged to feel inferior. Yet Janey did not permit aggression and helped them to face reality. She emphasized cooperative effort, and her pupils were making some progress in this regard.

But Sally could not help but hurt feelings, raise resentment, and cause hostility among her group, as long as she was sarcastic and blamed the children when things did not go well. Defensive herself, she was not a good adult model. She could expect discipline problems, poor achievement, and general deterioration of pupil morale. Weaker children might be hurt by it; others might not develop positive personality attributes as they might in someone else's class.

This chapter is about classroom morale, that is, the general feeling among pupils and teacher of friendliness and cooperation, the ability to tolerate some hard work and temporary frustration, and consideration of others. Morale encompasses a teamwork feeling, an expectation of accomplishment, and a willingness to participate. It refers to security and feelings of belonging, to a belief in fair play, and a respect for oneself and others. The level of classroom morale is largely set by the teacher's behavior and attitudes.

Morale depends upon the quality of classroom interaction, which means any communications among teacher and pupils and refers equally to smiles, frowns, the placing of a friendly hand upon a pupil's shoulder, verbal requests, praise, or reprimands. This quality, too, is largely a function of the teacher's behavior, as we shall see.

Classroom interaction, being public, affects many pupils besides those directly involved. Pupils learn vicariously by seeing how the actions of other pupils are handled by the teacher. Fearful children may become anxious if others are threatened by teacher (or peers), even though they are not directly a part of the interaction itself. Pupils identify with each other. They develop attitudes, feelings, and behavior displayed by others, which may be healthy and desirable—or not.

We hasten to observe that (as in Janey's case) the morale and interaction in the classroom is not entirely the result of the teacher's behavior. Pupils differ, and hers were typically problem cases. Teachers do not always *act*—they must also *react*—and thus *pupils* determine to some extent how classroom morale is maintained. Yet the teacher is the adult and has the advantage of being a trained status leader. Presumably even the most difficult children can be helped by the teacher.

What kinds of classroom interaction are most desirable? How

can high classroom morale be obtained? Are there any general principles that can help the teacher? Is it possible to attain adequate academic achievement yet develop "group spirit" in the classroom? Or does competitive effort in attaining grades tend to make each classroom an aggregate of individuals, rather than a group in the truest sense? How can the teacher maintain control and demonstrate leadership without stepping on some of the children from time to time?

Leadership Style, Morale, and Achievement

Most readers will recall the song in which there was mentioned "reading and writing and 'rithmetic, taught to the tune of a hickory stick." Perhaps some readers will recall stories told to them of how, in rural schools, the teacher had to be able to thrash every child and of how the bigger boys might "run the teacher out of the school."

Historically, the teacher was supposed to be an authority, not only in his subject but also in the way he handled his classroom. He was a despot. Pupils were required to be completely silent, to be entirely respectful, to follow the teacher's directions absolutely, and not to have ideas of their own. Some teachers, it is true, were kindly despots. But the usual method of evaluating the teacher was to visit his room to see how orderly it was, both in regard to pupils and materials.

Later the trend to "democratic" teaching was instituted. Teachers became more pupil-oriented. Pupils were allowed a voice in some decisions in the classroom; they were allowed to have ideas and to express them; they were encouraged to help plan units and projects and ways of proceeding; they were allowed certain leadership in the room; and so on. It was a humanitarian approach to the classroom, and most people have felt that it was a desirable change.

A few went even further. Some became so "pupil-centered" that children were not even expected to study if they did not want to, and quite recently A. S. Neill (1960) has somewhat fostered this approach, and it is being taken up by certain schools in our country. Under his original plan, children were expected to "learn what they felt a need to learn," somewhat analogously to the cafeteria experiments in which small children were found to choose voluntarily foods that had high nutritional value.

On the other hand, this system drew criticism. Some classes were considered so pupil-centered that they seemed entirely disorganized, and critics felt that the pupils learned little, if anything, of value. Teachers were said to have abdicated their positions as leaders, and to be acting entirely in a *laissez-faire* manner.

To add to the confusion surrounding how the teacher should act is the ethical argument over the extent to which children should be subject to controlled change of their behavior. B. F. Skinner suggested in *Walden Two* (1948) that it might be possible to produce whatever characteristics were wanted in children through a selective reinforcement process. C. R. Rogers, in rebuttal (Rogers & Skinner, 1956), argued that children should be helped to achieve freedom to be individuals, rather than be programed into whatever behavior authorities, no matter how benign, might desire for the good of society and the individual pupil.

All in all, either historically or at the present time, almost any variant of teacher leadership style has been tried out or suggested. The problem has, however, been oversimplified. Let us examine some relevant studies.

"AUTHORITARIAN" VERSUS "DEMOCRATIC" TEACHER BEHAVIOR

There has been considerable study of the question whether the teacher should remain essentially an authoritarian leader or whether a democratic posture is more desirable. It is really a question of social and academic values resulting from leadership patterns. Which sort of leadership yields most generally desirable results? What are the advantages or disadvantages of either pattern?

An early classic study by K. Lewin, *et al.* (1939) employed systematic alternating of leadership behavior in boys' clubs; leaders were instructed to maintain essentially rigid authoritarian, democratic, or *laissez-faire* roles. Results indicated that under authoritarian leadership a slightly greater amount of work was accomplished than under democratic leadership but that under *laissez-faire* conditions almost nothing was accomplished. The authoritarian leader, who was highly directive and repressive, however, engendered resentment in many boys and fear in others. Under this pattern there were aggressive behavior, submissive behavior, and scapegoating. When the leader left the room (by design), work ceased, in contrast to the behavior of the personally involved "democratic" boys. Playing, mischief, and absenteeism were more characteristic under authoritarian leadership (see Figures 2 and 3).

It might be concluded from this study that either authoritarian or democratic leadership resulted in productivity, but, when discipline, hostility, group morale, dependence, and other social variables were considered, democratic leadership seemed most advantageous.

Other studies have attacked much the same question, some having been made in the school setting. Essentially the question asked is "Is there a best mode of teacher leadership that will encourage learning and at the same time aid in developing excellent pupil morale, socialization, and personality development?" Or, one may wonder, must one goal be submerged in favor of the other? For example, when one tries to encourage personality development, mental health, and self-actualization (see Chapter 1), does he fail to inculcate the necessary "discipline" required for excellent subject matter learning?

R. C. Anderson, in an excellent review and critique of literature related to the authoritarian–democratic–*laissez-faire* dimension, finds that there are confusing results among the various research, and is able to come to no general conclusion. His position is:

The evidence available fails to demonstrate that either authoritarian or democratic leadership is consistently associated with higher productivity. In most situations, however, democratic leadership is associated with higher morale. But even this conclusion must be regarded cautiously, because the authoritarian leader has been unreasonably harsh and austere in a number of investigations reporting superior morale in democratic groups. In the educational setting, morale appears to be higher under learner-centered conditions, at least when anxiety over grades is reduced.

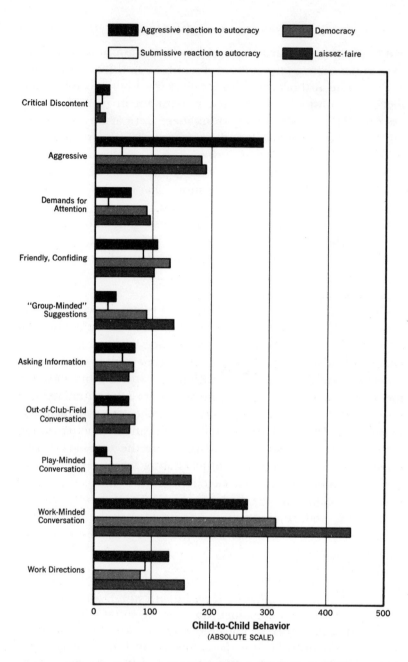

FIGURE 2. Four patterns of child-to-child relationship

SOURCE: Ralph K. White and Ronald O. Lippitt, "Leader Behavior and Member Reaction in Three 'Social Climates,'" in Dorwin Cartwright and Alvin Zander (eds.), *Group Dynamics: Research and Theory* (2nd ed.; New York: Harper & Row, 1960), p. 551.

The authoritarian-democratic construct provides an inadequate conceptualization of leadership behavior. When a satisfactory body of knowledge about learning in social situations is available it will then be possible to describe the behaviors which a teacher can exhibit to achieve a given learning outcome. It seems reasonable to suppose that leadership styles or teaching methods emanating from knowledge about learning will have a higher probability of meeting criteria of effectiveness than do *a priori* styles or methods. (Anderson, 1959, p. 213)

If democratic-authoritarian dimensions are not adequate conceptualizations, perhaps the problem can be reformulated. Let us now briefly consider the work of E. J. Amidon and N. A. Flanders.

DIRECT AND INDIRECT INFLUENCES

The well-known work of Flanders (1960) suggests relationships between teacher modes of behavior and the activities and personality characteristics of their pupils. Flanders defined "direct" influence techniques as lecturing; giving the teacher's own ideas, opinions, or information to children; giving directions; criticizing children; and justifying the teacher's own authority. "Indirect" methods of influence embraced the ability to accept the feelings of pupils; willingness to praise and encourage; and the questioning of pupils with intent that they should respond (as opposed to rhetorical questioning). One might consider direct influence as teacher-centered and indirect influence as learner-centered. There is some resemblance to the dimensions of democratic-authoritarian leadership, although certainly far from synonymity.

Flanders found a relationship among clarification of learning goals, pattern of teacher control, and dependence or independence of pupil behavior. Under *indirect* control it was found more likely that pupils *whose goals were clear to them* would be more independent and would initiate questions and discussion—and that classroom atmosphere would reflect high morale. In general, direct influence plus ill-defined goals tended to foster dependent pupil behavior.

Amidon and Flanders later (1963) summarized the results of

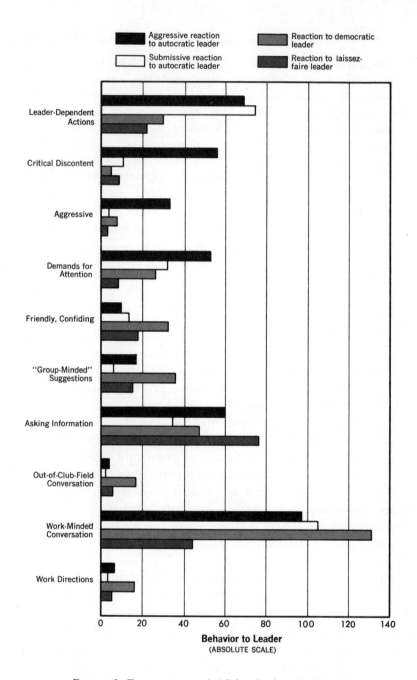

FIGURE 3. Four patterns of child-to-leader relationship

SOURCE: Ralph K. White and Ronald O. Lippitt, "Leader Behavior and Member Reaction in Three 'Social Climates,'" in Dorwin Cartwright and Alvin Zander (eds.), *Group Dynamics: Research and Theory* (2nd ed.; New York: Harper & Row, 1960), p. 550.

other studies of direct and indirect influence as it affects pupils. After conducting considerable research, they concluded:

It becomes clear that the concept of teacher flexibility was more predictive of teaching success than was the concept of direct-indirect influence. It was found that the teachers of classes in which achievement was above average differed from the teachers of below average classes in their ability to shift their behavior as it was necessary. That is, they could be just as direct as any teacher in certain situations, but they could be far more indirect in other situations. This ability, which is rarely found among teachers categorized as direct, meant that the teacher had the capability to make his own behavior appropriate to the requirements of the class situation at the moment. (p. 57)

It is now more apparent why older studies of teaching modes conflicted. The teacher's behavior cannot be simply a function of his own orientation and training but must also be governed by the nature of his classroom group. Furthermore, the particular goals of the teaching process must be considered and decisions made on the basis of his own hierarchy of values; that is, sometimes he cannot further all his teaching goals at one time and must therefore choose which goals to maximize.

We saw in Chapter 2 that there seems to be no generalized teaching ability. We now see that there can be no one "good" teaching behavior but that the teacher must vary his procedures with the situation.

Nor will all teachers be equally "good" for all pupils. We turn next to some studies to document these points further.

GROUP CHARACTERISTICS AND LEADERSHIP MODES

F. E. Fiedler (1962) and his colleagues have carried out a number of studies of leader attitudes and their effects on group climate, creativity, and other variables. Among the instruments employed for assessing leader attitudes is the scale known as Esteem for the Least Preferred Co-Worker (LPC). This scale yields a score defined as the "favorableness with which a subject described the *poorest* co-worker he ever had" (p. 308) and might be viewed as an estimate of a leader's general willingness to think well of others in a group situation.

In the 1962 article, the aim was to assess the relationship of group creativity to leader attitude, creativity being defined as "group interaction leading to an original solution of a problem or to a more effective recombining of given elements into new forms" (p. 308). Three laboratory studies and one study of natural groups were reported; they provided evidence that leaders who perceive their least preferred co-worker favorably tend to be most effective under pleasant and relaxed group conditions. Under stressful or unpleasant group conditions, however, and there is an important difference here, leaders who perceive LPC unfavorably are more effective.

This research seems to tie in successfully with remarks of B. M. Bass (1960), who concerns himself with initial effectiveness of groups as related to needs for leadership. If a group faces a difficult problem, many obstacles block the paths to its goals, and there is much frustration, considerable leadership must be provided before maximum need satisfaction or group effectiveness is attained. On the other hand, if the group is effective at the moment, if there is satisfaction, and if few or easy problems face the group, then relatively little leadership is required.

Therefore, if the classroom is to be considered a group working together, rather than as a collection of individuals communicating with the teacher more or less independently, it is probable that a more direct and firm leadership style is required to bring the group to effectiveness under stressful or unpleasant conditions. But once successful group activity is taking place and major stresses are removed, creativity, morale, and desirable group climate can best be furthered by a minimum of teacher control.

By implication, in the early days of a new class or when there are wide differences among group members, when disciplinary situations arise, or under other situations in which the group cannot successfully cope with its problems, the teacher may have to behave differently from the way he might prefer; he might need to exercise firm control, even though he might prefer to be more democratic in order to foster creativity, group problem-solving, or social interaction. The latter goals must be forgone until the prior problems can be resolved. If the teacher cannot make this shift in behavior, it may be appropriate to place the class under another teacher.

Teacher Personality Characteristics and Their Effects on Pupils

Teachers ordinarily must be "what they are." Personality characteristics change slowly, if at all. Aside from leadership method, is there something in the teacher's personality that is related to how he affects pupil behavior? A number of studies have examined personality dimensions of teachers in this regard. We shall look at some of them.

Among the studies that have considered the "warmth" of the teacher as a factor in achievement and morale is that of C. M. Christensen (1960), who found that pupils who perceived the teacher as warm and friendly did better in vocabulary and arithmetic than did those pupils who did not see the teacher in this way. M. L. Cogan (1958) found that teachers who appeared likable and approachable also seemed to require more work of their pupils and to generate more self-initiated pupil work. These studies suggest that teacher warmth is related to school achievement. However, D. M. Medley and H. E. Mitzel (1959) found teacher-pupil rapport related to teacher friendliness but not closely related to achievement.

Seeking to explore further some of the relationships between teacher characteristics and pupil behavior, N. E. Wallen and K. H. Wodtke (1963) found:

1. Achievement gain in reading vocabulary was positively correlated with the extent to which the teacher was viewed by observers as stimulating. (See the illustrative material on Ann.)
2. Liking for school was positively related to the teacher who was less achievement-oriented, possibly because the teacher who is highly achievement-oriented might tend to frustrate poorer students. (Note the illustrative material on Sally as a possible example.)
3. Liking for school was related to warmth and permissiveness in the upper grades, but lower-grade children seemed to need more structuring. (See material on Janey.)
4. The extent to which the teacher was achievement-oriented had a positive relationship to class ability to plan effectively in group problem-solving tasks, but this orientation tended to break down group relationships.

5. Supportive teacher behavior tended to foster more friendly group interaction. (See material on Ann.)
6. Supportive teacher behavior was negatively correlated with test anxiety.
7. There was moderately good correspondence between the perceptions of teacher behavior by pupils and by adult observers after second grade.
8. The permissive teacher fostered more pupil-initiated behavior. (See material on Ann.)

The impression gained is that teachers who are achievement-oriented fail to produce as high group morale as teachers who are more pupil-oriented. This idea needs some clarification. Let us first consider what is meant by "achievement orientation" and "pupil orientation."

Achievement orientation suggests that the teacher is primarily concerned with having his pupils learn the subject content and skills of his class. In general (although not necessarily) such a teacher tends to act as the organizer of knowledge, dispenser of information, director of pupil activities, and evaluator of learning outcomes. Success or failure of pupils is based upon learning achievement. The goals of teaching are essentially cognitive, rather than social or emotional in character. Emphasis is usually (although, again, not necessarily) on getting correct answers, striving to meet norms or standards, on passing tests, and on doing acceptable written or oral work.

Pupil orientation emphasizes changes in pupils' behavior in social and emotional areas, as well as cognitive outcomes. Content and skills taught are not based upon norms so much as upon their relationships to pupil abilities, backgrounds, and personalities. Pupil interaction with others, development of self-esteem and security, recognition of individual differences and of values beyond the cognitive are characteristic of this orientation.

In Wallen and Wodtke's study there was speculation that achievement-oriented teachers might frustrate poorer pupils. Or perhaps the achievement-oriented teacher fails to consider the needs of the individual pupils and how their social and emotional relationships affect learning. The achievement-oriented teacher may, because of his emphasis on content, overlook competition among pupils, anxiety engendered by marks and grades, and other factors related to individual motivation and group morale.

One wonders whether a teacher may not be interested in and able to foster both the cognitive and affective outcomes of learning. As we shall see, a number of studies have attacked this problem. One general area of study has shed some light on the findings reported. It is the area of differences among pupils' personality characteristics and how these characteristics are related to teacher personality and leadership mode.

Interaction of Teacher and Pupil Personalities

The present writer (Ringness, 1963) tends to support the views of Wallen and Wodtke in some respects but offers a different hypothesis for the morale problems sometimes attending achievement orientation. In interviews of bright high-achieving and bright low-achieving junior high-school boys who were matched on the variables of socioeconomic status (SES), academic load, classroom placement, age, and intelligence, two prevailing attitudes were found: The high achievers tended to choose as favorite teachers those who were academically competent; the low achievers tended to favor teachers for personality attributes like "fairness," "friendliness," "humor," and "kindliness." As will be discussed more fully later, the orientations of the boys seemed quite different, for the low achievers were affiliation-oriented (interested in popularity and friendships), whereas the high achievers were achievement-oriented. The teacher's effectiveness is thus not likely to be equal for all the groups with which he must deal.

TEACHER PERSONALITY TYPES

L. M. Heil and his colleagues (1960) tried to discover what teacher attributes seemed most desirable in working with different kinds of children. Both pupils and teachers were studied in various ways and classified by personality type. The classifications follow:

TURBULENT. ■ This teacher is turbulent in feelings and thought. He is relatively insensitive to others, he seems tense, and his impulses are close to the surface. He does not appear to need acceptance by others, to identify with others, or to have leadership ambitions. Lacking empathy, he appears blunt, impulsive, and unpredictable. He has a strong fantasy life and may be verbally aggressive. He prizes independence and desires freedom to do unconventional thinking. He may be somewhat exhibitionistic.

The turbulent teacher may be quite critical and outspoken. One might suspect that this sort of teacher, interested in ideas, innovations, and in independence, would be quite creative and stimulating to pupils but that he would confuse or frighten some and induce hostility in others. He probably would not foster warm interpersonal relationships with or among the children.

SELF-CONTROLLED. ■ This teacher feels most secure when things run smoothly. He prefers to keep his thoughts and feelings to himself and prefers not to get into "hot" arguments or to be around those who forget themselves and talk freely. He is ambitious and wants leadership responsibilities but prefers to manage rather than to create. He is submissive to authority and authoritarian toward others. He accepts responsibility and executes the ideas of others well.

This teacher plans carefully but is likely to be disturbed when plans do not go well and may be rigid in making on-the-spot changes. He is interested in being with people and is sensitive to how others react to him. In the classroom he focuses on structure and order and is work-oriented. He is warm toward the children and fosters interpersonal relationships.

FEARFUL. ■ This teacher is fearful both of the environment and of his own impulses. He is dependent and seems quite helpless. He has a severe conscience and likes to have rules to abide by; by the same token, he is irritated if others fail to abide by the rules. Because of his fears, he is relatively immobile in thinking and academic work. He is apparently most comfortable in dealing with things, rather than with people. In the classroom, this type of teacher is likely to be anxious and variable in his behavior toward children. He depends upon the reactions of others, rather than upon his own values and philosophy, and, as a result, cannot provide much structure in the classroom.

PUPIL PERSONALITY TYPES

In Heil's study, twenty male and thirty-five female teachers of fourth, fifth, and sixth grades from nine metropolitan schools were classified among these three types.

The pupils of these teachers were classified according to personality types.

CONFORMING. ▪ These pupils tend to conform to social standards and adult values and to emphasize mature behavior and control of their impulses.

OPPOSING. ▪ These pupils feel disappointed in themselves and others and frequently have problems with authorities. They tend to be oppositional and somewhat pessimistic.

WAVERING. ▪ These pupils are fearful, anxious, and indecisive; they change their attitudes and behavior according to the situations in which they find themselves.

STRIVING. ▪ These pupils have a high need to achieve and to obtain recognition for achieving. They are competitive, especially in scholastic activities.

Figure 4 shows the relative achievement gains for different kinds of teachers and different kinds of children.

Findings from this complex study differed, depending upon what was examined. For children's growth in "friendliness," the self-controlled teacher was superior and the turbulent teacher least successful. Children under self-controlled teachers had the highest perception of authority as controlling and effective. Under the self-controlled teachers the opposers and waverers had their highest intellectual aspirations. Children under fearful teachers had the highest perception of authority as ineffective and the lowest intellectual aspirations. The waverers, in particular, seemed to have high feelings of provoked hostility and anxiety under fearful teachers.

On an achievement test, conforming children made more progress under turbulent teachers, but other types of children did better under self-controlled teachers. When specific academic areas were examined, however, children under the turbu-

lent teachers seemed to make their greatest progress in arithmetic and science (relatively impersonal subjects), and children
under self-controlling teachers made their greatest gains in
reading and communication.

On the whole, turbulent teachers appeared to be most effective with conforming and striving children and quite ineffective
with opposing and wavering children. Self-controlling teachers
obtained consistent achievement with all kinds of children, and

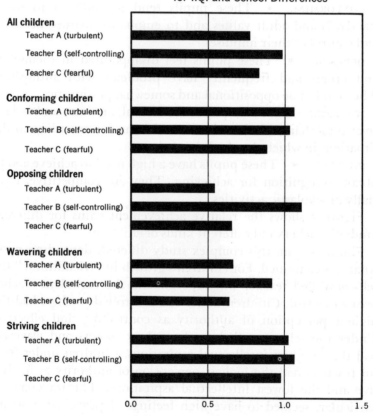

FIGURE 4. Relative achievement gains for different kinds of teachers and
different kinds of children

SOURCE: L. M. Heil, M. Powell, and I. Feifer, *Characteristics of Teacher Behavior Related
to the Achievement of Children in Several Elementary Grades* (Final Report, Cooperative
Research Project SAE-7285) (New York: Brooklyn College, 1960), p. 53.

fearful teachers were ineffective with all kinds of children except strivers (who apparently work hard regardless of the kind of teacher).

Essentially, Heil and his colleagues show that teacher personalities, with differing interests and goals, interact differentially with various kinds of pupils. They suggest that much more work needs to be done in examining the kinds of pupils and teachers that fit best together and what specifically causes results like theirs. Apparently all teachers cannot be all things to all pupils—there is probably no "ideal teacher."

DIMENSIONS OF TEACHER LEADERSHIP

Another interesting study with somewhat similar intent is that of C. W. Gordon and L. M. Adler (1963), who defined goals of the classroom system and related several dimensions of teacher leadership to the accomplishment of these goals.

It was considered that some teachers might wish to maximize the goal of academic achievement, others might pursue social and emotional development, some might emphasize good conduct, and still others might deal with some combination of the three.

Dimensions of teacher leadership were defined accordingly, and teachers were categorized according to the ways they were perceived by their pupils.

TASK DIMENSION. ▪ This dimension of teacher behavior is the extent to which the teacher organizes classroom activity to promote academic learning. Material learned is repeated and reviewed; pupils are shown when they respond correctly and what is wrong if they are not correct.

AUTHORITY DIMENSION. ▪ When the teacher wishes pupils to accept his decisions uncritically and to accept imposed tasks, he ranks high in the authority dimension. To the extent that he delegates initiation of activities and decisions to the class, committees, or individual pupils, and to the extent that he defers to pupil opinion he is low in the authority dimension.

EXPRESSIVE DIMENSION. ▪ The teacher who ranks high in this dimension strives to help pupils identify with school goals by being warm and affectionate with them, by being helpful and fair, by encouraging and praising them. He tries to make the class enjoyable and the work interesting. He tries to suit the class to individual interests and capacities.

To assess the effect of teacher emphasis on the goals implied by these dimensions, pupil productivity, morale, compliance, volunteer work, and classroom order were assessed. Productivity was measured by performance on reading, writing, and arithmetic achievement tests. Other dimensions were assessed with questionnaires and interviews. The classes of seventy-four teachers of seventh, sixth-seventh, and seventh-eighth grades were included; more than 2,000 pupils were studied.

In brief, the teacher who was medium in the expressive dimension, medium or high in the task dimension, and low in authority seemed to maximize pupil efforts. He is the teacher who tries to be warm and helpful to pupils and to suit work to their individual interests and abilities to a moderate extent, but who is medium to high in structuring and centering on subject content and tends to place responsibility for pupils' decisions and activities on the pupils, rather than seeking uncritical acceptance of teacher decisions. Under such a teacher pupils are likely to show highest morale, compliance, interest in volunteer work, and classroom order and productivity. Such a teacher seems to conform to the general concept of a democratic teacher and is one who expects pupils to study and to learn. This mode was less effective in producing classroom order, however.

Teachers who were low in the task, authority, and expressive dimensions produced *no* good pupil effects. Such teachers are like the *laissez-faire* leaders described by Lewin, Lippitt, and White and seem to produce similar effects.

Teachers high in the authority, medium and high in the task, and medium in the expressive dimensions obtained learning gain and class order. They did not obtain compliance with assignments or high morale, however. This rather authoritarian type of teacher seemed to produce effects quite related to those marked in other studies: outward conformity and some achievement but low morale and a tendency to try to circumvent or escape tasks.

IMPLICATIONS

It seems clear from the studies mentioned that there is no one method of teacher-pupil interaction that is successful in every situation or with all pupils.

There are some traits, however, that in most studies have appeared significant insofar as pupil morale is concerned. For example, teachers who tend to place responsibility for pupils' decisions on activities on the pupils themselves, who listen to pupils' ideas, who sometimes defer to pupils' wishes, and who do not attempt to obtain uncritical acceptance of authority tend to foster better morale. The teacher whose personality is warm, helpful, and considerate also is able to foster a good group climate.

But there is a difference between eliciting pupil morale and pupil achievement; the two do not necessarily accompany each other, although they are not mutually exclusive. If achievement is to be fostered, the teacher must also have a degree of task-orientation; pupils must understand that they are in the classroom to learn. It is the way learning tasks are approached that is significant for morale building.

Flanders' concept of flexibility (1960) is also important. The teacher must approach his task in a way that suits the occasion. For example, teaching objectives differ; the freedom necessary to foster creativity might be out of place when teaching purely factual material. The teaching behavior appropriate to fostering group problem solving may be quite different from that appropriate to fostering individual problem solving.

The concept of flexibility embodies the idea of behaving differently according to the needs of the pupils being taught. Conforming pupils need structure and direction, but others need freedom to push on by themselves. The fearful child may need a firm classroom structure to protect him, but the oppositional child may need more chances to be heard.

Finally, it should be noted that personality traits are relatively stable. It is apparent from the studies discussed that some teachers work better with some kinds of children than with others. Some seem to work best with bright, creative pupils whereas others do well with slower children. The abilities, backgrounds, and personality characteristics of the children should be considered when assigning a teacher to his position.

It is trite—but probably true—to say that in morale building and in efficient teaching of content, the teacher's biggest problems are assessing the needs of the group, correlating these needs with society's demands, and effecting the best climate possible for capitalizing on both. For this reason, teachers would do well not to look for "the best" method of teaching but to experiment and modify their expectations and techniques according to the immediate classroom situation.

Improving Group Morale

We are now ready to consider briefly some of the factors in group interaction. Bass (1960) makes the point that changes in behavior are fostered by interaction, rather than by individual or isolated activity; to the extent that it is possible, maximum interaction should be fostered in the classroom. The social reinforcements provided by an interacting group, the opportunities to understand others' values and points of view, the chance to obtain new ideas—these and other benefits are more likely when the group acts as a group effectively.

For the class to act as a group, rather than as an audience, depends partly on its training and partly on its morale. Group morale is more than the sum total of the positive feelings of the members, for it implies a cohesiveness, a willingness to pull together and operate as an integrated unit, and a spirit in which the abilities and leadership capabilities of one member are complemented by those of another.

The *group*, as we are concerned with it, is a face-to-face aggregate of a relatively small number of people working together for a common goal. Whether the goal is set by a status leader (like a teacher) or by interaction of group members, there must be an element of common concern and common direction. The class may or may not represent a group, or it may be a group for only part of the time. It is possible for the class to be little more than a collection of individuals placed together for similar tasks. Also the class can have within it several small groups, which may be drawn together because of common interests outside the classroom. There can also be an "in-group" and several students who are considered outsiders by this group.

It is not always possible (nor even always desirable) for the class to work together as a group. Class members should, however, get along well with one another and with the teacher, and in many learning situations it is advantageous for class members to act in concert for the good of all. Examples are class projects, demonstrations, group problem solving, and discussions.

The advantages of group morale are obvious. Motivation to achieve tends to be higher when morale is high. Leadership and followership are shared. All feel pleasure in group achievement. There are fewer discipline problems and less loafing. There are mutual support, less anxiety, and less individual feeling of guilt if things do not go well. In addition to satisfaction in achieving, social reinforcement is offered, and needs for affection, belonging, status, and recognition are met. Ideas can be expressed, tensions reduced, and communication furthered.

There is some risk in overemphasizing group cohesiveness, however, and this point will be amplified in later chapters. The group can establish norms unsuitable to some individuals, and force their conformity. Independence, creativity, self-actualization, and other values can thus be stifled. One way to improve individual personality development, as well as to provide opportunities for the advancement of society, is to insist on the individual's "right to be different." The group, as we see it, should work well together. It should not stifle outsiders or dissenters, however. A successful group tolerates dissenting points of view.

Let us now consider how group morale can be fostered.

MEETING THE NEEDS OF THE GROUP

A group does not develop simply because the teacher urges class members to act as a group. Furthermore, although group decisions tend to result in changes in the behavior of group members (Lewin, 1953), it can only happen when the group's needs are met. Understanding these needs is important if the teacher is to provide the proper conditions for group formation.

FREEDOM TO COMMUNICATE. ■ In any group, it is essential that communication be free and that group members not feel threatened when expressing feelings and opinions. The perceptive teacher understands that, although there may be outward conformity to majority feelings and ideas, some group members may have different feelings but be unable to voice them for fear of being ostracized by other members or the teacher. Highest morale can be achieved only when members feel free to express negative opinions, fears, and disagreements. Frequently members may even have to work through defensive behaviors and display feelings of guilt or hostility before they can accept others and become real group members. Only when they can express themselves honestly and openly can group progress be made.

In early stages of group formation, the teacher thus fosters the members' freedom to express themselves and helps them to clarify their feelings and ideas, some of which may not be clear even to themselves. He may try to help members understand why they feel as they do and how others feel. The teacher does not suddenly become a therapist, but he does recognize that complete group feeling cannot be obtained until members are able to communicate clearly and openly with one another and with the leader. The teacher's own attitude must therefore be open, inquiring, and permissive—keeping in mind the realities of the schoolroom, of course; that is, feelings must be expressed but in acceptable ways. The opinion of each member must be heard and respected; no one should be ignored, threatened, or ridiculed. Before decisions are made, each member's ideas must be weighed on their own merits. Ideas should be obtained from all and consensus sought, rather than simply majority opinion.

SATISFACTION OF INDIVIDUAL MEMBERS' NEEDS. ■ If each member cannot feel that through group activity his own needs will be met, he will psychologically, if not physically, withdraw from the group. The common goals should provide for individual needs as well as those that are shared. Therefore, the group must provide for a variety of roles on differing levels of academic and social competence. For example, a class Valentine's Day party may offer a variety of activities, including planning the party, obtaining refreshments, inviting guests, and even, for the less verbal or socially competent child, a chance to cut paper decorations for the Valentine box.

SHARING OF LEADERSHIP. ▪ When varying abilities are needed, the leaders should be chosen on the basis of their competence in the work to be done, rather than placing leadership entirely in the hands of one person or choosing leaders on the basis of popularity.

GROUP PRESTIGE. ▪ Group achievement must be respectable, even if more direction is needed from the teacher or other leaders. No group can attain high morale if members feel that others do not esteem it. It is difficult to maintain group prestige if the group is made up of obviously unfit people, which is why classes made up of low achievers are so difficult to manage. Classes that are dumping grounds for the unfit usually have little morale, whereas honors-program classes frequently work well as groups. The difficult project (or class) will be more respected than will the easy one, and when qualifications for membership and achievement are high members are respected accordingly.

COOPERATION RATHER THAN COMPETITION. ▪ The cooperative spirit can be furthered by continual expressions of "we feeling" and references to common needs and the common goal.

CHANNELING GROUP INTERACTION. ▪ If certain pupils monopolize discussions, if some do not exercise opportunities to participate, and if undue weight is given to some opinions, morale will not be high. The teacher or other leader must be responsible for seeing that interaction includes all members.

INTEGRATION OF EVERYONE INTO THE GROUP. ▪ Cliques, in-groups, and outsiders should be brought into the total group situation; on occasion, deliberate breaking up of cliques may be necessary. Minorities should not be permitted to continue if there is any way they can be helped to become full group members.

NEGATIVE INFLUENCES

Following are some factors that can operate against group morale and thus minimize the group's achievement:

A POOR LEADER. ▪ A World War II study of the Office of Strategic Services showed that the type of leadership provided the group was one of the strongest influences on group morale. A study of bombing crews also showed that, when the plane's commander was respected and liked, the crews were more efficient and less susceptible to emotional breakdown because of hazardous missions.

In the classroom, the leader must be the teacher. His characteristics as a person have been discussed in Chapter 2, but here we shall consider some other possible negative influences.

For example, the teacher may inadvertently fail to consider his class's feelings. When he frustrates too many individuals, when he employs such tactics as mass punishment, when he uses threats to get his students to study, or when he is manifestly unfair, it may happen that the class is welded into a group—but a group that probably has in common a dislike for the teacher. This type of unity is especially likely when pupils feel that the teacher cannot be trusted: Perhaps he breaks confidences or is inconsistent in his handling of pupils. The teacher who has pets cannot foster high morale, nor can the teacher who has obvious grudges against certain children. The teacher who engenders fear or who tries to make pupils dependent upon him can hardly develop a spirit of "we." The self-centered, defensive, or hostile teacher has problems of his own and cannot give much support to his students.

On this point we like to mention the teacher who was faced with teaching a subject for which he felt poorly prepared. His remark to the class was: "Well, I am no science teacher, but if you'll bear with me, we'll all learn together." This attitude won the understanding and loyalty of the class, and, as the teacher was willing to take suggestions from his students, a fine group spirit developed.

DIVERSE CULTURAL AND SOCIAL BACKGROUNDS. ■ When a class is too heterogeneous in background, ability, values, or other attributes, it is difficult for it to develop into a group. Classes in which students are from varying socioeconomic backgrounds may be harder to work with than if they were more homogeneous. When some students have a great deal of ability in a subject and others do not, it is difficult to find activities in which all can participate.

There is considerable controversy about what to do with

older boys and girls who do not wish to be in school yet, because of laws, must remain. There is the argument that they should not be placed on the labor market, as they will be unable to find work or to advance even if hired. On the other hand, such youths may be highly disturbing influences in the school— uninterested, rebellious, or hostile. Various alternatives to school have been suggested, including youth camps, service in the armed forces, part-time jobs, and the dropping of the compulsory attendance age. So far there has been no completely satisfactory solution; these youths remain in school and may contribute to poor school and classroom morale.

The background of the teacher is also important. If he is from a very different cultural milieu from those of his pupils, he may fail to understand them or they to understand him. It has been advanced that teachers who must work with underprivileged children should have had at least somewhat similar backgrounds to theirs and thus not only understand their attitudes and mores better—but be able to serve as successful "examples" to them.

UNFAVORABLE EXTERNAL CONDITIONS. ▪ Teachers must sometimes deal with overcrowded classrooms, inadequate materials and equipment, and similar environmental problems. It is difficult to provide high classroom morale in the face of such conditions, for they tend also to detract from the morale of the school as a whole. Other external problems include pressures from parents, overly structured syllabi and curricula, time pressures on teacher and pupils, and the teaching-staff morale.

The intent of these remarks is simply to indicate that the teacher is not the sole determinant of the level of group morale in his classroom. He can work only within the framework provided him. It is sometimes surprising that teachers can do as well for their classes as they do.

ASSESSING MORALE

An excellent early group of studies was done by J. W. Wrightstone and his associates on the social climates of classrooms (1951). The Pupil-Teacher Rapport Scale, developed for the City of New York, was employed in the classroom to give a picture of group morale (see Appendix A). Categories of pupil behavior to be observed were:

1. such self-initiated pupil activities as voluntarily bringing in clippings, exhibits, and books;
2. such cooperative activities as helping other students or teachers;
3. praising or criticizing activities or work of others;
4. leadership activities like organizing, directing, or controlling new combinations of people and things;
5. such work-study habits as using time wisely, working efficiently, and clearing away materials.

The degree of social interaction, its quality, the interest and enjoyment of class members, the role structure, physical and emotional aspects of the group, and activities and feelings of the teacher were all assessed. This device and others, like the scales of J. Withall (1960) and R. F. Bales (1950) can all give clues to the quality of classroom interaction.

In addition, of course, evaluation of the products of the group, information observation, and information informally provided by pupils help the teacher assess his group spirit.

Appendix A may be helpful to the teacher in this way: He can rate a random class session according to the variables, allowing "1st" for himself. He can then request a colleague, supervisor, principal, or other adult familiar with teaching to rate "2nd," and he can, if possible, obtain a third rater. Comparison of ratings and discussion with raters should prove valuable, especially if there is difference of opinion.

A second way to employ this scale is to rate the class on three different days or have it rated on three occasions. A comparison over these periods of time may throw considerable light on the prevailing classroom modes.

Appendix B is a modification of Bales' Interaction Process Analysis. Someone makes note of comments made during classroom discussion. Every remark by pupil or teacher should be categorized "A-1," "A-2," and so forth and entered on a prepared chart. (Obviously the validity of such a rating depends somewhat on practice.) The illustration shows that discussion was always between teacher and pupil, rather than among pupils. Mary S. was certainly negative in reactions, Joe J. was essentially positive, but most of the class had not participated as far as the chart had been continued. Not only the pattern of discussion, but also characteristic teacher and pupil patterns, can be assessed with this method.

Appendix C shows how pupils perceived their teachers; it provided the basis for categorizing teachers in the Gordon and Adler study. Perhaps the teacher can find value in asking the questions of himself.

Continual evaluation—formal or informal—will help the teacher keep in touch with the state of his class's morale and how it is changing. Teachers get general impressions, of course, of how things are going. But such instruments as these scales or even careful observation can point to things that may otherwise be overlooked. Not only the general progress of the class as a whole, but also the actions of individual pupils should be scrutinized: Perhaps a given child has steadily become more negative in his classroom comments, perhaps another child has begun to drop out of discussions, or perhaps another youngster has quite suddenly shown himself to be a leader.

Use of these scales can be especially effective if we can get other observers with whom we may compare notes. These rating devices can do a lot to improve teaching practices.

□

REFERENCES

Amidon, E. J., and N. A. Flanders. *The Role of the Teacher in the Classroom,* p. 57. Minneapolis: Amidon, 1963.

Anderson, R. C. "Learning in Discussions: A Résumé of the Authoritarian-Democratic Studies," *Harvard Educational Review,* 29 (1959), 201–15.

Bales, R. F. *Interaction Process Analysis.* Cambridge, Mass.: Addison-Wesley, 1950.

Bass, B. M. *Leadership, Psychology, and Organizational Behavior.* New York: Harper, 1960.

Christensen, C. M. "Relationships Between Pupil Achievement, Pupil Affect-Need, Teacher Warmth, and Teacher Permissiveness," *Journal of Educational Psychology,* 51 (1960), 169–74.

Cogan, M. L. "The Behavior of Teachers and the Productive Behavior of Their Pupils: I. Perception Analysis," *Journal of Experimental Education,* 27 (1958), 89–105.

Fiedler, F. E. "Leader Attitudes, Group Climate, and Group Creativity," *Journal of Abnormal and Social Psychology,* 65 (1962), 308–18.

Flanders, N. A. *Teacher Influence—Pupil Attitudes and Achievement* (Final Report, Cooperative Research Project 397). Ann Arbor: University of Michigan, 1960.

Gordon, C. W., and L. M. Adler. *Dimensions of Teacher Leadership in Classroom Social Systems* (Final Report, Cooperative Research Project 1084). Los Angeles: University of California, 1963.

Heil, L. M., M. Powell, and I. Feifer. *Characteristics of Teacher Behavior Related to the Achievement of Children in Several Elementary Grades* (Final Report, Cooperative Research Project SAE-7285). New York: Brooklyn College, 1960.

Lewin, K. "Studies in Group Decision," in D. Cartwright and A. Zander (eds.). *Group Dynamics: Research and Theory,* pp. 287–301. Evanston: Row, Peterson, 1953.

Lewin, K., R. Lippitt, and R. K. White. "Patterns of Aggressive Behavior in Experimentally Created 'Social Climates,' " *Journal of Social Psychology,* 10 (1939), 261–99.

Medley, D. M., and H. E. Mitzel. "Some Behavioral Correlates of Teacher Effectiveness," *Journal of Educational Psychology,* 50 (1959), 239–46.

Neill, A. S. *Summerhill: A Radical Approach to Child Rearing.* New York: Holt, Rinehart, Winston, 1960.

Ringness, T. A. *Differences in Attitudes Toward Self and Others of Successful and Non-Successful Ninth Grade Boys of Superior Intelligence* (Final Report, National Institute of Mental Health Post-Doctoral Research Fellowship). Los Angeles: University of California, 1963.

Rogers, C. R., and B. F. Skinner. "Some Issues Concerning the Control of Human Behavior," *Science,* 124 (1956), 1057–66.

Skinner, B. F. *Walden Two.* New York: Macmillan, 1948.

Wallen, N. E., and K. H. Wodtke. *Relationships Between Teacher Characteristics and Student Behavior—Part I* (Final Report, U.S. Department of Health, Education and Welfare, Office of Education Contract 2-10-013). Salt Lake City: University of Utah, 1963.

Withall, J. *Teacher Education-Mental Health Project* (National Institute of Mental Health Contract 2M-6624–C2). Madison: University of Wisconsin, 1960.

Wrightstone, J. W. "Measuring the Social Climate of a Classroom," *Journal of Educational Research,* 44 (1951), 341–51.

———. *Pupil-Teacher Rapport Scale.* New York: Bureau of Educational Research, 1950.

SUGGESTIONS FOR FURTHER READING

Amidon, E. J., and N. A. Flanders. *The Role of the Teacher in the Classroom.* Minneapolis: Amidon, 1963.

This work describes the "interaction analysis" technique in some detail and discusses the philosophy of and research into its development and usage. As the "Flanders technique" is one of the most promising means of assessing teacher-pupil interaction, it is well worth examining closely in terms of both practical and research use.

Bany, M. A., and L. V. Johnson. *Classroom Group Behavior.* New York: Macmillan, 1964.

The entire book is devoted to group dynamics as applied to the class-room. The four sections are concerned with the background of group behavior; some of the characteristics of classroom groups; methods for changing group behavior; and a discussion of some applicable research. Bany and Johnson provide illustrations of actual situations that aid in understanding the principles. In addition, they supply references that can lead the reader to other appropriate sources. We might emphasize that this topic is being extensively researched and that the application of group dynamics to the school setting has only recently become scientific (and carefully studied).

Seidman, J. M. *Education for Mental Health: A Book of Readings.* New York: Crowell, 1963.

A section on teacher personality and behavior contributes additional research and authoritative discussion related to the present chapter. R. M. Porter discusses student attitudes toward child behavior problems; J. S. Kounin, P. V. Gump, and J. J. Ryan III discuss classroom-management studies; H. Rosenfeld and A. Zander cover the influence of teachers on aspirations of students. A section on social behavior provides articles by M. Sherif on superordinate goals in the reduction of intergroup conflict that may relate to social problems reflected in the school; by N. A. Flanders and S. Havumaki on teacher-pupil contacts involving praise and effects on students' sociometric choices; by M. A. Dineen and R. Garry on the effects of sociometric seating on classroom cleavage; by A. Phillips and L. A. D'Amico on the effects of cooperation and competition on the cohesiveness of small groups; and by E. Amidon on aiding the isolates in children's groups. Such articles extend considerably the knowledge and understanding of interaction and morale that we have treated in this chapter.

4

CLASSROOM CONTROL
AND
MENTAL HEALTH

There are more than 2.5 million serious crimes in the United States each year. Serious crimes have increased 13 per cent per year, which is a rate of increase three times that of the population growth. People under eighteen years of age committed 37 per cent of serious crimes solved by police. Arrests of young law violators increased 17 per cent in 1965 over 1964. These figures come from the annual report of the Federal Bureau of Investigation (1965). There can be no question but that young people are less controlled and less socially adjusted than in the past and that this problem is increasing rapidly.

Schools are facing an increase in vandalism, theft, defiance, aggressive acts, even noting a rise in teen-age drug and alcohol problems. Not only are such problems becoming more frequent, but they are appearing in privileged city areas, suburbs, and rural communities, as well as in deprived metropolitan areas.

These facts are not meant to frighten teachers but to suggest that school personnel needs to take a careful look at school discipline and classroom control practices to see whether or not present methods are as useful as possible. It is granted that parents, police, and other community agencies must be as con-

94

cerned (or even more concerned) as the schools. Yet schools are supposed to help socialize children. Are they doing their best?

This chapter is concerned with the dynamics of disciplinary practices. It also attempts to relate control practices to pupils' mental health. We shall try to shed some light on the causes of poor discipline and hope to make some useful suggestions about ways to develop the kinds of classroom control that seem most desirable.

For one statement of the problem, read the following true account; then turn to our discussion:

AN EXAMPLE OF SCHOOL DISCIPLINE AND MORALE

When young Mr. T. obtained the position of supervising principal in a small school, he felt it would be helpful to interview the retiring incumbent, in advance of assuming control. In this way he hoped to gain a preview of existing problems as well as of strong points of his new school, so thus to be able to develop some of his policies and plans before arriving on the job. Accordingly, he met Mr. L., the retiring principal, who, although pleasant, was pessimistic. Mr. L. was elderly, a person to whom the years had not been kind, and was looking forward only to retirement. Nevertheless, Mr. L. was proud of the ways he handled his disciplinary problems.

"There is the chair leg, in the corner," said Mr. L. Seeing that this was less than enlightening, he went on to explain, "In this school you have to watch out for some pretty tough boys. Big, too. Some of them carry knives and they can get rough. But I know how to handle them. I keep that chair leg over there, and they know it. If they come at me, I'll rap them over the knuckles, or do whatever I have to do. When you take over, be just as hard as I am. Then you won't have any trouble."

Such an introduction to a new job does not make one feel at ease. However, Mr. T. felt that he should have full knowledge of whatever problems did exist, and that when he knew "the worst" he might be able to plan his actions more appropriately. He pressed for further information.

It developed that at school dances some of the older girls had brought their alumni boy friends, and there had been drinking and rowdyness; accordingly, there were now no school dances. The boys had been "acting up" in the gymnasium during the noon lunch hour, so the gym was now closed to them at that time. The merchants of the town did not like this, however, for some of the students congregated in the stores, with resulting confusion and some shoplifting. Some students spent part of the noon hour driving their cars recklessly about town.

There were writing on the walls, gouges in the woodwork, broken windows, tire marks on the school lawn, and a general air of defiance of authority. Partly for this reason, it was difficult to obtain and hold good teachers, and the curriculum suffered accordingly. Only one year of shop courses was offered; chemistry and physics were taught in alternate years; the library was overcrowded; control in study halls was lax. Extraclass activities also suffered, and the only going concerns were the school annual and basketball and baseball teams.

We invite you to consider what might be done in such a situation to improve school control and to enhance school morale. What Mr. T. actually did will be reported near the end of this chapter.

Desirable School Discipline

INNER CONTROLS ON BEHAVIOR

On page 70 a study concerning high- and low-achieving junior high-school boys was mentioned. Other findings will be reported here. In this study (Ringness, 1963), it was found that low achievers reported more school and family problems than did high achievers and in addition had more "nervous symptoms" and a lower sense of personal worth. It will be recalled that low achievers tended to have greater orientation toward peer affiliation than did high achievers; the latter were more oriented toward academic achievement. Interviews with these boys suggested that a desire for peer affiliation was probably both a cause and an effect of poor home relationships, low sense of personal worth, and "nervous symptoms," for the low-achieving boys' families did not take kindly to poor school achievement and tended to be somewhat punitive. At the same time, poor family relationships in many instances tended to cause the boys to seek peer affiliations and group support in excess of that sought by their high-achieving peers.

Another study (Ringness, 1965) showed that high achievers were more responsible, self-controlled, tolerant of others, and socialized than were low achievers. That such personality characteristics are related to disciplinary problems, as well as to school achievement, was attested by further data showing that low achievers were more rebellious, less conforming, and less willing to accept the school model for docility and "good behavior." They reported beliefs that most pupils only worked hard enough to "get by" and that they themselves cared less about what teachers thought of them than did high achievers.

In a word, these studies and others that will be described in Chapter 5 indicate that many low achievers are less well socialized than are high achievers. They also represent a good share of the "problem youngsters" in any school. At least one kind of child who contributes to school disciplinary problems is somewhat irresponsible, does not identify well with the school or with teacher values, and is somewhat undercontrolled, intolerant, and nonconforming.

It is commonly supposed that the best school discipline comes from within the child as a result of socially oriented motives or values, rather than being imposed from without. A child should conform to reasonable standards of behavior because he *wants* to—he understands and accepts the need for socially acceptable actions. He should not be "good" simply because he fears to be "bad." He should accept responsibility for his actions as a matter of course and not expect special inducements for desirable behavior.

Now, although it is true that inner controls are desirable in the child, they do not come about automatically, nor are they always adequate for the decisions he may be forced to make. To support progress toward maturity, it is necessary that parents and schools provide controls for the child until such time as he has developed controls of his own. Enough external control must be applied by parent or teacher so that the child conforms to society's demands until he learns to accept social values and finds means of self-control.

Too stringent external control, however, makes the child

dependent or rebellious. The proper amount is that which helps him conform suitably to the demands of his society without producing undesirable side effects. Quite obviously the teacher has to be in command of his classroom. His stepping in when needed may be a valuable support to his pupils. It helps protect children from fear of acting out their own impulses and also from fear of what might occur if they lost control of themselves. It also reinforces in children behavior taught to them by their parents and provides them with the security of knowing that others will not be permitted to act aggressively toward them.

When the teacher shows confidence that children will control themselves and accept responsibility but indicates that, if necessary, he will exert pressure, conditions favorable to maturing are enhanced.

The basic intent of desirable classroom control is to help children understand how to satisfy their needs in the context of those of society, to play acceptable roles, and therefore to receive more of the rewards offered by society to those who contribute to its welfare. Framed in this positive manner, reasons for acceptable behavior can be more readily seen by the child, and he is more able to resist temptation to misbehave. Pupils can thus learn to accept responsibility for their own conduct and to respect their own rights and those of others.

This approach is quite different from the punitive, threatening, and essentially degrading kinds of classroom control employed by some teachers, in which it is implicit that they have given up trying to help the child learn in a positive way and only hope to prevent him from doing things that disturb them.

PUPIL PERSONALITY AND CONTROL TECHNIQUES

Personalities of children are different. They may not respond similarly to techniques applied indiscriminately on a group basis. For example, G. G. Thompson and C. W. Hunnicutt studied the effects of praise and blame on extroverts (their spelling) and introverts (1944). They found that repeated blame was more effective than praise in increasing work output of extroverts and that repeated praise was more effective with introverts. Some of the children in both groups who were repeatedly blamed became increasingly emotionally upset by this, however, and some ceased entirely to try. Disciplinary efforts must be aimed quite specifically at the kind of child involved. A look from the teacher will suffice to quiet some, whereas others require more vigorous handling.

Another factor of importance is that of consistency of control. Although it is true that the teacher may tolerate more informality under certain circumstances than under others (a classroom party compared to a formal testing situation) and although it is also true that the method of control may vary from child to child, there should be consistency in reinforcing the same acts (positively or negatively) from day to day. That is, one should not ignore an act one day, punish it the next, and laugh at it on the third day. Furthermore, all children should be reinforced for the same standards of behavior. Otherwise, there will be little opportunity for children to learn what is acceptable behavior and what is not. Children who are continually asked to adjust to new situations, as when different teachers have differing standards of discipline, may not only fail to learn, but may also be frustrated and break the control patterns of both teachers.

Control patterns or classroom rules should not be too confining or too rigid. Such control may cause children to become dependent, frustrated, or fearful of the teacher. In some classes children almost automatically become anxious; guilt patterns may develop when the teacher is unduly threatening or demanding.

As stated earlier, children must learn to accept a useful set of social norms; these norms must be useful to the child and not merely to society. There is some danger in insisting upon conformity if the child does not understand why he should accept the demands placed upon him. Insisting on passive obedience to adult demands does not help a child. Conformity may cause one to lose the courage of his own convictions, as M. L. Hoffman (1955) shows. He found that children who conform strongly tend to score lower on measures of "ego strength" than those who are nonconforming; they score higher on measures of parental dominance, overconcern for the well-being of parents, overidealization of parents, strict moralism, positive attitude toward authority, success striving, and conservative attitudes in political and religious areas. Such children have been raised by overauthoritarian parents. They are frequently liked by adults, but they tend to be dominated by others. They may fear competition and have strong feelings of guilt and self-doubt. They are somewhat submissive and may be suggestible. They can find it more difficult to achieve mature independence. Too much strictness may thus have negative consequences. A happy medium is needed.

In regard to conflict, a frequent cause of poor personal or social adjustment, the school needs to keep in mind that school values may not be those of the home or of the peer group. Good discipline does not intensify these conflicts but attempts to promote a mutually agreeable solution. Failure to do so may result in children overconforming, losing their ability to identify with the school mores, and becoming frustrated, irritable, and guilty.

In regard to guilt, when a child must be reprimanded or punished, he should not be made to feel forever branded as a culprit. He must be shown how to atone for his misbehavior so that guilt and anxiety (or hostility, if he does not accept his guilt) will not be maintained. The teacher should show that he can accept the child, even if he cannot accept his behavior. Furthermore, control practices must distinguish between what is "wrong" or "bad" in a moral sense and what is "wrong" only because the child failed to reach a standard of attainment. The child must not attach a moral value to inability to succeed at a task; he must not be made to feel guilt over such failure. Failure is a natural consequence of living and occurs when one attempts a task beyond his present capabilities. Fear of failure, guilt, or feelings of rejection because of poor achievement have ramifications in motivation, self-acceptance, and defense mechanisms. Too many teachers imply that inability to achieve is the result of "not trying" or "not paying attention"—which may indeed be the case. But many children try, fail, and then feel not only inadequate but also morally wrong. Poor mental health is thus virtually assured. Finally, in disciplinary situations, the child's self-esteem must not be damaged. Sarcasm, ridicule, shaming, and other negative approaches may make him feel inadequate, rejected, or unworthy. Damaged self-esteem leads to all sorts of problems—the end result, of course, being deteriorated mental health and inability to cope.

Some Reasons Children Misbehave

In the last analysis, one usually finds life most satisfying if he assumes roles acceptable to society. If he conforms reasonably to the sanctions of his culture and thus receives the rewards, protection, assistance, and encouragement it can offer, some of his personal goals are reached. He is then freer to attempt within the social framework to seek self-actualization. For example, the better one can assume such prized roles as those of the athletic hero, the excellent student, and the energetic young businessman, the more social reward he is likely to have for his behavior and the more likely are his needs for status, recognition, and material rewards to be satisfied. But when one assumes roles that conflict with those allowed by society, he may find himself in danger, for behavior that does not satisfy social demands is punished by others. The child who forsakes the struggle for legitimate reward in school may find himself temporarily satisfied by the juvenile gang, but in the long run he fails to gain needed rewards and may be severely punished by the larger social group. Should he then forsake the demands of the culture for a set of mores of the gang subculture, he is unlikely to achieve successful, happy living.

Most children realize this fact. Why, then, are some children such problems to their parents or schools, even when they know they will suffer for their nonconformity? Why do some children persist in behavior that is punished by society, in spite of all that is said (and done) to them?

FAILURE TO LEARN SOCIAL BEHAVIOR

Sigmund Freud (1949) was one of the first to call attention to changes in style of response as the infant advances to early childhood. He thought that the infant was essentially a selfish being at the mercy of his own bodily needs and desires. Immediate gratification was seen as necessary if the infant was not to feel fear, anxiety, or frustration; the infant might thus complain loudly if he were hungry at two o'clock in the morning, caring (or knowing) nothing about his parents' need for sleep. This demand for immediate gratification through direct channels was explained by Freud as living according to the *pleasure principle*. Although expected in infants, such a way of life is not viewed as desirable for older children and adults, even though some adults are somewhat infantile and manifest demanding, impulsive, overly impatient, or too dependent behavior.

The infant begins to learn, however, even during the first year of life, that all his wants cannot be immediately satisfied. He learns to delay his demands, in accordance with the "reality principle"; he may thus try to suppress his desires for a time or to find indirect ways of attaining his goals. For example, he learns to live according to a schedule, to consider the wishes of others, to be cooperative instead of selfish, and so on. Should such learning fail to occur, the child is in frequent difficulty, for he tries to meet his needs at society's expense and is punished by society for this course of action. The sociopath (sometimes called "psychopath") is a youth or adult who seems to have utterly failed to conform to the reality principle; something has caused him not to learn to relate and adjust to the rights of others. Most people do not develop in such extremely maladjustive ways, yet if one examines one's own behavior he may find ways in which he has not become completely socialized. For example, there may be times when someone fails to obey laws, when he manipulates or "uses" others for his own purposes, when he is actively aggressive against others, when he is unduly demanding, or when he fails to tolerate delay and acts impulsively.

Among the reasons for failure to progress in social learning may be overindulgence of the child's demands, or unrealistic gratification of his desires, so that he has no need to consider others and act in a more mature manner. Or perhaps overcontrol of the child may make him more dependent so that he lacks strength to act on his own initiative and to assume responsibility. Inconsistency on the part of the parents in stating and enforcing sanctions may also contribute to immaturity, for the child is then faced with alternative interpretations of his behavior. He becomes confused about what is required of him and, because of inadequate learning, fails to become adequately socialized.

J. Dollard and N. E. Miller (1950) discuss some of the conflicts in early childhood that may relate to lack of social development. For example, there has been a question about whether infants should be fed "on demand" or on a fixed schedule. When he is hungry, the child cries. If he is not fed but left to "cry himself out," the child can learn that there is nothing he can do to change such painful circumstances, and a basis may be laid for apathy and "not trying something else" when in trouble. Again, if the child is left to cry, hunger mounts more strongly with the passage of time; if the child is *then* fed, he may learn that violent outbursts are rewarded. The child can thus learn to employ violent expressions, even when only mild hunger is experienced, and he learns to overreact and to be apprehensive.

On the other hand, if fed promptly, the infant learns to relax at the approach of its mother, and eventually even the mere sounds or presence of the mother can produce feelings of well-being; the mother becomes a person with whom the child identifies, and her desires can be internalized by the child.

Conversely, if the child is fed when he is not hungry (as may happen when he is fed on a schedule), the reward value of the food decreases, and the child may learn not to care if others are there or not—conceivably he could become low in social feeling. If he is punished for crying when hungry, a hunger-anxiety conflict may occur.

Such reasoning applies in other situations also: toilet training, childish fears, early sexual experimentation, and the like. As early patterns of responses tend to continue—indeed, to become a way of life—it is important that early training be carefully considered.

A. Bandura and R. H. Walters (1963) stress the influence of identification and modeling in social learning. As children tend to identify and accept the mores of people who provide rewards for them, the *kind* of model provided by parents (and later peers and teachers) has much to do with their social behavior. Impulsive parents may thus have impulsive children; hostile parents may have hostile children; anxious parents may have anxious children; and compulsive parents may have compulsive children. Of course, should the child fail to identify with the parents or with any other model, he may react against values and behaviors exhibited by them.

J. F. Feldhusen, J. R. Thurston, and E. Ager (1965) studied 384 children from the third-, sixth-, and ninth-grade levels. Defining children as "socially approved" (industrious, productive, good-natured, ambitious, cooperative, truthful, and so forth) or "socially disapproved" (disruptive, bullying, temperamental, overly dominant, tardy or absent without excuse, insolent, lying, cruel, and so forth), they used various devices to assess home backgrounds and family interactions. Table 4 shows some of the differences found significant.

This discussion seems to emphasize one main point: Socialization of the child depends primarily on demonstrating to the child the values of society's rewards, hence the desirability of incorporating society's behavior standards and mores. A positive approach works much better than do such negative approaches as punishment; the latter usually fails in its purpose, particularly if the child does not fully understand the reasons for it.

Children often come into the school with inadequate inner controls and inadequate socialization. The school can help most by demonstrating to the child the values of conforming to reasonable adult standards. Appropriate positive reinforcement, provision of identifying figures and models, and helping the child find real satisfactions in school are of primary importance. Conversely, the child who is isolated, frequently derided or punished, and subject to experiences of failure has little inducement to accept the values of the school. We shall pursue these points further, after suggesting some other reasons for misbehavior.

In our illustration of the retiring school principal's actions against his students (p. 95), it was clear that punitive measures "did not work" but simply resulted in retaliatory action of the students against the principal and the school. This happened partly because many innocent students suffered along with the culprits, partly because the goals of the students were not being met, but perhaps primarily because no inducements

TABLE 4. Ratings on 5 Glueck Factors for Behavior and Location

FACTOR	GROUPS	RATING CLASSIFICATIONS AND FREQUENCIES			CHI-SQUARE
		Erratic or Overstrict	Lax	Firm but Kind	
I. Discipline of child by father	Approved	24	31	137	23.52*
	Disapproved	57	42	93	2 df
	Urban	35	22	135	19.97*
	Rural	46	51	95	2 df
		Unsuitable	Fair	Suitable	
II. Supervision of child by mother	Approved	6	26	160	29.06*
	Disapproved	14	66	112	2 df
	Urban	7	36	149	8.63†
	Rural	13	56	123	2 df
		Indifferent or Hostile		Warm or Overprotective	
III. Affection of father for child	Approved	29		163	17.26*
	Disapproved	65		127	1 df
	Urban	34		158	8.80*
	Rural	60		132	1 df
		Indifferent or Hostile		Warm or Overprotective	
IV. Affection of mother for child	Approved	17		175	14.02*
	Disapproved	45		147	1 df
	Urban	21		171	6.94*
	Rural	41		151	1 df
		Some or None		Marked	
V. Cohesiveness of family	Approved	46		146	35.54*
	Disapproved	104		88	1 df
	Urban	54		138	18.39*
	Rural	96		96	1 df

* Significant at .01 level of confidence.
† Significant at .05 level of confidence.
SOURCE: J. F. Feldhusen, J. R. Thurston, and E. Ager, "Delinquency Proneness of Urban and Rural Youth," *Journal of Research in Crime and Delinquency*, 2 (January 1965), 36.

were being offered for acceptable social behavior. We shall later discuss better alternatives for aiding children to acquire mature, responsible behavior.

CONFLICTING ROLE DEMANDS

There are various roles that the child is expected to enact, for example, son, pupil, athlete, Boy Scout. These roles may coincide, or they may conflict. If the role of son conflicts with that of peer or if the role of student conflicts with that of gang member, there is always a question of which role will be emphasized; essentially the child tends to identify with the role that provides him with most rewards, but there are problems when he desires rewards offered by conflicting roles. (For example, many children do not achieve so highly in school as we should expect from examination of their earlier achievement scores or I.Q.s. This discrepancy can result from a desire to identify with peer groups, whose achievement norms may be very mediocre. Or some children can take satisfaction from irritating the teacher if they can gain status with the peer group by being known as "taking nothing from nobody.")

Problems frequently arise with children from subcultures that are at variance with the "middle-class" culture portrayed by most schools. For example, in some "high-risk" areas children are taught to fight physically, lest they be called "sissies," yet fighting may be frowned on in the school play area; learning to discriminate and to control one's behavior may be difficult for such children. In some families, swearing may be looked upon with no particular disgust and, among the peer group, may be a mark of status; yet swearing is punishable at school. Such cultural differences in standards suggest that the teacher needs a thorough knowledge of the mores of his school population area. He must begin "where the child is" and by gradual efforts perhaps move the child toward more acceptable standards; yet he must do so without damaging the relationships of the child (or the school) to the home. If standards differ too widely and if too much pressure is put upon the child, damaging conflicts can arise. Equally, if the child finds school reinforcements different from those of his home, he can only be confused and may fail to mature appropriately.

An extreme example appears in the book *The Blackboard Jungle* (Hunter, 1963) , which shows that most pupils cannot be successfully coerced into obeying rules and trying to learn. The work described in this book had to begin with the children's subculture itself. Some of the pupils asked for nothing more than to be let alone and resented assignment of even the simplest tasks. Until they could learn to tolerate the school situation, they could not be required to try to learn. The film, *The Quiet One,* similarly shows how children from deviant cultures, many of whom have been hurt emotionally, cannot be forced to participate in school situations until they are able to trust and accept the teacher and the school itself. Pressure on such children only increases the threat they already feel; this increase in turn increases anxiety, resentment, and negative forms of behavior.

SCHOOL CONDITIONS

This book is concerned with school conditions that contribute to poor mental health or poor adjustment. Many of these conditions contribute to poor discipline, and poor discipline and poor mental health are closely allied. Later chapters will discuss stresses upon pupils and will include discussions of grouping, marking practices, motivational practices, and others. For this reason, we shall content ourselves here with merely noting that the curriculum, in its broadest sense, may contribute to poor school discipline, either because it is poorly suited to the requirements of certain pupils or because it is poorly administered.

When children fail to receive sufficient satisfaction from school, many fail to identify with the school; both disciplinary and achievement problems result, and some children eventually drop out of school entirely. Bright children, as well as dull ones, sometimes find their assignments meaningless ("Mickey Mouse," "busy work") ; others find themselves unable to achieve success. Some deem the teacher unfair and find ways to release their hostility at his expense.

Some children are placed in classes in which they have no interest or for which they are unfit; the general tendency to aim most high-school students toward college and to teach accordingly is an example, although recent trends at upgrading technical and vocational schools are a refreshing step toward making school more suitable for all youth. Some students are bored with too easy assignments; others are frustrated with work that is too difficult. Yet schools tend not to recognize the difference between *quality* of task and *quantity* of task and tend in effect to teach all students at the same level. The classroom may be overcrowded, there may be insufficient materials, organization of activities may be poor, or the teacher may lack understanding of his subject—or of children.

This last lack, of course, was clearly part of the problem in Mr. T.'s new school. The gymnasium had been closed, and students had no opportunity for noon-hour recreation and were really forced to spend their free time about town. The curriculum was certainly inadequate to meet the needs of most students, and the extraclass-activity program was woefully lacking. The library and study halls were poorly administered. All in all, it was not surprising that students tended to identify negatively with their school.

PERSONALITY CONDITIONS OF CHILDREN

Among the personality conditions that may contribute to inappropriate classroom behavior are desires for independence, attention, and status; feelings of guilt; habitual frustration and resentment; continued anxiety; and even neuroses, psychoses, and organic problems.

R. Dreikurs (1957) makes much of the fundamental desire to belong, or the security of knowing one is valued and desired. Although this desire is strongly related to the peer group, especially during adolescence, basic security begins at home. As the child enters school, he may seek a feeling of belonging similar to that he had at home, or, if this feeling was not attained at home, he may attempt to compensate through the school.

In his book, Dreikurs suggests that, if the child cannot attain a feeling of being a valued member of his group, he bids for attention in a desire for evidence of his worth as an individual. This seeking of attention may be manifest in a number of ways. Some children may seek attention through achievements in academic, athletic, social, or other areas and may be competitive and even compulsive in their efforts to gain the plaudits of others. Some seek attention by trying to be attractive or cultivating the teacher. But some seek attention inappropriately by becoming nuisances or by sullenness. Some poor learners are in reality seeking attention, for such behavior brings attention from teacher and peers.

Dreikurs recognizes a progression of deteriorating behavior (see Figure 5). If children are thwarted in attention seeking by being punished, shamed, or ridiculed, they may resort to more serious misbehavior. They may rebel and engage in what he terms a "struggle for power" with the teacher, challenging him through their misbehavior. They imply that the teacher cannot "make them learn" or even "make them behave." They are thus proving their worth by manipulating the teacher. This behavior, too, was seen in the illustration at the beginning of this chapter (p. 95).

If the teacher uses extreme force in trying to win the "struggle for power," the child may become vengeful and employ vicious kinds of behavior. The eventual turn of strong pressures upon the child may lead to complete discouragement and inability to live a successful life. Needless to say, children who seek revenge or who are deeply discouraged need professional help and should be referred to appropriate sources.

Some children become class "clowns," trying to mask basic feelings of inferiority or insecurity. Some attempt to gain status with the peer group by "goofing off" in the classroom. Some are hyperactive because of anxiety. Some, failing to gain acceptance in the peer group, become resentful and sullen. In each case, there is a reason for the behavior, and handling of the problem should be related to the reason, if it can be found.

One more type of problem behavior demands specific mention. It can loosely be called "aggressive," in the sense that it appears hostile, angry, resentful, or irritable; bothers other people; or is turned against property as in vandalism. Aggressive children, in this sense of the term, are likely to bully others, to be defiant, and to be difficult to live with. Teachers tend in turn to feel angry and become punitive.

It is difficult to see aggressive behavior as a symptom and still more difficult to realize that it can be caused by feelings of rejection, inadequacy, or even legitimate rebellion at truly intolerable conditions, but such is frequently the case.

It should be noted that aggressive behavior has an advantage, in a clinical sense, over withdrawing or escapist behavior, as it represents an attack on a problem rather than an admission of defeat. The aggressive child may be helped to rethink his methods of trying to overcome his problems; the withdrawn child may lack motivation to overcome his problems at all, and helping him may be more difficult.

Later we shall discuss some methods of dealing with problem behavior.

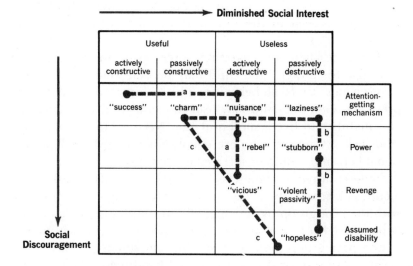

FIGURE 5. Schematic diagram of Dreikurs' concept of deteriorating pupil behavior (from lack of feeling of belonging).

Note that the child may proceed toward diminished social interest, toward social discouragement, or toward both. For example, he may proceed along the path represented by the broken line "a," "b," or "c." "Success" and "charm" are construed as actively constructive and passively constructive behavior respectively. "Nuisance" and "laziness" are parallel destructive counterparts.

SOURCE: Rudolf Dreikurs, *Psychology in the Classroom* (New York: Harper & Row, 1957), p. 15.

TEACHER PERSONALITY AND BEHAVIOR

We have devoted a chapter (Chapter 2) to discussion of the teacher as a person and shall only note here that the teacher frequently "gets what he asks for" from his pupils. The teacher who engages in Dreikurs' "struggle for power" with the children, who is sarcastic, uses ridicule or shame, or is unduly touchy or punitive, induces resentment to the point at which most pupils (even the "good kids") will rebel and become hostile. Some teachers act as if they have no concern for the feelings of pupils. Some hold grudges. Others are rejecting. Some are so threatened by the children that they become rigid and barricade themselves behind their desks. Such teachers may be impersonal, cool, and aloof to children and may become unduly anxious at minor infractions of the rules. Some, by their very actions, seem almost to induce problems; for example, as we saw in Chapter 2, one teacher frequently dashed weeping from the room, thereby inducing some of the boys to find ways to bring about this interesting phenomenon. Another teacher would throw things at the pupils. (Chalk, pencils, and erasers were no problem, but her downfall came when she threw an ink bottle, which hit the wall and broke, splashing several children.)

Reasons for the teacher's behavior are rooted in his motives, his training, his cultural heritage, and his emotions—just as are those of his pupils' behavior. It is obviously necessary to recruit and train as many competent and mentally healthy people as possible for the teaching profession.

Some Learning-Theory Principles

The approach of this book is somewhat eclectic, but, in the main, practices suggested to the teacher evolve largely out of a *learning theory* context. A. Bandura and R. H. Walters (1963) offer an excellent discussion in this area. In essence, the paradigm for learning theory consists of stimulus, response, and reinforcement, in that order. A stimulus elicits a response, and, if that response is confirmed by a reinforcement (or reward), when the stimulus again appears the same response should again be elicited.

The terms "stimulus" and "response" are complex, and definitions vary according to author and context. As they are employed here, stimuli are any phenomena to which the individual reacts. They may come from the external environment in the form of sights, sounds, or other sensations; they may also, however, come from within the individual in the form of ideas, emotions, or internal sensations like muscular pain. Responses are essentially reactions of the individual to stimuli—they may be overt movements, ideas, emotions, and so forth. These definitions are essentially circular in a sense, of course, but as long as the reader understands that stimuli are any phenomena that elicit behaviors and that responses are the behaviors elicited, the principles discussed should be clear enough for present purposes.

Reinforcements may be positive or negative. They are essentially the perceptions of the consequences of one's behavior as pleasant or unpleasant.

Responses that are not reinforced tend not to be elicited again by the stimulus; this result is termed *extinction*. If negative reinforcement (punishment) follows the response, the response will be *inhibited;* that is, the response will be held back although the tendency to make the response will still be there. When negative reinforcement is used, therefore, the reinforcement (or threat of reinforcement) must be present, or the response may again be elicited. Negative reinforcement is not a good way of controlling behavior, therefore, in a disciplinary sense. If it is followed by the organism's trying an alternative response, however, the alternative may be reinforced, which can be desirable. One other point must be made: When negative reinforcement or punishment is employed to control behavior, it is important that such reinforcement occur near the beginning of the act we wish to inhibit; if punishment occurs after the act is completed, the risk is run that the organism simply learns not to get caught—that is, to avoid the punishment.

This discussion has been quite technical. Let us illustrate.

Suppose a man is training a puppy. He whistles; the pup

pricks up his ears and may come toward the man. When the dog comes near, the owner pets him, speaks kindly to him, and perhaps offers him a tidbit. Before long the dog will come to his owner each time he whistles. It will not be necessary to reinforce the dog every time, just some of the time; but if the man fails to reinforce him at all, the time will come when he will whistle and the dog will fail to come. This process is extinction. It is clear that positive reinforcement induces approach (or adient) behavior.

Now, if a mischievous youth whistles and the pup comes and he then speaks harshly to the dog or strikes him, the dog will learn not to come to that person when he whistles. He probably will, however, come when his owner calls. Negative reinforcement thus teaches avoidance behavior. Whether that behavior extends to everyone who whistles or merely to the youth who punished will depend upon how well the pup learned to *discriminate* between stimuli emitted by the youth and by the pup's owner. If no discrimination occurs, the dog will be in conflict, having been positively and negatively reinforced for the same response.

Now, it was noted that *stimuli* can come from the environment, that is, from without the individual, or from within, in the form of ideas, emotions, or biological states, for example. Equally, *reinforcements* can come from without—the smiles of the teacher, an "A" on the report card, a dollar bill for work completed—or from within, as with a sense of satisfaction for having attained a goal, complied with the dictates of conscience, or otherwise lived up to self-expectations.

One other aspect must be considered: vicarious reinforcement. It is not necessary to learn appropriate responses directly, for one can learn from observing what happens to others when they make certain responses to stimuli. For example, children learn a great deal from watching other children. If one child "talks out of turn" in a classroom and is reprimanded, the other class members are aware that if they talk out of turn they may also expect reprimands. If one child is praised for a good piece of work, others are vicariously reinforced to do good work.

Reinforcers vary among people. To someone who is hungry, food may be a stronger reinforcer than is something to build his self-esteem, so that a hungry bum is willing to suffer indignity to get a free meal. On the other hand, self-actualizing people may be less affected by reinforcements provided by others than are people who lack feelings of security.

Some people's desires for self-esteem cause them to respond favorably to getting their names in the newspaper, but to others this result would be hardly reinforcing; the latter might respond better to reinforcements of money, rank, or prestige.

In school, the teacher must take into account the kinds of reinforcers that help to govern the behavior of each pupil. Some children work hard at a task for a smile of approval, whereas others need gold stars for achievement. Some need special privileges as inducements, and others may find money a stronger reinforcement. Small children may respond well to such concrete reinforcements as candy, toys, or small prizes, but older children and adults more frequently respond to evidence of success, status, and esteem. The teacher therefore needs to examine the range of reinforcers at his disposal and may wish to vary them in accordance with his understanding of his various pupils. Although he will want to be fair in dispensing available reinforcers, it is apparent that all pupils will not respond to the same ones; he therefore should vary his techniques within the limits dictated by the classroom context.

Methods of Classroom Control

SOCIAL REINFORCEMENT

As the term will be employed here, social reinforcers are those evidences of approval, affection, esteem, or success that are awarded through others' remarks, gestures, nods, smiles, or other behavior, as distinct from concrete reinforcers that have value in their own right (food, money, toys). The latter, it is true, may be provided because of someone's approval of one's behavior, but they are far less personal in meaning and depend much less upon the relationship of dispenser and recipient.

When one tells a child that he has been very thoughtful and that it was nice of him to offer a chair to a visitor, such social reinforcement usually causes the child to be inclined to repeat the act. When one frowns and shakes his head at a child for talking out of turn, the negative reinforcement should cause him to inhibit such behavior. Whether such acts of the teacher (or parent) are actually construed as reinforcers by the child depends in part, however, upon the degree to which the child "identifies" with that teacher or parent. Failure to identify may cause social behavior to lack reinforcing value or may even cause what is intended as positive reinforcement to be construed as negative reinforcement.

Let us consider further what is meant by "identification." Ordinarily children form positive emotional attachments to their parents and strive to please them and to be like them. Parents are able to provide material things for their children, play with them, and offer all sorts of pleasurable things to them. Children usually come to view parents with affection, and evidence of approval or disapproval by parents is socially reinforcing. In the same way, children may learn to identify with various peers and with the teacher.

Because of parental rejection, harshness, inconsistency, or other attitudes, however, the child may lose his identification with parents or fail to achieve it at all. In this instance, the approval or disapproval of the parents may be taken much more lightly than would otherwise be the case. The writer is aware of one instance—admittedly extreme and certainly not admirable—in which a child so failed to identify with her parents that she became extremely negative toward them and their wishes. The foolish parents for a time governed the child's behavior by asking her to do precisely the opposite of what they wished, so that, for example, they might tell her not to eat her breakfast, expecting that she immediately would consume all of it as rapidly as possible. The writer's studies of high- and low-achieving junior high-school boys showed that low achievers did not identify as well with parents' and school values as did high achievers. If the teacher does not become an identifying figure for his pupils, the positive social reinforcements he can offer are meager. Such teachers frequently then depend upon attempts to threaten, force, or punish their pupils into appropriate behavior, with consequent deterioration of discipline and learning efficiency.

There are other factors related to the efficacy of social reinforcement that deserve mention here. For example, certain personality variables in children cause reinforcers to have differential effects. S. Rachman (1962) summarized a number of studies that are germane. Among them were the findings of L. Jacubzak and R. H. Walters (1959) that dependent children are more easily influenced by social reinforcers than are independent children and those of G. Lesser and R. Abelson (1959) that (under certain circumstances) children with histories of failure are more likely to display social imitation and respond to social reinforcement than are children who have been successful. Looking at these findings a bit differently, self-confident, independent children may be reinforced less by the opinions of others than are children who are more anxious to please because of feelings of inadequacy or lack of self-confidence. Self-confident children may be reinforced to a greater extent by their own self-evaluations or perhaps by such less personal reinforcers as college scholarships, football letters, and the like.

Sometimes a reinforcer is less effective because the child is satiated. (One chocolate soda may induce a certain amount of work; two sodas may for most of us be one too many.) It has been found that to introduce desired behavior a good practice is to reinforce such behavior every time it occurs; once the behavior has been well learned, however, intermittent reinforcement produces better results. For example, praise given too lavishly tends to decrease in value. For this reason, praise should be given only for definitely continuing improvement. Teachers sometimes notice that some bright children attain high marks without really extending themselves. The marks, in turn, are not particularly prized. In such an event it might be wise to withhold such marks unless the children produce well in accordance with their own abilities, rather than in comparison with the performances of their fellows. Marking and grading offer many problems, of course. We shall discuss pros and cons of this reinforcement technique in Chapter 7.

In more extreme instances, it may be necessary to institute a little actual deprivation. (A hungry pigeon works harder for food than does one that has had a full meal.) Deliberate with-holding of reinforcers for a time, even when they have been earned, may make them more desirable.

Care must be taken to distinguish between the withholding of reinforcers because desired performance has not been elicited, on one hand, and punishment, on the other. Sometimes privi-leges are so easily attained that they seem to become rights, rather than privileges, in which instance their loss is viewed as punishment.

For example, most school authorities believe that participa-tion on an athletic team is a privilege, and that only high-caliber students should have this privilege of representing the school. Participation on athletic teams also brings its own re-inforcers in the form of sweaters, emblems, and awards, as well as the plaudits of student body, adults, and newspapers.

In order to participate, however, the student is expected to do academic work commensurate with his abilities. If he fails to do passing work, he is considered ineligible and is (at least tempo-rarily) dropped from competitive athletics.

Ineligibility brings many problems. Sometimes the student does, indeed, try harder in class in order to regain his team position. Others help him, even to the extent of tutoring. Pleas may even be made to faculty members for special help for him or for lenience. But sometimes he becomes resentful, rather than motivated to try harder at his studies.

There are many possible causes for the latter attitude, but among them may be the feeling that the athlete is being punished for failure, rather than that he is being reinforced to attain a desired result. The failure to make such a distinction arises from a mix-up in the values of the athlete, certain adults, peers, and others. People may feel that he is so necessary to the team that he should be allowed to participate, that athletics is more important than study, that the school will suffer defeats without him, and so on. On the other hand, once it is clearly established in the minds of faculty, students, and community that athletics (as distinct from physical education) is a reward for good school citizenship and academic effort, the problem should be greatly lessened.

Another illustration arises in connection with the child who habitually disrupts class with attention-seeking behavior—he clowns, talks out of turn, is sassy, and so on. It is possible to study in class, but it is equally possible to study by oneself. It is wise for the teacher to treat participation in class study as a privilege to be enjoyed by those who cooperate; if the privilege is not earned, the child must study alone.

This approach is in line with the ideas of Dreikurs, who suggests that the desire to be with the group is strong in most children and that isolation soon causes most of them to want to win their way back into the group. The child who is a disruptive influence is therefore told: "We'd like to have you in the group, but since you are not ready to help the group, I'm afraid you will have to study alone." The child is then allowed to study in an office, study hall, or other isolated area—but, it must be emphasized, he is not told that he is being removed from class as punishment or that he is bad but that he has failed to earn group privileges. The implication is that he is removing himself because he does not care for being in the group and that, when he desires to be with the group and to contribute, he will be welcomed back.

Studies of young children by J. L. Gewirtz and D. M. Baer (1958) seem to suggest similar implications of deprivation. They found that frequency of social behavior was greater after social deprivation than after nondeprivation or satisfaction.

PUNISHMENT OR NEGATIVE REINFORCEMENT

Punishment is the attempt to inhibit a response by supplying unpleasant consequences. There are problems with punishment, for its use is essentially based upon fear and therefore teaches avoidance behavior. Punishment can help the child to inhibit certain behaviors, but it does not deal with the motives leading to the misbehavior. Furthermore, it does not reinforce desirable responses, nor does it usually provide the child with a clue to what he *should* do. For these reasons, punishment is not a dependable way of managing misbehavior; yet in our culture it must be occasionally employed, if only for purposes of expedience. Punishments range from simple verbal censure to corporal punishment, and the school may even suspend or expel a child for a serious incident of misbehavior.

A more serious indictment of punishment is that it may produce concomitant learning that is undesirable. The purpose of punishment is to deter behavior but not at the expense of the child's self-respect, of inducing guilt feelings and anxieties, or of deterioration of the feeling of belonging of the child. The too heavily punished child may suffer in mental health. In addition, he almost certainly develops negative feelings about the entire situation in which he was punished, which may include the teacher, the subject, the classroom, and even the particular peers with whom he was involved; this process leads to avoidance behavior.

With some children it may be more useful simply to try to extinguish undesirable behavior through nonreinforcement. Rachman (1962) says:

> The use of social reinforcers in eliminating undesirable behavior should follow a pattern of non-reinforcement rather than aversive conditioning.[1] At the risk of over-simplifying we may state it this way: an undesirable response is more likely to be eliminated if it is met by no reaction at all than if it is met with a negative or punishing reaction.

Yet punishment cannot be entirely avoided; children are used to punishment at home and may think that lack of punishment signifies weakness on the part of the teacher. They may be sometimes unable to reduce feelings of guilt if they do not suffer punishment (expiation), and a few may increase disciplinary problems until firmly handled.

Some words must be said about threatening. It is clear that threats must be carried out if they are to carry weight. Furthermore, when the reinforcing agent (teacher) is not around, he may expect the threat to be ineffective; threatening punitive teachers usually find that when they leave the room more or less chaos results.

REINFORCING ALTERNATIVE BEHAVIOR

In any situation there is likely to be something positive as well as negative. "Reinforcing alternative behavior" simply

---

[1] Aversive conditioning means to teach the child to dislike the behavior you wish him not to choose, that is, to avoid making that response.

means emphasizing the positive. When Johnny interrupts some-one to disagree with him, the teacher can emphasize that it is good to have ideas and to think for oneself but that it is not good not to permit others to have their say. Emphasis on dis-criminating how and when to disagree and reinforcement of critical thinking can thus improve pupil behavior, and the effects of the censure will more likely be fewer interruptions, rather than resentment, frustration, and inhibition of ideas along with inhibition of interrupting.

DEALING WITH MOTIVES OF CHILDREN

Some disciplinary problems are the results of failure to re-ceive suitable reinforcements, hence failure to identify with and model after school values.

One of the basic motives is to belong. Let us illustrate. In a midwestern city of 150,000 a study was made of adolescents who tended to hang around the downtown area in the evening (Committee on the Role of Leisure Time Programs, 1959). Much of their behavior was rude, and some of it was delinquent or predelinquent—beer drinking, wild driving, sexual experi-mentation, fighting, and shoplifting. To learn more about this street-corner society, a young social worker went into the area and made contact with most of the young people. They were found to congregate in various-sized groups, rather flexibly, but the total population on a given night was around 200. He found that such youths were not truly delinquents but that most talked with more bravado than they acted with, trying to gain status among themselves.

Almost none of these students identified with his high school, and most saw graduation only as a ticket to better jobs than could otherwise be obtained. When asked about a local basket-ball game, a typical response was "Who is playing?" showing a lack of feeling for their own school's team. Many such youths were school dropouts; others were potential dropouts. None was a member of a youth club in school or the community. Most felt that teachers were too strict, school subjects uninteresting, marking practices unfair, and other students uninterested or rejecting.

The key to such behavior apparently lay in the feelings of isolation and rejection by peers, teachers, and the school milieu in general. Although their behavior may itself have been one cause of rejection, their failure to integrate successfully into the broader school society was also partly the fault of others. As is commonly the case, a "vicious spiral" came about, in which feelings of rejection caused antischool and antipeer attitudes, which, in turn, resulted in further rejection by the larger school society. Congregating on street corners was an attempt to gain feelings of acceptance and status outside the school context.

The Vanishing Adolescent (Friedenberg, 1962) makes the point that school is the habitat of youth. Thus school problems may not always be school problems as such; they may be problems occurring within the school confines simply because youth, by law, must be in school.

Youths who are isolated may be helped in some ways. Perhaps they may be inducted into certain extraclass activities through which they may gain status, for example, racing on drag strips, rifle clubs, and other activities that may demand less team-sports skill. In one community, a number of isolated rural youths gained prestige by forming a forestry club and establishing a school forest. In another community, some youths were aided in beginning a small profit-making business.

Special counseling is generally needed, however, if the youths in question are genuinely unacceptable to the peer culture, for it may be their own attitudes and behaviors that make them so. Such children should, perhaps, be helped to work at part-time jobs or forestry camps, or even to join the armed forces and complete high school while in service.

Schools must provide ways that all can achieve successfully, so that status can be legitimately attained over a wide spectrum (too frequently a small percentage of students earn all the honors) ; work must be tailored to levels of ability and interests of students, and other needs must be met. We shall continue to deal with this subject throughout the book; here we shall content ourselves with this reminder that the total school situation must be examined if children who misbehave because of lack of positive reinforcement and identification are to be helped.

DEALING WITH AGGRESSIVE BEHAVIOR

There are some special measures that must be considered in dealing with highly aggressive or hostile, acting-out children.

In dealing with aggressiveness there are two aspects: immediate need, often for superficial treatment, to protect others or school property, and careful study to get at the cause of such behavior and help begin remediation. The aggressive child cannot be allowed to work off his frustrations indiscriminately, nor can he be allowed to interfere with others. Nevertheless, as studies of the treatment of prisoners have shown, harsh punishment does not end aggressive behavior but tends only to harden the youthful criminal. In fact, ability to tolerate any punishment that can be imposed may be a mark of status in the eyes of the offender and his friends.

IMMEDIATE NEEDS. ■ Children who act out their problems through aggressive behavior should be immediately restrained for their own good as well as that of others. Sometimes restraint may mean physical handling of the child, or it can be a sharp command ("Take your seat!") or a movement toward the child. In any case, he must be restrained, lest the consequences be even more serious for the school situation, as well as for him, in terms of resentment, fear, guilt, self-deprecation, and other feelings. Frequently such children are sent to detention rooms, the guidance office, or the back of the room; this treatment allows both child and teacher to "cool off" so that the problem can be approached constructively. When a child is in the grip of strong emotions, no punitive measure should be instituted. Furthermore, he should not be made "an example" to other children; this approach is ineffective, is unfair, and generally does not "work."

It is possible that sending the misbehaving child to the guidance office or to the back of the room may be construed as punishment by the child and his peers. It is true that the teacher who takes such action is reacting to a scene perpetrated, at least in part, by the child who has been removed. There is no use in trying to pretend that classroom order has not been disrupted. Mentioning to the child and to the class that tempers have been raised and that no helpful decisions can be made until people have cooled off should, however, make it clear that all that is being sought is an opportunity for self-control to return; decisions will be made later.

PREVENTIVE MEASURES. ▪ Children who are habitually hostile or aggressive should be kept occupied at some useful task under surveillance. Speaking to them, physical proximity of the teacher, changes in work task, moving seats, allowing drinks from the water fountain, and similar tactics may help them to release tension before it builds to the "boiling over" stage and to keep behavior and emotions under control.

The pet peeves of such children should be avoided, for any frustration makes it harder for them to control their feelings. For example, some children feel threatened or resentful at being asked to work at the chalkboard, perhaps because they feel that they are a source of amusement to the others. The teacher can avoid insisting that they perform this task. Others become resentful at inability to do assigned work; for them, more careful assignments may be the answer. They can achieve some degree of success by being given appropriate tasks. G. M. Allen (1960) achieved some success by simply letting his "adjustment" children copy from the blackboard, even though the material was put to no further use. Steps should be taken to see that these children are not labeled "stupid," teased, treated sarcastically, or otherwise deflated or inflamed.

The teacher must accept the child, even though the behavior cannot be tolerated, and must try to remain emotionally uninvolved. Behavior must not be seen as a personal threat to teacher prestige. Fairness is essential, and the aggressive child needs opportunity to be heard when conflict seems imminent.

Physical activity is useful in discharging pent-up emotions, and many aggressive children find real pleasure in displaying their strength or physical prowess. Such children can put their strength to legitimate use in many ways. Lifting things for the teacher, working with the custodian, helping direct younger children in hallways or on street corners, engaging in strenuous sports—all may be preventive measures.

Care in seating, attention to classroom routine, consistency in discipline, and friendly and humorous handling all help prevent angry or hostile emotions arising.

CHANNELING IMPULSES. ■ Useful channels for aggressive impulses may be devised. The defense mechanism of sublimation may apply as when hostile impulses are turned into creative channels and mark the reformer, the aggressive businessman, the soldier, or the professional ball player.

A sense of humor and the opportunity to make others laugh may provide status and help release tension. The dance, art, music, writing, talking out one's feelings, physical and manual activity in auto mechanics or shop work can all be useful.

AIDING SELF-RESTRAINT. ■ The aggressive child may profit by identification with a person whom he respects and because of this relationship may be aided in self-restraint. Often such children do better under male teachers. Teachers who are given aggressive children to work with should be people who are not frightened by aggressiveness and who can restrain the children, at the same time playing down situations and, hopefully, being able to find something in the children to like.

Poor behavior should not be overemphasized; real, even though inept, attempts at improvement should be recognized. Conversely, such a child should not be cultivated exceedingly. The problem is to help the child develop feelings of worth and belonging, without reinforcing his aggressive tendencies.

As we have noted, many aggressive children need to gain feelings of self-confidence, of being liked and wanted, and of being accepted. Such feelings can be furthered in the classroom in several ways. Perhaps the child can be given opportunities to be a leader. He may be given jobs that serve the class. If he is a follower, he should be given credit for being a good follower. His good points should be given publicity—his failings should be handled privately as far as possible and without emotion.

Something should be said about the shaping of behavior through what is called *successive approximation*. This concept means that one need not expect (nor, perhaps, even hope for) behavior to change in the desired direction "all at one time." But small movements in the desired direction may be relatively easy to obtain. If each such small movement is reinforced, eventually the intended result will be obtained in its entirety. One thus does not try to stem disciplinary problems by remaking children in one fell swoop, but one works gradually to extinguish undesired behavior and reinforce what is wanted. Teachers may raise antagonism by moving too quickly; they also may be quite unrealistic.

GROUP HOSTILITY AND AGGRESSIVE BEHAVIOR

M. Horwitz (1963) has shown that group hostility toward the teacher can be successfully managed by certain methods. Before these methods are discussed, the causes of hostility should be considered. In most instances, hostility in the classroom is the result of frustration of the students. When motives of the pupils are thwarted and tasks are imposed that conflict with their needs, frustration and hostility may result. Though it is true that hostility may simply reflect anger because of some real or imagined unfairness of the teacher or because conditions outside the classroom are generalized to the classroom (as when resentment against parental or police authority is displaced to the teacher), pupils usually are not hostile unless there is a marked difference between their goals and the demands of the classroom.

Teachers can often inadvertently set a task level that is too difficult for pupils and may keep them working at this task even when their efforts do not bear fruit. The reverse may also be true when pupils are ready to move forward long before the teacher senses this readiness. Some school work is tedious, and some tasks must be undertaken even when it is clear to all that these tasks are boring or tiring. When students are overdirected or subjected to highly authoritarian control, when test grades seem unduly low, when the teacher does not permit some freedom to move about or otherwise to release tension, and when threats and punishment are frequent, hostility may arise. Not only some of the pupils, but even whole classes, may become hostile.

The most workable solution, of course, is to discover the source of the hostility and then to remove the cause. If this method is not possible, perhaps other techniques will be successful.

One method sometimes used is that the teacher seeks to prohibit overt hostile actions, even though the feelings may remain. For example, ". . . among the modes of control which have been considered are prohibiting hostile actions but encouraging verbalization, punishing both action and verbalization, additionally punishing hostile thoughts by inducing guilt" (Horwitz, 1963, pp. 203–4). Unfortunately, as Horwitz explains, such methods may cause hostile activity to decrease, but there is also a tendency for other activities, including productive effort, to decrease. It is the opinion of this writer that the reason is that the tension represented by the hostility has not been removed; it takes energy from other tasks and also represents a competing motive. It would seem better to reduce hostility than to suppress its expression. The teacher can thus reduce hostile feelings by explaining to students why they must try to cope with a frustrating situation, what benefits they can reap, that the teacher is in sympathy with the students, that the frustration is for their own good, and that the frustration will be removed in a short time. He tries thus to make clear that his frustrating activities are not mere whims or hostile impulses of his own.

The teacher might also point to the class's progress and suggest ways to improve efficiency in the frustrating task. Temporary release tactics like "breaks," humor, positive encouragement, and verbal acknowledgment of pupil difficulties by the teacher may help. Teachers with whom children identify and whom they trust can expect more tolerance than teachers who are perceived less favorably.

In some instances, simply by observing the activities of the pupils, the teacher can avoid frustration. Frequent signs of inattention, boredom, or minor disciplinary infractions should warn the teacher that something is wrong and that he needs to alleviate the difficulties.

Tolerance of frustration can perhaps be improved as B. F. Skinner suggests in *Walden Two* (1948) by deliberately planning short periods of frustration to help children learn not to become emotional and to attain self-control. Skinner's point of view is that, when students learn that it is better to accept frustration unemotionally and that loss of self-control may only result in further frustration, they will gradually discard undesired responses to thwarting. In school we do actually employ this tactic, as when the teacher refuses to dismiss the class until everyone has been quiet in his seat for a minute or so. (Obviously, the frustration must not be overdone lest it produce the opposite effect, emotional outbursts.)

The reader may wonder how such "self-control" relates to the matter of releasing emotions constructively. In the present discussion we are attempting to *prevent the arousal of unpleasant emotions* in response to frustration—that is, we are trying to reinforce patience, sense of humor, understanding, and good will in opposition to hostility and aggression. We are also, however, trying to reinforce the withholding of emotional expression in circumstances in which such expression would be inappropriate. This behavior is one mark of socialization and maturity. One cannot always immediately express his anger and must wait until an opportune time arises. But if he represses his feelings too frequently or for too long, the conflicts engendered between his behavior and his emotions may cause problems.

AN EXAMPLE OF SCHOOL DISCIPLINE AND MORALE (CONTINUED)

Upon taking over the principalship, young Mr. T. began to try to improve morale and discipline. His first move was to try to capture good feelings from the students. At the initial assembly, he announced that the privileges which had been denied would be reinstated, and that they would be continued; he expected the student body to cooperate, since he had confidence in his pupils. He also stated that he would work—with their cooperation—to try to improve the school curriculum, recreation and sports programs, clubs, and other activities.

He suggested that more athletics be instituted, that a school band be organized, that typewriters be procured and typing classes offered, and that a hot lunch and noon-hour recreation program be developed. He reinstated dances and urged the performance of class plays. A broader curriculum was contemplated, he indicated, and students would have more choice of subjects.

At the same time, Mr. T. indicated, students were expected to work for these innovations and not to take uncalled-for advantage of changes. If no improvement of behavior was found, some of the privileges might be withdrawn, but this was not expected to be necessary.

Some changes, of course, could not come about in one "grand

reform." Immediate steps were, however, taken to bring some of them about, and the students, noticing faculty efforts, cooperated admirably. Discipline and morale rose markedly, and the few lapses that occurred did not receive the support of the majority of the students.

This case could have been entitled, "What Good Is a Chair Leg?" for that implement disappeared into the furnace, and no one mourned its loss. It may seem trite, but it was found that most students wanted to behave, cooperate, and achieve and took pride in so doing. When convinced that the school staff had their interests at heart, they helped the staff to achieve the kinds of control that are most desirable.

The reader will no doubt be able to refer to other methods that might have helped in handling the initial situation. For example, perhaps privileges and advantages should not have immediately been handed out but kept as reinforcements for demonstrated changes in student behavior. On the other hand, immediate positive steps had to be made to improve morale enough to induce students to change "for the better." On the whole, however, Mr. T.'s move was in the correct direction—he instituted positive reinforcements instead of negative reinforcements; he kept pupil goals in mind; he assumed that pupils desired to accept school values and that they would identify with the school; and he tried to be a model of desired behavior and an identifying figure for the students.

□

REFERENCES

Allen, G. M. *Undercover Teacher*. New York: Doubleday, 1960.
Bandura, A., and R. H. Walters. *Social Learning and Personality Development*. New York: Holt, Rinehart, Winston, 1963.
Committee on the Role of Leisure Time Programs (Madison Delinquency Prevention Study). *The Hard to Reach Project*. Madison: Unpublished report, 1959.
Dollard, J., and N. E. Miller. *Personality and Psychotherapy*. New York: McGraw-Hill, 1950.
Dreikurs, R. *Psychology in the Classroom*. New York: Harper, 1957.
Federal Bureau of Investigation. *Crime in the United States*. Washington, D.C.: Government Printing Office, 1965.

Feldhusen, J. F., J. R. Thurston, and E. Ager, "Delinquency Proneness of Urban and Rural Youth," *Journal of Research in Crime and Delinquency,* 2 (January 1965), 32–44.

Freud, S. *An Outline of Psychoanalysis.* New York: Norton, 1949.

Friedenberg, E. A. *The Vanishing Adolescent.* New York: Dell, 1962.

Gewirtz, J. L., and D. M. Baer. "Deprivation and Satiation of Social Reinforcers as Drive Conditioners," *Journal of Abnormal and Social Psychology,* 57 (1958), 165–72.

Hoffman, M. L. "Some Psychodynamic Factors in Compulsive Conformity," *Journal of Abnormal and Social Psychology,* 48 (1955), 383–93.

Horwitz, M. "Hostility and Its Management in Classroom Groups," in W. W. Charters and N. L. Gage (eds.). *Readings in the Social Psychology of Education,* pp. 196–212. Boston: Allyn & Bacon, 1963.

Hunter, E. *The Blackboard Jungle.* New York: Pocket Books, 1963.

Jacubzak, L., and R. H. Walters. "Suggestibility as Dependent Behavior," *Journal of Abnormal and Social Psychology,* 59 (1959), 102–7.

Lesser, G., and R. Abelson. "Personality Correlates of Persuasibility in Children," in I. L. Janis and C. I. Hovland (eds.). *Personality and Persuasibility.* New Haven: Yale University Press, 1959.

Rachman, S. "Learning Theory and Child Psychology: Therapeutic Possibilities," *Journal of Child Psychology and Psychiatry,* 3 (1962), 149–63.

Ringness, T. A. *Differences in Attitudes Toward Self and Others of Academically Successful and Non-Successful Ninth Grade Boys of Superior Intelligence* (Final Report, National Institute of Mental Health Post-Doctoral Research Fellowship). Los Angeles: University of California, 1963.

————. *Non-Intellective Variables Related to Academic Achievement of Bright Junior High School Boys* (Final Report, Cooperative Research Project S–035). Madison: University of Wisconsin, 1965.

Skinner, B. F. *Walden Two.* New York: Macmillan, 1948.

Thompson, G. G., and C. W. Hunnicutt. "The Effect of Repeated Praise or Blame on the Work Achievement of 'Introverts' and 'Extraverts,' " *Journal of Educational Psychology,* 35 (1944), 247–66.

SUGGESTIONS FOR FURTHER READING

Dreikurs, R. *Psychology in the Classroom.* New York: Harper, 1957. *Dreikurs and his associates have written several books, articles, and pamphlets that emphasize the points to which we have briefly referred. Based essentially on Adlerian psychology, the material in this book stresses the importance of the sense of belonging. Dynamics of teacher control tactics and their effects on pupils are considered. Principles mentioned have been employed in various school systems with good effects. Interestingly enough, this approach somewhat resembles a learning-theory approach, in that Dreikurs uses what some might see as extinction tactics and positive reinforcement but prefers to stay away from negative reinforcement.*

Schorling, R. *Student Teaching,* chap. 4. New York: McGraw-Hill, 1949. *For the teacher who wants "practical tips" on classroom management,*

Schorling discusses preventive teacher acts aimed at heading off trouble before it arises; constructive tactics aimed at building good behavior habits; and remedial tactics aimed at correcting problems that have arisen. He does not go deeply into theory of management or causes of behavior but is useful in suggesting things teachers can do.

SCHOOL ACHIEVEMENT
AND
MENTAL HEALTH

In Chapter 1 the idea was advanced that the relationship between pupil adjustment and school achievement is complementary. The pupil with good mental health has some of the prerequisites for adequate achievement, but the pupil with poor mental health has problems that can interfere with success in school.

The pupil who succeeds in school tends to have feelings of self-worth and other favorable attitudes. He develops skills that help him meet stress, and he becomes more self-actualizing.

Poor mental health may be accompanied by so much anxiety that performance suffers; concentration may be poor, energy level low, perception interfered with, attention span limited, and behavior impulsive. Other problems may also exist to interfere with achievement. Poor achievement can produce anxiety, hostility, or discouragement. Defensive maneuvers, originally directed at school tasks, can become habitual and be used in other stressful situations. The pupil can fail to identify with adequate sex and role models. His emotional learning may be undesirable, and he can become dependent, fearful, rigid, and over- or underconforming.

This chapter considers some of the relationships between

mental health and school achievement and suggests measures both to prevent deterioration of mental health and to remedy any that may have taken place. Improvement of learning is also considered.

We shall first discuss the prediction of school achievement— problems in determining what pupils should be expected to achieve. We can move from there to examining high and low achievement and related adjustment variables.

Problems in Prediction of Achievement

If one knew all the pertinent factors affecting the achievement of a given boy or girl, he could predict what that child would achieve with considerable accuracy. Because relevant factors have not been completely established on the basis of research evidence, to say nothing of the difficulty of discovering and interpreting them for each child in the actual teaching situation, predictions for children's performances usually fall far short of perfection.

Two of the most common measures employed in predicting school achievement are the child's scholastic aptitude or intellectual abilities, as estimated on some form of "intelligence test," and the child's present or beginning level of achievement in the school subject under consideration (Thorndike, 1963). That is, how well Johnny will do in school this year depends considerably on his starting point in reading (or other subjects with which the teacher is concerned) and his intellectual abilities. For example, a bright child who, for one reason or another, has a poor background in a given academic area should not be expected to progress as well in that area as one who is better prepared initially. (This disparity is noticeable when children from privileged areas are compared with underprivileged children in reading skills or other school tasks that stress verbal or semantic competence.)

But measures of present attainment and intellectual ability fail to predict as accurately as one might desire. Thorndike suggests some of the reasons. For example, there is always the possibility of errors of measurement of past or present ability and attainment. There is the problem of heterogeneity of criteria: Grades from one teacher or scores on one standardized test need not necessarily reflect the same attainment as grades from another teacher or scores on a different test. Intervening events—protracted illness, an extended vacation, movement from one house to another—may lower (or sometimes increase) achievement over what is expected.

Finally, there are problems of motivation, emotional health, and related attitudinal and cognitive variables that affect the degree of achievement. It is these problems with which this chapter is concerned. Knowing something about these factors in relation to the individual child may not only improve ability to predict his achievement but may also offer opportunities to improve achievement over what one expects for the child. It should be taken into account that these variables relate to the child's previous, as well as present, school achievement.

HIGH ACHIEVEMENT

Other things being equal, a mark of "A" is considered to indicate above-average achievement in comparison with some standard, even though an "A" in one class does not necessarily mean the same thing as an "A" in another. Similarly, a standardized test score in the 95th percentile also usually indicates superior attainment. (Such standards are, of course, based on some normative group, which may or may not be appropriate when considering any given child.)

High achievers may be high in all areas or simply in one or two where they have particular interests or abilities.

Toby is an example. She is a young lady in high school who seems to "have everything." She is a "straight-A" student in all her classes and additionally takes dancing, art, and music lessons. Toby is popular with almost everyone and belongs to a number of school and out-of-school organizations, in which she usually has positions of leadership. During summers she has a job as counselor at a youth camp and has now become a senior nonprofessional helper. Toby expects to attend college and is certain of obtaining a scholarship to at least one. With all this achievement, she enjoys life, is in excellent health, and is making the most of her opportunities.

Toby is one of those people who seem to dominate the choice

positions in student bodies. Teachers frequently remark that a relatively small proportion of the student body seems to be "in everything," and the fact that these students are so active does not hinder their school achievement in any way. Such pupils have learned to use their time efficiently and to act in ways that please others as well as themselves. Many are truly self-actualizing. Most are mature and well socialized.

LOW ACHIEVEMENT

Just as with high achievement, some pupils achieve poorly because of personal characteristics and backgrounds. Some children, for example, have relatively low intellectual ability, and others have poor cultural backgrounds or other handicaps. And, just as high achievers seem usually to have many other desirable qualities, those who achieve poorly seem also to have other undesirable qualities.

Miles is a case in point. He was studied by a counselor while he was a freshman in a small high school. Miles' parents were deceased, and he lived with a great-uncle who was considered the ne'er-do-well of the village. Miles had an unkempt appearance; he always seemed dirty, his clothes were uncared for, his hair was never trimmed neatly, and he usually needed a shave. He wore thick lenses because of nearsightedness, and his gait was awkward. Somewhat surly and withdrawn, he was unpopular and frequently the butt of pranks.

Small wonder that Miles, with dull normal intelligence, rarely attained a school mark of "C" and that he frequently failed courses. Having been held back one grade twice in elementary school, Miles was considered a very poor scholar. Eventually he dropped out of school.

Special provisions may be needed for such pupils. They are low achievers in every sense of the word.

"OVERACHIEVEMENT"

The term "overachievement" has come in for a great deal of criticism, for it seems to imply that someone is doing better than he is able to do. "How *can* one overachieve?" is the question frequently asked.

As the term will be employed here, overachievement means

simply that a child is achieving higher than would be predicted on the basis of attainment in the past and scores on tests of intellectual ability. In school practice, the overachiever is usually identified as the pupil who attains higher marks than pupils of similar abilities and backgrounds.

Now it is true that some children become enthusiastic over their classes and simply work harder than others. In a sense, they are "overachieving." We need not be concerned about such children in most instances, for they are simply highly motivated, healthy people.

But there are also children who are unhealthy overachievers. These children are also overworkers, not so much because of enthusiasm as because they are anxious. There may even be a somewhat compulsive aura to their activities. They do not do *better* work than do others, in the sense of higher-*quality* work, but they tend to stress *quantity*. They may do *more* work than required; their high marks may come partly from extra-credit assignments. They may take extra pains to turn in neat work, to polish their notebooks, and to use their very best handwriting or typewriting, even when the nature of the assignment does not call for this degree of precision.

Because it is apparent that overachievement may be either healthy or unhealthy, the teacher would be wise to observe the characteristic behaviors of overachievers carefully, rather than to rely upon marks and grades or standardized test results alone.[1]

This discussion also highlights one reason that studies of overachievement sometimes bear conflicting results—researchers have failed to consider that overachievers may be of different kinds.

One kind of overachiever is illustrated by the "case" of Clarence. At the time he was studied, he was a high-school senior taking a course in physics. He reported one day that he hoped to go on to college and become a physics teacher. This stated ambition bothered the teacher, for Clarence's measured I.Q. was approximately 100, and he did not seem to be "college

[1] Keep in mind what has been said about test error, problems of criteria of achievement, and other problems in predicting achievement.

material." When Clarence further mentioned that he would need a scholarship or else would have to work to support himself and that he eventually intended to earn a Ph.D. degree and become a research physicist, the teacher felt that counseling was in order.

Clarence was doing "B" work in physics, partly because he turned in masterpieces of notebooks, in which his careful drawing, neatness, and illustrations were outstanding. He was willing to do extra laboratory assignments and was capable of quality work as far as the mechanical aspects of experiments were concerned. On the other hand, he did rather poorly on the mathematics problems assigned, and his test results were mediocre. Another factor obscuring his lack of ability was that his high school sent few students on to college, so that the physics course was not as rigorous as in many schools.

Clarence told the teacher that he spent four or five hours every night on his physics ("You can ask my folks if you don't believe me") and an hour or so on the remainder of his subjects. This prevented him from having much social life. Clarence was not popular with other students; generally speaking, they tended to ignore him.

Asked how he expected to do college-level work, support himself by working while in college, and keep up in all of his studies, Clarence showed little grasp of his intellectual mediocrity. He was willing to listen to the teacher, however. He changed his goal to that of becoming a mechanic; he is now the chief repairman for the Board of Education, working on trucks, lawn and road machinery, and the like. When last heard from, he was respected, happy, and successful in his position.

"UNDERACHIEVEMENT"

Underachievement, like overachievement, represents a failure to predict the pupil's performance from available data. Unlike overachievement, however, underachievement is never likely to be healthy; it may represent poor social adjustment, adjustment to a deviant social group, personal problems, or other variables. The underachiever is almost always in trouble or bound for trouble, simply because the schools and society in general look upon underachievement with considerable disfavor. As a result, many problems arise for the child, his parents, and the school itself.

The recognition of underachievement is complicated by the problems to which we have referred previously. It is further complicated by the fact that the underachiever sometimes does well on standardized tests of achievement but attains poor school marks; in such an event, the child may not be underachieving so much as he is being a problem to the teacher in some way—discipline, truancy, attention seeking, or other nonconforming behavior.

On the whole, underachievers do not do as well as others of similar abilities and backgrounds.[2] They are frequently characterized as lacking in motivation. They are termed "lazy," and teachers complain that work that is turned in is often late and is usually carelessly done. Typically, such children make little effort to please their teachers but may be defiant and rebellious.

Bill is a case in point. The boy was first studied in fourth grade. At that time his measured I.Q. was 155. He was large for his age and exceedingly fat, rather than chunky. Bill wore thick glasses and blinked frequently. He was genial to the persons studying him and was even somewhat patronizing. He indicated that he preferred books to people and that he sought no friendships with others in his classroom. Bill attained "A"s without really trying because of his high intellectual ability, and his teacher said that she was unable to find work to keep him challenged. Bill was no problem in the classroom, but he contributed nothing to projects or group discussion.

When he was in the eighth grade, Bill turned up in another study. This time his measured I.Q. was only 125; he was earning "C"s and "B"s and was considered an underachiever. His social adjustment had not improved, and he was cordially disliked by some pupils because of his "superior attitude." The veneer of complacency had disappeared, and Bill now showed a number of such nervous symptoms as a tic in one eye, habitual covering of his mouth with his hand, and inability to concentrate.

---

2 Pupils who achieve adequately may still be underachievers if they do less well than predicted; their high marks may be achieved with little effort if such marks are based on comparison with other children of less ability.

Bill is now in counseling to determine more clearly the causes of his difficulties and to try to help him adjust better to school and peer life, as well as to improve his academic achievement. Such potential ability is prized by society and can be of immense worth to the individual who possesses it; it should not be wasted.

Personality Factors and Academic Achievement

The discussion that follows offers a sample of some of the studies relating achievement in school to personality attributes. Although lack of space prohibits a comprehensive review of the literature, the studies included here are representative and show trends in findings that seem to be generally accepted.

Most studies have compared high and low achieving pupils *who have approximately equal intellectual abilities and quite similar backgrounds.* Essentially, these studies can be considered similar to those of over- and underachievement if one defines above-average achievement as overachievement. Because researchers have employed various terminologies, however, the reader is warned to be alert for differences in the ways findings of studies are reported.

Boys are studied more frequently than girls, for boys are considered to underachieve three to four times as often as girls; furthermore, referrals to clinics because of emotional, social, and achievement problems are much more frequent for boys than for girls.

Bright children are studied more frequently than are average or dull children. One reason is that bright children are expected to achieve highly, and, when they do not, parents and schools quite naturally wish to know why. Bright children underachieve more than do others, partly because they have more "room to underachieve," partly because schools are more closely geared to average pupils, and partly because bright children can do reasonably well in school without having to extend themselves.

In examining the findings of the studies reported here, the reader is again reminded that results are based on *group* data; for this reason, findings may be useful in curriculum building and in seeking causes for underachievement in individual pupils, but it is still vitally important that each child be studied as an individual. There are wide differences in characteristics among children who are lumped for study as high, average, or low achievers.

EMOTIONAL ADJUSTMENT

In studying emotional adjustment of pupils as related to school achievement, J. C. Bledsoe and K. C. Garrison (1962), G. R. Boyd (1960), and E. Frankel (1960) found little or no differences between high- and low-achieving subjects. J. V. Pierce and B. H. Bowman (1959) did, however, find differences favoring high achievers on the California Personality Inventory, as did the present writer (Ringness, 1963).

L. D. Goodstein and his colleagues (1962) suggest that there is no consistency among measures of achievement as related to measures of adjustment. D. P. Hoyt and W. T. Norman (1954) consider that poor adjustment may be characteristic of either high or low achievers.

What is one to believe? The present writer tends toward a position similar to that of R. G. Taylor (1961), who (as we shall see) tends to view high achievers or overachievers as generally better adjusted than low achievers. This belief does not mean that *all* high achievers are well adjusted.

In most instances high-achieving subjects are reinforced by society for their efforts and develop positive attitudes toward self and others and toward school and adult values. Yet some, while pleasing society, may fail to consider personal needs. As the example of Clarence illustrates, some may neglect rest, recreation, social activities, and other physical- and mental-health requirements. Indeed, perhaps *average* achievers may be healthier than either high or low achievers.

Taylor (1961), basing his remarks partly on a study by W. W. Farquhar (1959), has interpreted over- and underachievers' patterns of adjustment as follows: Both over- and underachievers may be anxious, perhaps highly so. The difference in achievement between the groups arises from the way the anxiety is handled. The underachiever seems less able to control his anxieties, so that they get in the way of academic pursuits.

Such pupils show conflict over their own conduct and over sex; they are highly emotional and reflect instability and maladjustment. The overachiever's anxiety, however, is directed toward achievement; high achievement is thus security- and esteem-building and guilt-reducing for the overachiever.

Achievement, for some, may be a defense. The overachiever may overconform, and he may seem compulsive, putting in more hours on his schoolwork than is required, but he attains anxiety reduction in the process.

The underachiever is less able to manage his anxieties. He fears failure but runs away and attempts to reduce his anxiety by such defense mechanisms as denial of inadequacy, rejection of school achievement norms, and compensation through social or other activities. He concentrates more energy on means to reduce anxiety than on achievement and is therefore academically ineffective.

Both over- and underachievers may thus be poorly adjusted; the prime difference seems to be in the ways they handle their problems. This point will be amplified in our discussion of interaction with peers, adults, and the school.

SOCIALIZATION

The present writer found in one study (Ringness, 1963) that low-achieving bright ninth-grade boys had more problems with family and school relationships, felt somewhat less personal worth, and admitted to slightly more "nervous symptoms" than did high-achieving bright boys. In another study (Ringness, 1965) high-achieving eighth-grade boys had higher California Psychological Inventory test scores on scales of sense of well-being, self-control, tolerance, dominance, and responsibility than did low achievers. In terms of the C.P.I. areas, high achievers were seen to be more ascendant or poised and more socialized than were low achievers.

A card-sorting task in the first study showed high achievers to be less nonconforming but more independent than low achievers, and another task showed them to be higher in parent identification.

In effect, low achievers simply were less mature than were high achievers—less willing to accept responsibility, more impulsive, less willing to conform to necessary mores, and more rebellious and intolerant than high achievers.

ACHIEVEMENT MOTIVATION

J. V. Pierce (1961) and others (Pierce & Bowman, 1959; Ringness, 1963) found that high achievers were more interested in academic achievement than were low achievers, as might seem quite natural. It was also found that low achievers were less realistic and less decided upon occupational and educational goals (Graff, 1957; Todd, *et al.,* 1962), although not all studies bore out this finding (Morgan, 1952; Rust & Ryan, 1954). But even though they may *verbalize* desires to achieve highly, low achievers do not carry out plans that satisfy these needs in the academic context as well as do high achievers.

AFFILIATION MOTIVATION

A number of studies suggest that low achievers are more interested in peer relationships, heterosexual relationships, and social activities than are high achievers. The low achievers seem to lean more on the affection of the group, and may find social activity a substitute for—and a cause of—poor academic attainment. One study found high achievers more independent than low achievers (Ringness, 1963); this finding suggests that they were more autonomous and self-directed and less at the mercy of their peer groups as far as setting standards and attaining them were concerned.

Taylor (1961) finds the overachiever to be more leader-like, responsible, and dependable—all of which is evidence of maturity—and the underachiever to be impulsive and easily influenced. He also agrees that the underachiever seeks to identify with a group from which he gains support and satisfaction. The overachiever gains satisfaction from scholastic success, but he may give up a certain amount of creativity and originality in conforming to the requirements of instructors to attain high marks.

SELF-ESTEEM AND SECURITY

The present writer's two studies found that low achievers have less feeling of personal worth and less sense of well-being than do high achievers. Taylor (1961) suggests that under-achievers are derogatory about themselves, unrealistic in their self-attitudes, and therefore more likely to have conflict in dealings with others. The underachiever may be too critical of others and may act aggressively or rebelliously. In general, the overachiever has positive feelings about himself and others, feels accepted by others, and views himself as efficient, persistent, and adequate (Shaw & Alves, 1963; Walsh, 1956).

W. B. Brookover (1962), in an interesting study of self-concept of ability as related to school achievement, found that pupils possess both general concepts of their over-all abilities and specific concepts of their abilities in certain school subjects. When intelligence was controlled for, Brookover found that both the over-all concept and the specific concepts were related to school achievement. Specific concepts were found to vary with school subjects and might be different from the over-all estimate. A student who thinks he has high abilities tends to achieve better than one who thinks he has less ability, whether or not such estimates are realistic in terms of actual ability.

Low-achieving boys, we have said, are less likely to accept school and parental definitions of pupil behavior than are high achievers. This failure may be a carry-over into school of the effects of the home situation. One study (Ringness, 1963) showed that high-achieving boys had more interaction with their fathers and admired their fathers more than did low achievers. It also showed that low achievers had significantly more home problems than did high achievers.

(The findings reported here should not be generalized to girls, as they were not studied. Typically, as girls have more contact with their mothers than boys have with their fathers, one might expect the mother's influence—for better or worse—to be stronger for them. Girls present many fewer problems of achievement and conformity to classroom standards than do boys; their greater contacts with mothers may be partly responsible for their acceptance of school mores and values. Confirmation of this notion must, however, await further research.)

Most pupils, high and low achievers alike, believe that teachers want pupils who are conforming and docile; few pupils believe teachers want them to be academically alert, challenging, or creative. This image is rejected by low achievers, who tend to believe that they are not like this model and furthermore claim that they don't particularly care.

It has also been found that most male pupils, choosing popular peers, feel that, to be popular, one needs more than academic competence; one must be athletic or have a "nice" personality. The scholar *per se* is considered "square." This feeling is not true for girls, however; it is generally accepted that a girl may be a good student without onus (as compared to boys), for academic achievement is accorded a place in the sex-role definition for girls.

Most pupils believe that the average pupil does little more than necessary to "get by." Few believe that pupils work "up to capacity." This belief relates to the findings concerning affiliation motivation, in that those who want to fit in with the gang may fear that achieving too highly will militate against them in the (male) peer group.

W. Morrow and R. Wilson (1961) and others (Pierce, 1961; Portland Public Schools, 1959) found families of high achievers to be less authoritarian, more permissive, and more supportive, although E. Drews and J. Teahan (1957) suggest that domineering mothers foster high achievement. To foster high achievement, evidently, parents must be democratic and supportive yet must provide sufficient motivation to achieve. Low achievers, in rebellion against authority, rebel against home and school together. In turn, parents are more punitive with them, in contrast to the advice and support given high achievers by their families in the few instances when school work goes poorly.

There is some suggestion that low achievers among boys have more masculine interests than do high achievers. This tendency is also reflected in school achievement, for they favor physical education, shop courses, and the like more than do high achievers.

RELATED FACTORS

As previously remarked, more bright children tend to underachieve than do average or dull children (Thorndike, 1963). A number of factors beside those already mentioned enter in. Peer values are geared more to the achievement of average children than to that of the bright ones. Teaching and academic tasks may also favor the average child. The dull child, striving to maintain status with adults and peers, may conform well and attempt to work up to his potential, whereas the bright ones may become more easily bored and may fail to see the importance of their school work. It has also been remarked that teachers frequently fail to understand how high the potential of bright students actually is and therefore do not expect enough from them. (This statement does not mean that teachers fail to recognize bright students or do not know their I.Q.s. It does mean that they fail to understand what an I.Q. of 125, for example, means in ability to achieve, compared to an I.Q. of 100. Assignments should reflect appreciation of both quantity and quality of intellectual differences.)

We have remarked that teachers' marks do not reflect a true picture of what may actually be attained by pupils if standardized tests are used as criteria of achievement. Thus R. S. Carter (1952) found that boys may be short-changed, as their more aggressive behavior may cause them to be less appreciated by the teacher than are girls. Because girls are more cooperative and conforming, they may attain higher marks than do boys with the same actual achievement.

Health is not a factor in differences between high- and low-achieving boys, except in instances of gross deficiencies or defects.

IMPLICATIONS

In examining a number of studies, several generalizations about the differing characteristics of high- and low-achieving pupils, principally boys, have been reached. It should be carefully noted, however, that, although such generalizations may hold for groups of people, they do not necessarily hold for any given individual. They are useful guidelines in helping us to study and to understand better the low achiever or the underachiever, but they tend to ignore individual differences. Although curricular implications exist in findings like those discussed, treatment of a given youngster must be based on a more thorough search of his own personal characteristics.

One thing seems quite clear, however. Low achievers are not

simply unmotivated in school. Their values, interests, backgrounds, and self-perceptions may all be quite different from those of high achievers. For this reason one cannot deal with low achievement simply by exhorting youngsters to stronger efforts, nor will threats or pressure be of much help. Some low achievers may feel inadequate, have many conflicts, or be anxious or tense. They develop many defenses. Their relationships with others may be dependent, aggressive, or withdrawing; they are not independent or leader-like in most instances.

We have also suggested that some overachievers who are too conforming and too anxious may rid themselves of some tension by classroom efforts and scholastic success. Although useful to society, this success may be at the child's expense, for such children may neglect their own needs. They may fail to gain independence and may continue to lean on authority. They may fail to seize opportunities for originality or creativity in their attempts to conform to known—and "safe"—school and adult models. They may fail to develop their own individualities and may not attain a desired degree of self-actualization.

It is not enough for teachers to know which children are achieving highly and which are not. It is equally necessary, from a mental-health point of view, to ascertain what is affecting high or low achievement and how the child's achievement is related to his other needs. The healthiest child is one who achieves near what is predicted on the basis of his intellectual ability, previous school achievement, and personal and social adjustment.

Dealing With Underachievement

The prevention and remediation of underachievement can be roughly divided into methods emphasizing improvement of social and personal adjustment, motivation, and attitudes and methods emphasizing educational or curricular variables. As already noted, there are probably no existing techniques that can be generally applied to all pupils, and underachievers are no exception to this rule. Each child needs careful study and probably a combination of efforts that include attention to both adjustment and educational factors. Nevertheless, as there are similarities among underachievers and because of problems of economy, certain group techniques may be employed.

CURRICULAR MEASURES

Research suggests that underachievement begins long before it is usually recognized. M. C. Shaw and J. T. McCuen (1960) showed that underachievement can be detected as early as first grade, and it tends to increase with succeeding grades, becoming statistically significant for boys at third-grade age. For girls, a drop in achievement becomes noticeable at sixth grade, with statistical significance attained at grade nine. There are a number of possible reasons for this sex difference in achievement, including the fact that elementary schools may be geared more closely to the feminine role and that boys may lack male identifying figures in the earlier grades.

Underachievement tends to increase with the age of the child. There are a number of factors that may influence this tendency: Smaller children are more dependent upon their parents and other adults and are therefore likely to be more conforming and amenable to their demands; in preadolescence and adolescence, however, children begin to lean more upon the values and attitudes of peers and to rethink their own roles and values. Some, during adolescence, may actively reject adult wishes, particularly if they have failed to find positive reinforcements through compliance. Again, with progress upward through the grades, more and more departmentalization tends to take place; scholastic stringency and emphasis on course content increase, as compared to earlier grades. Because of departmentalization, teachers deal with many more children than does the teacher of the self-contained classroom and may be less able to understand individual children and provide for their differences.

The teacher's first step in prevention or remediation of underachievement might be to examine carefully, by use of standardized tests and direct observation, the accomplishments of all pupils to discover whether or not they are in line with the children's potential. Such an examination allows one to deal remedially with initial underachievement and also to gain some idea of the relevant factors at the grade level at which underachievement is first recognized, so that preventive steps may be taken.

For example, it is known that some children learn better with visual stimuli than with auditory or tactile stimuli. On the other hand, there are learners who do better with either of the latter than with the former. It is possible, through the use of tests, to determine which may be the case for each pupil. He can then be presented major material according to his best medium, but training can also be given to improve his use of other sensory media. Again, some underachievement arises from cultural deprivation, in which the child fails to learn language skills (vocabulary and sentence construction, for example) at home as well as does the average child. Work in progress suggests that specific vocabulary building (and concept building) can help prevent lowered achievement from this cause.

Some boys and girls have high verbal abilities as measured by such intelligence tests as the WISC. Others have high performance in nonverbal abilities. Those with high verbal abilities have most chance to succeed in the usual academic courses; on the other hand, work might be geared to the nonverbal abilities and interests of boys and girls who have them. Crafts, laboratory work, shop courses, physical education, instrumental music, and similar courses might thus be upgraded in prestige and used to keep such pupils motivated, to provide evidence of success, and to lead to more academic courses.

It has been suggested that the school norms for achievement at the junior high-school level appear to be those of mediocrity and doing enough to "get by"—and that scholars *per se* are considered "square." Pupils tend to view teachers as demanding the conforming, docile pupil rather than the creative, intellectually active, or independent pupil. Here is a whole area for exploration and experimentation. What reinforcements can be offered for high academic attainment other than teacher praise or censure and school marks? Would it be feasible (see Chapter 4) to use privileges, concrete rewards (especially in lower grades), and other reinforcements to induce underachievers to work to capacity and to enhance the image of the achiever?

Underachievers do not identify with the school as much as do high and overachievers. Can ways be found to help them to attain feelings of belonging and to locate people in the school with whom to identify? On the latter point, it is suggested that male teachers be provided for at least part of the curriculum at *all* grade levels, not only as identifying figures, but also as masculine models for boy pupils.

As with our discussion of discipline (Chapter 4), identification and desirable behavior are more likely when reinforcements are positive and when the adult model is friendly, cheerful, and accepting. In contrast to threats and other pressures to get children to work at school tasks, the school should emphasize any positive reinforcements available.

Responsibility can be taught. Children should be given opportunities for decision making. When decisions are "wrong," children should be allowed to face the natural consequences—failure, the requirement to rework their decisions and follow them in revised form, and so on. Teachers should imply that they are present to help pupils but not to take responsibility for pupils' work. Teachers should express to children a willingness to provide help but only if the pupil asks for it and is willing to utilize that help constructively. When a teacher offers unwanted help, he may raise resentment and take away independence and acceptance of responsibility. It is true, of course, that lowered self-confidence, feelings of guilt, and other undesirable attitudes and emotions may result from failure too frequently experienced. The point made here is that failure may be a result of not trying; in such a case, the teacher is actually contributing to failure, for the child is not being required to take responsibility upon himself, and, in conditions where teacher help is not available, the child may lack the necessary experience to deal with problem situations.

Pupils should not be reinforced for shoddy work. It is incumbent upon each teacher to estimate accurately what each pupil can do and to require him to do it. "Encouragement" should be offered only for effort; false praise should never be given. Although more will be said later, in Chapter 9, marking practices should not be entirely based upon standards or in comparison to the work of other children but should reflect some idea of the abilities of each pupil. For example, bright children are typically underestimated and may be given work that fails to reflect their true abilities. Extra work given to such children may not represent extra quality so much as extra quantity, in which event bright children are not encouraged to utilize their abilities to the extent that they should if they are to develop optimally. Such considerations should be kept in mind in individual assignments.

Opportunities for independence should be offered, and pupils should not be required to be too conforming. In fact, creative and divergent thinking might well be stressed. Emphasis should be shifted, whenever possible, away from considering whether a pupil is "right" or "wrong." After all, some problems have no solutions, whereas others have many; furthermore, one way to learn is to make mistakes and to learn from them. Therefore many "rebels" might learn to be healthily independent rather than simply nonconforming, a desirable quality in today's children and youth. Teachers can help children to differentiate between independence and nonconformity—a desirable step in helping children to attain self-actualization without having to experiment in socially undesirable ways.

WORKING WITH PARENTS

Studies have shown that parents of high achievers are generally more supportive, willing to advise and help, more respectful of children, and more willing to tolerate independence than are parents of low achievers. It has been noted previously that many underachievers, usually boys, find difficulty in accepting authority. In many instances their failures at school reflect a transference reaction to faulty use of authority in the home. Either in rebellion or because of anxieties, such children are thus unable to achieve successfully, which in turn usually brings forth more pressure from parents for them to achieve, creating a vicious cycle of nonachievement, parental dissatisfaction, negative child attitudes, and both educational and mental-health problems.

It is desirable to have parent study groups—perhaps beginning with parents of preschoolers and continuing into early elementary years—related to school achievement, mental health, and similar questions of interest and importance to them. Additionally, parents may be counseled individually concerning their children. In some instances it is possible to provide some understanding of what is taking place, as Chapter 13 discusses in greater detail. When parent counseling fails to bear fruit, however, the child's school environment may be modified; for example, he might be placed under a strong, supportive teacher who can be an identifying figure for him. As this problem usually arises with boys, male teachers are recommended.

COUNSELING TECHNIQUES

In a study of underachieving high-school boys and girls of I.Q.s ranging from 90 to 139 (mean I.Q. 109), B. J. Bosdell (1962) randomly assigned subjects to five treatment conditions: individual counseling, group counseling, combination group and individual counseling, study-skills instruction, and no treatment or control grouping. Those in group counseling were seen once a week for a fifty-five-minute class period; those in study-skills training received equal time; those in individual counseling were seen for half-periods each week; and those in combination counseling received a total of a period and a half each week.

Study of personality change showed that, although there were no statistically significant changes in the combination, individually counseled, and group-counseled subjects, there were consistent trends in personality improvement. Students in the study-skills group scored the same on personality measures as they had done before treatment; those in control groups showed slight negative trends on measures of personality.

In improvement of study habits and attitudes, individually counseled students showed more change than did the group-counseled and control groups; those in study-skills groups also improved more than did group-counseled pupils. In fact, the only negative changes were in group-counseled students. In grade-point average improvement, individually counseled and study-skills pupils improved more than did group-counseled or control children. Some group-counseling clients and controls changed negatively.

Bosdell suggests that there were individual differences among the skills of the counselors that might have had some effect upon the efficiency of group counseling. Her main finding was that there are differential effects in counseling, depending upon the primary goals of the counselors, for example, attitude change or improvement in achievement. Study-skills instruction was considered valuable in working with underachievers.

It is reasonable to conclude that individual counseling may frequently be more useful than group counseling and that, when subjects get no treatment, they tend to continue their negative trends in achievement and in personality traits. Results are differential, depending on the purpose of the counseling. There are some peripheral implications in this study: For example, as group-counseled clients changed negatively in study habits, attitudes, and grade-point average, it is possible that they may have been reinforcing one another's negative attitudes toward academic achievement; they may have felt singled out, on display, and acted accordingly. If this interpretation is correct, the common school practice of placing low achievers together in the same classrooms probably militates against optimum achievement, even though study skills may be taught. This study reinforces the value of tutorial remedial instruction and individual counseling on attitudes and mental-health problems.

H. G. Stern (1961) also cites the need for personal support through counseling and points out the value of academic, vocational, and adjustment counseling at the high-school level. She stresses the importance of the attitudes of teachers, as some are notably unsympathetic and punitive toward underachieving pupils. As working with underachievers is not considered the task of the counselor only, but also involves teamwork with the teachers, the latter's attitudes are highly important to the counselor's success with pupils. Such specialists as the school psychologist, remedial-reading expert, school social worker, visiting teacher, and representatives of community clinics or other agencies can also help underachieving pupils.

A. R. Meeks (1961), working at the elementary-school level, stresses the need for the school to differentiate between boys' and girls' maturation and motivation as related to their readiness for learning. Counseling can also help children to handle relationships with their parents more successfully.

STUDY SKILLS AND REMEDIAL INSTRUCTION

Aside from study-skills instruction, as mentioned in B. J. Bosdell's research (1962), and aside from the remedial efforts of the teacher, the school program may be modified to provide remedial classes, special schools, tutoring by subject specialists, tutoring by pupil "big brothers," programmed instruction and teaching machines, specialized homework, and so on. What is recommended for a given child should be based on the diagnostic study of his needs by either a qualified teacher, a remedial specialist, or a school psychologist. Efforts may range from dealing with basic word recognition in reading, through help in budgeting study time and learning to concentrate, to changes in media of instruction, and including efforts to modify attitudes, motivations, or mental health.

The concept of a "total approach" to slow learners and underachievers has been fostered in such special situations as the Psychology Clinic School of the University of California at Los Angeles. This school, working mostly with boys who are of near average or higher intelligence, provides a special setting in which a variety of efforts at remediation are undertaken. After careful study of each boy and assessment of personality, academic, physical, and social data, remediation may be planned in individual or group settings. Individual counseling on personality or academic problems may take place; there may be placement in remedial classrooms under trained teachers, or there may be individual tutoring. Recreation provides opportunity for change in personal and social attitudes and behavior. Family counseling may be used. In the instance of certain boys, referral for therapy may be made to clinicians. As most of the boys are poor readers, specially devised textbooks, elementary in reading level but mature in content, are provided. Many of the students can enhance their ability to learn through tactile means, so that students are asked to write the reading words and in other ways make use of tactile and kinesthetic senses. This total approach is expensive, of course, and may not be within the grasp of some school systems, yet its value in helping young people to learn to achieve successfully and to return eventually to the public-school setting has been amply demonstrated.

The use of remedial programmed materials—either teaching machines or programmed instruction books—in various subjects is currently being fostered. Such programming permits the child to proceed at his own pace, to gain immediate confirmation of response, to be active in learning, and to achieve success by small but consistent movements toward the learning goals. It is probably also true in certain instances that such devices, being impersonal—compared to the teacher, classmates, or tutor —provide enhanced opportunities for children who are threatened by learning in social settings.

EFFECTS OF IDENTIFICATION AND STUDY

M. Krugman and I. H. Impellizzeri (1960) found, interestingly, that, when gifted students in New York City were studied, the mere fact that some of the students in the program were included was enough to focus attention upon them by parents, teachers, counselors, and the pupils themselves. This attention, in turn, seemed to stimulate some students to improved efforts.

Whether identification of bright students, especially of underachievers, involves the "Hawthorne effect," in which mere attention given to them is enough to make them feel "special" and hence to motivate them at least temporarily, or whether apprising students of their real, but unsuspected, abilities tends to set more adequate goals is not always clear. It is also possible that the study of a child implies a mild threat or admonition, suggesting that he should accomplish more. In any case, study of a child, with feedback to him and to his parents, is frequently useful in modifying his attitudes and improving his behavior.

THE DROPOUT PROBLEM

An estimated more than 700,000 students drop out of school each year, most of them at the secondary level. Many of these students have been characterized as "slow learners," and most come from culturally deprived, "high risk" socioeconomic areas, a large proportion in large cities. A number of explanations for dropouts are currently being offered, but the prime factor seems to be inadequate language development and consequent inability to read or write at levels expected in the usual classroom (Bayley, 1963) .

It must be pointed out that, although the most frequent dropout I.Q. is from 75 to 90, most tests given pupils are of the paper-and-pencil type and tend to emphasize these students' lack of verbal ability. As many of these students are from subcultures that are not always adequately tested by the usual instruments, it frequently is not intelligence *per se* that is at the root of the learning problems but its *manifestation* in verbal areas.

In the homes of many such children there is no father; a frequent concomitant is that home life is disorganized, with no regular mealtime and therefore no family interaction at the table or, indeed, at any other place. Language skills are not practiced, and there is a cumulative loss in the child's language development, which militates against school learning. Furthermore, most school textbooks and other materials tend to emphasize a kind of life that is not typical for these children, with consequent disinterest, frustration, and inability of the pupil to identify with the material presented. Add to these problems the attitude of many teachers toward these children—low expectations concerning their abilities and motivations—and one can see that the dropout is essentially a culturally caused problem.

Many school systems place emphasis on "vocational" courses, which are valuable. But experience shows that the dropout's greatest problems in life after school will come from inability to read, write, and calculate effectively. In too many classes these students are given primarily rote material, and little attention is devoted to comprehension and the ability to think for oneself. Reading problems are rarely adequately treated. In turn, many of these children become disheartened, and in their boredom and frustration they tend to become disciplinary problems.

Many school systems have made attempts to deal with the problems of potential dropouts. For example, Farmington, New York, has provided a special program (Abramowitz, 1964) in which dropouts take many of the same courses as do more successful pupils but in smaller doses and in "highlighted" versions. Speed of progress is adjusted to ability and current status. Each day's work is treated as a special unit, so that one can be absent or fail to master one day's assignment without jeopardizing succeeding days' work. Furthermore, with material given in small amounts, it is more likely to be mastered, and students can thus have the positive reinforcement of achieving success. Review of previous days' work is provided, and comprehension tests are given daily; new vocabulary is provided at the beginning of every lesson. Reading is done in the classroom under supervision. Grades are not recorded, and pupils are asked to evaluate their own progress. Homework is minimized, and what is given is given as clear-cut, positive assignments, as these students are used to sloughing off.

Abramowitz mentions that, when classes like these were first instituted, the students displayed the characteristics of truants but that, after a few months, their attitudes changed, and they began to feel that school might do them some good. Some even began to like school for the first time in their lives.

New York City has several programs that aim at preventing students from dropping out of school. There is the School to Employment Program, which supports seven schools in which students obtain individual guidance and a regular curriculum in the morning but hold jobs in the afternoon (which are paid, supervised, and provide school credit). The Co-operative Program aids students in obtaining work in various municipal agencies while still in school. Operation Return provides two high schools for students who have dropped out. The Higher Horizons Program attempts to deal with problems in slum areas where, not only is the dropout helped through guidance, but his cultural life and that of his parents are also dealt with. In the latter program, remedial classes and after-school study opportunities are provided.

St. Louis attempts to deal with cultural deprivation by working directly with the home and parents and finds many formerly slow-learning pupils much better motivated and able to achieve in school.

The potential dropout has problems that begin early in elementary school; indeed, some enter school with several "strikes against them." Emphasis thus shifts to dealing remedially with problems long before they become acute, although attempts are made to help these children at any possible point in their school careers.

Essentially, the curriculum offers the most hope. Arbitrary grading and failure or nonpromotion should be eliminated. There should be a broad, flexible curriculum, designed for individual differences. Unrelated courses and lessons should be eliminated. Material should be arranged logically and chrono-logically and should be related to pupils' needs and interests. And, because children differ, some should be provided with more structure and restriction, whereas others need more free-dom. Some require remedial instruction of special kinds. There is thus no panacea for the school dropout problem, but there are many things that can be done.

THE TEACHER'S ATTITUDE TOWARD THE UNDERACHIEVER

We have referred to the teacher's attitude before; we shall expand briefly here. The teacher's attitude is important, not only because it may cause him to be punitive or to feel negative toward the child and thus compound the problem, but also because the child's attitude toward himself is affected by the ways others seem to evaluate him. Such evalution is a promi-nent factor in motivation to achieve.

The professionally minded teacher considers underachieve-ment as a problem to be attacked in a professional manner. He views underachievement as a symptom of underlying difficulties related to home, peers, school, or personal mental health that must be discovered and treated appropriately. Off-the-cuff at-tempts to "motivate" the underachiever rarely bear real fruit, and threat and punishment simply tend to promote unfavorable attitudes and emotions in both teacher and child. When the teacher is able to view poor achievement as a problem for both himself and the pupil, he is less likely to be threatened by the failure of his efforts with a given child and thus more able to accept the child and deal with him successfully.

We have seen that most underachievers do not feel overconfi-dent but are seeking to obtain security, self-esteem, the status, and respect they lack. Some use defenses of rebellion, with-drawal, or apparent rejection of the values of the school. Many feel a compelling need for others' respect and for self-respect. Lacking self-confidence in their own worth and abilities, they are anxious and cannot help but employ defenses, some of which are irksome to the teacher.

Once convinced by demonstration that they can do better, many underachievers improve greatly.

Nevertheless, like other categories of human behavior, underachievement varies widely with individuals. Remedial efforts must be based on careful study of the child and must be as comprehensive as possible.

☐

REFERENCES

Abramowitz, J. "How to Reach Potential Dropouts Before They Quit," *School Management,* 8 (1964), 64–7.

Bayley, M. "Efforts to Solve the Problems of Dropout," *School Life,* 46 (1963), 11–6.

Bledsoe, J. C., and K. C. Garrison. *The Self Concepts of Elementary School Children in Relation to Their Academic Achievement, Intelligence, Interests, and Manifest Anxiety* (Cooperative Research Project 1008). Athens: University of Georgia, 1962.

Bosdell, B. J. *Evaluation of Counseling Treatments with Underachieving High School Students* (Cooperative Research Project 1263). Grand Forks: University of North Dakota, 1962.

Boyd, G. R. *Classroom Adjustment of the Underchosen Child Through Changes in Teachers' Attitudes and Behavior.* Troy, Ala.: Troy State College, 1960.

Brookover, W. B., A. Patterson, and S. Thomas. *The Relationship of Self-Images to Achievement in Junior High School Subjects* (Cooperative Research Project 845). East Lansing: Michigan State University, 1962.

Carter, R. S. "How Invalid are Marks Assigned by Teachers?" *Journal of Educational Psychology,* 43 (1952), 218–28.

Drews, E., and J. Teahan. "Parental Attitudes and Academic Achievement," *Journal of Clinical Psychology,* 13 (1957), 328–32.

Farquhar, W. W. *A Comprehensive Study of the Motivational Factors Underlying Achievement of Eleventh Grade High School Students* (Research Digest 846–8458). East Lansing: Michigan State University, 1959.

Frankel, E. "A Comparative Study of Achieving and Under-Achieving High School Boys of High Intellectual Ability," *Journal of Educational Research,* 53 (1960), 172–9.

Goodstein, L. D., J. O. Crites, and A. B. Heilbrun, Jr. *Personality Correlates of Academic Adjustment* (Cooperative Research Project 805). Iowa City: State University of Iowa, 1962.

Gowan, J. C. "The Underachieving Gifted Child," *Exceptional Children,* 21 (1955), 247–9.

Graff, F. A. *Occupational Choice Factors in Normally Achieving and Underachieving Superior Twelfth Grade Boys.* Doctoral Dissertation, University of Connecticut, 1957.

Hoyt, D. P., and W. T. Norman. "Adjustment and Academic Predictability," *Journal of Counseling Psychology,* 1 (1954), 96–7.

Krugman, M., and I. H. Impellizzeri. "Identification and Guidance of Underachieving Gifted Students in New York City," *Exceptional Children,* 26 (1960), 283–6.

Meeks, A. R. "What Can Be Done at the Elementary Level," in L. M. Miller (ed.). *Guidance for the Underachiever With Superior Ability* (Bulletin No. 25, OE–25021), pp. 31–42. Washington, D.C.: U.S. Department of Health, Education and Welfare, 1961.

Morgan, H. W. "A Psychometric Comparison of Achieving and Non-achieving College Students of High Ability," *Journal of Counseling Psychology,* 16 (1952), 292–8.

Morrow, W., and R. Wilson. "Family Relations of Bright High-Achieving High School Boys," *Child Development,* 32 (1961), 501.

Pierce, J. V. *Sex Differences in Achievement Motivation of Able High School Students* (Cooperative Research Project 1097). Quincy: University of Chicago Quincy Youth Development Project, 1961.

Pierce, J. V., and P. H. Bowman. *The Educational Motivation Patterns of Superior Students Who Do and Do Not Achieve in High School* (Research Project 208–7136). Chicago: University of Chicago, 1959.

Portland Public Schools. *The Gifted Child in Portland.* Portland, Ore.: Public Schools, 1959.

Ringness, T. A. *Differences in Attitudes Toward Self and Others of Academically Successful and Non-Successful Ninth-Grade Boys of Superior Intelligence* (Final Report, National Institute of Mental Health Post-Doctoral Research Fellowship). Los Angeles: University of California, 1963.

———. *Non-Intellective Variables Related to Academic Achievement of Bright Junior High School Boys* (Final Report, Cooperative Research Project S–035). Madison: University of Wisconsin, 1965.

Rust, R. M., and F. J. Ryan. "The Strong Vocational Interest Blank and College Achievement," *Journal of Applied Psychology,* 38 (1954), 341–5.

Shaw, M. C., and G. J. Alves. "The Self-Concept of Bright Academic Underachievers: Continued," *Personnel and Guidance Journal,* 42 (1963), 401–3.

Shaw, M. C., and J. T. McCuen. "The Onset of Academic Underachievement in Bright Children," *Journal of Educational Psychology,* 51 (1960), 103–9.

Stern, H. G. "What Can Be Done at the Secondary Level," in L. M. Miller (ed.). *Guidance for the Underachiever With Superior Ability* (Bulletin No. 25, OE–25021), pp. 43–56. Washington, D.C.: U.S. Department of Health, Education and Welfare, 1961.

Taylor, R. G. *Personality Factors Associated With Scholastic Achievement.* Paper presented at American Personnel and Guidance Association convention, Denver, March 30, 1961.

Thorndike, R. L. *The Concept of Over- and Under-Achievement.* New York: Columbia University Teachers College, 1963.

Todd, F. J., G. Terrell, and C. Frank. "Differences Between Normal and Underachievers of Superior Ability," *Journal of Applied Psychology,* 46 (1962), 183–90.

Walsh, A. M. "Self-Concepts of Bright Boys With Learning Difficulties," *Teachers College Studies in Education,* pp. 1–79. New York: Columbia University Teachers College, 1956.

SUGGESTIONS FOR FURTHER READING

Crow, L. D., and A. Crow. *Mental Hygiene for Teachers—A Book of Readings*. New York: Macmillan, 1963.
This book takes the stand that some low achievers are underachievers but that others lack abilities or cultural background. In Part 7, H. M. Williams discusses the "slow-learner problem" and indicates that retarded children have special needs. M. D. Fantini looks at ways to make learning exciting for slow learners, and E. Arnholter describes the values of social drama for retarded adolescents. In Part 8, problems of the gifted learner are discussed; the reader will recall that some of these children are underachievers and that others may have anxieties, frustrations, or other problems. E. H. Grotberg, G. Kaluger, and R. Martin discuss some of the problems of gifted learners, adding point to our contention that high achievement does not necessarily reflect optimal mental health.

Miller, L. M. (ed.). *Guidance for the Underachiever With Superior Ability* (Bulletin No. 25, OE–25021). Washington, D.C.: U.S. Department of Health, Education and Welfare, 1961.
Here is a condensed but valuable survey of the methodology of guidance practices with underachievers. Research support is presented, and problems are discussed. This bulletin would be particularly valuable for those in remedial or counseling positions.

MOTIVATION AND EMOTIONS IN THE CLASSROOM

In Chapter 4 we discussed some principles of learning, relying strongly on a discussion of stimulus, response, reinforcement, imitation, and identification. It must not be assumed, however, that learning does not involve other variables too. Indeed, human learning, hence human behavior, is highly complex and involves a number of factors. In this chapter we shall primarily consider motivation, feelings, and emotions. We shall begin with a consideration of motivation, an exceedingly complex and somewhat controversial subject.

Importance of Motivation to Behavior

The importance of motivation becomes clearer when we consider the following statement by Herbert Thelen:

It is possible for a child to go through a programmed text, making all the required responses correctly, and then not remember any of the ideas he has been dealing with. It is possible for a child to work through a chemical experiment in the lab manual and still not be able to say what he has seen and what principle it illustrates. It is possible for a child to study spelling for seven years and still not be able to spell. It is possible for a man to engage in churchly activities all his life and still be spiritually unwashed; for a business-man to engage in one business activity after another and end up broke. (And for a professor to study education for twenty years and still not have any different or new ideas than he started with.) It is one thing to engage in activities, producing socially demanded and acceptable behavior; it is another thing to learn anything from the experience—except, possibly, how to play roles. (1964, p. 33)

Thelen implies that it is not only the activities in which one engages but also the reasons for engaging in them that contrib-ute to the outcomes. What one learns from a situation depends in no small part on why he entered into it. What he pays attention to, how he interprets what he senses, what responses he chooses from his repertoire, and how he interprets any reinforcements must depend partly upon his motives. Whether or not he uses what he has learned depends on his motivation, and what he expects from similar situations is also a function of his motives.

Much of the meaning of a given act thus depends upon the motivation to perform that act; to understand what another's actions mean, it is necessary to have some understanding of his motives. For example, one may see a high school freshman walking down the hall wearing a green felt cap. One might hypothesize that he is seeking attention or that he is cold, rude, or untutored. But when one learns that freshmen in this school are required at all times to wear "beanies" in the school colors, the act takes on a different meaning. The boy is now seen to be conforming to regulations and appears socially adjusted. A given act can quite obviously come about for differing reasons.

Conversely, a given motive may produce many kinds of behavior. A boy who is interested in a girl may do all sorts of uncharacteristic things. He may walk with her and offer to carry her books. He may give her a ride in his automobile. He may ask a friend to indicate to the girl that he is interested in her. Or, depending on his age, he may act the clown in front of her, show off, tease her, or even pretend that he does not like her.

Motivation has a number of functions: It activates behavior

and helps determine which responses will be made; it maintains behavior; it causes the organism to discriminate between various stimuli, responses, and reinforcers.

The kinds of motives that initiate or continue behavior may be mentally healthy or not. In addition, the resulting behavior may represent desirable or undesirable means of achieving reinforcement. Conflict of motives and inability to discriminate are causes of much emotional distress. Therefore, one function of therapy or remediation is to teach the individual to discriminate more clearly between his motives and the related stimuli, responses, and reinforcers. Another function is to help him find ways to reduce conflicts and to attain his goals in ways acceptable to himself and society or, if his motives are unacceptable, to find ways to change or extinguish them.

Here is an example of a child whose behavior is maladaptive. It will be obvious that not much can be done to help her until more is learned about what is motivating her actions.

Debbie is a real child. The material presented here was originally handed in to a professor by a student teacher as a study in observing children. Not all the information gathered will be presented, but the problems she noted will be shown in sufficient detail to arouse questions.

The student teacher wrote:

In room K-3 of G—— School we find a shy, withdrawing child. Her name is Debbie, she is five years old, and is a new student in the room. I started observing her because of her unusual quietness. We were warned that she had not spoken since she entered kindergarten at a different school in September. It was now March. For two weeks she was observed quite closely and not much change occurred in her behavior. In the beginning, we understood, other children in the class wanted to take care of her, but after a few days with no response on Debbie's part, the others lost interest and left her alone. Her behavior was characterized by wandering about the room, looking at everything, seeming very alert and aware of what was going on, refusing to do any type of art work, and complete absence of speech.

She listens when a teacher is talking, and from her score on a reading test, seems to be getting the information presented in kindergarten. She does not appear physically afraid of the others, for when they sit, she follows and sits; when lining up, she does also. She sometimes smiles, but this is the only emotion she ever shows.

After discussing the problem with my cooperating teacher, we decided to try to force her to speak, by asking questions and insisting on an answer. This was tried one day, but Debbie clenched her fists and refused to answer. When the teacher insisted, Debbie turned away. We tried on other occasions, without result.

We tried to help Debbie with her drawing by actually taking her hand and moving it. We found that once she was started, Debbie would carry on by herself, without the teacher's help. We are using this technique in regard to most of her assigned tasks—we start her, and hope she will carry on. We have had some success, but there is a long way to go.

At this point we can only speculate on Debbie's motives for such behavior. Does she enjoy attention? If so, she is gaining it from the teachers, although perhaps not in ways she might prefer. Is she too concerned with being correct? Such concern might account for her grudging willingness to draw after being started by the teacher and her copying the lining-up or sitting behavior of the others. Does she wish to do things in her own way and therefore resist direction? This explanation might account for her failure to respond to the other pupils, her lack of speech, and her unwillingness to answer the teacher's questions.

It would be difficult to form any conclusions at this stage, however, and Debbie must be studied much more thoroughly, preferably by experts. But it can be said that, when more is learned about Debbie's motives and the closely related feelings and emotions, her behavior may be much better understood.

The Relationships of Motives With Mental Health

HEALTHY MOTIVES

Mental health, as defined in Chapter 1, includes desires to further the social good; to be independent and to accept responsibility for one's own actions; to solve problems rather than to vacillate or employ defense mechanisms; and to achieve self-actualization. Healthy motives lead the individual to seek ways of accomplishing his own goals within a socially acceptable context. A healthy individual thus does not act in a completely selfish manner; nor does he blindly conform to the wishes of others without considering how he may also achieve his own goals. Healthy motives maintain the organism and permit growth and development.

It is perfectly possible, of course, to have healthy motives yet to employ them in unhealthy ways. We all probably like to seek the attention of others, but there are desirable and undesirable ways of so doing. For example, a child may seek attention from the teacher by raising needless questions or by bringing presents, both undesirable means of satisfying a legitimate motive. Such acts lead only to social disapproval, with possible consequent negative feelings toward self and others. On the other hand, there are desirable ways of seeking attention: for example, employing one's talents constructively, showing oneself to be outstanding in an acceptable way, and showing interest in others.

On the whole, if a child's motives are healthy but his behavior is maladaptive, he is probably easier to work with than if he has unhealthy motives.

UNHEALTHY MOTIVES

Some motives are unhealthy in the sense that they lead to problems for the child or for others with whom he deals. If his motives are essentially destructive, it is necessary to try to find ways to deal with them, as well as with his actions.

For example, many children are overconforming. They seem to want to abase themselves before others. They continually deride themselves and their accomplishments. They lean on others and may even consort with those who are harsh, derogatory, or contemptuous toward them. There are many possible reasons for such behavior. One is that, if they give in most of the time and show themselves to be noncompetitors, others will be less likely to do them harm. Indeed, some people may become their protectors. Most of us are kind to the "underdog." Another possibility, however, is that such children feel considerable guilt. They may actually feel themselves to be unworthy and may be seeking punishment. Such children are usually depressed. They seem to wish to do themselves harm or to have others punish them.

At the other end of the spectrum, dominance and aggression can be healthy characteristics—or not—depending on the reasons for them. If the basic motive is to stand up for one's rights or to attack a problem wholeheartedly, aggressiveness can be perfectly healthy. But if motivated by a desire to harm others, out of hate, fear, or self-aggrandizement, obviously this tendency is unhealthy.

Masochistic behavior, sadism, extreme withdrawal—all represent maladaptive behavior that is likely to be motivated by unhealthy feelings and emotions.

UNCLEAR MOTIVES

Psychoanalysts have long contended that many actions are motivated by desires that are unclear to the actor; perhaps the real motives have been repressed or disguised. Such motives would be those one really would not wish to recognize in himself. For example, parents being what they are, children may both love and dislike them. Because it is not socially acceptable to hate one's parents, such feelings must be repressed or disguised. A child may sometimes try to compensate for them by being oversolicitous of his parents or perhaps by taking out his hostile feelings on someone else. (The mechanism of *displacement* consists of transferring one's feelings to people or situations other than the person or situation that is really causing the difficulty. Teachers are thus sometimes recipients of hostile behavior initiated by a child's reactions to his parents in the home.)

Sometimes not understanding the "real" reasons for one's actions can cause trouble. One of the goals of clinical therapists (of several schools of thought) is therefore to try to help the patient understand the true nature of his motives and how to deal with them constructively.

CONFLICTING MOTIVES

Again we must credit psychoanalysts for first calling clinical attention to the problem of conflicting motives. Motives may conflict because of the nature of our social living (for example, there is the problem of pleasing others without submerging oneself) ; because of inadequate or erroneous early learning (when is it "right" to inform on someone who is doing something wrong?) ; because of ambivalent feelings about something or someone; because one has two attractive goals that cannot both be attained; or for many other reasons.

Among the common conflicts in life is that between dependence and independence, which usually occurs during adolescence when the youth is aware that he must learn to make his own way in the world, when he realizes that his own ideas and desires are legitimate, but when he also knows that he is still dependent for physical and moral support upon his parents and other adults. Another common conflict arises from differences in social norms between peers and school authority. Two studies already mentioned showed that an achievement norm of mediocrity and of doing just enough to get by was fostered by the peer group (Ringness, 1965) , in contrast to the standards of excellence demanded by parents and teachers. Other conflicts in youth range all the way from whether one should be honest or cheat to get a good mark, through some quite complicated conflicts in which a boy may wish to undertake a vocation or avocation usually considered feminine, yet does not wish to appear a sissy (hair dressing, clothes designing, or nursing, for example) .

Such conflicting motives can lead to frustration, anxiety, fear, guilt, and depression. In this sense, motive conflicts can be unhealthy.

Further relationships between the nature of motivation and mental health will be brought out later in this chapter.

Here is an example that illustrates some of the points we have mentioned in connection with healthy, unhealthy, unclear, and conflicting motives.

A student teacher reports:

Jay is in sixth grade—he is a withdrawing boy, a victim of cerebral palsy. He can keep pace with the slower portion of the class if allowed time to work without pressure and if instructions are organized and explicit. He becomes frustrated if he cannot complete his work. On the one hand, he wants badly to be a part of the class and to enter into all activities; on the other hand, Jay has difficulty in speaking and in many physical efforts such as walking, writing, or even sitting upright. He has to move carefully and quite slowly, and even though he tries hard, his work is frequently messy because of poor psychomotor control.

I have been trying to reinforce Jay's feeling of confidence and self-respect. We had been working on the Middle Ages, and I planned a dramatic improvisation of the different members of the social classes of that time. The idea was to use creative dramatics; the children would do the production by themselves, with each character self-created. Jay was voted to be the minstrel.

Jay stayed after school with me for two nights to plan his part. The first night we found sources in the library describing minstrels, their instruments, and songs. Next we went to the music room to find an appropriate instrument and decided on a tambourine. We discussed what the minstrel should do; the class had him scheduled to play before the king. Should he sing, hum, or recite?

Jay wanted to sing, and I encouraged this form. A song about Robin Hood was Jay's choice. I found a record in the library about Robin Hood. One song happened to be the music of the theme song of an old TV serial about Robin, and Jay recognized it; I copied two verses for him and he memorized them. We practiced the tune a couple of times, using verses and the tambourine. I was getting as excited as he was by this time! The show had been unfortunately delayed a week—but finally went on . . .

It went amazingly well. The performance surprised the class and I think it surprised Jay, himself. The praise it brought him from his classmates gave him a feeling of satisfaction and peer acceptance in addition to added evidence that he could actively take part in class. It proved to him that he could be before the group with confidence.

The idea of dramatic usage was to allow students to be someone else—in Jay's case, a minstrel. Although I don't think playing someone else through acting should be used as a shield, I do think it helped a great deal in expression, so that it was a positive technique.

Quite obviously, Jay wanted to participate yet was afraid to because of physical infirmities. He wanted to express himself and thus gain self-esteem and social reinforcement, yet he was fearful of doing badly and accomplishing the reverse of what he desired. He was using defenses, essentially that of fantasy (in this case, play acting) , to get him through his "ordeal." On the other hand, he was motivated to use desirable constructive effort.

Essentially Jay was mentally healthy, and his work was adaptive. Consider, however, what might have been the result with a less perceptive student teacher.

The Nature of Motivation

GENERAL FORMULATION

There are two main kinds of motivating forces: the basic, inherited, biological drives and the learned or acquired drives or needs.

In the history of the individual, biological drives are the original motivational forces. These include hunger; thirst; avoidance of pain; need for rest, elimination, and oxygen; and others. Most of the biological drives are aimed at producing behavior to ensure life; if one does not eat, he eventually starves to death, and, if he takes no note of pain, he may wound himself without being aware of it. (The sex drive, of course, does not neatly fit into this formulation, for it is not necessary to satisfy one's urges in order to survive. It is obvious, however, that complete lack of satisfaction of this drive in everyone would result in annihilation of the human race, and in this sense it *must* be satisfied as must any other biological drives.)

Drives are aroused by stimuli, and these stimuli may be internal. For example, a complex group of internal reactions takes place to make us thirsty; not only do we respond to a relative dryness of the mouth or throat, but there also seem to be brain cells that are sensitive to relative lack of water in the tissues and "tell us" we should drink. Stimuli may also be external, and it is interesting to note how many pupils stop at the water fountain in the hall for a couple of swallows of water but do not make the trip around the corner if the fountain is not on their way. Briefly, people are motivated by the biological drives and act to reduce these drives, causing the activating stimuli to be removed.

Biological drives tend to operate until satisfied, and in most (but not all) instances tension continues to mount and goads us into action. These drives are not learned and therefore cannot be extinguished through procedures that affect learned motives. But they can compete with one another, and temporary substitutes can be made on occasion—as when a hungry dieter smokes a cigarette or drinks a cup of coffee instead of eating. To some extent drives can be at least temporarily overridden by acquired motives, as when a sailor in a lifeboat gives his food ration to a friend. They are modifiable to a degree; one develops preferences for certain foods or drinks and for eating at certain times of day.

Acquired motives are those gained through a learning process: the motives to achieve, to gain acceptance by and affiliation with others, and to attain status and recognition. In addition to the motives, themselves, one learns ways of satisfying them—that is, to seek certain reinforcers. Acquired motives, because they are learned, are especially susceptible to modification—much more so than are the biological drives. Motives and related reinforcers become quite specific. The child may thus desire not only to receive affection but also to receive it from certain people. He may at first be quite satisfied with evidence of love from his parents; later he may desire friendship from his peers, which, if not forthcoming, cannot be replaced by parental love.

Because motives can be modified, it is probable that everybody is motivated somewhat differently.

There are other implications. First, if motives are learned, reinforcement for related goal-seeking behavior must occur—frequently while learning is taking place and somewhat less frequently later, to maintain the behavior. For example, if a child seeks affection from his peers, he must at least occasionally be reinforced by evidences of their friendship; if none is forthcoming, his motives and behavior may change, and he may become disinterested in others, may withdraw from social contact, or may even become hostile. The child whose motives include the desire to succeed in school may eventually learn not to care about school success if he fails too frequently to be reinforced for his efforts; the continual failure of a child may eventuate in a lack of desire to keep on trying.

Reinforcement need not always come from the environment.

A child may study to please the teacher or to earn a grade, but, if actual study of the subject becomes intrinsically rewarding, he may pursue his subject long after his teacher has ceased to be a current influence. Such is the case with many pupils who eventually become teachers themselves; they have found school activities so pleasurable as children that they have continued to desire them as adults.

Inner reinforcements are related to goals, value systems, and expectations of self. If behavior is evaluated as successful, the child in effect reinforces himself. For example, when one extends aid to another, he tends to feel satisfaction with his act, even though the other may prove ungrateful. To illustrate further, one pupil may prove highly satisfied with a grade of "C" in a subject if he expected to receive a "D"; another, expecting a "B," would not be satisfied with the "C."

MOTIVES AS A HIERARCHY

A. H. Maslow (1954) has suggested that within a person certain motives tend to take precedence over others. Some motives tend to activate behavior more powerfully than do others. Biological drives thus tend to take precedence over all others; safety motives are next in importance and so on, according to the following hierarchy:

1. biological drives ⎫
2. safety motives   ⎬ maintenance-directed
3. affectional motives ⎪
4. status motives   ⎭

5. self-actualizing motives ⎬ growth-directed

The most basic drives are listed at the bottom; as they are satisfied, it becomes more likely that the person will respond to motives on the next level.

Of this list, the self-actualizing motives enhance the individual; all others maintain him. Although this hierarchy is a generalized formulation and does not invariably apply and although it may differ a bit with individuals, it does help in understanding behavior. The important point seems to be that, in order to employ motives aimed at growth and development, one's more basic motives must first be satisfied. The average person cannot be as careful of his safety when he is hungry as he otherwise would be; he cannot extend affection to others if he does not trust them; and he cannot exercise a high degree of self-direction if he is worried about what others think of him.

Maslow relates the levels of motives being reinforced (or "gratified," to use his term) to mental health as follows:

. . . if we assume that the healthy organism is . . . need-gratified and therefore released for self-actualization, then we have thereby also assumed that this organism develops from within by intrinsic growth tendencies . . . rather than from without, in the behavioristic sense or environmental determinism. The neurotic organism is one that lacks certain satisfactions that can come only from the environment and is less autonomous and self-determined, i.e., more shaped by the nature of the environment and less by its own intrinsic nature. Such relative independence of environment as is found in the healthy person does not, of course, mean lack of commerce with it; it means only that in these contacts, the person's *ends* are the primary determiners, and that the environment is no more than means to the person's self-actualizing ends. This is psychological, if not geographical, freedom. (1954, p. 116)

Maslow thus implies that the healthy person is more dependent on his inner reinforcers than on the evaluations of others or on concrete rewards. This reliance is understandable, for such inner reinforcers (value systems, long-term goals, expectations of self) are more likely to have been tested through experience and the individual is thus less at the mercy of the *immediate* environment. But these inner reinforcers, too, have been learned at some time in the past; once learned, they may govern behavior in the face of current negative environmental reinforcements. It is for this reason that the healthy, self-actualizing person can see the faults of his society and can make attempts to correct them. Essentially, the healthiest person is the one whose maintenance-directed motives present relatively ew unsolved problems so that he is able to attend more to the ends he himself is seeking.

SOME FACTORS IN MOTIVATION

Basically motives can be divided into approach and avoidance dimensions. This distinction means that there are motives to employ behavior to gain something and motives to employ behavior to avoid or escape something. One acts to gain food and avoid pain, to gain applause and avoid humiliation, to gain friendship and avoid the hatred of others.

Motivation can be defined as the desire to gain or avoid a given positive or negative reinforcer. But how do various things become reinforcers? In some cases, direct experience is all that is needed. When one touches a hot stove, he quickly learns aversive behavior. The stove is a negative reinforcer, and one develops the motivation to avoid touching hot stoves with his bare finger. On the other hand, when one is given candy and finds its taste good, candy becomes a reinforcer and induces motivation and resulting behavior to obtain and eat candy.

The learning theorist argues that, given some such natural reinforcers, it is simple to develop other reinforcers either by stimulus generalization or by conditioning. In the case of stimulus generalization, if the child finds smiles from his parents a source of positive reinforcement, he is soon also reinforced by the smiles of others. In the conditioning process, the words, smiles, and other instrumental acts of the parents gain reinforcement value because they occur when the child is being fondled, fed, or otherwise reinforced in regard to biological or early acquired drives and motives.

Reinforcers do not motivate behavior endlessly; or perhaps we should say that most things are not permanent reinforcers. For example, a youth may work hard to earn money for a bicycle; to a young adult, the thought of a bicycle is not reinforcing—he now much prefers an automobile (or motorcycle).

Reinforcers differ for different people, partly because of differences in the culture, the availability of such various reinforcers as food, and the child's ability to attain reinforcers. The strengths of different reinforcers change with circumstances. The small child may be strongly reinforced by parental approval, but the adolescent may be more influenced by peer values and the adult by his own value systems.

We should consider satiation and deprivation briefly. The term "satiation" essentially means that a given reinforcer has lost its ability to motivate behavior, as in the example of the boy and the bicycle. The loss can have a number of causes, perhaps the main one being that other motives are competing or that other reinforcers are more appealing. It should be noted that obtaining reinforcers requires expenditure of effort; when the effort expended meets more negative than positive reinforcement, effort tends to decrease or cease. For example, it is fun to swim, but we stop when we are tired.

Sometimes a child seems entirely unmotivated, or, more properly, we can find no reinforcer that causes him to study or work or whatever else we think he should do. In this event, deprivation is sometimes useful (see Chapter 4) —that is, removing his reinforcers so that he will be motivated to work for them. If this measure seems harsh, consider the "spoiled child," who is usually quite unhappy. Having "everything," he has few satisfactions in life and is discontented. We agree, however, that a parent or teacher who uses deprivation must be humane and quite clear about what he is doing.

For example, teachers sometimes reduce children's motivations to achieve by doing too much for them. They explain too much, provide too much individual help, and so on. The child is unable to make his own decisions or to make efforts without direction, which results in his feeling that what he does learn is not the result of his own efforts; it is therefore not highly reinforcing. Furthermore, he fails to see why he should exert any effort, for the teacher will shortly appear to help him (or do the work for him). In some instances he actively resents the teacher's help and bows out of the learning situation.

For such children—indeed, for all children—it might be wiser to wait until the child actively seeks assistance, after striving "on his own." The assistance would then be reinforcing and the teacher viewed as a helpful friend, rather than as a coercer or belittler of the child's own efforts.

Finally, we again emphasize that all motives are not clear to us. One may defensively disguise his motives both from others and from himself. The mechanism of rationalization, in which one invents acceptable reasons for behavior instead of admitting the real reasons, is such a disguise. For instance, one can rationalize his purchase of an expensive automobile instead of a cheaper one on the ground that it will "last longer, be safer, and have higher resale value," although his real motive is to attain social prestige. Freud considered such rationalization to be unconsciously motivated, but it is our belief that—at least at first—rationalization is a conscious process aimed at excusing one's behavior, convincing oneself that he should act on his rationalized motives rather than on the original less acceptable reasons.

In substance, what *appear* to be motives for acts may not be the actual motives. Teachers should be on guard lest they assume children to have motives that they do not have and lest they confuse defense mechanisms (of which we shall say more later) with underlying motives.

Motivation and School Practices

LEVEL OF ASPIRATION

Striving is partly determined by expectations. In research studies, expectations for achievement have been termed the "level of aspiration" (LOA) and have been measured by giving children tasks, telling them how well they performed, and then asking them how well they expect to do on similar tasks.

P. S. Sears (1940) and others have shown that LOA is related to success and failure experiences but also to certain personality variables. Children who are mentally healthy and who have mainly successful experiences tend to predict LOAs that are slightly higher than their present levels of attainment; this estimate is realistic, as most people do indeed improve performance in succeeding trials on the same tasks. Children who have had repeated failures or who are less mentally healthy may predict LOAs that are unrealistically high or extremely low. In the first instance, it may be that they are hoping (gambling) for a lucky break or that they want credit for at least aiming high.

Low LOAs probably represent discouragement and fear of failure.

V. J. Crandall and his colleagues (1962) made an interesting study of LOA as related to free play. Children were asked to state what they expected to accomplish on an intelligence test. They were also allowed a period of free play in which, if they chose, they could indulge in intellectual activities or in non-intellectual play. Previous intelligence-test results were obtained, and the childen were observed in their free-play situations.

It was shown that boys' stated expectations of intellectual success (expected scores on intelligence tests) were positively associated with their intellectual achievement but that the expectations of girls were either negatively or not significantly related. The researchers suggested some reasons for this sex differential. Possibly boys and girls are rewarded differently by parents and teachers. Boys may be more often criticized when their stated expectations do not fit actual performance, but girls who are less intellectually competent may be rewarded for saying they would try whether or not their achievements reflected their efforts; competent girls, on the other hand, might be criticized for stating high (even though realistic) goals and thus showing "unfeminine" boasting.

Girls who stated high LOAs tended to engage in intellectual free play, but boys did not.

The degree to which the children themselves thought that they were responsible for their successes or failures, rather than owing them to outside influences, was assessed. The more intellectually competent boys felt that they were "masters of their fate" more often than did low-achieving boys, but girls' assignments of responsibility were more variable.

Whatever LOA represents, therefore, it does not always predict achievement. When a child tells a teacher that he will do well or that he expects a given level of accomplishment, his statement cannot be taken at face value. Boys and girls differ; bright children differ from less bright children in how realistically they assess their LOAs.

As related to mental health, it seems that the child whose LOA is frequently erroneous would be worthy of further study by the teacher; a tendency toward erroneous self-assessment can foster lack of realism, and it is desirable that a child become realistic. The child who expects more of himself than he is able to deliver may suffer frustration and discouragement, which can lead to anxiety, lowered self-esteem, and other unpleasant feelings. The child who aims too low is probably anxious and is able to gain far less from his activities than he otherwise could. We need to help children realize their potentials and to provide work at which they are challenged yet usually manage to succeed.

ACHIEVEMENT MOTIVATION

One of the obviously more important motivations in school is the motivation to achieve. This motivation may be directed toward school tasks; on the other hand, it is equally possible that motivation to achieve may be expressed in other ways. We noted in Chapter 5 that bright high-achieving boys possessed higher motivation to achieve intellectually than did low achievers; this finding is echoed by D. C. McClelland (1965), who notes that there is a small but significant relationship between achievement motivation and performance, although other factors beside the motivational variable enter into actual achievement.

Motivation to achieve depends partly on one's culture. For example, a study by D. A. Kolb (1965) found that training in achievement motivation was more effective for boys from upper socioeconomic-status (SES) classes than for those from lower SES classes. J. A. Kahl (1952) suggests that the upper SES class values education more than does the lower SES class. Accordingly, it is probable, as Kolb suggests, that the underachieving upper-class boy finds himself at odds with his subculture and that there is parental and school pressure on him to achieve well in school. The lower-class underachiever, however, does not face such a strong academic value orientation and therefore faces less pressure to achieve and does not feel so out of place in his subculture if he does not achieve. Whether such SES differentials occur because the lower-class families believe that they are unable to achieve or out of defensiveness cannot be stated;

programs to increase motivation to educational achievement among the underprivileged, however, are now being studied.

McClelland (1965) suggests that Americans have a problem relating achievement motivation to popularity. (The present writer, it will be recalled, found that among boys academic achievement *per se* was considered "square" [Ringness, 1963; Ringness, 1965b].) Sears (1963) showed that girls are permitted to be both achievement-motivated and popular but that boys are not, again suggesting a difference in role expectations for girls and boys.

There are interfamilial differences also. For example, dominant fathers have sons who are low in achievement motivation (McClelland, 1965), whereas boys with high motivation to achieve have warmer, more democratic, and more encouraging fathers (Rosen & D'Andrade, 1959).

It is clear that school curricula and the reinforcements offered for academic achievement must vary with sex, SES, and other factors related to values placed on achievement. That schools are not always successful is apparent to any teacher. We noted earlier (Chapter 5) that some bright students fail to identify with the school and with teacher values. Most of our bright boys felt that the peer norms for achievement were those of doing just enough to get by. We have also noted previously that some children find little interest in school tasks, that the elementary-classroom climate seems more favorable to girls than to boys, and that "masculine" activities are lacking in many school situations. Such variables are related to pupil adjustment, as well as to school achievement, and we shall suggest some possibilities for improving them a little later on in this chapter.

Motivation to achieve can be viewed from another point of view, which, like LOA, is related to the child's expectation of success or failure. J. W. Atkinson (1958) has said that the "incentive value" of a task, the degree to which it is challenging and motivating, is a function of both the reward possibilities for successful completion of the task and the difficulty of the task itself. He discusses the concepts of "hopes for success" and "fear of failure." A task in which one expects to succeed quite easily with little risk of failure may thus have small incentive value; it is so easy that its accomplishment provides little feeling of satisfaction. Such is the case with tasks not difficult enough to challenge pupils, commonly termed "busy work," "Mickey Mouse," or "baby stuff."

On the other hand, tasks may be so difficult that failure seems almost inevitable to some pupils. Such tasks also have little incentive value, and pupils will avoid them. An appropriate task is considered to be one in which there is strong hope for success but in which a certain risk of failure is present.

Risk-taking behavior is not the same for all pupils. McClelland (1965) mentions that people who are highly motivated to achieve tend to prefer medium risks. C. H. Mahone (1960), working with high-school students' choices of occupations found that those high in fear of failure tended to lower their goals unrealistically below their potentials.

Motivation to achieve, the incentive value of a task, and expectations for success are thus seen to vary considerably. On the whole, bright children usually accept challenges better than do dull children; boys are more willing to take risks than are girls; young children are less willing to take risks than are older children; fearful children are less realistic and set lower (or unrealistically higher) goals than do confident children. These generalizations do not necessarily hold true for individual children, of course; the problem for the teacher is to determine each pupil's potential, helping him to see this potential realistically and then helping him to attempt tasks that will be rewarding without being unduly threatening.

The dilemma is clear, but the solutions are not so clear. Too much anxiety, fear of failure, and frustration rob pupils of confidence and decrease motivation to achieve; on the other hand, success too easily bought provides little incentive to learn. The need is to find tasks paced so that completion itself is rewarding. Completion, in turn, can lead children to engage in the task for its own implicit values.

TEACHER TRAITS AND MOTIVATION

Tables 5, 6, 7, and 8 reveal responses of eleventh-grade and senior students who were queried concerning teacher characteristics or behaviors that motivated them or hindered their motivation. Some of these factors are modifiable; others are more

TABLE 5. Eleventh-Grade Students' Opinion of Teacher Motivating Factors

Motivating Factors	Frequency
Sense of humor	52
Talked on our level	35
Variety in subject	27
Knowledge of subject	22
Made us work	19
Friendly	19
Interested in individual	18
Respect for our intelligence	17
Gave help at any time	16
Understood his boys	16
Made course interesting	13
Good discipline	11
Fair grader	10
Not overly strict	10
Broadminded	8
Outside media used	8
Teacher interested in subject	8
Extra credit	6
Dedication to career	6
Respected our opinion	6
Oral quizzes	5
Good disposition	5
Every student was equal	5
Explained subject well	4
Taught useful things	4
Organized	4
No teacher's pets	3
Announced quizzes	3
Reward for good work	3
Inspired the students	3
Written homework	2
Angry only when necessary	2
Informal	2
Teacher earned respect	2
Required reading	1
Reasonable tests	1
Well-groomed	1
Gave benefits of doubt	1
Total	375

SOURCE: R. A. Patton and P. A. De Sena, "Identification Through Student Opinion of Motivating and Nonmotivating Qualities of Teachers," *The Journal of Teacher Education*, 17 (1966), 43.

TABLE 6. Eleventh-Grade Students' Opinion of Teacher Nonmotivating Factors

Nonmotivating Factors	Frequency
Boring	38
Unfair grader	37
Overly strict	36
No sense of humor	33
Too much homework	25
Partial to certain students (i.e., teacher's pets)	25
Thought himself perfect	21
Couldn't explain on our level	20
Bad temper	19
Sarcastic	17
No interest in students	16
Use of physical means	15
Bad quizzes (i.e., unannounced, hard, lengthy)	15
Little knowledge of subject	14
Held grudges	14
Thought he was too good (i.e., better than students)	12
Followed regulations too closely	12
Lack of respect for our opinion	12
Useless material	9
Picked on students	9
Hard to understand	9
Unfriendly	9
Did not command respect	9
Would not answer questions	7
Sloppy appearance	6
Tried to make course hard	5
Lacked teaching ability	5
Bad physical condition	5
Strayed from subject	4
Poor notes	4
Expected too much	4
Hurried to complete material	3
Went too fast (i.e., too fast on lectures, etc.)	3
No reward for good work	3
Egotistical	3
Too friendly	3
Suspicious of good grades	3

SOURCE: R. A. Patton and P. A. De Sena, "Identification Through Student Opinion of Motivating and Nonmotivating Qualities of Teachers," *The Journal of Teacher Education*, 17 (1966), 43–4.

(TABLE 6 CONTINUED)

Nonmotivating Factors	Frequency
Used profanity	3
Lazy	3
Impatient	3
Unorganized	2
Too holy	2
Sadist	2
Disallowed respect for other teachers	1
Hypocritical	1
Bad breath	1
Talked about his unhappy childhood	1
Pittsburgh accent	1
Bragged about his family	1
Total	504

nebulous and may be harder to change. Note that personal characteristics, as well as teaching competence or command of the subject, are mentioned, primarily in regard to nonmotivating factors.

INTRINSIC VALUES OF THE TASK

Probably one of the most difficult jobs for the teacher is to find ways to interest children in their work. Obviously if children engage in a school task only for reasons unrelated to the task itself—to please the teacher, to avoid a low mark, to earn $5 from parents—when the class has been completed, pupils will no longer follow that academic subject. How does one induce the kind of interest in literature, history, or another subject that will cause the learner to pursue the subject as a hobby, reading interest, or even vocation?

Granted the incentive value of a school task plays a part, so that tasks of correct incentive value lead to feelings of self-satisfaction when accomplished, but that is only part of the story. As teachers know, it is important to relate school subjects to pupil interests. The study of history can be handled so that special topics and related readings can be found for pupils with such varied interests as cartooning, home building, and hunting or fishing. Furthermore, classroom activities can be designed so that some pupils enjoy the status of engaging in drama, chairing committees, and so on. Movies, field trips, and other activities can provide reinforcements not forthcoming in the typical school day. To the extent that positive, rather than negative, reinforcements can be provided, interests and motivations to achieve can be fostered.

TABLE 7. Composite Total of Seniors' Opinion of
Teacher Motivating Factors

Motivating Factors	Frequency
Dedication to career	30
Explained subject well	26
Made course interesting	24
Knowledge of subject	23
Sense of humor	21
Interested in individual	18
Teacher interested in subject	14
Respected our opinion	13
Announced quizzes	11
Gave us help at any time	10
Every student equal	9
Reasonable tests	8
Understood student	8
Inspired the student	8
Fair grader	6
Extra credit to help grade	6
Variety in subject	6
Respected our intelligence	5
Friendly	4
Informal	4
Angry only when necessary	3
Teacher earned his respect	3
Outside media used	3
Good disposition	3
Talked on our level	3
Made us work	2
Total	271

SOURCE: R. A. Patton and P. A. De Sena, "Identification Through Student Opinion of Motivating and Nonmotivating Qualities of Teachers," *The Journal of Teacher Education*, 17 (1966), 44.

Mental health, as noted earlier, is closely related to motives. Because of the number of years children remain in school, motivation for school tasks should become rooted in interest in the tasks themselves, rather than in desires to please teachers, avoid punishments, and the like. Both from an achievement and from a mental-health point of view, the kinds of reinforcement employed should be considered.

TABLE 8. Composite Total of Seniors' Opinion of
Teacher Nonmotivating Factors

Nonmotivating Factors	Frequency
Boring	48
Lacked teaching ability	43
Wouldn't answer questions	13
Little knowledge of subject	10
Thought himself better than his students	10
Unfair grader	10
Did not respect our opinion	9
Unorganized	9
Hard to understand	9
Expected too much	8
Too much homework	7
Thought himself perfect	6
Picked on students	6
Partial to certain students	6
Use of physical means	6
Couldn't explain on our level	5
No interest in students	5
Bad temper	3
Overly strict	3
Hard quizzes	3
Useless material	3
No sense of humor	3
Sarcastic	3
Impatient	2
Too holy	2
Went too fast	2
Followed rules too closely	2
Total	236

SOURCE: R. A. Patton and P. A. De Sena, "Identification Through Student Opinion of Motivating and Nonmotivating Qualities of Teachers," *The Journal of Teacher Education*, 17 (1966), 44.

POSITIVE REINFORCERS IN THE SCHOOL SETTING

To the extent that pupils identify with the teacher, the teacher becomes a model. To that same extent, the teacher can act as a social-reinforcement agent for the pupils. We have discussed desirable characteristics for teachers. We must now consider some of the positive reinforcers that the teacher has at his command. In regard to the following comments, it should be noted that the reinforcements to which various children respond will be somewhat different, as will the children's motives.

First of all, the teacher has his comments, both oral and written, to use as positive reinforcers. His evaluation of a homework paper is an important factor in reinforcement. School achievement and attitude improve when comments are written on students' work (Page, 1958), and they need not all be favorable. Comments help in various ways: They show that the teacher has thought enough of the pupil's work to evaluate it, that he has taken an interest in the individual pupil's work, that he believes the assignment important, and that the pupil who does good work will receive credit for it. Contrast work dignified by a comment with the amount of "busy work" children are sometimes assigned, in which the teacher takes no evaluative interest—workbooks that are not examined, papers that are not graded, and the like. Oral comments, smiles, nods of encouragement, recognition of good pupil ideas, and so forth provide the same kind of reinforcement.

When sufficient positive reinforcement cannot be given— when a pupil's work is generally poor—one must first consider whether or not the assignment was appropriate and well understood, whether or not the lesson was well taught, and whether or not the pupil's attitude has begun to deteriorate. In any of these cases it is likely that modification of teaching technique is needed. When a given pupil, in contrast to the group, consistently does poorly, he should be studied as an individual. On the whole, it is likely that in most classrooms too little positive reinforcement is provided. This lack leads to discouragement, defensive pupil behavior, and negative attitudes toward the subject and teacher.

Another kind of positive reinforcement is concrete rewards, to be employed until some of the intrinsic values of the school tasks begin to be recognized by the pupils. Certainly gold stars, football letters, band pins, typing medals, diplomas, and report-card grades have a legitimate place in positively reinforcing effort. The only danger is that pupils work for such reinforcements without ever finding intrinsic value in the work itself. Positive reinforcement in the form of special treats, movies, trips, released time for individual study, and similar techniques may be employed usefully. Pupils can be allowed some choice of things to read, songs to sing, games to play, and ways to carry out units and projects.

All in all, one principle stands out in importance: "Nothing succeeds like success." When pupils are given worthwhile work at levels they can deal with and when they achieve success in their work, inner reinforcements related to self-esteem, confidence, security, and other personality variables enhance the motivation of the pupil; in such instances there is less need for reinforcement by the teacher.

At this point we should mention the possibilities implicit in programmed instruction. It has been stated that learning steps in programmed materials should be small enough so that there is about a 90 per cent chance that the pupil will make the correct response for each item. In this way, positive reinforcement (being correct) is very likely. Furthermore, in this form of instruction, reinforcement is immediate. Here is another method by which low achievers can be helped to find positive reinforcement in the school setting.

NEGATIVE REINFORCEMENT IN THE SCHOOL SETTING

Negative reinforcements are frequent in the school day. Not only do teachers' comments frequently devalue pupils' efforts, but children are also subject to kidding, ridicule, and the laughter of their peers when they make mistakes or otherwise do poorly on their assignments. Some children tend to garner most of the concrete rewards. Others suffer most of their school lives because they are handicapped, culturally deprived, not up to the work, not accepted by peers (or teacher), or inferior in looks or health.

The usual tendency of the small child is to participate in school tasks (as a member of the classroom social group) and to succeed. When motives to affiliate, to achieve, and to gain status and acceptance are frustrated, however, a number of negative reactions can occur.

Some frustrated children simply withdraw psychologically or even physically from the classroom. Daydreamers, truants, and dropouts are in this category. Others become hostile; being frustrated themselves, and blaming others for at least part of such frustration, they react against the real or imagined source of their problems. Some simply make trouble—they are discipline problems. Others become sarcastic, tattle, bully other children, or otherwise verbally show their hostility. Some become agitated; being anxious, they cannot concentrate and may become hyperactive. Some develop compensatory behavior. They seek attention, attempt to prove themselves in other than academic areas (including vandalism), try to deflate school and teacher values, or become class clowns.

In all cases, children who receive mainly negative reinforcements tend to do less well in their work and in their social relations than do others. A common example follows: A child does poorly and becomes somewhat anxious and defensive. The teacher places even more pressure on this child. In turn, his work and his attitudes deteriorate, and the situation worsens. If a child is threatened and anxious, more pressure can but hurt him more. In effect, for good school achievement and pupil mental health, it is better to reinforce positively when possible, and to induce behavior aimed at problem solving and cooperative effort, than to reinforce negatively, for the latter leads to avoidance behavior.

One other point should be made. A. Bandura and R. H. Walters (1963) note the comparative effects of lack of reinforcement upon behavior. If a child is doing something for which he has hitherto been positively reinforced, the absence of comment can be interpreted as negative reinforcement. But if he has been doing something for which he has been punished, the absence of comment can be construed as permission to continue the behavior, or as positive reinforcement. Consistency in the teacher's reinforcement pattern thus becomes necessary. The need for consistent reinforcement probably exists more during the child's initial learning of what behavior is desired and what is not; once he clearly understands, it should not be necessary to reinforce every example of behavior, and, indeed, there is some evidence that intermittent reinforcement can be as effective as, or more effective than, continuous reinforcement.

The Role of Emotions

The emotions of fear, anger, and happiness—or more complex emotions like shame, remorse, disgust, or exaltation—are partly biological and partly intellectual in character. Strictly speaking, one should discuss *emotions* only as biological states, and the term *feelings* should be employed for intellectual recognition of emotions. For convenience, the term "emotion" will be used in this chapter in a looser sense—the reader will understand that it includes *both* the cognitive and biological components (feelings and emotions).

Although everyone experiences varying degrees of emotional arousal throughout his life, probably no situation of which he is conscious exists without some emotional tone. He may not always be aware of precisely how he feels or of what is causing him to feel that way, but there is some degree of affect at all times.

Emotional responses are aroused by stimuli—internal or external, cognitive or physiological. One thinks of something beautiful, and a reaction of pleasure ensues; or he may be coming down with a cold and have a depressed feeling. He may be aroused to guilt by the knowledge that he has inadvertently shot through a stop sign, or he can react with pleasure at the sight of his wife or children. Sometimes his responses conflict, and a state of uncertainty or even anxiety may result. Essentially, the emotions determine which stimuli become positive or negative reinforcers.

In order to show more clearly the effects of strong emotion, we cite the following illustration of emotional reactions from Cannon (1929) :

One may be confronted by a threatening dog as he walks homeward in the evening. He perceives the dog as dangerous and immediately recognizes his own fear. At the same time, biological changes take place. Cannon suggests that these biological changes are rooted in man's historical past, when he was more primitive than he is today. At any rate, when one sees an angry dog, he must prepare either to fight with it or to run away. In either case, his muscles require extra energy. To provide this energy, extra oxygen is needed, and it is supplied by rapid, deep breathing. More blood sugar is needed for fuel to provide energy, and the liver therefore releases part of what it has stored in the form of glycogen. To carry the oxygen and sugar to the muscles, the rate and strength of the heartbeat increase. Because the blood supply is limited, digestion slows or ceases. Perceptions of the sense organs appear to become more acute. Blood composition changes so that clotting will occur more quickly in case of wounds. And a number of other bodily changes take place.

All these somatic changes are under the control of the autonomic nervous system, which produces these effects by stimulating nerves in the various organs, and activating production of hormones. The autonomic nervous system is not under conscious control, and the somatic responses cannot be governed by the individual.

In some emotional reactions there is a depressing effect and in others an arousing effect; in all probability, for most emotional states, there are varying degrees of both. An interesting biological adaptation has occurred in the course of our evolutionary development: Because it is necessary to act quickly in the face of danger, the arousal effects of strong emotion take place very quickly; return to equilibrium is slower, however, and one may remain aroused for some time after he is cognitively aware that the danger is gone and that he need no longer react emotionally. Continued arousal of strong emotions puts a strain on the body somewhat analogous to racing the motor on a car. Although the strain can be withstood for a time, prolonged strain may produce damage—one way that emotions can produce poor physical health, as in the case of psychosomatic illness.

Emotions as Motivating Forces

Emotions can be broadly classified as pleasant or unpleasant. One wishes to prolong pleasant emotional states and tries to rid himself quickly of unpleasant emotional states. In this sense, emotions not only determine what stimuli become positive or negative reinforcers; they themselves may also be viewed as relatively continuous stimuli to motivate behavior. For example, anxiety is an unpleasant emotional state; anyone experiencing it seeks to reduce it. In this sense, then, anxiety may be construed as a drive.

Emotions can be conditioned. That is, certain stimuli that originally aroused no particular emotion can eventually cause anger, fear, or other emotions. It is not necessary that one clearly recognize which stimuli produce these effects, and, indeed, in a neurosis the *origin* of the anxiety and the *current stimuli* arousing the anxiety may not be clear to the sufferer. Furthermore, through stimulus generalization, new stimuli, because of some association with or resemblance to the original stimuli, may arouse certain emotions.

For example, one sometimes finds that he "dislikes certain people on sight," even without having previously met them. Dislike is a mild form of anger, of course, and the problem is to discover why one is angry without apparent cause. The answer may lie in the fact that there is some (perhaps subliminal) likeness in the other person that triggers the same reaction we had to someone else in the past. A person with a whining voice may thus bring forth the same hostility that a whining parent brought forth years ago, even though the resemblance is otherwise not notable.

Conditioning comes about through the effects of a situation upon one's behavior. Small children do not fear moving automobiles and must be taught to do so. The actions of their parents may teach them to be afraid of cars, as when parents jerk a child out of the street and themselves show fear. Frequently, too, the parents will show anger, producing some fear

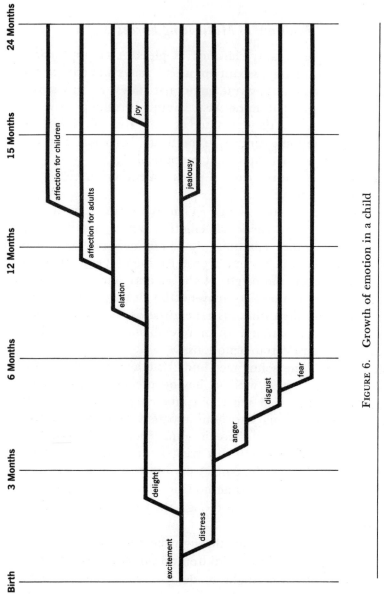

FIGURE 6. Growth of emotion in a child

SOURCE: Adapted from Katharine M. Banham-Bridges, "Emotional Development in Early Infancy," *Child Development*, 3 (1932), 340. Copyright 1932 by The Society for Research in Child Development, Inc.

in the child, so that by generalization the child learns caution toward streets and automobiles.

K. M. Banham-Bridges (1932) has diagramed the presumed development of emotions (see Figure 6). The tiny infant is believed to be capable only of reacting to any stimulus. Shortly, however, he begins to show both avoiding and approaching behavior, or negative and positive affects, or feelings. Later he learns to differentiate his emotions in more complex fashion. In general, however, we may classify emotions as those that produce *approaching* responses, or desire to engage in close contact with the stimulus situation, and those that produce *avoiding* responses, a tendency to withdraw or to become aggressive. For example, happiness tends to produce a desire to continue whatever activity is involved; anger or fear tends to produce attack or escape, either of which gets rid of the aversive stimulus. When there are conflicting emotions or when the emotions are not clear, confused—and even "irrational" or superstitious behavior—may occur.

Emotions in the Classroom

There is an emotional tone to everything that goes on in the classroom. Because emotions that produce approaching behavior tend to motivate children to attend to their tasks, every opportunity should be found to make school pleasurable, thrilling, exciting, and happy. Equally, for purposes of engaging pupils in their tasks, rather than creating aggression or withdrawing, it would be desirable to keep threat, anger, fear, frustration, and other negative experiences out of the classroom whenever possible.

This program is difficult to follow. As a result, in too many classrooms there is little opportunity for the kind of pleasurable emotion that might be provided by humor, warmth, accomplishment, and the like. Many classrooms—perhaps for disciplinary reasons—are sterile, quite cold, and relatively lacking in emotional expression. Worse, in many rooms there is "motivation" by threat, fear of failure, censure, a hostile and driving tone. We need only to note the enthusiasm with which small children enter school and compare it with the feelings of many of them in their later school years to see that the emotional content of many classrooms is inappropriate. In one sense, the classroom with negative emotional tone is inefficient. In another sense, it does not contribute to good mental health.

Our second point is that emotions are felt and should therefore be permitted expression. It is natural for everyone to feel anger, frustration, or anxiety sometimes, as well as to feel joy, excitement, and pleasure sometimes. Emotions that are not expressed are still felt; both intellectual and somatic aspects of emotion exist, and it will manifest in one way or another. The child who is not permitted to express anger may thus develop anxiety, guilt, psychosomatic symptoms, or escapist or aggressive behavior. By not permitting fears to be expressed, we cause the child to feel unsupported and possibly to feel incompetent or unworthy. Now, it is not the fact of the emotion that is the problem, as the teacher sees it, but the manner in which the emotion is expressed. It seems, therefore, that the school should make clear to children that it is normal and permissible to feel various emotions but that they must be expressed in socially acceptable ways. The child who is hostile might express his feeling in a reasonable way by having a talk with his teacher. The child who is fearful might express it and gain the teacher's support.

Finally,[1] it is not what happens in the classroom but what the child *expects* to happen that may arouse anxiety or other strong emotions. For this reason, expectations of success, acceptance, and pleasure should be emphasized; good teachers habitually stress them, suggesting the satisfaction in learning to read or announcing that classes will certainly do well on achievement tests. Good teachers also keep in mind that emotions can be generalized from one situation to another, and they make clear, when children are chastised for being disciplinary problems or for doing poor work, that the "slate is clean," so that the negative effects of criticism will not carry over into future activities.

---

[1] Much more will be said about the emotions and their relationships with school practice in Chapter 7. In this chapter, we have been most concerned with emotions as motivating factors.

□

REFERENCES

Atkinson, J. W. *Motives in Fantasy, Action, and Society.* Princeton: Van Nostrand, 1958.

Bandura, A., and R. H. Walters. *Social Learning and Personality Development.* New York: Holt, Rinehart, Winston, 1963.

Banham-Bridges, K. M. "Emotional Development in Early Infancy," *Child Development,* 3 (1932), 324–41.

Cannon, W. B. *Bodily Changes in Pain, Hunger, Fear, and Rage.* New York: Appleton, 1929.

Crandall, V. J., W. Katkovsky, and A. Preston. "Motivational and Ability Determinants of Young Children's Intellectual Achievement Behavior," *Child Development,* 33 (1962), 643–61.

Kahl, J. A. *Adolescent Ambition.* Doctoral dissertation, Harvard University, 1952.

Kolb, D. A. "Achievement Motivation Training for Underachieving High School Boys," *Journal of Personality and Social Psychology,* 2 (1965), 783–92.

McClelland, D. C. "Toward a Theory of Motive Acquisition," *American Psychologist,* 20 (1965), 321–33.

Mahone, C. W. "Fear of Failure and Unrealistic Vocational Aspiration," *Journal of Abnormal and Social Psychology,* 60 (1960), 253–61.

Maslow, A. H. *Motivation and Personality.* New York: Harper, 1954.

Page, E. B. "Teacher Comments and Student Performance: A Seventy-Four Classroom Experiment in School Motivation," *Journal of Educational Psychology,* 49 (1958), 173–81.

Ringness, T. A. *Differences in Attitudes Toward Self and Others of Academically Successful and Non-Successful Boys of Superior Intelligence* (Final Report, National Institute of Mental Health Post-Doctoral Research Fellowship). Los Angeles: University of California, 1963.

———. "Affective Differences Between Successful and Non-Successful Bright Ninth Grade Boys," *Personnel and Guidance Journal* (February 1965a), 600–6.

———. *Non-Intellective Variables Related to Academic Achievement of Bright Junior High School Boys* (Final Report, Cooperative Research Project S–035). Madison: University of Wisconsin, 1965b.

Rosen, B. C., and R. G. D'Andrade. "The Psychosocial Origins of Achievement Motivation," *Sociometry,* 22 (1959), 185–218.

Sears, P. S. *The Effect of Classroom Conditions on the Strength of Achievement Motive and Work Output in Elementary School Children* (Final Report, Cooperative Research Project 873). Stanford: Stanford University, 1963.

———. "Levels of Aspiration in Academically Successful and Unsuccessful Children," *Journal of Abnormal and Social Psychology,* 35 (1940), 498–536.

Thelen, H. A. Quoted in *Phi Delta Kappan,* 46 (1964), 33.

SUGGESTIONS FOR FURTHER READING

Allport, G. W. *Pattern and Growth in Personality,* chaps. 9, 10. New York: Holt, Rinehart, Winston, 1961.
Allport discusses the concept of functional autonomy of motives in some detail. Not all motives are functionally autonomous, and Allport shows why some are and some are not. Allport is quite eclectic in his approach, and the entire book is an excellent discussion of pertinent factors concerning the nature of personality.

Combs, A. W., and D. Snygg. *Individual Behavior.* New York: Harper, 1959.
Combs and Snygg emphasize the role of the self and the self-concept in behavior. Their position is that motivation consists essentially of the needs to maintain or enhance the self. They do not negate the role of reinforcers or other environmental influences but stress the individuality of man. From Combs and Snygg's point of view, it is necessary to understand how each person perceives himself and his individual "world" in order to understand the nature of his motives and behavior.

Shaffer, L. F., and E. J. Shoben, Jr. *The Psychology of Adjustment.* Rev. ed. Boston: Houghton Mifflin, 1956.
This book is a basic reference on the nature of adjustment, factors related to adjustment, emotions, motivations, and related variables. It contains extended statements on motivational theory and the emotions and is useful for providing a comprehensive point of view on problems of poor mental health, defense mechanisms, and the like.

FRUSTRATION, CONFLICT, AND ANXIETY

In this chapter we shall discuss additional dynamics of behavior. We shall be concerned with some of the effects of frustration, conflict, and anxiety and how teachers may deal with them in the classroom. As these feelings frequently result in defensive or escapist behavior, we shall also consider defense mechanisms and their dynamics. It should be noted, however, that the presence of any of these personality dynamics does not in itself indicate poor mental health; in fact, most people could see themselves reflected in these illustrations. But it is true that continued stresses arising from frustration and conflict can be harmful and that anxiety sometimes can be neurotic. It is also true that defensive behavior can represent poor mental health or even lead to it, as we shall see.

We shall illustrate with the case of Jimmy, who is in the fourth grade. The following true anecdotal record shows many interrelationships among feelings, behavior, and personal and social adjustment. Jimmy was studied in connection with a student teacher's laboratory assignment.

As soon as I started teaching (after lunch) Jimmy started jumping around, interrupting discussion, and not giving anyone else a chance to say a word. He had a comment on everything and although I asked him to be quiet and give others a chance to contribute, his behavior did not change. Finally I walked up to his desk, rapped my knuckles on it twice, and told him he would have to settle down and raise his hand like the other children if he wanted to be called on. From that time on he was somewhat quieter, even though he continued to be hyperactive the rest of the day. After recess we had free individual reading, and since this was one of Jimmy's favorite activities, he behaved well and read quietly—usually about Yogi Bear.

My cooperating teacher has had trouble with Jimmy all year. It seems that his attention-seeking behavior is a bid for approval. He wants me to praise every small bit of work he completes, and if I don't do so, he compliments himself and approves his own work. Such sentences as "I read well, don't I? Yes, I do" are common.

During discussion Jimmy shouts his answers; his ideas are worthwhile, but the manner in which he interrupts to present them causes the rest of the pupils to ignore most of what he says. This angers him and he talks even louder and moves around more.

He alienates himself from his fellow pupils more and more each day. He forces his way into group situations and demands the major share of attention. He is usually not courteous to his peers and calls them names, yells, and laughs at them.

I have noted that Jimmy sucks his thumb and frequently coughs in a jerky little way when reading. He is oblivious to these behaviors; to me, they seem outward manifestations of nervousness.

Notice the evidence of frustration, hostility, anger, and insecurity. Also notice defensive behavior like playing down others, complimenting himself, and attention seeking. He attempts to compensate for his insecurities by bullying others or deriding their accomplishments; he requires constant reassurance of his own worth. His anxiety and frustration seem to interfere with his ability to concentrate, and he is unable to organize his work well.

The student teacher has done quite a good job in describing Jimmy's actions, though she has been interpretive, rather than objective. One must not overlook some of the positive behaviors shown by the boy—he likes to read, he has good ideas, his written work is interesting. Although the symptoms seem serious enough so that Jimmy probably could be termed "maladjusted," it is true that some of his problems are being at least partially induced in the classroom. In fact, Jimmy may fail to be challenged, may be bored, and may in turn react to his frustrations aggressively. Some of Jimmy's behavior may be quite natural under the circumstances; it does not *all* suggest personality problems.

We shall come back to Jimmy at the end of the chapter to show what was done for the boy. The reader might ask himself at this point how he would handle Jimmy's problem behavior.

Definitions and Effects

DEFINITIONS

Frustration is a state of emotional arousal in which there are usually elements of anger and disappointment. It will be recalled that, once one is motivated, he tends to remain motivated until he attains his goal and is reinforced or rewarded. A number of factors in the environment or within the individual may, however, intervene so that the goal is not attained. The result is frustration; several kinds of behavior can result, and we shall discuss some of them shortly.

Conflict is the result of competing motives that cannot all result in goal-directed behavior and reinforcement—or of the presence of alternative choices of goal-directed behavior, alternative goals, or some combination of the two. Conflict tends to arouse emotions, frequently including anxiety. It can contribute to poor mental health if it results in behavior that fails to reduce anxiety or gets the individual into difficulties with his environment—or if it results in feelings of inadequacy, guilt, or fear. Until conflict has been resolved, one cannot attain his goal and reinforcement cannot follow; emotional tension is therefore not reduced. Several categories of conflict have been identified by Miller (1944) ; we shall discuss them shortly.

Anxiety is a term with many definitions and usages, and the reader is urged to consider carefully how his writers have employed it. Here it will refer to an unpleasant emotional state in which there is a vague element of fear, aroused by the anticipation of some unpleasant future event. It occurs before actual fear-eliciting stimuli are present, and in many instances people experiencing anxiety are unable to tell why they are anxious. There are also instances in which the cause of the anxiety *can* be distinguished. In "test anxiety," for example, anticipation of a test produces emotional reactions. Extreme anxiety can manifest itself in trembling, perspiration, increased rates of heart beat and breathing, and other discernible physiological reactions, as well as in feelings of dread, fear, depression, and confusion.

Anxiety can be elicited by both inner and outer stimuli, some of which may be at the subliminal level. For example, when one does something that does not accord with his values, he experiences guilt, but he may also experience anxiety, the latter perhaps because of the fear of possible consequences should his act be discovered by others. Anxiety can be aroused by environmental conditions, as when one enters a situation in which he will be evaluated by others, when he is not certain of how he will perform (as in a football game), or when he is uncertain of the outcome of the situation. Anxiety may also be caused by concern about one's ability to control one's impulses, ability to satisfy one's motives, or some combination.

In "neurotic" anxiety the stimuli that set off the reaction are likely to be at considerable psychological distance from the original cause of the anxiety, and in treatment there is thus posed the difficult problem of discovering what the original cause is. For example, one may be anxious in the presence of authority figures without realizing that his anxiety initially arose from harsh treatment at the hands of his father.

INTERRELATIONSHIPS

It is patent that frustration, conflict, and anxiety may be (and usually are) closely related within the personality dynamics of the individual. For example, conflict may result in frustration, for failure to make appropriate choices can result in inability to attain a desired goal. Conflict can also produce anxiety, for one may realize that, if appropriate decisions are not made, unpleasant consequences may result. For that matter, he may be so situated that, no matter what choice he makes, some unpleasant consequences are likely to follow.

On the other hand, frustration may result in conflict, as when one's way to a given goal is blocked and he must therefore choose between abandoning his goal, changing his behavior, changing his motives, or doing without the reinforcement he is seeking.

Anxiety may be not only the result of frustration or conflict but also the precursor. The child who is anxious about a school test may suffer conflict over whether he should take the test, find a means of delaying taking the test, attempt to do his best even though failure seems likely, and so on. He may find that anxiety so interferes with his performance that he does badly, which in turn may leave him frustrated in efforts to make a high grade.

We shall now discuss briefly some of the results of frustration, conflict, and anxiety. We shall then turn to the defense mechanisms, and later we shall consider some ways of dealing with these emotional states.

Results of Frustration, Conflict, and Anxiety

FRUSTRATION

In the ordinary sequence of events, a person can usually find ways to attain his goals and receive the expected reinforcements. Frustration may occur, however, either because he has aimed higher than his abilities or the situation justify or because his methods for attaining his goals are inadequate.

In the case of such biological drives as hunger, motivation continues to mount, and behavior related to the drives may therefore be intensified. The really hungry person thinks about little else but food. In an amusing experiment with conscientious objectors in wartime, food was withheld for a period. As a result, the men planned menus, replaced pin-ups of girls with pictures of food, and showed other evidence of strong preoccupation with food.

Acquired motives may or may not continue to increase in strength. There may be initial increased motivation, but frustration that is too great or continued too long may act to modify the motive.

A variety of responses may thus accompany frustration. A person may simply intensify his efforts to attain his goals, using extra energy in his efforts to overcome obstacles. This form of behavior is common among athletes, who strive even harder when their teams are losing. On the other hand, frustration may simply continue if efforts to deal with it are not adaptive—producing the familiar phenomenon of "butting one's head against a stone wall." Emotive behavior may also increase, as when the golfer angrily throws away his club after flubbing an easy shot.

A person may also learn to live with temporary frustration, hoping to achieve satisfaction at a later time. This adaptation is frequently useful, especially when environmental conditions are the cause of frustration. For example, a boy may intensely desire to engage in sports but may have to delay satisfaction until a broken leg is healed.

Another approach is to alter goals to achieve satisfactions that are more easily obtainable. A person may modify his behavior to circumvent the obstacle to his goals. Or he may explode in outbursts of anger that decrease his ability to cope with the situation. This last response is sometimes seen in children who have difficulties with their school assignments. They tear up their homework papers, throw tantrums, or weep and complain.

A child may learn to fear the obstacle and withdraw from the situation, or he may employ defenses to reduce his emotional tension. An example of the latter is the "sour grapes" mechanism, which takes its name from Aesop's fable in which the fox disclaims his desire for grapes that are too high for him to reach "because they were sour and not good to eat anyway." Similarly, when a school subject is too difficult (or too easy) for a student, he may rationalize that it lacks value or that the teacher is uninteresting.

Any of these kinds of behavior may be employed by anyone, regardless of his mental health, but long-term frustration may result in maladaptive behavior. Character disorders, neurotic states, and psychosomatic problems can result from frustration.

One of our school mental-health goals is to help children

learn to deal successfully with frustration. Another is to avoid constantly frustrating them in the curriculum. The teacher can sometimes reduce obstacles to attainment of goals, particularly in learning problems. He can also aid the pupil by teaching appropriate responses to frustration, as we shall see later.

CONFLICT

N. E. Miller (1944) has postulated four forms of conflict: double approach conflict; double avoidant conflict; approach-avoidant conflict; and double approach-avoidant conflict. The first two forms of conflict are relatively less important in terms of mental health than are the latter two (which differ essentially in their complexity). In double approach conflict two or more alternatives are approximately equally desirable; this form of conflict is easily resolved, as a simple choice provides the desired reinforcement. A parent, teacher, or other adviser can help most children to make such choices if they are unable to do so for themselves. Double avoidant conflicts exist when each of two alternatives is distasteful, as when one does not wish to study but does not wish to fail the course either. The desire is to escape both unpleasant alternatives, which results in attempts to avoid the conflict situation entirely. In school, for example, children vacillate and waste time, trying not to study but also not to displease the teacher unduly. When pressed, however, they usually accept the "lesser of two evils."

Approach-avoidant conflict and the more complicated double approach-avoidant conflict exist when a given act, object, or person is regarded with ambivalence or when several alternatives are regarded with ambivalence. For example, one may desire to perform in a stage play in order to attain the applause of the audience, yet he may suffer "stage fright," even panic, as the time for the performance draws near. If he actually does engage in the performance, however, and if he receives the coveted applause, his approach tendencies are strengthened and his avoidant tendencies weakened. If, on the other hand, his avoidance tendencies equal or exceed his approach tendencies, considerable anxiety can arise, leading to maladaptive behavior. In this event his performance, if he undertakes it, may be inept; as a consequence, his avoidance tendencies may sharply increase.

Similarly, anxiety is raised when a child both fears and loves his father or when he releases sexual tension through masturbation but feels guilty as a result. Some resolution must be found, for this sort of conflict tends to generate a great deal of emotional tension that can result in neurotic behavior, psychosomatic illness, or inappropriate use of defense mechanisms. Furthermore, it may result in lowered feelings of self-confidence and self-esteem, depending upon the causes of the conflict. For example, inability to muster courage for a fight may result in the child's feeling that he is a coward. He may wish to prove that he is a "hero" or a "man"; but beside suffering loss of esteem by others, because of his backing out, he may feel guilty as well.

Miller has shown that as a goal toward which one is ambivalent is approached, both the avoident and approach tendencies are increased—that is, both the negative and positive aspects of the goal are felt more strongly. But Miller also argues that the *gradient,* or rise, of avoidant tendencies increases more sharply than does that of the approach tendencies. There may come a point, therefore, at which the individual's negative feelings toward the goal are stronger than any hopes he may have for positive reinforcement by its accomplishment; in this event, he may never actually reach the goal and will fail to receive the reinforcement.

It is possible to resolve such a conflict in several ways. Either the value of the goal or the motivation to attain it can be increased. For example, industry offers high pay to people who engage in dangerous work. For children, the rewards for winning a football game may surpass the discomfort and fear of injury in participation; the fun of swimming may surpass fear of the water; the desire to please a parent may overcome dislike for vaccinations.

The avoidance potential can also be decreased. For example, a child can be prepared in advance for what he will encounter, and strong suggestions that discomfort will be less than he fears can be made. We try to reduce anxiety connected with examinations by helping children learn how to study for them, by giving them "dry runs," and by de-emphasizing the importance of tests in grading report cards. Children who are afraid of dogs may be less afraid of small puppies; those who are afraid to talk in class may be willing to read instead. Supportive behavior by others, the provision of reinforcements as the goal is approached, appeals to moral courage, and other means are also used.

There is danger, however, when conflicts are not resolved. Unless one learns to resolve them, he must learn to live with them. As long as strong conflict can be avoided or when one aspect of the conflict can be, at least temporarily, ignored, perhaps little harm may be done; yet it is better to reduce or resolve the conflict if at all possible.

ANXIETY

The reader is urged to refer again to the definition of "anxiety." We are concerned here with some of the effects of anxiety, especially on performance in learning.

Anxiety is learned, but it is difficult to extinguish. There are a number of reasons why. First, anxiety is a strong force, a force usually aimed at avoidance. One tends to stay away from known anxiety-producing situations; extinction is therefore not likely because, for extinction to take place, anxious behavior must be present but not reinforced. A second difficulty in extinguishing anxiety is that one does not always know all the stimuli that elicit the anxiety; indeed, one problem for therapists is to determine which stimuli the client may be sensitive to. Finally, anxiety can sometimes be reduced, at least temporarily, without eliminating its causes. For example, humor, rationalization, and even superstitious ritual serve to reduce anxiety in some situations; the mechanism of displacement permits temporary reduction of anxiety through avoidance of stimuli from the object of displacement. The child who is made anxious by a demanding father may displace some of his feelings to teachers. Then by negating their values, hence their evaluations of him, he is able to reduce some of his anxiety. This pattern seems common among some underachievers.

We are concerned here with how anxiety affects behavior. We shall turn to a formulation much like that of C. L. Hull (1952) to try to explain some of the behavioral phenomena associated with anxiety.

Consider, first, that a person may have learned many different responses to a given stimulus in the course of his lifetime. For example, the printed word "teacher" may be related to the memory of several specific teachers; a generalized stereotype of teacher; feelings of respect, fear, pleasure; or other responses. The command of an army officer to charge the enemy may bring forth such possible responses as obedience, anger toward the enemy, fear of being hurt or killed, desire to escape the fight, and others.

But learned responses are not always elicited by the stimuli. Typically one response is elicited, and other possible responses are not. If the reader, for example, wishes to try a little "experiment," he can ask his friends to write down all the uses they can think of for a common brick, to write down all the adjectives they associate with "school," or some similar exercise. It is usually found that certain responses tend to occur more frequently than do others among members of a group but that the range of responses is quite extensive. Some responses are more common because they have been reinforced for most of us at some point in our cultural background. Less common responses can be produced, however. The likelihood of a given response's being elicited is related to how well it has been learned—how frequently it has been made and reinforced. Responses (or more properly, response tendencies) are believed to be thus ordered in a hierarchy.

Response tendencies are believed not to eventuate in actual responses until they gain strength enough to overcome a "response threshold." That is, most responses of which one is capable are not usually made, as they have been inhibited and better-learned responses take precedence. But if strong motivational conditions are present, all response tendencies seem to be strengthened, and multiple responses to a given stimulus may be elicited.

As anxiety may act, as does a drive, to motivate behavior, strong anxiety may cause, not only the dominant response, but other responses also, to be elicited by given stimuli.

Responses may be compatible with one another, and the mode of response may thus be strengthened under conditions of high anxiety. On the other hand, they may be competing or incompatible, in which instance it may be desirable to keep the motivational level low so that only the wanted response is elicited; otherwise disorganized inefficient reactions are elicited.

Consider the problem of stuttering. One theory about the causes of stuttering is that of conflict; the stutterer both does and does not want to communicate his ideas. When he is asked to respond to a question in class, he has a tendency to answer; he also has wishes not to answer because he fears being wrong, being ridiculed, being pitied for stuttering, or seeming inadequate.

When relaxed, the stutterer may communicate quite adequately and without impediment, but in a state of high anxiety he may experience the conflict described. The two responses are incompatible, which may be the cause of the verbal inefficiency we call "stuttering."

Proponents of this theory treat stuttering in two ways: They try to help the patient learn to relax and to extinguish the anxiety response; they also try to reinforce the speaking response so that it will become dominant over the avoidant response even in anxiety situations.

Many studies tend to confirm this generalization. For example, K. W. Spence (1960) considers that a strong drive acts as a multiplier, which means that the strongest response in a hierarchy becomes even more dominant than it was and so on.

Spence used the Manifest Anxiety Scale to estimate the degree of anxiety (or emotionality) of his subjects in a variety of studies. This instrument, developed from clinical recommendations, shows the degree to which people will admit to overt emotional symptoms suggestive of strong emotionality or anxiety. In some studies Spence placed subjects under experimentally induced pressures and involved them in tasks with the aim of examining differences in performance between subjects who were high on the anxiety scale and those who were not. From these studies he was able to suggest differential efforts in regard to competing and noncompeting responses, when anxiety is severe.

For example, if the first response in a hierarchy is the correct (or desired) one, severe anxiety increases the likelihood that the response will be made. Should the first response be incorrect, anxiety (strong drive) would cause performance to deteriorate, for that incorrect response would gain an even greater tendency to occur. It is true that, if a second response in the hierarchy were to be the correct response, strong anxiety might cause it to be elicited along with the incorrect first response—in which event the second, correct response might be reinforced and in turn become the first response in the hierarchy. In general, however, Spence suggests, when there are competing responses of which only one may be correct, a lower drive or anxiety level is to be preferred. When responses are not competitive, mild anxiety or other higher drive level may improve over-all performance.

It may be inferred by the teacher that, in initial learning when pupil responses are as likely to be incorrect as correct, students should be kept as much as possible from feeling anxious or threatened. On later occasions, when material has been learned correctly, a higher degree of motivation (as in competitive drill) may enhance performance.

S. B. Sarason and his colleagues (1958) seem to agree; they apply the principle of interference with performance under strong drive to the highly anxious pupil who, when presented with unfamiliar stimuli to which he must respond, tends to be illogical in his thinking.

N. Keys and G. Whiteside (1930), relating anxiety level to school learning, found that anxious children averaged more than one year retardation in age-grade standings. Later studies seem to confirm their finding. R. Wirt and W. Broen (1956) found reading-achievement scores inversely related to high-anxiety scores when intelligence was controlled for. H. Reese (1961) found high anxiety inversely related to arithmetic scores, and B. Philips (1962) found that pupils with low anxiety had better scores on two standardized achievement tests. For an excellent review of the findings on the effects of anxiety on school performance the student should consult Sarason (1960); in general, we may accept the notion that the higher the pupil's anxiety level, the more interference there will be with *complex* learning performances.

Anxiety may become almost chronic in pupils who have had many fear-producing or guilt-producing experiences. Such pupils are less able to tolerate stressful situations than are others. On the other hand, pupils who are usually not particularly anxious may be made so by constant threats, sarcasm, or highly critical remarks; in such instances it is likely that performance will suffer rather than improve.

F. F. Lighthall states:

Teaching strategies based on threat of punishment (for example, poor grades, change of curriculum or teacher, and expulsion) undoubtedly accomplish the intended effect on children of creating fear. This has potential for causing growth or retardation *depending on the reaction to fear* elicited by the strategy. If the reaction is a sharpened attention to specific weaknesses and increased efforts for improvement and mastery, then no one could oppose the strategy. Far more likely in such a strategy, however, is withdrawal reaction which is the first step toward repression and anxiety. Therefore, whenever it appears necessary or desirable to use some threat or "warning" to induce involvement, the teacher should take careful note of the child's reactions. If the threat fails to have its intended effect, it probably has backfired and contributed to the child's tendency to avoid and forget rather than to approach and mastery. (1964, p. 28)

We have not so far discussed the effects of anxiety on mental health *per se*. Numerous studies have shown that highly anxious pupils blame themselves more for failure than do less anxious pupils (see Doris, 1959) ; they tend to have poorer self-concepts and are less popular with peers (Horowitz, 1962) ; they make more negative self-references (Sarason & Ganzer, 1962; Sarason & Ganzer, 1963) . Anxiety is, after all, a condition of emotional stress. Its consequences, especially if pupils are anxious in a variety of school situations, cannot help but harm the mental health of pupils. Furthermore, interference with adaptive behavior tends to bring increased problems to the child—and the teacher.

The Defense Mechanisms

The term "defense mechanism" comes from psychoanalytic psychology and refers to a kind of behavior that is habitually employed to deal with frustration, conflict, anxiety, or inability to attain desired reinforcements. Defense mechanisms represent attempts to help maintain self-esteem in the face of failure, or to relieve oneself from guilt in the eyes of others or himself, and to escape anxiety-provoking situations. These mechanisms can be defensive, in the sense of actively coping with the situation or with one's internal drives and motives, or they can be escapist in that one attempts to avoid unpleasant inner or external phenomena. Such mechanisms may be consciously employed at first, but eventually they become habitual and are used without our full awareness.

Defenses are employed by everyone, usually in quite "normal" ways, but they are useful only in avoiding or relieving anxiety or other emotional tensions temporarily, for they do not solve the problems with which one must cope. They may be useful temporary bridges to help one deal with stressful situations, but if they are employed excessively or inappropriately or if they cause further problems, defenses can be maladaptive. For example, *fantasy* was used by Jimmy in order to escape engagement in class discussion, an apparently anxiety-provoking situation. He was temporarily relieved of tension by reading and thinking about Yogi Bear, but this relief did not enable him to learn to enter into discussions; instead it made him a problem for the teacher, and he failed to learn from the other pupils and to make his own ideas known. Jimmy's defenses are a clue to his problems. Once they are understood more clearly, he can be helped to a more realistic, problem-solving way of life.

In some instances, excessive reliance on the defenses can lead to neurotic behavior or even to more severe disturbances. The ultimate result of fantasizing, for example, can be a life completely divorced from reality. Autism and certain forms of schizophrenia are characterized by complete withdrawal from contact with others in "life" completely based within oneself. Some psychologists and psychiatrists have argued that such complete withdrawal is the result of extreme anxiety about dealing with the external world, but this argument is probably an oversimplified statement of causation.

Although defense mechanisms are frequently purposefully learned, at least at first, they *can* be learned without our knowledge or volition. For example, a child who has learned to "state good reasons" for his conduct may tend to rationalize to the point at which he hides his true motives even from himself. The child who is highly motivated to be liked may learn to sublimate his aggressive impulses and to withdraw from controversy simply because such behavior may be reinforced in our society.

Most readers have had opportunities to become familiar with the defense mechanisms. For this reason, we shall merely identify them briefly. Further information can be found in selections listed under "Suggestions for Further Reading" at the end of this chapter.

Identification is psychological acceptance and affiliation with a person or institution from which reinforcement is forthcoming. It usually leads to imitation and acceptance of the values of the object of identification. Mutual support is provided among those who identify with one another. We have already mentioned that bright underachieving boys tend to identify with their peers, rather than with the teacher or other adults.

Introjection is acceptance and internalization of the values and mores of those with whom one identifies, partly to obtain positive reinforcement and partly to avoid negative reinforcement. Essentially this process at first involves imitation or emulation; later the person may no longer realize where his values and mores came from. This shift is seen in schools where children from differing socioeconomic classes adhere to different values. Teachers, of course, often hope that children will introject such values as academic achievement, self-discipline, and mutual helpfulness. Whether or not they do depends partly upon whether or not they identify with the teacher. Some may identify instead with undesirable peer-group elements and may introject values incompatible with those of the school.

Projection is attribution of one's own motives to others; one may then obtain a certain amount of "justification" for his own behavior. The child who has a desire to cheat on a test may attribute this motive to "everybody." The child who is prejudiced may consider that others are prejudiced against him.

Rationalization is the justifying of one's own or others' conduct that is basically unacceptable to either oneself or to society.

In this way one defends against feelings of guilt or unworthiness. The lazy child may rationalize that "school isn't that helpful, anyway."

Compensation involves striving to overcome thwarting and consequent feelings of inadequacy by exerting extra effort to achieve one's goals or by shifting to similar but not identical goals that may be easier to attain. The average child may win excellent grades by exerting extra effort; the handicapped child learns to engage in activities compatible with his problem, as when the blind child learns by listening rather than by reading.

Displacement is the removal of feelings and emotions from the original, threatening object to one that is less threatening. It can be considered as stimulus generalization of a sort. For example, the child may fear or be angry at a punitive parent; he may then apply these same reactions to all in authority, including the teacher. But, as the teacher is not in fact the parent, the child's feelings toward the teacher probably will not be as strongly felt as toward the parent. As will be discussed later (Chapter 11), children who are made anxious by such stimuli as authority figures can be helped through the process of extinguishing their anxiety with the least threatening authority figures, then in regard to the next least threatening, and so on. This process seems to work more successfully than does trying to deal with the conditions of strongest anxiety first.

Sublimation is the reduction of threat and guilt by turning undesirable feelings, emotions, and motives into socially desirable channels. For example, aggressive behavior may be turned against "crime." One is still aggressive but in an acceptable way.

Undoing is removal of guilt feelings through attempts to atone. It is valuable for teachers to help children relieve any guilt feelings and thus to enjoy more positive feelings toward themselves. For example, when a child marks up a desk, allowing him to refinish it is probably better than punishing him, if he is sorry that he misbehaved.

A *reaction formation* is an attempt to control "unworthy" feelings or to deal with "unworthy" motives by reacting against them. For example, the child who feels hostile toward other children may try unusually hard to be pleasant and helpful to them. The child who is tempted to cheat may take unusual measures to be honest—and may also concern himself with trying to prevent others from cheating.

Denial of reality enables one to protect oneself against external or internal threat by refusing to recognize real occurrences, motives, and feelings. Some children deny their excellent intellectual abilities—"I'm not really that smart"—which permits them to excuse shoddy work or laziness. Sometimes children caught in misbehavior will say, amusingly, "I'm not doing anything."

Fantasy also enables one to escape from dangerous situations, as well as to enjoy feelings of adequacy, reinforcement, and power without realistic bases. When children daydream in the classroom, we can be fairly sure that they find reality either anxiety-provoking or frustrating. The answer is not to punish them but to help them find value in classroom participation.

Insulation is a form of protection against feelings of inadequacy or other threats through avoidance of emotional involvement. It is especially visible (apparent) in unwillingness to become highly involved in seeking goals: If one does not care, he will not be hurt by failure to attain his goals. Class clowns sometimes offer examples of insulation, for humor may preclude serious involvement (and also produce secondary gains in attention from others) .

Regression is reversion to earlier habits. One gains by not being expected to assume responsibilities commensurate with his present stage of development. Regression is essentially dependent behavior. The present writer noted an extreme instance in a kindergarten child, who, upon being pushed to achieve, reverted to baby talk and gave up control of elimination; needless to say, this child required expert treatment.

Repression is the relegation to the unconscious of actions, thoughts, or feelings that one feels guilty or fearful about. (If relegation is carried out with full awareness, the mechanism is termed "suppression.") Sigmund Freud considered repression a basic component of neurotic behavior, and, because the individual was therefore not conscious of the reasons for his problems, a "cure" required the uncovering of repressed thoughts and feelings. One can also view repression as the inhibition of thoughts or feelings that are painful and therefore negatively reinforcing. One tends to forget his failures or his inadequacies and to remember his successes (although not always) .

Psychologists have sometimes posited mechanisms other than those we have included in the preceding list; they have also explained the dynamics activating the mechanisms in ways relating to specific personality theories like psychoanalysis, self theory, and others. We shall take the position that the mechanisms merely represent kinds of behavior that have been initiated by trial and error, imitation, or purposeful problem-solving and that have been reinforced frequently enough to become habitual. They will continue as long as they protect the individual from inner or outer threats or otherwise accomplish their purposes. To phrase it differently, as long as they are reinforced, they have utility and will be continued. Frequently, because of stimulus or response generalization and passage of time, their origins have been forgotten. Many times we employ these mechanisms without being aware that we are doing so. As they are not essentially problem-solving behavior, their indiscriminate use can lead to further difficulties for us.

The teacher needs to be well aware of defense mechanisms operating in his pupils (and in himself) . They can serve as clues to the fact that something is troubling the child and sometimes can point to the source of the trouble, which can then be handled. As excessive use of the defenses does not solve problems, it may be necessary to call the child's attention to reality and to show him better ways of handling his difficulties. It is patent that behavior cannot always be taken at face value, so that the teacher cannot necessarily accept the child's explanation of why he does what he does, especially as the child may not even be aware of his own defense mechanisms. The defense mechanisms can thus be clues to alert the teacher to what is wrong and should be carefully studied. Extreme or frequent use of them requires remedial efforts.

Let us refer back to Jimmy for a moment. It seems likely that Jimmy's quietness during free reading represents a number of mechanisms. He was insulating himself from reality and apparently enjoying a certain amount of fantasy. He failed to identify with the teacher and with his peers. His remarks, sarcasm, and name-calling toward other pupils can be seen as displacement of angry feelings to them, as well as expression of direct hostility. He may have been attempting to compensate for feelings of insecurity or rejection by playing others down.

Jimmy's behavior was dependent, in that he wanted the teacher to provide constant support and attention; it was immature, of course, and, if he had previously been more mature, we would see such behavior as regressive. The fact that Jimmy praised himself, although his work was frequently poor, might be viewed as denial of reality, fantasy, or lack of identification with the teacher's values. Sucking his thumb also sounds like regressive behavior.

All in all, Jimmy's behavior cannot be termed healthy, coping, or problem-solving. We shall discuss further findings about Jimmy later in this chapter.

Dealing with Frustration, Conflict, and Anxiety

FRUSTRATION

In Chapter 4 we discussed hostility as a manifestation of frustration. There are, of course, other possible manifestations of frustration. For example, mild frustration may simply result in intensified efforts to reach a goal, and in this instance it can be beneficial. Stronger frustration, however, may result in a change of motives—the child who never is reinforced for being kind to others may eventually not wish to be kind. Emotional outbursts, guilt feelings, self-devaluation, withdrawal from social contact, and failure to engage in problem-solving activities are some other possible reactions.

There are two means of dealing with frustration. One is to attempt to alleviate frustrating circumstances; the other is to help the pupil learn to tolerate frustration. Both have advantages and disadvantages.

Attempts to prevent or alleviate frustrating circumstances may help to improve classroom morale, discipline, motivation, and school achievement. But they do not help children learn to tolerate situations that may frustrate them throughout life or to deal with them constructively.

Attempts to teach frustration tolerance can aid the child to be constructive in many frustrating circumstances in his life. Everyone meets such situations, and there is value in learning to react adaptively. On the other hand, one can become over-tolerant of frustration. Calm acceptance of frustration can become apathy and may allow the individual to seek less from life than he should.

In Chapter 9, we shall discuss some common stresses among children in school; other chapters touch upon peripheral causes of frustration.

Some ways to teach tolerance of frustration and ways to handle frustrating circumstances follow:

First, the teacher can teach suitable emotional reactions and help the child to relax under frustration by precept, example, and supportive behavior. For instance, consider the child who has tried many times to solve a difficult mathematical problem and is becoming emotionally upset by his failure to do so. The teacher can, first of all, not allow himself to become angry or upset. He can sympathize with the child's difficulties, but, in his supportive efforts, he must be careful not to reinforce the child's feelings; that is, he should not implicitly agree that the child has a right to emotional outbursts. Sometimes simply putting a hand on a child's shoulder or a finger to the lips "shushing" him is sufficient.

Second, the teacher can encourage the same child to take a little time to calm down and relax. He can reinforce calmness, patience, and self-control.

Third, the teacher can point to what the child *has* accomplished: a good beginning or at least discovery of what will not "work."

Fourth, the teacher can suggest possible changes in attack on the problem. Frustration and anger may narrow horizons in problem-solving activity.

Fifth, the teacher can reinforce motivation and be encouraging and optimistic about eventual solution of the problem.

Sixth, the teacher can attempt to remove threat induced by failure to solve the problem—not only material threats like lower marks but also threats to the child's self-esteem and feelings of adequacy.

Seventh, the teacher can negatively reinforce unadaptive behavior.

As we saw in Chapter 4, B. F. Skinner (1948) believes that frustration tolerance can be taught. The constant exposure of the child to mildly frustrating situations, with positive reinforcement for adaptive behavior and intensification of frustration for unadaptive behavior, can presumably increase frustration tolerance. This approach is, essentially, teaching self-control. Or, as Freud would say, it fosters movement from the pleasure principle—the demand for immediate gratification—to the reality principle, or recognition that delay of gratification may frequently be necessary.

CONFLICT

It is important to keep in mind that conflicts should be resolved and that decisions must be lived with, for better or worse. Failure to resolve conflict usually leads to increasing emotional tension and lack of adaptive behavior.

Conflict is common in the life of everyone. The ability to resolve conflict is therefore important, and schools can aid pupils in learning it.

It is evident that the teacher or the child may not always be clear about the nature of a conflict or, indeed, whether or not a conflict actually exists. There are a number of kinds of behavior that do suggest conflict, and careful study of the child and his situation may also suggest the nature of a specific conflict. For example, vacillation, unwillingness to act on his own, leaning on others for advice and decisions, conflicting reactions to school situations (apparent in verbalization or emotional behavior), dependence, and extreme lethargy may all be signs. Counseling the pupil may help to clarify the nature of conflict.

In double-approach conflicts, schools can help children make decisions by clarifying the consequences of various choices. For example, if a child cannot both play football and be in the marching band, the short-term and long-term effects of each choice can be discussed. If he must choose between two courses of action in a moral question the teacher can show how others have solved similar problems and can perhaps suggest a suitable choice for him. Practice in actual and hypothetical decision making can be given. For example, the *NEA Journal* has stories for children in which conflict situations arise, allowing for class discussion of the merits of various decisions.

In double-avoidant conflict, it is again useful to point out the implications of each alternative. It can also be shown that, whatever the choice that is made, some unpleasant consequences may follow and that the child must learn to live with his decisions nevertheless. A typical example is the unwillingness of a child to study. He does not want to fail his tests, but he finds studying distasteful. Accordingly, he is likely to employ many defense mechanisms to reduce his emotional tension. The teacher can reinforce the idea that sometimes one has to do things he really would rather not do; if this approach is not successful, the child may be allowed to face the consequences of a decision not to study. Teachers who urge or argue with the child too much deprive him of the opportunity to make his own decisions and to live by them; they tend to increase emotional tension and to make the child feel threatened.

Perhaps approach-avoidant conflict and double approach-avoidant conflict are more common than are other forms: in stage fright, for example, in tackling difficult tasks, in entering athletic activities, or in engaging in leadership activities. It will be recalled that hopes for positive reinforcement may cause the child initially to move toward the goal but that, as the goal is approached, the fear of negative reinforcement mounts more strongly and retreat begins. It may then be necessary for the teacher to nudge the pupil more strongly toward the goal by enhancing the positive effects of an attempt to reach it, by playing down the negative aspects, or, in the case of double-avoidant conflict, by increasing the negative aspects of not proceeding toward a desirable goal.

Consider the instance of a young man who wishes to become a lawyer but feels uncomfortable in speech class. He can be made more comfortable about public speaking by such tactics as explaining that others have overcome similar problems too; by offering strong positive reinforcement for even participating in speech (for example, high marks for effort); by reinforcing even the writing of a speech, not to mention its delivery; and by trying to make certain that any speech he may present will be good enough to arouse the applause of his peers, thus positively reinforcing his efforts.

The principle of successive approximation is important. That is, the young man does not have to enter the situation all at once. He can be allowed to talk first to one other classmate, then to a small group, and then to the entire class. Or he can be allowed to act as a member of a committee or group making reports before he proceeds alone. Or he can speak for one minute, then for two minutes, and so on. Similar tactics are used in teaching swimming—the beginner starts in shallow water, perhaps simply learning to lie on his stomach and kick his legs. Later we teach him to float, to use his arms, and, finally, to breathe properly, exhaling under water. Eventually he may become an expert swimmer and even a high diver.

Teachers can also work with conflicts in the motives of children and sometimes with moral conflicts, through individual counseling. Serious conflicts, however, may require the services of a specialist.

The ultimate goal, we have noted, is to teach the child to recognize and resolve his own conflicts. It implies that the more the teacher can provide opportunities for children to make their own decisions and solve their own problems, the more they can learn to cope with conflict situations. It is only when the child is involved in situations with which it is beyond his ability to cope that teachers should intervene.

ANXIETY

There are a number of steps the teacher should take in dealing with a child's anxiety: First, he needs to discover, if possible, what makes the child anxious. In this event, he may be able to prevent anxiety from arising. Second, he needs to help the child to reduce his anxiety. Third, he needs to reduce the threat value of stimuli that induce anxiety. Fourth, he needs to enhance the child's ability to function, even while he is anxious. Fifth, he needs to do what he can to help chronically anxious children overcome their anxiety.

Let us take the example of a child who becomes highly anxious at the thought of taking tests. He "blows up" on tests and fails to achieve scores anywhere near representative of his usual achievement in class.

One may discover that several factors are operating. For example, the child may be subjected to pressures from home to achieve high marks. He may be insecure because his parents never agree that he has done well enough at any task. He may have had some failures that have resulted in lack of confidence in his ability to do well. For these reasons, any evaluative situation causes him tremendous anxiety.

In turn, anxiety interferes with performance, so that he is negatively reinforced in his anxiety over tests. This downward spiral may continue until the child refuses to try to achieve and either avoids tests, shows emotional and psychosomatic problems, or simply makes perfunctory efforts in tests. He has, in effect, already condemned himself to failure.

There are many techniques the teacher may try.

He can try to take pressure off the child by talking with the parents and by de-emphasizing the importance of tests to them and to the child.

He can provide positive reinforcement when the child takes a test, even though the child does poorly.

He can treat tests as evidence of what one *can* do, rather than of what one *cannot* do and can use them as learning devices for the child *and to find out himself* what has not been adequately taught.

He can provide practice tests to help habituate the child to taking tests and to help him become "test wise."

He can help the child to prepare adequately for tests, so that he is less apprehensive.

He can teach the child to relax his body, to employ a sense of humor, and to focus on the task rather than on himself.

He can attempt to build over-all self-confidence and esteem through positive reinforcement.

He can encourage the child to talk about his feelings, which may reduce anxiety.

And he can gradually help the child, through precept and example, to overcome some of his tension.

These methods are not sufficient to deal with neurotic anxiety, the causes of which are usually difficult to discover. That is, although we can work with the symptoms of such anxiety, we cannot prevent its occurrence unless we are able to determine its source, which may be either environmental, internal, or both. This job is for clinical experts.

A Further Report on Jimmy

The student-teacher reporting on Jimmy continued:

Jimmy needs affection, we think, and requires more approval from peers and authority. He receives little warm attention at home. His parents have never inquired about his progress, nor have they ever appeared for parent-teacher conferences. As a result of feeling left out at home, Jimmy tries to gain what he lacks from the school environment. Since a classroom setting cannot provide complete compensation for lack of approval and attention and affection at home, Jimmy becomes frustrated. As a teacher, I cannot give him constant attention and support, nor would this be of permanent help to him.

I have taken a stronger stand in regard to Jimmy's disciplinary problems. I have set limits on the amount of time he is allowed for any particular assignment, and at the end of that time have checked to make certain he has progressed.

This has worked out fairly well, since Jimmy knows he is responsible for those tasks assigned him. In this way, wasted time is becoming less and less and progress is improving.

Also, I have simply brought Jimmy to order by telling him to "sit down" and "be quiet" in no uncertain terms. Often I stand near his desk when talking to the class. By the way, his desk was moved to the front of the class and this has helped. It causes him to be more attentive, for he is within notice of his classmates and myself.

Finally, we had the school psychologist in to observe Jimmy. We had several reasons: Jimmy's lack of organization, his nervousness in the absence of any apparent environmental cause, and his constant bids for attention and approval. The psychologist suggested that Jimmy receive professional help. He not only found Jimmy's behavior beyond normal expectations but also noted other evidence of probable emotional disorders. In following through, we have asked the parents to come in for a conference, and they have finally agreed to do so.

In terms of what we know about Jimmy, the reader is asked to raise questions. For example, were the teacher's actions desirable? What else might have been attempted? What was being reinforced? Was Jimmy anxious? If so, what was done to help him be less anxious? What was done about Jimmy's apparent frustrations? What was done by the school to offset problems Jimmy had at home?

□

REFERENCES

Doris, J. "Test Anxiety and Blame-Assignment in Grade School Children," *Journal of Abnormal and Social Psychology,* 58 (1959), 181–90.

Horowitz, F. "The Relationship of Anxiety, Self-Concept, and Sociometric Status Among 4th, 5th, and 6th Grade Children," *Journal of Abnormal and Social Psychology,* 65 (1962), 212–4.

Hull, C. L. *A Behavior System.* New Haven: Yale University Press, 1952.

Keys, N., and G. Whiteside. "The Relation of Nervous Emotional Stability to Educational Achievement," *Journal of Educational Psychology,* 21 (1930), 429–41.

Lighthall, F. F. *Anxiety as Related to Thinking and Forgetting.* Washington, D.C.: National Education Association, 1964.

Miller, N. E. "Experimental Studies of Conflict," in J. M. Hunt (ed.). *Personality and the Behavior Disorders,* I, 421 ff. New York: Ronald, 1944.

Philips, B. "Sex, Social Class, and Anxiety as Sources of Variation in School Achievement," *Journal of Educational Psychology,* 53 (1962), 316–22.

Reese, H. "Manifest Anxiety and Achievement Test Performance," *Journal of Educational Psychology,* 52 (1961), 132–5.

Sarason, I., and V. Ganzer. "Anxiety, Reinforcement, and Experimental Instructions in a Free Verbalization Situation," *Journal of Abnormal and Social Psychology,* 65 (1962), 300–7.

———. "Effects of Test Anxiety and Reinforcement History on Verbal Behavior," *Journal of Abnormal and Social Psychology,* 67 (1963), 513–9.

Sarason, S. B., K. Davidson, F. F. Lighthall, and R. Waite. "Rorschach Behavior and Performance of High and Low Anxious Children," *Child Development,* 29 (1958), 277–85.

Sarason, S. B., K. Davidson, F. F. Lighthall, R. Waite, and B. Ruebush. *Anxiety in Elementary School Children.* New York: Wiley, 1960.

Skinner, B. F. *Walden Two.* New York: Macmillan, 1948.

Spence, K. W. *Selected Papers: Behavior Theory and Learning.* Englewood Cliffs: Prentice-Hall, 1960.

Wirt, R., and W. Broen. "The Relation of the Children's Manifest Anxiety Scale to the Concept of Anxiety as Used in the Clinic," *Journal of Counseling Psychology,* 20 (1956), 482.

SUGGESTIONS FOR FURTHER READING

Coleman, J. C. *Personality Dynamics and Effective Behavior.* Chicago: Scott Foresman, 1960.
Chapters 5 and 6 include a discussion of adjustment processes and an excellent résumé of the defense mechanisms. This book is devoted to a treatment of adjustment aimed primarily at the college student himself. It provides many illustrations and examples of how one's adjustment can be improved.

Dollard, J., and N. E. Miller. *Personality and Psychotherapy.* New York: McGraw-Hill, 1950.
This book offers a fairly technical, although entirely readable, discussion of kinds of conflict, results of conflict, and a theoretical framework for considering the conflicts we have mentioned in this chapter. Dollard and Miller use diagrams to illustrate approach and avoidance gradients and considerably extend our discussion about stability and other characteristics of conflict. It is based on research findings, some of them with animals.

Sarason, S. B. *Anxiety in Elementary School Children.* New York: Wiley, 1960.
Sarason is a leading authority on the study of anxiety. This book, based on research, discusses the question of children's anxiety in detail and provides suggestions that can be useful to teachers and others who work with children. Assessment, causes, and effects of anxiety are covered.

8

COURSE CONTENT
AND TEACHING METHOD
AS RELATED
TO MENTAL HEALTH

Miss Johnson, teaching a unit called "How Is the Ocean Studied?" used an experiment to try to help her children develop skill in observation and deduction. She got some laboratory apparatus consisting of a graduated cylinder filled three-quarters full with water and a small model of a Cartesian diver.[1] Placing him in the cylinder, she then fastened a rubber sheet over the top with a strong rubber band. When the rubber sheet over the mouth of the cylinder was pressed, the diver sank to the bottom. The question "Why did this happen?" was raised. The principle to be learned was that the increased pressure on the water forced some water into the diver, who therefore became less buoyant. She reported the results of this lesson as follows:

Most children were able to grasp Archimedes' principle, that a body immersed in a liquid is buoyed up by a force equal to the weight of the liquid it displaces. However, they were not satisfied with a simple understanding that pressure on the cylinder forced

[1] A Cartesian diver is a small model of a man, hollow and open at the bottom. He is placed in the water in such a way that the air he contains is just sufficient to balance him, with a tendency neither to sink nor to float. One can use a small bottle, open end down, to demonstrate the same principles.

water into the diver so that he displaced less water and decreased buoyancy caused him to sink; they wanted to go farther. They were curious as to what would happen if they now added salt to the water. Would the diver still do his trick? Many decided that he wouldn't, while others supported the idea that he would. The extended experiment was tried, and it was determined that the diver still would dive, but increased pressure on the rubber covering was needed. Salt water, being denser than fresh water, produces more buoyancy, which has to be overcome before the diver will sink.

This led to a discussion concerning salt versus fresh water. One child had been to the Great Salt Lake, and mentioned the ease of floating in it. Another child had noticed a difference in waterlevel marks on a ship coming from the ocean into the Great Lakes, and a discussion concerning the need for shipping companies to take this difference in buoyancy into consideration ensued.

I felt that we were successful, not only in regard to the objectives specifically stated, but that we were able to generalize and transfer our knowledge to extended areas. Motivation was excellent, and you should have heard the scholarly class discussion!

The reader may say to himself, "Sure, the kids learned about buoyancy, and they were interested—but what has *that* to do with mental health?" It is our purpose, in this chapter, to suggest some relationships. We contend that all content can be a valuable vehicle for contributing directly or indirectly to mental health goals.

Mental-Health Goals and School Subjects

In Chapter 1 two concepts were stressed: the need to teach preventively and constructively for optimal pupil development and adjustment; and, the intimate relationship between school achievement and mental health of pupils. We also considered the concept of self-actualization and how it is related to mental health.

To the extent that a teacher can improve a child's abilities to cope with his physical and social environment, to understand himself and his world, and to utilize his assets to his best ability, the teacher helps strengthen him against stresses he will meet

nd gives him tools for building a better life. Some objectives to
seek in course content and manner of teaching are

1. aiding the child to identify more clearly and to understand
   problems presented by today's world;
2. assisting the child in learning how others have tried to solve
   their problems and those of society as a whole;
3. helping the child to engage in reality testing, and to compare
   reality with what he previously thought was true or wished
   were true;
4. helping the child to gain enhanced competence in necessary
   social skills;
5. aiding him to enjoy success, to gain motives for study, exploration, critical thinking, and other cognitive skills;
6. helping him to become creative and to express himself;
7. showing him how to solve problems, and to be oriented toward
   solving problems;
8. showing him how to use constructive methods when frustrated,
   anxious, or in conflict;
9. urging him to identify with successful, interesting figures in
   literature, school, or community life about him;
10. providing him with opportunities to gain self-enhancement,
    esteem, recognition by others, and a feeling of security regard-
    ing the present and the future.

In school every child may be expected to learn much about
himself, his abilities and his limitations—and he should learn to
accept the latter. He may find ways to improve upon his
deficiencies and to set his goals realistically. He should learn to
meet stress and frustration constructively and to employ his
feelings and emotions to enhance his life and those of others,
rather than be hurtful. Each young person should become more
aware of what to expect in future growth and development and
should anticipate and prepare to solve problems arising from
maturation. He should learn to be independent, creative, and
to move toward self-actualization. He should be able to develop
a useful philosophy of life and habits of putting this philosophy
into practice.

This approach, quite evidently, is nothing more than the
"pupil-oriented" approach about which teachers talk and which

many believe they try to employ. Content and method are determined by their probable effects on *changes in the pupil,* rather than by a blind feeling that content is valuable for its own sake. It is our purpose to try to clarify the differences in these points of view, and to suggest some ways of teaching which can be useful for both teaching content and fostering pupil growth, development, and mental health.

EVIDENCE ON TEACHING FOR MENTAL HEALTH

The question naturally arises: Can teaching methods and course content influence pupil mental health and personality development? That is, can children learn to understand themselves and others better because of appropriate teaching? Can teaching really promote better social adjustment? Can one teach for such objectives without jeopardizing other teaching goals?

Studies by R. H. Ojemann (1959), F. S. Stiles (1959), and others (Muuss, 1959; Ojemann, 1953; Zelen, 1954) have shown that teachers can be oriented toward highlighting for pupil·discussion and evaluation human relationships appearing either in classroom interactions or in course content. Teachers themselves learn better how to understand their pupils (and themselves) and how to manage their teaching more effectively in terms of *all* of their objectives.

LIMITATIONS OF TEACHING FOR MENTAL HEALTH

As mental-health problems are not always caused by inappropriate learning, they cannot be completely prevented or alleviated by teaching. For example, medical help is needed in organically connected problems. The school cannot relieve the pressures from problem home situations, which may become quite unbearable. Teachers cannot do anything to help the mentally retarded gain normal intelligence (although they can help such children to live more satisfactory lives on their own levels). A few children need intensive therapy, and the school cannot provide it for them in the regular classroom.

Teaching for mental health thus primarily implies that the school is functioning on a preventive level and is working with reasonably normal children in reasonably normal circumstances; teaching is no substitute for other measures that must be instituted when problems are serious. Schools emphasize the so-called "positive approach" and try to help children to develop in a healthy manner, rather than taking a remedial approach toward those who are poorly adjusted, although the latter, too, may benefit from this form of teaching.

Course Content and Mental Health

THE NEED TO IMPROVE COURSE CONTENT AND METHODOLOGY

Ojemann (1953) has said that much course content is not realistic in relation either to stated objectives or to what pupils are likely to find in "real life" outside school. For example, in the typical school reader, failure at a task is likely to be unheard of, and the hero of any story usually attains his goals. Yet failure is a concomitant of high aspirations, and one must learn how to meet failure or else not attempt difficult tasks.

Much school literature stresses platitudes about the rewards for just behavior, good character, hard work, and thrift; yet such rewards do not always appear in reality. Still, children must learn to adopt worthwhile value systems, even though their adherence to values may not always be rewarded by others.

Course content also stresses the wisdom of parents and other adults and the need for children to conform to their mandates and advice; yet children might be better off doing more independent thinking. Children are unrealistically pictured as conforming and anxious to please, and there are few illustrations of normal hostile or aggressive behavior.

There is relatively little about girls in the literature, but much about boys and men (especially in classes of history and science). Minority-group and underprivileged children and those from other than the middle SES class are relatively neglected also.

Because of these inadequacies, the child may have difficulty relating what he gains in school to what he finds in the newspapers, radio, or television. In mass media events are often treated with journalistic slants which may confuse the naïve child; in some cases there is sympathetic treatment given to criminals and income tax evasion, and much publicity given to such adult delinquencies as price-fixing, bribery of officials, and disrespect for the law. If the curriculum does not take cognizance of such practices, the school may be considered as quite apart from actual living. Conversely, the child may find that some of what he learns in school is treated lightly by his parents, who can no longer factor trinomials or figure square roots and who have forgotten the participants in the War of the Roses.

In school one may learn about vaccinations, but while it is in our power to conquer smallpox, many parents fail to see that their children get necessary booster treatments. The child may learn about the actions of the United Nations, yet fail to acquaint himself with the issues in his own city government, and how one might proceed to make his voice heard by the governing bodies. He may learn about automation, yet fail to see how this affects the need for his own education, and the kinds of vocational opportunities which will be available to him.

Children may also fail to get help in understanding their own lives. A child may realize that he is not well accepted by others, yet fail to learn that his own actions contribute to his unpopularity. He may not learn why he is afraid to speak in class discussions and what steps he might take to rid himself of such fear. He may fail to understand how his own attitudes place him in conflict with adults, and to respect the opinions of others.

Education, to be functional, must find application outside the formal course activities and content. It must, in essence, be related to actual problems of living. We shall illustrate the kind of teaching we believe to be functional; we do not negate the theoretical or the abstract, but insist that school must apply to the present and the actual more than it does; when this applicability is not considered by the teacher, school loses much of its vitality and meaning for the pupil.

AN ILLUSTRATION OF FUNCTIONAL TEACHING

Driver-education courses have tended to stress knowledge of correct driving procedures, appropriate laws, and reasons for accidents. Sometimes "scare" films have been shown, in an attempt to induce caution in youthful drivers. However, it is not ignorance that seems to cause automobile accidents so much as improper attitudes and emotional behaviors. That is, most people could drive more safely than they do, were they so motivated.

In our illustration, the class in driver education was discussing why certain automobile accidents occurred late at night on country roads. The newspapers had recently printed stories about three different accidents in which teenagers' cars had ended in ditches, one of them seriously injured.

The teacher began by asking what might cause three different drivers to lose control of their cars when alone on safe roads under good driving conditions. He received such suggestions as, "They didn't know the road," "They drove too fast," and "They weren't watching what they were doing."

Not satisfied, the instructor pursued. "All of these boys had driving licenses and they had had a course in driver education. They must have had driving skill. Could it be that their feelings or attitudes might be at fault?"

The class was interested. They countered with such notions as the desire of some students to show off, especially with their girls, or the attempt to be funny, as when steering with their knees. Beer-drinking was also mentioned.

"So," remarked the teacher, "these seem to be ways to gain attention and to impress others and maybe prove something about being a man?"

The class agreed.

"But," suggested the teacher, "this suggests to me that such fellows must not really feel that they are successful and that others accept them. If they really felt adequate, they wouldn't have to keep proving it."

"Well," said one boy, "maybe such fellows do feel as if other people didn't think they were real great. Come to think of it, maybe they weren't."

Discussion continued in similar vein. Mention was made of constructive ways to demonstrate courage and ability, such as in athletics, or in drag-strips and rallies. The teacher was able to suggest other poor driving attitudes and feelings, such as anger and hostility, inconsiderateness, or even intense anxiety. In this way, he hoped, students would begin to look at the reasons for accidents from a motivational and emotional point of view. They might begin to see certain driving practices as rather immature, and form collective attitudes which could foster better driving throughout the peer group.

In the illustration, notice that there is a concern for motivation, including status seeking, recognition from others, and desire for popularity. Immaturity and lack of responsible behavior are mentioned; developmental level, self-esteem, and other variables enter the discussion. At the same time, personalities are avoided, and threat and moralizing are kept out of the picture. No student is forced to identify himself or his friends, and he is free to examine his own driving attitudes in the privacy of his own thoughts. Mature values are stressed, and students are taught to think of how they may satisfy their needs more successfully. Furthermore, although teacher-led, a large share of the discussion comes from the students.

It is this sort of teaching that we consider functional. Varying with the subject, grade level, and goals, the techniques are directed to consideration of emotions, values, and motives. Although factual content and problem solving are included, the lesson does not rest merely with them.

We shall now consider some content areas, in order to suggest their possible value in helping to develop positive mental health. Space forbids consideration of all school subjects, and it is hoped that the reader, recognizing that the following discussions are merely illustrative, will make his own applications to areas not discussed.

THE SOCIAL SCIENCES

Again we look to Ojemann (1953) for an exposition of the need to improve content, in this case that of the social sciences, especially at upper grade levels. He discusses some civics books that deal with crime and suggests that, although in most texts there is discussion of such protective devices as the police force, detection of criminals, the courts, and the prisons, there is little treatment of causation of crime other than mention that underprivileged neighborhoods may be contributing factors.

Ojemann considers such an approach primarily factual in nature. It does not seem to attack questions that provide fundamental understanding of how crime comes about, what treatments might be more useful than those we now employ in prevention and handling of criminal behavior. He would like to see questions such as the following asked:

Are the ways in which the police and courts handle the criminal such that after they apprehend him they try to find out what caused

the behavior and then take the causes into account in their reaction
to him? Do they try to find out in a given case whether the causes
are such that the criminal can be rehabilitated into a self-respecting
cooperating individual? Or if he cannot be rehabilitated, is he then
effectively isolated? In other words, do the present systems that
society has developed study the criminal to find out what factors
underlie his behavior and base their treatment on those findings?

Furthermore, if criminal behavior is caused, then real protection
from the criminal requires that the community find out and change
those conditions that produced him. Real protection—both in the
sense of protection from direct damage to life and property that
the criminal may inflict and also in the sense that taking care of
the criminal is a drain on other citizens—such protection comes
when the people in the community are aware of the forces that tend
to produce crime and seek to change those forces. (1953, p. 102)

Criminologists (but not always the courts) *do* take interest in
questions such as these, although this orientation may not
always appear in textbooks. Law enforcement workers are beginning to recognize that closing a tavern may merely move the
disturbance to a new environment but does not really force
hoodlums to stop; ticketing for speeding does not ensure that a
person will drive better, but merely makes him more careful
when policemen are around. Basic motivations and contributing factors of various kinds must be considered when dealing
with persons who break the law.

Thus textbooks may—or may not—raise fundamental questions and issues about the nature of human behavior. To the
extent that they do not do so, they may be missing an opportunity to help children learn values, ways of interacting socially,
understanding of selves and others, and acceptance of responsibility and foresight.

ELEMENTARY-LEVEL TEACHING. ■ Because children in early
grades may not understand many of the broader questions
about social living, an approach to understanding human behavior must be made through studying familiar figures. The
work of the milkman, the postman, the farmer, and others in
the community may thus furnish vehicles for understanding the
interdependence in our society, and the values and contributions made by such persons. (Incidentally, the teacher himself

may not always be aware of such contributions, and may have only a limited idea of what it means to live in a different subculture, or to have a different occupation. One student teacher known to the writer had come from a large metropolitan area. Her assignment happened to be in a rural community. When she started to discuss with her fourth graders some of the aspects of farm living, she suddenly discovered that she had never been on a real visit to a farm. She asked one of the children whether she could visit with them on a Saturday, and soon discovered that she had held many misconceptions of farm life, including the belief that farming required little professional competency or specialized education! This discovery was profitable to her—and, by extension, to her classes.)

Many topics in elementary books deal with home and family relationships, and their dynamics should be pursued whenever possible. For example, not all families have adequate incomes. Yet most readers for elementary-school children stress middle-class living and show advantages that many do not enjoy. (Many modes of living are desirable, however, and the "good life" does not require large material outlay. This point is not always clearly made or clearly understood by children.)

Other examples may come from the home lives of class members. Rules children observe, things they like to do, privileges they are awarded, trips they have made—all may lead to discussions of social living. Free writing, free drawing, incidents from the school room, and other sources provide material for discussion. The teacher may prepare little narratives suggesting possible problems faced by children, which offer take-off places for group problem solving.

Social studies encompasses topics in elementary psychology, geography, history, economics, government and politics, and many other aspects of living. If geared to the child's level, opportunities for personality development, social adjustment, and reality testing are presented.

SECONDARY-LEVEL SOCIAL SCIENCES. ▪ In addition to courses in social problems or courses of somewhat similar intent, the study of history deserves mention here. History is full of great men who had tremendous decisions to make, who worked their ways upward against odds, and who faced opposition and adversity. The study of history is the study of people, individually and in groups. It is also the study of ideas, and involves philosophy, politics, economics, and science. Reasons for historical movements and their outcomes are important in understanding the present and its problems.

Not only in history, but in most other subjects as well, the study of biography can add interest and understanding. Biography is not as widely employed as it might be, and texts do not give as much space to outstanding personalities as formerly. Neither do we celebrate our national holidays as we used to, with the result that pupils may fail to realize a personal stake in issues and problems that historical personages have met. For example, a study of the Civil War might require supplementary biographical readings, including source materials, when possible. Such materials provide understanding and appreciation that are hard to provide in more broadly oriented texts.

Of course, many of our historical leaders have not always been exemplary, and this point is worth emphasizing. Furthermore, many of our "great men" have had problems that they could not surmount or failures in certain aspects of their lives (for example, Abraham Lincoln's career as a storekeeper). Such biographical material not only serves to enrich courses but can also provide springboards for discussions that can be clearly related to present-day problems.

Another possibility that enhances thinking, furthers problem solving, and aids understanding is the "what if?" technique. For example, one teacher asked, "What if France had refused to help us during the Revolutionary War?" Another asked, "What if the Norsemen had maintained flourishing settlements in North America when they arrived many years before Columbus?"

FINE ARTS

Art and music can offer much to personality development and mental health; pleasant emotions can be fostered, tensions can be released, creativity and self-enhancement can be encouraged, and understanding of others improved through these activities.

Great painters, musicians, dramatists, and dancers create

moods. A fine work of art can lead to discussion of what was intended by its creator, of the conditions in which it was produced, of how the artist captured the character of his subject, and so on. Artists can be highly perceptive of human personalities and problems, and their work can lead to sympathetic understanding of human behavior and emotions.

When a child indulges in a creative effort in the fine arts, he may not only gain pleasure and pride in accomplishment or recognition, but he may also be able to communicate feelings that he cannot express verbally. Artistic studies also help to develop aesthetic values and provide pleasurable sensations as one deals with beautiful sights, sounds, or feelings.

One can express angry emotions through drawing, painting, dancing, or acting. The same is true of fears, happy emotions, and thoughts about oneself and one's world. The "case" of Karen and Bobby, to be discussed shortly, is a good example of how such expressions can aid us in understanding the child's feelings and how he views his world.

In regard to diagnosis and remediation, teachers should not expect to reach the refined conclusions about artistic productions attained by the specialist in mental health. Careful observation of children's drawings, the ways in which they interpret acting roles, their dances, and their songs can, however, help the teacher understand pupils better. Let us use drawing and painting as an example, for such productions are everyday occurrences.

For example, choice of characters in a drawing may be important. Does the child draw fearsome creatures, unhappy scenes, or aggressive action? Or does he deal with pleasant human relations, happy events, and comforting places? What are his characters doing—are they fighting, crying, running away? Or are they playing, singing, or working? Which characters receive most emphasis? In what attitudes are they customarily portrayed?

Children who are low in verbal abilities may express themselves better and with more satisfaction through their hands, as in crafts and industrial arts classes, as well as in fine arts. Some who are not gifted intellectually may still find satisfactions in making something of value, or something that gives pleasure to others. For example, one mentally retarded adolescent gained security and recognition by being able to play almost any popular song requested of her at the piano, although her technique was not masterful. It is because of the satisfactions in working with the tactile mode, pride in concrete accomplishment, and opportunity to express oneself to others, that arts, crafts, music, and similar subjects are so useful in therapy in mental institutions.

THE "CASE" OF KAREN AND BOBBY

Wishing to illustrate what may sometimes be gained from children's drawings, the present writer asked a psychologist friend to have his children make some pictures. Figures 7, 8, and 9 were drawn by the friend's children, together with other pictures not reproduced here.

Karen is the youngest child and is six years old. Bobby is seven, and Bill is eight. The family is happy and enjoys sports and taking trips together. There are no particular problems.

Figure 7. This picture was drawn by Karen. She clearly identifies with her mother, for she has drawn the female figures similar in size and style, especially their hair. She drew them first, starting at the left edge of the paper, suggesting that they were more important to her than were the male members of the family. Notice, too, that the males are smaller than the females. Bill is correctly shown larger than Bobby, but Dad takes a somewhat subordinate role. Everyone is smiling, which suggests that Karen believes her family to be a happy one.

Figure 8. Here Karen has drawn her father, her mother, and her self—as princess, queen, and king. Notice again Karen's closeness to her mother. Father is missing an arm and appears to have but one eye—apparently he does not receive such detailed attention from Karen as do she and her mother. Karen has often remarked that she wishes to be both a queen and a nurse when she grows up—these ambitions are reflected by the attire and by the doll. When told that princesses married kings and that kings would be hard to find, Karen remarked that she would be certain to find one and in the meantime would be glad to wait. She thinks well of her parents, ascribing royal roles to them. Karen apparently has high goals and enjoys a bit of pleasant fantasy in anticipation of attaining her own stature as a queen.

Figure 9. Bobby drew upon his imagination for this scene. He is a youngster who expresses anger when he feels it but is also able to express a great deal of affection. Notice that in the scene there is a certain ambivalence of mood. There is constructive action, shown by the gravel pit and mechanical shovel, but there is also aggression shown by the rock throwing, shooting, and armored car. The airplane appears to be rescuing someone. This combination of warlikeness and interest in machinery is quite typical of boys Bobby's age.

COMMUNICATIONS SKILLS

Communications skills are found in language arts, reading, speech, literature, and other classes, depending on the pupil's grade level. Reading, because it is basic to the study of most other school subjects, is vital to mental health. Reading prob-

FIGURE 7. "My Family" by Karen

FIGURE 8. "Mommy, Dad, and Me" by Karen

lems may be caused by inability to concentrate, by anxieties leading to "blocking," or by frustration, and poor reading ability can in turn cause frustration in other academic work. Poor readers are found in high school as well as in elementary school, so that when poor achievement and related poor social and emotional behavior are found, reading skills must be carefully checked, and remediation instituted when the need is apparent.

Reading, literature, writing, and speech classes can foster positive personality development and good mental health (Schramm, *et al.,* 1961). Modern literature teaching tries to help students understand what writers are trying to say, how their works come about, how their ideas and feelings compare with those of others, and how the writings might apply to students' lives. The teacher tries to interest pupils in *ideas,* rather than in mechanical or pedantic preparation of content. Proper choice and presentation of good literature can be intellectually stimulating, aesthetically desirable, and highly practical. Free-time reading, library research, and the building of the student's personal library help to foster such goals. In contrast

FIGURE 9. "A Scene" by Bob

to the influence of comic books, "cheap" novels, and other
undesirable literature (Lovaas, 1961; Maslow, 1954), good literature provides them with models and identifying figures who
can help them grow emotionally as well as intellectually.

Inability to communicate well how one feels and to understand how others feel is characteristic of some mental health
problems. (As a result, psychotherapy tends to stress improvement of communication; the therapist endeavors to help the
patient discover how he feels and formulate this understanding
so that he can communicate to the therapist. Some therapists
also believe that the mere talking about one's problems can lead
to self-analysis and improvement in mental health. Because we
hide unpleasant or threatening thoughts from ourselves as well
as from others, we find ourselves unable to communicate them;
the lifting of such repression is therefore of therapeutic value.)

Not only do people have difficulty in communicating their
real feelings to others, hence fail to be their "real" selves—or
"congruent," as C. R. Rogers (1958) terms it—but they fail to

understand how others feel. One tends to attribute his own ideas to others; he projects upon them his own interpretations of how they must think and feel. As a result, here again he does not communicate on a clear, realistic basis. The resulting social interaction is thus inadequate.

For many children, improvement in expressing their ideas and feelings, learning to better understand how others feel, and gaining a better idea of what they, themselves, communicate about themselves to others, would result in improved social relationships. Many are too defensive. Some are highly inhibited. Some fail to really listen to others. Communications skills might help to solve such problems.

SCIENCE AND MATHEMATICS

Our initial illustration (page 222) was about a science class. We showed how children were learning to observe, to hypothesize, to generalize and apply, and to evaluate. We showed how curiosity was stimulated, and how problem solving and reasoning were encouraged. These are goals for positive mental health. Coping skills are frequently highly cognitive, and the ability to cope with problems is important in building adequate personalities.

Although many scientific "truths" are substantially enough proved so that they must be precisely learned and applied, science is by no means entirely exact. The same is true of mathematics, which is continually providing new insights. Thus while there are certain satisfactions (and challenges) in following a problem-solving process to a common conclusion with that of the authorities, there is also considerable room for divergent or creative thinking. Furthermore, desirable attitudes can be fostered in science and mathematics, e.g., the willingness to accept solutions to problems, even though the answers may be distasteful; the willingness to reserve judgment, to test conclusions, to seek facts rather than opinions, to critically weigh the ideas of others; and the willingness to tolerate frustrations and learn from mistakes. When these school subjects are taught from the viewpoint of the thought processes involved, rather than mere exposition of content, such values can be fostered.

HOME ECONOMICS

Both the content and activities of this field offer possibilities for personal and social development. Since improved health and personal appearance can contribute to self-confidence and acceptability to others, the topics studied in home economics classes are "naturals" for fostering mental health. When a dowdy girl transforms herself into a charming person, when proper nutrition improves physical condition, or when the learning of etiquette improves self-confidence in social situations, good adjustment is fostered.

Perhaps one of the greatest contributions home economics can make to mental health is that of studying marriage and child care. A strong emphasis in the mental-health movement is that of prevention of mental-health problems by providing optimal home environments to infants and children. This, in turn, starts with the making of a good marriage. If today's young people can become better parents than were their parents' generation, a great deal can be done in this preventive mode. The study of boy-girl relationships, sex, choice of marital partner, the needs of children, and similar subjects can contribute to such constructive efforts. The inclusion of boys as well as girls in home-economics classes would seem to be a desirable trend, especially from this standpoint.

OTHER SUBJECTS

We have touched upon only a few of the school subjects which are taught. We have no wish to slight any, and have no value judgments concerning the merits of any content or teaching areas. It is quite obvious, for example, that physical education can contribute to mental health in many ways, including learning the value of teamwork, having opportunities for leadership roles, and gaining confidence that comes with successful effort. Music can lead to improved expression of oneself. The study of agriculture may involve the study of human relationships. It is the hope of the writer that each teacher can find in his subject the content and activities which lead to improved pupil adjustment, utilizing the above illustrations only as examples of a few of the means for so doing.

Extracurricular Activities and Mental Health

It is quite obvious that extraclass activities, which include YMCA and YWCA and Boy Scout and Girl Scout activities as well as school clubs, forensics, musical organizations, athletics, and others, can foster mental-health goals just as can class-time activities.

A difference exists, however, in that the activities are both voluntary and exclusive. Several kinds of dangers exist, as well as several possible advantages, in inducting children into such activities. It is clear that many children and youths who might profit from the companionship, service, recognition, and fun aspects of extracurricular programs do not volunteer for them, because of shyness, lack of feeling of belonging, cost, lack of time, or other reasons. As a result, those children who are already adequate tend to be those who enter into and profit most from such activities. It is also clear that a high degree of ability, acceptability, a certain social-class status, or other prerequisites operate in regard to a number of such activities—so that cliques and in-groups are fostered to the detriment of those who are kept out. It is easily documented that such problems exist.

Any activities sponsored or abetted by the school should make provision for all children who desire to participate, and those who "most need" such activities should be helped to participate. If the present program cannot provide for certain kinds of children, it is obvious that expansion is needed.

Learning Activities and Mental Health

THE "CAUSAL" APPROACH

One way to help students gain the insights from their lessons that have been recommended is for the teacher to use the "causal" approach. This term, employed by Ojemann, *et al.* (1955), R. E. Muuss (1960), and others, refers to a difference in attitude and practice from the more typical "surface" approach used by many teachers.

The surface approach and causal approach differ in the following ways:

1. In the surface approach the teacher responds to behavior, to what happens, and is angry or pleased or otherwise reacts emotionally to *what the child does*. In the causal approach the teacher tries to understand *why* the child acts as he does and strives for objectivity.

2. In the surface approach the teacher tends to label a behavior "good" or "bad," "moral" or "immoral." In the causal approach the teacher avoids hasty interpretations and evaluations of behavior until he understands its purposes and meanings to the child.

3. The teacher using the surface approach makes such generalizations as "All ten-year-olds are like that," or, "What can you expect from slum children?" In the causal approach the teacher looks for the specific clues that trigger each child's behavior. He recognizes that each child responds individually to each situation.

4. The surface approach prompts the teacher to use rule-of-thumb procedures, "tricks of the trade," and stock solutions to problems. In the causal approach he varies his methods according to his understanding of the causes of the pupils' behavior.

5. The teacher employing the surface approach fails to consider that behavior is caused by the interaction of many factors. The causally oriented teacher recognizes that behavior is complex and that therefore control of behavior may also be complex.

6. In the surface approach the teacher fails to consider the later effects of his techniques, merely assuming that they will be successful and not produce detrimental side effects. In the causal approach the teacher follows up his acts with future observation to see whether he has helped the child or not. If the latter seems to be the case, the teacher alters his tactics.

7. The surface approach is characterized by a rigidity of techniques, whereas the causal approach is flexible.

In summation, the causally oriented teacher tries to think diagnostically. Although he may make mistakes, continued attempts to do so will sensitize the teacher to clues to child behavior and will suggest alternative hypotheses and ways of handling problems. The emphasis of the causal approach is on the pupil as a learner, rather than on subject matter for its own sake. Granted the need for certain common knowledge, this knowledge will not be useful unless accepted and applied by the learner. By trying to view the learning situation from the point of view of motives, meanings, social interaction, and implications, the teacher thus learns to employ the causal approach but does not need to "take on" any particularly "new" teaching behavior. That is, he simply looks at the teaching situation in a somewhat different way.

CHANGES IN PUPIL PERCEPTIONS

Ojemann (1955) and others (Snider, n.d.; Hawkins, 1959) have shown that pupils can learn to employ the causal approach, as well as teachers. Helping them to do so depends on how the subject is taught. Even elementary-school children as young as kindergarten, however, are able to grasp the basic idea and put it to serious use.

Although much of the experimental work by Ojemann and others was done in social studies classes and in the primary and intermediate grades, the basic concepts can be applied to any level or teaching field. Teaching that has incorporated these objectives (although not necessarily phrased in the same language) has met with successes in such classes as those of the core curriculum in Evanston, the Horace Mann School, and in various colleges. Essentially such classes attempt to orient students toward individual and group problem solving, improvement in human relations and understanding of the dynamics of group interaction, the study of oneself as an individual, and self-direction in personal improvement. Acceptance of responsibility, openness to ideas of others, and improvement in decision making are other outcomes. Most such classes emphasize teacher-pupil planning, evaluation of progress by both the individual student and the class, and the use of content material related to real issues in the lives of the pupils.

If we seem to confuse training in human relations with teaching for mental health, one must recognize that, although not entirely synonymous, both goals have much in common. As one learns to improve human relations, he minimizes his conflicts with others; he also learns how others have handled problems similar to his. He learns to examine his own motives and is freer to develop more mature social and emotional behavior. Success gained through such insights contributes to an enhanced self-concept and frequently to greater acceptance of others. Adaptive, rather than maladaptive, behavior tends to be strengthened.

CREATIVITY

Although it is clear that everyone must attain a degree of communality with others so that a cohesive society can exist, it is undoubtedly true that most of the needed changes in social living and the majority of contributions to enriching our lives are made by creative people. Creative people are, in many ways, self-actualizing; they tend to be independent, willing not to conform when independence seems desirable, prone to experiencing life in their individual ways, and are able to transcend the ordinary.

From the point of view of conforming to the concept of "normal," creative individuals do not fare too well. They may have more conflicts, or more severe conflicts, than others; many show signs of stress in their efforts to achieve their creative goals. On the other hand, they may outshine less creative people in many desirable traits and abilities.

DEFINITION OF CREATIVITY. ▪ E. P. Torrance (1963) suggests that creativity is

. . . sometimes contrasted to conformity and is defined as the contribution of original ideas, a different point of view, or a new way of looking at problems; whereas conformity is defined as doing what is expected without disturbing or causing trouble for others. . . . Creativity has been also defined as a successful step into the unknown, getting away from the main track, breaking out of the mold, being open to experience and permitting one thing to lead to another, recombining ideas or seeing new relationships among ideas, and so on. Such concepts as curiosity, imagination, discovery, innovation, and invention are also prominent in discussions of creativity. (1963, p. 4)

In regard to identifying creative behavior, Torrance says that included are

> . . . originality in behavior (e.g. unusual solutions, unusual answers, and unusual approaches to problem solving) ; imagination (e.g. fantasy and story-telling) ; nonconforming behavior (not bothered by pressures to conform) ; unusual perceptiveness of relationships; an overflow of ideas; experimentation; unusual flexibility in meeting emergencies; unwillingness to give up; constructiveness; daydreaming and preoccupation with an idea or problem; and going beyond assigned tasks. (*Ibid.,* p. 12)

CHARACTERISTICS OF CREATIVE PEOPLE. ■ Creative children seem to gain a reputation for having wild or silly ideas and their work is frequently off-beat. They are frequently humorous and playful (Torrance, *et al.,* 1960) . Because of characteristics such as these, they may irritate teachers, especially when they disrupt conforming activities planned for the group. Also, some teachers cannot tolerate divergent points of view, especially if they, themselves, are not creative; these teachers are threatened and there is friction with the child.

Creativity and intelligence are not necessarily synonymous. It is generally conceded that the more intelligent one is, the more ideas he can muster for his creative talents; on the other hand, some bright children are not creative, since their efforts are directed toward convergent, rather than divergent thinking and activity.

F. Barron (1958) suggested that creative people are especially observant; they often express "part truths, but the part they express is the generally unrecognized, by displacement of accent and apparent disproportion in statement they seek to point to the usually unobserved" (1958, p. 4) . They appear to be independent and value clear understanding, going to great lengths to seek such understanding. They lead more complex lives and deal more with fantasy and imagination. They are flexible and broad in their awareness of themselves. Barron suggests that "the creative person is both more primitive and more cultured, more destructive and more constructive, crazier and saner, than the average person." In other words, the creative person is more of an individual; however, he may be viewed by others as somewhat lacking in balance.

Notice the close interrelationship between autonomy, self-actualization, and creativity. All seem to need to break away from the confines of others' thinking and of dependency upon the evaluations of others. A. H. Maslow agrees (1954). He states that the creativeness of the self-actualized man is related to the native and universal creativeness of unspoiled children and implies that all of us are creative at birth, but lose this quality as we develop. When behavior is viewed as an expression of a healthy personality, then anyone will seem creative (but not all can be creative to the same degree). Self-actualizing people are creative, since they are less inhibited, less constricted, and less enculturated, hence seem to see the true and real more easily.

J. W. McKenney (1964) stresses that creative people may appear one-sided. They do not seem well-rounded, and they resist reshaping.

In essence, the creative person has an idea he is pursuing; he is highly motivated, and will go to considerable lengths to pursue his goals. In one sense, he may be somewhat socially less well-adjusted than others; in another sense, however, because he does not overconform, he may be better adjusted than average.

FOSTERING CREATIVITY. ▪ J. P. Guilford (1959) refers to divergent, as opposed to convergent, thinking in his model for structure of intellect. Divergent thinking, of course, is not the only characteristic of creative thinking, but seems to be a basic ingredient. Creative behavior includes originality, of course, but also involves an attempt to solve a problem—that is, there is an element of purpose behind it. An act is not creative merely by being different—in some way it must be aimed at doing something better than it was done before. This suggests that convergent thinking, evaluation, and, in B. S. Bloom's (1956) terms, analysis, synthesis, and evaluation objectives must be sought.

It is frequently considered that small children, especially in their play, seem highly imaginative. They appear to be more creative than older children, and it might be that creative acts are natural to people, but that our efforts are stifled as we mature. Torrance (1963) feels that blocks are thrown in the way of children's creative efforts. In addition to stifling spontaneity and initiative, parents and teachers continually refer to "reality," and play down imagination and fantasy. The peer-oriented culture, too, emphasizes conformity. American culture emphasizes success, pointing to the need for few errors and the penalties of failure; it equates divergence with abnormality or delinquency; work is not supposed to be play; and there seems to be misplaced emphasis on sex-role differences. In the schools, he suggests, there is overemphasis on the acquisition of knowledge, finding known answers to problems, reliance on textbooks and other authorities. The lecture system, departmentalization of subjects, and the closely prescribed curriculum block creative effort in that they not only foster conforming learning activities, but tend to preclude seeing new relationships among content. Too, there is too infrequently sufficient time for the child to experiment in his efforts to be creative.

To illustrate, the writer at one time taught geometry in high school. The Pythagorean theorem concerning the relationships between the legs and hypotenuse of a right triangle was taught "from the book," and the various parts of the proof were memorized. He penalized students for failure to conform to the prescribed proof. One day a young person came in with a different proof. He offered this as original, wondering if it could be acceptable for extra credit. Careful examination showed that this proof, indeed, was valid. The boy was rewarded.

It was not until later that the writer learned that there were some seventy known proofs to this theorem and that the pupil's proof approximated one of them. From that time on, students were urged to develop their own figures and proofs of theorems, and even to try to find theorems of their own. It was eye-opening to see what they could do, once freed from "authority." (And, incidentally, motivation to study geometry increased tremendously.)

Creativity can be fostered in many ways. The essential ingredient is to show that creative efforts are prized, and that penalties will not be forthcoming if solutions to problems are not always satisfactory. The teacher must, himself, prize originality, and insofar as he can, be a model for creative effort.

It is difficult to be creative without "something to be creative about." This statement has several implications: First, background is needed; new relationships cannot be sought, if there is a lack of knowledge to work with. This suggests that a wide acquaintance with the media in which one is working is essential. Thus writers should read widely, artists should see many paintings, musicians should read and hear many composers, and so on. Secondly, it is useful to help students find problems as starting points. Some of J. P. Guilford's tests of fluency, for example, suggest means for stimulating ideas. (How many uses can you find for a brick? What would we need to change if all the people in the world were three feet tall? Where, in the house, can one best hide a twelve-foot length of clothesline?)

Businesses find success in the "brainstorming" technique. Meeting in small groups, salesmen, engineers, and others speculate concerning their products. How could this product be made better? More cheaply? Of different materials? How could it be better designed to appeal to more users? No ideas, no matter how wild, are discarded, for they may be the starting point for some really creative effort.

Time is required for creativity, and it must be provided. Reinforcement for perseverance, productivity, and fluency should be provided. Examples of the creative efforts of others, the sensitizing of pupils to feelings and emotions as well as cognitive material, the critical appraisal of existing efforts—all can suggest needed changes and ways one might proceed.

In essence, just as "correct" responses, essentially convergent thinking, can be reinforced, so can divergent thinking. If this philosophy and value system is really followed, rather than merely given lip service, we will do much to free children for creative efforts of all kinds, as well as to free them for being individuals rather than carbon-copies of whatever prevailing stereotype exists at the time.

GROUP ACTIVITIES

A number of goals can be sought through such group activities as projects, discussions, panels, and the like. Social interaction may be enhanced, pupils may learn more about others and their ideas, and they can try out their own ideas on others.

Communication and other social skills can be improved. A feeling of belonging; an opportunity to gain self-esteem, status, and recognition; chances to identify and to imitate—all may be fostered in group situations.

H. J. Klausmeier (1953) states that group activities provide opportunities for a favorable relationship between students and teacher and for enhancing motivation by establishing purposes and group goals. Some of the broader types of problems such as are met outside the school in social groups (for example, home, church, neighborhood, community) can be discussed; ways of attacking these problems can be learned or improved on.

Self-actualization also can be fostered in group activities. Clarification of the ideas and feelings of others permits one to learn to what extent his own ideas and feelings are different, and to what extent it is necessary or expedient to conform. Because one can recognize and clarify social problems in group situations, it is possible to find a greater understanding of and identification with society as a whole. It is partly by learning what others are like, and by comparing oneself with them, that self-actualization may be fostered.

This is not a book on teaching methodology *per se* so we shall not delve into ways of handling discussions or other teaching practices. But we should like to make a special point here that group activities are useful for teaching affective as well as cognitive skills. Not only can one learn by imitation, but groups can reinforce various ways of reacting emotionally. Attitudes are learned and values are developed.

Affective behavior implies experiencing feelings and emotions, rather than just talking about them. A way of providing such experiences deliberately is role-playing, in which problems are posed and pupils act out their feelings and ideas. Sometimes prepared dramas can be of help. The writer has had some success using those supplied by the National Association for Mental Health (Gilmore, 1958; Stirling, 1955).

VALUES AND PURPOSES OF INDIVIDUAL ACTIVITIES

Individual activities such as studying at one's seat, library research, programmed instruction, or the language arts laboratory are also useful in fostering development of healthy behavior. The development of coping skills, independence, responsibility, individual problem solving, creative activities, self-evaluation, and ability to respond adequately to frustration can be fostered through individual activities by precept, example, and proper reinforcement. Klausmeier (1953) refers to satisfying the "need for mastery over things," and for helping able and retarded students by providing opportunities to differentiate tasks. The building of independence is stressed.

Essentially the above paragraphs have suggested that both group and individual activities can be beneficial for mental health and personality development. The task of the teacher is to arrange the situations with these goals in mind, and help pupils engage in their tasks in desirable ways.

GROUP VERSUS INDIVIDUAL EMPHASIS

Man is a social being. He depends for many of his satisfactions on the acceptance and support of the group, hence it is incumbent upon him to learn to live successfully with others. However, he is also an individual, and must not be submerged by paying too much attention to satisfying the group, at the risk of failing to satisfy himself. Optimal adjustment would suggest that each person learn to live his own life in a satisfying way, within the context of society; that is, he should be able to satisfy both the social group and himself by the same set of behaviors.

It must be recognized, however, that this is not always possible, for society itself has many conflicts. For this reason, it is not always possible to be autonomous and self-actualizing as desired. Compromises must be made by most of us. It is the ability to most satisfactorily make such compromises and to adapt to situations successfully that probably represents the best "adjustment."

□

REFERENCES

Barron, F. "The Psychology of Imagination," *Scientific American*, 199 (1958), 150–66.
Bloom, B. S. (ed.). *Taxonomy of Educational Objectives. Handbook I: Cognitive Domain*. New York: Longmans, 1956.
Gilmore, L. *Which Way Out?* New York: National Association for Mental Health, 1958.

Guilford, J. P. "Three Faces of Intellect," *American Psychologist,* 14 (1959), 469–79.

Hawkins, A. S. *A Primer in Human Behavior for Kindergarten and First Grade.* Iowa City: State University of Iowa Preventive Psychiatry Program, 1959.

Klausmeier, H. J. *Principles and Practices of Secondary School Teaching,* pp. 276–8. New York: Harper, 1953.

Lovaas, O. I. "Effect of Exposure to Symbolic Aggression on Aggressive Behavior," *Child Development,* 32 (1961), 37–44.

McKenney, J. W. "Identification of Creative Persons," *Classroom Teachers Association Journal,* 60 (1964), 5–7.

Maslow, A. H. *Motivation and Personality.* New York: Harper, 1954.

Muuss, R. E. "The Effects of a One- and Two-Year Causal Learning Program," *Journal of Personality,* 28 (1960), 479–91.

Ojemann, R. H. *Developing a Program for Education in Human Behavior.* Iowa City: State University of Iowa Preventive Psychiatry Program, 1959.

———. "An Integrated Plan for Education in Human Relations and Mental Health," *Journal of the National Association of Deans of Women,* 16 (1953), 101–8.

Ojemann, R. H., E. E. Levitt, W. H. Lyle, Jr., and M. Whiteside. "The Effects of a 'Causal' Teacher-Training Program and Certain Curricular Changes on Grade School Children," *Journal of Experimental Education,* 24 (1955), 95–114.

Rogers, C. R. "Characteristics of a Helping Relationship," *Personnel and Guidance Journal,* 37 (1958), 6–15.

Schramm, W., J. Lyle, and E. B. Parker. *Television in the Lives of Our Children.* Stanford: Stanford University Press, 1961.

Snider, B. C. F. *Relation of Growth in Causal Orientation to Insecurity in Elementary School Children.* Iowa City: State University of Iowa Preventive Psychiatry Program, n.d.

Stiles, F. S. "Developing an Understanding of Human Behavior at the Elementary School Level," *Journal of Educational Research,* 43 (1959), 516–24.

Stirling, N. *Tomorrow Is a Day.* New York: American Theatre Wing, 1955.

Torrance, E. P. *Creativity.* Washington, D.C.: National Education Association, 1963.

Torrance, E. P., J. E. Bowers, H. J. Rodig, N. Palmuth, and P. R. Krishnaish. *Minnesota Studies of Creative Thinking in the Early School Years.* Minneapolis: University of Minnesota Bureau of Educational Research, 1960.

Zelen, S. L. *Effect of a Causal Learning Program.* Iowa City: Child Welfare Research Station, Preventive Psychiatry Project, 1954.

SUGGESTIONS FOR FURTHER READING

Bonney, M. E. *Mental Health in Education,* chaps. 12, 13. Boston: Allyn & Bacon, 1960.
These chapters discuss classroom grouping, pupil participation, group discussion, and role-playing activities.

Kaplan, L. *Mental Health and Human Relations in Education*, chap. 13. New York: Harper, 1959.
Chapter 13 discusses the teaching of mental hygiene, mentions some resource materials, and evaluates the effects of mental-hygiene education.

Mouly, G. J. *Psychology for Effective Teaching*, chaps. 13, 18. New York: Holt, Rinehart, Winston, 1960.
These chapters discuss attitudes and character formation and also provide a "psychological re-orientation" of the modern classroom.

Phillips, B. N., R. L. Duke, and M. Vere DeVault. *Psychology at Work in the Elementary School Classroom*, Part I. New York: Harper, 1960.
The chapters in Part I deal with classroom organization, small-group discussions, patterns of interpersonal relationships, and factors in cohesiveness of small groups.

9

COMMON SOURCES
OF STRESS
IN SCHOOLS

A stress may be defined as a condition resulting from frustration, conflict, or pressures placed upon an individual. It may be primarily a result of the person's own motives and behaviors, or it may be induced by his environment. Although some stresses are primarily physical in nature, we will confine ourselves to psychological stress conditions, which usually result in strong emotional tension. Because of their individual characteristics, some pupils face greater and more continued stress than others; equally, some pupils are more able than others to cope with the stresses they meet.

As everyone meets periods of unusual stress at times, learning to deal with such conditions efficiently is important. The ability to do so is, indeed, one criterion of the healthy personality. But stresses can be too severe and may extend beyond one's abilities to meet them, and then deterioration of mental health is bound to occur. Everyone has a "breaking point" where, if pressure continues, behavior deteriorates. For this reason teachers should both wish to help pupils learn to deal with stress, and hope to avoid causing unnecessary stresses themselves.

Stress is cumulative in its effects. Just as "little drops of water wear away the hardest stone," so can apparently minor stresses eventually break through one's defenses. Sometimes this process can be quite dramatic as the following story, related by a teacher, will indicate:

We had an incident at our school the other day which caused me to consider how little we frequently know about our boys and girls. One of our kids took a sock at a teacher, and really beat him up. The teacher preferred charges and Pete is now in jail.

This was the culmination of a series of defiant acts on the part of Pete, and it wasn't the first time he had tried to get tough around the school, although most of his fighting was with boys outside of school.

The way it came about was this: Pete had just turned in his math paper, at the desk, and on his way back to his seat he stopped to look out of the window. Mr. Jones asked him to take his seat, but Pete just stood there. So then Mr. Jones ordered him to sit down, but Pete wouldn't. When Mr. Jones came up to him, Pete got sort of angry looking and defiant, and when the teacher put his hand on Pete's shoulder, Pete swung at him and really bruised him.

Two of the other boys grabbed Pete so he couldn't do any more damage, and they walked him down to the office. Pete wouldn't apologize and didn't seem sorry, so much as sort of desperate. He said that he was tired of "people picking on him all of the time" and "wasn't going to stand for any more of it."

Later, when we knew more about it, we understood the problem better. One clue came from the principal's secretary. She is an older woman, and apparently she and Pete had a pretty friendly relationship. Pete would sometimes come in and talk to her, and tell her about his problems, which were generally centered about his home and family. He would tell her how his father would tell him—not ask him—to do something, and if Pete didn't follow through, he would be physically handled by his father. And his mother was "always nagging" at him to do this or that. This seemed like normal complaining, until it happened that one day this secretary said something like "Pete, I feel about you just like one of my own sons, and I'm trying to help you." At that Pete became livid and he more than cussed her out.

You can see what has happened. Constant friction with his parents has made Pete sensitive to others, and he cordially dislikes, if not hates, his parents. So far, he had not transferred these feelings to the teachers directly, that is, in the form of action. He'd mostly kept his feelings pretty well bottled up inside him. But he'd steadily been getting more frustrated and irritable, to the point where he couldn't take a direct order from anyone, and resented being made to do anything. Finally, he just exploded.

The reader will appreciate the need for some therapeutic counseling to desensitize Pete to authority relationships, so that he can take orders without becoming angry. It is also clear that Pete may have to be removed from the home situation unless the parents can be aided to deal with him in ways that do not continually irritate him. Pete must be helped to learn to control his behavior. Though it is permissible for pupils to have feelings, it is not permissible for them to "act out" their angry feelings with danger to themselves or others. Finally, because his experiences in this school may have produced feelings in Pete and others that would be almost impossible to erase, it should be carefully considered whether or not Pete should be placed in a different school situation.

The teacher who was involved with Pete needs some training in understanding others. A more sensitive person would have realized that Pete was in a rather desperate emotional state and would not have pushed him into loss of control; the sensitive teacher might have found ways to help Pete save face, to relax a bit, and perhaps even to get Pete to discuss his problems with the teacher or counselor at a later time. It is also debatable whether or not Pete should have been placed in jail except, possibly, for safe-keeping. His problems require clinical help, rather than punitive measures.

Children sometimes are placed in situations that produce anger, fear, humiliation, discouragement, and depression. We shall concern ourselves with some of these conditions as they apply to the school setting, but the reader can make his own applications to other situations that produce stress of which he may be aware. A few of the common stress conditions in schools that we shall consider are grouping policies; promotional policies; tests, marks, and grading; and school-related stresses arising from socioeconomic class factors.

Common Curricular Stress-Producing Conditions

J. Holt (1964), in a provocative book based on his experiences as a teacher and his efforts to see why stress experiences occur, makes a strong case for the notion that children's goals in school are not usually those of wishing to learn, but to "get the right answers" and to "please the teacher." He feels that children develop a number of strategies to do this, many of which have little to do with real learning or understanding, and few of which are related to motivation to pursue a school subject further, when coercion has been removed. In a word, Holt suggests that pupil behavior is frequently based on fear. For example, he says:*

. . . The strategies of most of these kids have been consistently self-centered, self-protective, aimed above all else at avoiding trouble, embarrassment, punishment, disapproval, or loss of status. This is particularly true of the ones who have had a tough time in school. When they get a problem, I can read their thoughts on their faces, I can almost hear them, "Am I going to get this right? Probably not; what'll happen to me when I get it wrong? Will the teacher get mad? Will the other kids laugh at me? Will my mother and father hear about it? Will they keep me back this year? Why am I so dumb?" And so on.

Even in the room periods, where I did all I could to make the work non-threatening, I was continually amazed and appalled to see the children hedging their bets, covering their losses in advance, trying to fix things so that whatever happened they could feel they had been right, or if wrong, no more wrong than anyone else . . . They are fence-straddlers, afraid ever to commit themselves . . .

What is most surprising of all is how much fear there is in school. Why is so little said about it? Perhaps most people do not recognize fear in children when they see it. . . . the subtler signs of fear escape them. It is these signs, in children's faces, voices, and gestures, in their movements and ways of working, that tell me plainly that most children in school are scared most of the time, many of them very scared. Like good soldiers, they control their fears, live with them, and adjust themselves to them. But the trouble is, and here is a vital difference between school and war, that the adjustments children make to their fears are almost wholly bad, destructive of their intelligence and capacity. The scared fighter may be the best fighter, but the scared learner is always a poor learner.

If it is true, and it really does seem likely, that many children are suffering from anxiety and fear in school, then it seems

* source: J. Holt, *How Children Fail* (New York: Pitman, 1964), p. 48.

logical to arrange the curriculum in ways that provide each child with maximum chances for success, and minimize the likelihood of failure. Furthermore, children need to learn to live with failure in healthy ways—which suggests that the penalties for failure should be reduced, but also that children should be helped to withstand stress. We shall begin by studying the effects of curricular practices on children's achievement and mental health.

GROUPING POLICIES

Pupils are frequently placed in school classrooms according to estimates of their abilities and achievements. There are honors classes, classes for the gifted, regular classes, remedial classes, classes for the emotionally disturbed, the mentally retarded; and, as of this writing, a number of classes are appearing for the culturally "impoverished" or educationally "deprived." Presumably special grouping improves both school achievement and social and emotional outlook of pupils. We shall address ourselves briefly to these questions.

GROUPING AND ACHIEVEMENT. ■ Deciding which pupils belong in the various classes is done on many bases, among them the recommendations of the regular classroom teacher who feels that a child is not profiting from the present grouping and testing by guidance counselors, school psychologists, or others.

It is patent that, no matter how children are grouped, insofar as abilities are concerned grouping will reduce differences in some dimensions, but may actually increase differences in others. Even in a so-called "homogeneous" group, abilities range almost as far as in a nonability-grouped class. This range suggests that children should probably be grouped in one manner for one purpose, and in another manner for another purpose; however, for economic reasons (among others) this sort of grouping is rather unlikely to be followed.

Given rather permanent special groups or classes, what is known about achievement? Studies differ in their findings. H. J. Otto (1954), reviewing much of the literature on grouping, reports that "homogeneous grouping" favors dull, average, and bright children in that order. On the other hand E. Drews

(1959) and M. Bell (1957) found homogeneous grouping to benefit most pupils.

Probably R. B. Ekstrom (1961) comes closest to explaining differential findings. She agrees that experimental studies of grouping have shown a great variety of experimental designs and no consistent pattern of results; but she is not surprised, for many of the experiments failed to control the type of teaching or to differentiate materials for different ability levels. Where experiments provided for different materials and for different methods of teaching at the various ability levels, results tended to favor homogeneous grouping. For example, bright students do not always fare better in special groupings—sometimes because nothing new or more profound is given them and they are simply given *more* work at the same average level of difficulty. Given curriculum enrichment, however, bright students flourish in grouped situations (Parker, 1956). Essentially, then, the value of homogeneous grouping seems to depend upon the differences in methods and materials from those employed in nonhomogeneous classes.

Among the alleged advantages and disadvantages of homogeneous grouping are the following:

ADVANTAGES	DISADVANTAGES
The child should feel more at home with his peers, as they are more like him in ability than are those in the regular class.	Children in slow groups may feel stigmatized; those in fast groups may feel superior.
The child will be challenged but will be given work he can successfully do.	Grouping may minimize some ability differences but may increase other differences.
Children can be tested over a narrower range of achievement, and evaluation can thus be more accurate.	Teachers may be reluctant to work with certain groups or may lack training required for work with some special classes.
Class members may find it easier to work together, for they may understand one another better.	Individual differences may not be recognized or valued, as pupils are grouped for like abilities.

ADVANTAGES	DISADVANTAGES
With a narrower range of abilities, teachers can plan and manage better.	Grouping practices may become formalized and rigid and fail to take into account pupil changes over time.
Children can progress in accordance with their development, rather than in lock-step.	Teaching may become subject-centered, formal, and uninspired, particularly with low-ability pupil groups.
Pupils may find it easier to engage in projects, panels, and the like, for their interests and abilities may be much more alike.	Because of demands placed on certain pupils (like the gifted), mental health may be threatened.
Unnecessary stress and frustration can be avoided. Feelings of adequacy, self-esteem, and reinforcements from success should improve mental health.	The pupil's entire academic and vocational career may be predetermined.

GROUPING AND PERSONALITY VARIABLES ■ It has been advanced that average or dull pupils may resent having bright pupils grouped in honors classes by themselves (Franseth, 1963); parents, too, may resent having their neighbors' children in more advanced classes than their own children, and considerable pressure may be placed on borderline achievers to work harder and avoid placement in "inferior" groups. (This, by the way, sometimes extends to parents doing their children's homework for them, and to having children trained for situations in which they will be tested and screened. The latter can also be seen in the instance of the bright child. Some prestige high schools and colleges are finding that standard intelligence tests must be replaced by specially designed instruments because answer keys to the usual tests are being sold, or children are being trained in the proper answers.)

It can be argued that the child with somewhat inferior academic ability can learn from his peers, and that he can keep up with them socially and physically. On the other hand, he may simply stand out from his peers as not being very bright; he may react by becoming the class clown, withdrawing, or acting in an aggressive or hostile way.

Gifted children, especially those who are extremely gifted, may have problems in gaining peer acceptance. In some instances they may be leaders in the regular classroom and be respected by other children, but on the other hand, they may not be socially accepted by their less-gifted peers and become lonely and isolated in the upper grades and in high school (Kaluger & Martin, 1960). Which outcome results appears to be a function of personality and talents other than those of academic achievement.

RECOMMENDED PRACTICES. ▪ The way grouping is carried out is important, primarily because individual abilities vary so widely. Some who are excellent at mathematics may be poor in reading. Some who are high in language skills may be poor in psychomotor abilities. Personality variables compound the difficulties. Each advantage or disadvantage must be multiplied by the number of children involved, so that probably no standard cut-off points or similar cut-and-dried procedures should be used in selecting children for the various groups. Essentially, placement of the child must depend not only on his pattern of intellectual, physical, and even cultural assets and liabilities, but on his emotional maturity, friendship choices, and the attitudes of pupil, parent, and teacher.

Placing a child in a special group must be tentative, so that if his transfer is unsuccessful, he may be returned to his original group or tried in another situation. Transfers into and out of a group should be possible at any time; pupils placed in special groups should be continually studied and re-evaluated to see what changes are taking place in their attitudes and behaviors and to make certain that their abilities are not being stereotyped by teachers because they have been in certain groups for a period of years.

A special word should be said concerning placement of "disturbed" children in special classes. Sometimes, of course, this is advantageous both to the child and to the teacher and peers in the classroom which he may have been disrupting by his emotional behavior. On the other hand, many disturbed children can and should learn to live with others and should realize they can learn well in a "normal" situation. Furthermore, when children are placed in special classrooms, there is always the problem of helping them develop in ways which will permit them to return eventually to more natural groupings; in the special room they are, after all, likely to miss some of the learnings that take place in the regular room, and problems of readjustment may occur. Similar questions may be raised concerning the borderline mentally retarded. Other things being equal, one likes to keep such children in regular, rather than special classes, unless the advantages of such placement are overwhelming.

PROMOTIONAL POLICIES

Promotional policies are actually a variation on the topic of grouping, for, as can easily be seen, strict promotional policies may cause a piling up of slow learners in the early grades and result in more selected groups in upper grades or in high school. There are two aspects that must be considered: retention in grade when the pupil has not reached norms for promotion and acceleration when he has surpassed expectations. We shall briefly examine each.

RETENTION IN GRADE. ■ Two questions must be asked: What does retention do for academic achievement? What does it do for mental health?

By retention in grade, we mean holding back some children, who do not accomplish the quality or quantity of work that would prepare them for the next grade level. It can be argued that, when a child is advanced without being ready, he will fall farther and farther behind his class, posing a problem for succeeding teachers. Not only will he be at a disadvantage in handling the advanced new learning, but he may also become so frustrated that he gives up. He may be looked down upon by his classmates as "stupid" or a "goof-off"; he may use defenses like clowning or misbehavior; he may also lose motivation if he knows that he will be promoted regardless of accomplishment.

Such arguments have some validity. Research fails to show much advantage in retaining the slow learner in grade, however. W. H. Coffield and P. Blommers (1956) found that pupils retained a year in grade typically gained only six months in educational progress during the repeat year and still failed to achieve the norm *for the grade they were repeating.* They continued to remain behind their original groups. In seventh grade they were about on a par with pupils who had spent one year less in school. Slow learners who are promoted and those who are failed usually perform at about the same levels.

There are a number of reasons. First, unless real remedial help is provided, the child is faced with the same frustrating tasks that he faced the "first time around." Secondly, he is bored by being asked to cover the same content he has already covered. Third, he usually finds himself with the same teacher, and both pupil and teacher may have some reservations about each other.

It should be kept in mind that even under ideal conditions, children do not learn the same things or to the same degree. Individual differences *increase* rather than decrease with progress through school (although the curriculum and some teachers' assumptions would seem to point to the opposite). Aside from ability, cultural background and other factors indicate that some children just never can learn as much as others in a given space of time. It is not uncommon for a high-school freshman class to possess individuals ranging from as low as fourth-grade reading ability to as high as that of the typical college senior.

T. L. Torgerson and G. S. Adams (1954) suggested another aspect of the problem, namely, the quality as opposed to the quantity of educational content and skills which can be learned by slow as opposed to average or superior students. They maintain that slow learners are unable to handle symbolic material satisfactorily or to think abstractly as well as the faster learners; they are relatively unable to handle complex assignments; they are less able to work independently and to evaluate their own work. They are slower in thinking and responding; have fewer interests, shorter attention span; and quite naturally, lack motivation for many school tasks that others may enjoy.

B. Bloom, *et al.* (1956), in their *Taxonomy of Educational Objectives,* have suggested several levels of learning tasks in terms of higher order skills and abilities. Thus the child may learn information, meaning, application, evaluation, synthesis, and analysis of content. It should not be thought that all pupils can equally well handle all of these levels; it makes more sense to place the slower pupil at a content and task level for which he may achieve success, rather than to expect the same things of all pupils.

Remedial work will be necessary for the child who fails to achieve, regardless of whether he is promoted or not. Remedial efforts for failing pupils may provide amazing success, especially if their problems are educational or cultural, rather than highly related to ability.

In substance, unless the child has transferred in from another school with a considerably different curriculum (as is frequently the case with pupils from foreign countries), or unless he has been ill or caused to miss a major share of the year's work for some other reason, there seems little justification for retaining him in grade. More can be accomplished by studying his assets and liabilities, and placing tasks at a level he can handle.

One more point: Too frequently schools stress the deficiencies of pupils. There may be, on the other hand, much more to be gained by stressing their assets and talents. If one works from the standpoint of utilizing individual abilities, at least one of the benefits is that one can stress positive reinforcement, rather than the negative reinforcement that comes with working with disabilities.

In regard to adjustment, S. W. Dimond (1959) mentions that unpromoted children are typically too much bigger physically than their classmates to remain long with the new group, and that they are discouraged at being separated from their friends. E. R. Steadman (1959) favors *selective* retention, calling attention to the important variable of peer acceptance. It is evident that for many pupils, lowered self-esteem, feelings of rejection, teacher and parental pressure, decreased motivation, and other socioemotional variables preclude successful retention except in the unusual circumstances just mentioned. (If threat of failure is the only way to motivate pupils, from a mental-health and achievement point of view one is better off not to try to motivate them at all.)

In general, there are both achievement and personality variables to consider, and it would seem that retention in grade does not usually improve achievement enough to warrant the risks to adjustment which are involved. Special attention to needed remediation seems much more warrantable.

ACCELERATION. ▪ Acceleration, too, should depend on the characteristics of the individual child. The writer remembers one girl who was promoted from seventh to ninth grade with complete success. She was physically and emotionally mature enough for this step, however; in church school she habitually associated with an older group; she and her parents both wanted the double promotion; and her intellectual ability and academic background warranted this move.

Universities have admitted youths as young as twelve and fourteen years old into the freshman program. Results have varied. Typically, the youth does not encounter academic problems, but he may suffer problems of social adjustment, inability to keep up in physical-education classes, difficulty in finding girls to date, and similar difficulties relating to size or maturity. Some resolve such problems by associating with age-mates outside the campus setting. Others, however, adjust very well to life with older students.

As there are other ways of aiding gifted students—for example, honors classes, permission to take college work by correspondence or tutoring, extra electives, individualized study, work-study programs, and the like—automatic double promotions should not be employed, and careful study should be made of individual cases.

EVALUATIVE PRACTICES

Evaluation means to place a value on something. When evaluating a student's work the teacher subjectively decides whether it is of high quality, comparable to expectation in regard to his ability, and acceptable so far as class standards are concerned.

Evaluation is not the same as *measurement*. Measurement, usually made by testing, means to discover where the student's efforts lie in relation to a certain scale. Thus in assigning a mark or grade the teacher must first *measure* the child's attainment, and then *evaluate* it to determine whether it is good enough or not. Evaluation, then, cannot be better than the quality of measurement upon which it is based; in addition, value judgments must be made about the measured outcomes.

TESTING PROBLEMS. ▪ Some tests are inappropriate. They place a premium on factual knowledge, so that those who cram and are gifted in memorizing earn the best marks. Factual knowledge should be tested, but if this is all that is measured, some of the other competences of the pupil may not be considered.

Tests may reflect biases or points of view from which pupils are not permitted to differ. To this extent they do not favor critical thinking, creativity, pupil autonomy, or self-actualization. Many tests call for socially acceptable beliefs in their answer choices, influencing students to slant their answers in certain ways. Such tests provide the teacher with acceptable results from pupils—but are essentially erroneous in their outcomes.

Many tests encourage guesswork. Students who actually prepare may suffer through the blind luck of their classmates. Essay tests may favor the highly verbal student who can make a good case for himself without having much knowledge of the subject.

Tests may be limited to tasks on which the child does poorly. Too often they are aimed at finding what the child *does not know* rather than allowing him to show what he *does know.*

There are other problems of tests related to their construction and use. The reader is referred to such standard works as J. C. Stanley (1965) concerning problems of test construction, reliability, validity, and content analysis. In addition to the problems of tests themselves, *testing conditions* may be inadequate, test results may be put to improper uses, and much threat, tension, and anxiety may ensue.

TEST ANXIETY. ▪ In addition to problems related to tests themselves, there may be even more serious problems relating to the testing situation. Many pupils cannot give a fair performance on tests because of the threat imposed; whether they are habitually anxious children, or whether they are made anxious by the consequences of testing, many children suffer from what has been termed "test anxiety."

Psychological interest in "test anxiety" has resulted in scales which are specifically aimed at finding children's reactions to test taking; I. Sarason's Test Anxiety Scale for Children (Sarason, *et al.,* 1960) and R. Alpert and R. Haber's Achievement Anxiety Test (1960) have been frequently used to make such assessments. Findings tend to support the notion that the higher the pupil's intelligence, the less likely he is to suffer from test anxiety (Sarason, 1963). This likelihood suggests that such anxiety is rather specific to the idea of testing itself, in the sense that brighter children tend to expect better outcomes from taking tests; they have, in the past, probably received more positive and less negative reinforcement in the form of grades and test scores than have children of lower intelligence. Girls tend to score higher on the anxiety scales mentioned above, but boys tend to have higher "lie" scores, suggesting that girls are probably not more anxious than boys but are simply more honest in admitting it.

All in all, it would seem desirable to reduce the stresses caused by testing by concerning oneself with finding ways to reduce anxiety in the testing situation (see Chapter 7), by making certain that the tests themselves are appropriate, and by seeing to it that tests are not used as threats or as the whole basis for making important decisions about children. Tests are, after all, only one kind of evidence about learning or other variables being assessed. If they can be viewed by children as means of diagnosing errors, as providing evidence of accomplishment, and as ways of discovering how the teacher can improve his teaching, much stress due to testing can be removed.

MARKING AND GRADING PRACTICES. ▪ Most teachers like to think that they have "standards" for their classes to meet. Such standards imply that

1. all students *can* do the work;
2. all students *should* do the work;
3. all material was adequately taught;
4. the evaluation of pupil achievement was adequate.

An example of the existence of such assumptions is found in the case of certain schools in which children are required to attain certain scores on standardized achievement examinations to earn promotions, without real consideration for the fact that children differ widely in background, ability, and interests.

The use of established standards may have a number of mental health correlates. For example, overemphasis on grades, unreasonable demands upon pupils to prepare for tests, emphasis on comparing pupils with each other, and similar practices may lead to discouragement, lowered self-confidence, frustration, insecurity, and resentment. Some pupils rarely obtain the positive reinforcement of good grades, but are too frequently negatively reinforced. Others are reinforced for little effort. As many college students know, the competitive aspect of grades places much pressure upon them. Such pressures may not be justified when results upon personality and mental health are considered.

For example, consider the remarks of some teachers in —— High School.

Miss J. says that she is "going to give Emma a 'B' this time, to encourage her, even though her work really isn't that good." On the other hand, "Peter cheated on the final examination," so Mr. L. is giving him an "F" for the six weeks. "George *could* do better," so Mrs. J. will stimulate him with a "C" instead of his usual "B."

One must not forget that marks have far-reaching consequences. What do marks convey to these students or to their parents? Emma may be encouraged by Miss Jones, but, as she knows she hasn't really done well, she may also become confused. Furthermore, if Emma received quite a bit of help from Jane and if Jane received only a "C," there would be resentment. Miss Jones' integrity is in question, and some of the other pupils may try to butter her up instead of trying so hard to do well.

Peter may learn not to cheat (or to get caught cheating), but it seems a little severe to proclaim to all that he learned nothing in Mr. L.'s class during that grading period. Will his humiliation, his resentment, and his parents' reactions justify that failing mark?

George may react as hoped, yet, unless the students know that marks are given on achievement as related to ability, the situation will be misrepresented.

The present writer does not propose to discuss the marking system in any detail, for books on measurement and on teaching methodology can be of considerable help to the teacher in suggesting better means of marking and grading. The intent, in this chapter, is to suggest some of the inadequacies that result in unnecessary stress on pupils, which have correlates in both mental health and learning. There are some general points, however, that relate to evaluative practices generally:

1. Goals for pupils should be clearly stated, and should be broad enough to encompass the varying abilities of the children.
2. Assuming that the pupils try to do their best, it should be possible for all to attain some positive reinforcement from the marking practices; therefore a variety of kinds of evidence should be employed in marking.
3. Children should be taught that failure is a normal concomitant of life, and that there is no moral component in it.
4. Some risk taking should be encouraged—pupils do not learn if they only attempt what they can already do. Therefore evaluation should be aimed at helping the child to evaluate his strengths and weaknesses realistically and should help him know how to improve.
5. Failure to learn should also be considered as a failure in teaching, and the teacher should work with the child on the basis of mutual attempt to improve the teaching-learning situation.
6. The child's accomplishment should be stressed, and his lacks of accomplishment should not be overemphasized.
7. Ignorance should not be treated as stupidity.
8. The teacher needs to preserve optimism about the child's abilities and future chances for success.
9. The dignity and self-acceptance of the child, and his acceptance by the teacher, peers, and parents, should be maintained.

Stresses from Social-Class Influences

Emphasis on the "Great Society" has focused in no small part on the culturally deprived and academically underprivileged child. Such projects as Head Start and the Elementary–Secondary Education Acts projects are aimed at helping children who find difficulty in competing in school (and life) with children whose socioeconomic class backgrounds have been more favorable. A number of studies have dealt with such factors and more are in progress. We shall consider some of the findings.

Although social class structure and the values attributed to the various social classes (SES) are now thought to be changing, there are some characteristics related to the school which are still of importance insofar as the adjustment of the child to the teacher and the teacher's values are concerned.

B. McCandless (1961) has found the topic of SES of importance and has written an entire chapter in his work on *Children and Adolescents* that he calls "Middle-Class Teacher, 'Every-Class' Child." McCandless points out what has long been well-known, namely, that most teachers are drawn from the middle SES class. He recognizes that the values attributed to this class are admittedly somewhat uncertain, yet probably the following beliefs are quite characteristic:

1. a belief in God coupled with church attendance (the majority of public-school teachers in the United States are Protestant);
2. the importance of personal cleanliness;
3. the value of thrift;
4. the conviction that intellect, rather than emotion, should control one's life;
5. the avoidance of expressing strong emotions including sex and aggression (guilt often accompanies such expression);
6. choosing avenues that are socially acceptable when aggression must be expressed (loud arguments, brawls, and fights are not permissible);
7. the correctness of sexual restraint;
8. the propriety of clean and correct language;
9. the importance of temperance in alcohol;
10. the practice of honesty in speech and action;
11. the value of hard work and self-discipline in achieving success;
12. the importance of doing one's duty;
13. the importance of learning for learning's sake.

On the other hand, McCandless notes that the majority of children in the public schools are not middle SES class. He contrasts in particular the values of the lower class, with those of the teachers; this group makes up 25 to 30 per cent of the public-school population. The lower-lower class is considered to espouse the following:

1. infrequent attendance at church (most are likely to be funda-
   mentalist or Roman Catholic) ;
2. indifference to cleanliness, partly because of less opportunity in
   meager living quarters to be clean;
3. indifference to thrift, again because of meager resources;
4. a belief in fighting for what one wants—essential to survive in
   a street culture;
5. encouragement of strong emotion;
6. physical as well as verbal expression of aggression;
7. unrepressed sex practices (this group does not have privacy) ;
8. blunt and unrepressed language;
9. alcohol as an escape from grim reality;
10. the value of honesty, though there is more temptation to steal;
11. cynicism about hard work and self-discipline, which have not
    won advancement for day-laborer fathers;
12. questioning the value of duty;
13. unimportance of learning, unless it shows "practical" results in
    terms of earning.

Notice that McCandless does not hold that these values and
attitudes are universal in the lower-lower class, nor that they are
immutable—rather, he suggests, considering the ways these
people must live, that they are quite natural. But the point that
such children are almost automatically in conflict—as far as
values are concerned—with the average teacher and curriculum
is well taken.

It is true, however, that SES class differences seem to be
growing fewer, at least for the upper-lower SES class and higher
levels. Mass media—including television, newspapers, and the
movies—as well as the schools, are acting to iron out differences.
Furthermore, as W. B. Brookover and D. Gottlieb (1963)
suggest, children do not necessarily espouse the values of their
parents, so that there is a mobility in values, as well as in class
position.

ACADEMIC ACHIEVEMENT

Theoretically the school should reduce differences among the
social classes by providing common experiences for all. Optimism on this point is not justified, however, for a study by F. C.
Smitter (1951) showed that by the time children from the
lower classes reach eighth grade, they are retarded approxi-

mately two years in school achievement. Vocabulary, reading, and arithmetic present the greatest difficulties, and the deficiencies increase with time.

The curriculum may not meet the needs of lower-class children. The high premium placed on language, the use of illustrations from middle-class lives, and low respect for nonacademic classes, which these children usually elect, are factors in making the typical school program seem unrealistic and useless to them. These children come from homes where communication is often placed on a physical level and where language is not prized, so they must virtually learn to communicate with words before they fit into the school program. By that time, they may have become retarded readers (Bossard, 1954). Here is one strong argument for the Head Start programs.

ADJUSTMENT

The lower-class child must adjust to two social worlds (Shaffer & Shoben, 1956), one centering about family, relatives, and friends and the other about school and its inhabitants. Conflicts and frustrations result. W. L. Warner, *et al.* (1948), found that, on personality questionnaires, middle-class subjects usually achieve higher scores on such traits as self-sufficiency, dominance, and emotional stability, whereas lower-class subjects show greater tendencies toward insecurity and irritability. Lower-class pupils indicate that they like school less, have more nervous habits like nail biting, have more trouble controlling their tempers, are less willing to leave home for college, worry less about being useful to society, and think less about ethical and religious questions than do middle- or upper-class subjects (Shaffer & Shoben, 1956). They frequently feel that teachers overemphasize good order and conduct and are overly strict (Kaplan, 1959). They tend to resent authority and try to circumvent the teacher. Teachers, in turn, react against them and show their feelings and biases. J. M. Rich (1960) suggests that such biases may be in effect even before children are grouped into classes.

It is possible, however, to overemphasize social-class differences among children. U. Bronfenbrenner (1961) sees that differences in child-rearing are less than formerly. He notes that patterns of child-rearing have changed for most groups in the last twenty-five years. Parents are now thought to be more permissive than formerly, freer in expressing affection, and less authoritarian. The result is that children are more conforming, anxious, and less aggressive than formerly, and more interested in security than in forging ahead on their own. There are also, he notes, stronger pressures to achieve competitively in school, which contribute to achievement-oriented children, who are more aggressive, tense, domineering, and cruel. Apparently we do not foster competitive achievement and socially oriented behavior with equal success. For reasons such as these, that is, changing value systems, we must be careful not to stereotype the child because of his family or social status. The teacher needs to recognize the various pressures on the child, the various competing value systems with which he must deal, and we must avoid superimposing pressures on him in addition to those to which he is already subjected.

Peer-Group Influences

The peer group has many influences upon the mental health and personality development of children. It may offer advantages such as a feeling of acceptance by others, development of leadership, experience in social interaction, and pleasurable recreation. Groups consisting of students motivated to help society as well as to enhance their members exert much worthwhile effort in and out of school. Among them are athletic teams, the band, orchestra, chorus, and newspaper, as well as such related groups as the Boy Scouts, Girl Scouts, YMCA, YWCA, and similar service organizations.

The peer group, however, may offer stresses as well as support. Not all children are able to attain the kinds of group acceptance that they want. For example, J. R. Frymier (1959) has shown that students new to a classroom or a school are at a disadvantage. He found that students who had been together in school for some time constituted an in-group or power faction, and that students new to the school were rejected for "no reason at all." The newcomers had to prove themselves in order to be accepted—by proficiency in athletics for boys, or, for girls, by possession of beauty, charm, and ability to dance well. In the case of lack of such attributes, new students were isolates. The old-timers, feeling somewhat threatened by new students, sought security by uniting with those who were familiar.

If students are not able to join an on-going group which is well-accepted, they may form groups of their own, some of which may be hostile to the older groups, or even antisocial in nature.

Peer groups do not always have codes of conduct which are acceptable to all members. In some cases the mores may be quite different from those demanded by adult society, so that members experience strong conflicts between peers and parents, and also with their own values. But groups exert pressures upon their members and isolate those who will not conform, and in such cases members must reject the values previously held, or else dispense with group membership. An example of this is the fostering of norms of mediocre school achievement, which prevents some children from doing well in school. They have the choice of popularity or high achievement, unless they are fortunate enough to be athletic, have "good personalities," or are otherwise attractive to the group without entirely espousing its values.

Schools do not always do well in fostering peer acceptance of students. For example, many school organizations are based on the premise that to belong, the pupil must be proficient in the particular activity. If, however, he lacks this proficiency, he is rarely provided opportunity to gain it. This is particularly true where special abilities—as in athletics—are concerned. We need to foster activities in which children with poorer backgrounds or abilities can gain status and recognition; an example of this was a school known to the writer which provided such unusual opportunities as the chance to participate in a weight-lifting club and in a forestry club which maintained a school forest and built a cabin for its members.

Sometimes entry into organizations depends upon the applicant's having an excellent social and moral background. In this case, the ideals of the organization, which are usually aimed at uplifting the members, are rather beside the point; they can uplift only those who need little uplifting, and those who might profit from good examples and precepts are excluded from membership.

Pupils tend to follow the lead of the teacher in acceptance of other pupils. Stresses from peer-group influences can be minimized if the teacher makes it a point to accept all pupils and works with the group in ways designed to gain acceptance for them. For example, some third-grade pupils in one school tended to look down at a small girl whose mother was a Chinese war bride. The teacher, however, was unwilling to allow this tendency to develop. She asked the mother whether or not she would be willing to visit the room and discuss Chinese ways; then the teacher worked one of the class units around to the subject of Asia. The mother came to the classroom, complete with Chinese clothing and a few articles, and so charmed the children that, from that point on, the little girl was one of the most sought-after children in the room.

Younger children can be aided in accepting the newcomer much as parents prepare them for the birth of a new sibling. That is, they can assume some responsibility for the care of the newcomer and for making him feel at home, with consequent reinforcements from the teacher, just as parents praise older children for their help and attitudes. Older children and youths, similarly, can act as "big brothers" or "big sisters" to help introduce the newcomer around and to help him learn mores and procedures. This system is routine in many schools. If "big brothers" are carefully chosen, their friendliness and prestige go far to obtain acceptance for the new child or youth.

Sex-Role Stresses in the School

In Chapter 5 we referred to the fact that teachers may give boys poorer marks than girls, even though on standardized tests there is no discernible advantage to either sex in academic achievement. Presumably this marking is partly because boys tend more toward "acting out" behavior and are more likely to be disciplinary problems than girls.

Many people are becoming quite concerned at apparent disadvantages to boys in the elementary schools. Among the disadvantages are the lack of appropriate sex-role models. Fathers have much less to do with the rearing of small children than do mothers, so that little girls have an initial advantage in learning how women act. When school is encountered, most of the teachers (especially in the primary grades) are women, and again small girls have models, and the boys do not.

Furthermore, the school culture is based on female norms. Boys tend to be active, somewhat aggressive, and noisy—but these virtues are not especially esteemed in schools. Girls seem to have the advantage of maturing somewhat earlier than boys do and are thus readier for school tasks. In addition, they are likely to be more verbal and to prefer school-type activities more than boys do.

The teachers, being women, may find it easier to understand the problems of little girls, for they can reflect on their own early experiences.

These remarks are rather broad generalizations, of course. Many psychologists and psychiatrists are, however, beginning to have grave fears about the masculine identification of boys and are worrying whether, on the one hand, boys may be too conforming and thus lacking in the aggressiveness, independence, and confidence they need or, on the other hand, boys may react against too much female example and control and become unduly aggressive and fail to identify with the school. (Others are concerned, however, that girls may be less feminine than formerly. Possibly sex-role differentiation is tending to disappear?)

Dealing with this sort of stress is a problem, especially in the elementary school. Too few men become elementary school teachers, and, possibly because of financial need, usually try to become administrators, counselors, or specialists of other kinds. The National Education Association (1965) has shown that, at all levels but particularly at the elementary-school level, men fail to make teaching a lifetime career. By the time they reach the age of fifty almost all men have moved out of the classroom.

Progress can be made in two directions. It can be possible to introduce more men into the school, as coaches, counselors, and in other specialties, as well as in the classroom. But perhaps more important, women teachers can recognize the problem stated above, and attempt to deal with it through class content, activities, and examination of their own attitudes and mores. (It may be stated in passing that this problem is not merely limited to the schools. Consider the sex differential in church-school teaching, in certain groups such as the Cub Scouts, playground directors, and the like. As a result, boys are thought to identify with an image of manliness gained more from films, TV, and books, whereas girls are thought to gain their image of femininity more from their own mothers.)

Academic Pressures on Pupils

As schools are presently constituted—in response to the demands of society—many pupils are "low man on the totem pole" right from the start. They fail to possess some of the abilities stressed by schools, and abilities they do possess are frequently ignored. (The movement toward technical and vocational high schools, and to continuation schools and community colleges, however, is beginning to counteract this trend.)

Consider the following report:

NO-HOMEWORK EXPERIMENT

Mr. Arnold is not alone in protesting what has been called the "post Sputnik, pile-it-on policy." As Neal Ashby pointed out recently in *Parade* magazine, many parents and educators are alarmed at the effects of homework pressures. "They see them taking a toll in tension, physical break-downs—cases among juveniles—and in mental crackups."

According to Mr. Ashby, a team of Stanford University professors is testing the idea of eliminating homework entirely in about a dozen West Coast high schools. He reports Dwight W. Allen, assistant professor of education and spokesman for the team, as saying, "We don't feel the home is the best place to do school assignments. The student isn't his best after school. Study conditions may not be good. Necessary resources—reference books and the like—are not often available."

The Stanford team is experimenting with a school day of from 8 A.M. to 5 P.M. that includes all school work and all extracurricular activity. Between a third to a half of students' time is left unscheduled. In this "independent study time," they may complete outside-class assignments, or work on personal study projects.

According to Mr. Ashby, up to one-half of the teacher's time, too, is unscheduled. "They are thus available to work with individual students who may be falling behind in a subject or pushing ahead on their own." (Ashby, 1965)

Piling on homework, emphasis on all pupils accomplishing the same academic tasks, emphasis on competition as a way of motivating, and stress on similarities of pupils rather than attention to individual differences abound in school practice. Emphasis on having all children conform to set standards, emphasis on the child's weaknesses rather than on his strengths, and the failure to make use of the child's abilities which may not be valued in "academic" courses tend to ensure that many children will have much more negative reinforcement in school and less positive reinforcement than is desirable.

Certain school subjects are considered more "respectable" than others. Students pursuing a college-bound curriculum are considered "better" students than those aiming for a service occupation, a technician's berth, or other noncollege occupations. In this, we do violence to the dignity of many pupils (and adults) and we tend to force many pupils into curricula for which they have little interest and no real fitness.

The field of intelligence testing has shown that pupils vary widely in their talents, even though they may have highly similar gross test scores. Achievement testing echoes this finding. Although the verbal component in an intelligence test score seems to be a better predictor of scholastic success than the performance component (Ringness, 1965), this fact should not be taken as evidence of "what should be" so much as evidence of "what is." That is, school is a place where premium is placed on high verbal ability, necessary for academic classes.

Yet this need not be so. The business world has predicted for some time that there will be a shortage of technicians, service personnel, and other types of workers who can deal with mechanical problems, develop high-level manual skills, or solve problems in which sensory and perceptual skills are involved (as in commercial art). Training people who possess less than top-flight abilities for professions is of less value. For example, university professors of science and mathematics have noted that many young people aspire to follow careers in these fields, primarily because of their prestige value; yet some of these young people have done well in such subjects in junior and senior high school more because of hard work than because of talent and might well be inadequate in the university and professional setting. These same young people might do super-latively in other forms of endeavor.

Artistic, recreational, dramatic, musical, athletic, and other abilities are in intense demand in today's world. Yet in some schools such subjects are either given only partial scholastic credit or are offered only on an extracurricular basis.

Now, it is true, of course, that some children may not have compensating talents. They may lack all forms of ability and background. One must try to help these children to live with their limitations. The teacher can help by reinforcing them for effort, for character attributes, and for cooperative behavior. It is also possible to help some of them develop special abilities or skills of value to the class, to provide a measure of esteem. For example, one high-school boy known to the writer became the curator of reptiles for the biology class, as he grew to know wooded areas where snakes, frogs, salamanders, and other such creatures could be found; he collected live specimens, took care of them in the class herbareum, and studied them enough so that he could discuss them with some (teen-age) authority. Eventually he did become a keeper for a city zoo, although he was not able to attend college and become a scientist or veteri-narian.

Improving Ability to Handle Stress

Up to this point, we have dealt with some of the common curricular and social stresses upon pupils and ways to avoid or minimize such stresses. The balance of this chapter will be devoted to considering ways to help children themselves handle stress situations. The following material should be considered in relation to other material presented in this book (see, for example, Chapter 4, material on frustration tolerance), since many different elements may be found overlapping or com-patible in any problem situation.

DEALING WITH EMOTIONS

J. C. Coleman (1960), an authority on human adjustment, makes the point that too often one fails to understand the causes for his emotions and is unwilling to accept them. Certainly emotions are realities and cannot be denied, and certainly they come about in certain situations because previous experiences have taught us particular emotional reactions to those situations. When one is aware of how he feels, why he feels that way, and accepts these realities, he is able to at least begin to deal with the emotional components in situations of stress.

Let us illustrate what is meant by referring back to the case of Pete, mentioned at the beginning of this chapter. It will be recalled that Pete hit his teacher because the teacher asked him—and then told him—to take his seat. Pete also used vile language to the school secretary who had been nice to him, when she mentioned that she felt about him just as she would about her own son.

It would not be difficult for us, or for Pete, to realize that in both instances he was angry. The problem is to discover *why* he was angry, *whom* he was angry at, and whether other emotions were involved. This is not so simple as it seems on the surface.

Pete was certainly angry at the teacher, and at the secretary, and the precipitating instances were fairly clear. He may not, however, have realized that his angry feelings were really a transference or generalization of anger learned from home situations in which his father employed harsh punishment and his mother nagged at him. His inability to tolerate direct commands or to allow someone to feel motherly toward him were essentially extensions of reactions learned in the home context—it is probable that it was the connotation, rather than the person, in the school situation that angered him.

It is also probable that Pete was angry at himself, first, for giving way to an emotional outburst, and, second, for being hostile to people who really were friendly and trying to be helpful. It is also probable that he had feelings of guilt and remorse, and felt considerably frustrated.

One step a counselor might employ would be to help Pete clarify the dynamics of his behavior, and then to find constructive ways to deal with emotionally arousing situations. Pete would probably be shown that his outburst was quite natural and that his feelings, though acceptable, could be displayed better.

Teachers can act similarly, to a point. They can help the

pupil—and themselves—to understand reasons for emotional displays of pupils by carefully noting the circumstances, trying to interpret the pupil's behavior, and exploring these factors with him. This method is ordinarily more useful than lecturing or punishing the pupil or asking for apologies. These tactics can often be useful in regard to fears, and other negative emotions; they are sometimes useful in helping pupils to better understand such positive feelings as joy and love.

Coleman also makes the point that one must try to learn to work *with* his emotions instead of fighting them. Pete, again, had tried to bottle up his negative feelings and hostility. Yet anger can lead to positive action. For example, teachers sometimes dislike certain pupils, without ever making really clear to the pupils why they feel this way. They try to hide their feelings and to "think positively" about the children, whereas an honest expression of anger, coupled with some discussion of how pupils might change this, can lead to improved pupil behavior and the avoidance of emotional arousal. Equally, teachers sometimes feel guilty about not liking all children equally well; this reaction, too, is not particularly healthy, since all children are not equally likeable. It would be better to recognize the existence of such feelings and try to find ways to change the pupils— or their own attitudes—rather than to continue this state of feeling.

Fear can be healthy. It is a signal that something is threatening and can be a spur to improved efforts to rid oneself of danger. Although Holt, as stated previously, feels that children's fears lead to less efficient behavior it is also possible that fear-producing situations can be conquered. For example, some children fear the water, hence hesitate to try to learn to swim. In this instance the fear is healthy, for it causes them to be cautious; on the other hand, swimming is healthy, and ability to swim may save one's life, so it is desirable that the child learn to swim in spite of such fear. Careful teaching can help him to do so.

It is also valuable, from a mental-health point of view, that the child learn to overcome his fear of the water as a means of mastering a potentially debilitating emotion; that is, one who gives in too frequently to his fears may develop avoidance tactics at any sign of danger, rather than a mastering, problem-solving attitude. Furthermore, because most children enjoy water sports, unless the child can learn to swim and enter in, much pleasurable interaction (and prestige) that could be gained is lost. Nonswimmers may be considered "sissies" and fail to gain acceptance by others; in turn, they may lack self-esteem.

If negative emotions must not be expressed against someone's person or property, as in the case of Pete, and if they should not be bottled up, allowing pressure to rise, what can be done? It is generally conceded that emotions should be expressed, rather than suppressed, but that such expression should be made in constructive ways. In Pete's case, his feelings could have been expressed to the teacher or secretary verbally. He could also have talked about his feelings to his guidance counselor, or he could have written about them. One can also reduce angry feelings by hard physical work or athletics, through music or art, or vicariously through role playing.

Fear and anger can sometimes be avoided or reduced by the use of humor. The class "clown," of course, makes use of this defense, but he uses it to excess. By refusal to take himself seriously and to let others take him seriously, he avoids the threat of failure—for he is not "really trying." Furthermore, if others laugh at him, he wins a certain amount of attention and regard, both of which are positive reinforcers. Most of us can, however, reduce emotional tension due to stress by using humor to a less debilitating degree. After all, our mistakes may really *be* funny! And who do we think we are, that we are perfect? That was a dumb remark we made, wasn't it? And so on.

Teachers, too, can reduce emotional tension in the classroom, as when during a test the teacher cracks a joke, or when a pupil is having trouble with his lesson the teacher "kids him along" a little.

One can also help students to tolerate stress by accentuating positive emotions which may come about. For example, even though a pupil's total progress may be disappointing, he can take some pride in having made *some* progress. Even though he may be fearful or anxious about making a speech, there are certain elements of pride and pleasure in having others listen to him.

Finally, a pupil can learn to understand what situations arouse negative emotions in him, and not only gradually desensitize himself to them by moving into such situations fore-armed, but he can, if necessary, learn to avoid those situations entirely.

BUILDING FEELINGS OF ADEQUACY

Stress tolerance may be partly a function of constitutional factors—that is, heredity and basic biological make-up may cause some persons to be generally more stable, better integrated, and stress-resistant than others. However, the ability to withstand stress seems more closely related to experiences during one's development that build self-esteem, independence, acceptance by others, and other positive ways of viewing oneself. Children from stable homes, who have not lacked support and encourage-ment, tend to be less easily upset by pressures placed upon them than are others.

People who feel adequate are less likely to feel stress from situations than those who lack self-confidence. How one with-stands pressures is partly a function of his expectations concern-ing the eventual outcomes. Thus the child who has generally met with success tends to be optimistic in most situations, and he is able to resist stresses with less trouble than the child who is basically fearful, anxious, and insecure.

It is possible to build feelings of adequacy in children in a number of ways. A teacher can help them gain a generalized self-evaluation which is positive. He can also build feelings of adequacy related to specific situations. He can also help chil-dren learn to find ways of coping with their problems, so that success experiences are more likely.

In building feelings of security, adequacy, and self-esteem, it should be remembered that our self-evaluations come only partly from our nonsocial experiences. Thus, while a child may gain some expectations of future success in solving mathematics problems "on his own," he probably gains the greater number of his evaluations of himself from the ways others show they regard him. Thus when others are supportive, complimentary, optimistic concerning his abilities, and otherwise show that they evaluate him highly, chances are that he will tend to evaluate himself highly. Such evaluations come not only from the home, but from the peer group and the school. (The reader is referred to the paragraph by Holt, page 255, in which children who had difficulties in academic work tended to think of themselves as "stupid.")

In addition to fostering generalized feelings of confidence and adequacy, the teacher can aid pupils to arm themselves against specific stress situations. For example, in regard to test anxiety, if the pupil learns means of studying for a test, strategies for taking tests, and an adequate command of his subject, this sort of anxiety should gradually decrease. In some instances it has been found useful to provide children with "dry runs," which are practice tests similar to the test which will count. When such tests are given, results can be discussed with pupils, providing them with better tools for dealing with the actual tests themselves.

Equally, in regard to school marking practices, when pupils are really informed about the meaning of a mark, how it is arrived at, and how they can earn excellent marks, some of the anxiety can be avoided.

In substance, stresses can be better handled if the pupil can be aided to

1. learn to analyze the sources of his anxieties, fears, and frustrations;
2. learn to find ways to prepare himself for stressful situations, so that emotions are not strongly aroused;
3. learn to find ways to control, reduce, or avoid emotional tension by understanding and working with, instead of fighting, his emotions;
4. build feelings of general self-confidence and expectations of positive outcomes;
5. learn to express emotions constructively;
6. alter his goals, if necessary, or even change to another environmental situation.

□

REFERENCES

Alpert, R., and R. Haber. "Anxiety in Academic Situations," *Journal of Abnormal and Social Psychology*, 61 (1960), 207–15.
Ashby, N. "Is Homework Necessary?" *Parade* (November 22, 1964), pp.

4 ff., reprinted in part as "No-Homework Experiment," *NEA Journal,* 54 (1965) , 22.

Bell, M. *A Comparative Study of Mentally Gifted Children Hetero- geneously and Homogeneously Grouped.* Doctoral dissertation, Indiana University, 1957.

Bloom, B., *et al.* (eds.) . *Taxonomy of Educational Objectives.* New York: Longmans, 1956.

Bossard, J. H. S. *The Sociology of Child Development,* p. 339. New York: Harper, 1954.

Bronfenbrenner, U. "The Changing American Child: A Speculative Anal- ysis," *Journal of Social Issues,* 17 (1961) , 6–17.

Brookover, W. B., and D. Gottlieb. "Social Class and Family Influences," in W. W. Charters, Jr., and N. L. Gage (eds.) . *Readings in the Social Psychology of Education,* pp. 3–11. Boston: Allyn & Bacon, 1963.

Coffield, W. H., and P. Blommers. "Effects of Non-Promotion on Educa- tional Achievement in the Elementary School," *Journal of Educational Research,* 47 (1956) , 233–50.

Coleman, J. C. *Personality Dynamics and Effective Behavior,* chap. 10. Chicago: Scott Foresman, 1960.

Dimond, S. W. "Who Should Fail?" *Nation's Schools,* 63 (1959) , 63–5.

Drews, E. *The Effectiveness of Homogeneous and Heterogeneous Ability Grouping in Ninth Grade English Classes with Average and Superior Students.* Lansing, Michigan Public Schools (Cooperative Research Proj- ect 608) , 1959.

Ekstrom, R. B. "Experimental Studies of Homogeneous Grouping: A Critical Review," *School Review,* 69 (1961) , 217–26.

Franseth, J. "Does Ability Grouping Make a Difference?" *Education Digest,* 28 (1963) , 15.

Frymier, J. R. "Acceptance and Rejection of New Students," *Progres- sive Education,* 34 (1959) , 30–2.

Holt, J. *How Children Fail.* New York: Pitman, 1964.

Kaluger, G., and R. Martin. "The Loneliness of the Gifted Child," *Elementary School Journal,* 61 (1960) , 126–32.

Kaplan, L. *Mental Health and Human Relations in Education,* p. 204. New York: Harper, 1959.

McCandless, B. *Children and Adolescents,* chap. 14. New York: Holt, Rinehart, Winston, 1961.

National Education Association. "The Selective Shortage of Teachers," *NEA Research Bulletin,* 43 (1965) , 72–7.

Otto, H. J. *Elementary School Organization and Administration,* pp. 201–2. New York: Appleton, 1954.

Parker, C. "A Measured Experiment with Mentally Advanced Children," *American School Board Journal,* 133 (1956) , 23–4.

Rich, J. M. "How Social Class Values Affect Teacher-Pupil Relations," *Journal of Educational Sociology,* 33 (1960) , 355–9.

Ringness, T. A. "Affective Differences Between Successful and Non- Successful Bright Ninth Grade Boys," *Personnel and Guidance Journal,* 48 (1965) , 600–6.

Sarason, I. "Test Anxiety and Intellectual Performance," *Journal of Ab- normal and Social Psychology,* 66 (1963) , 73–5.

Sarason, S. B., K. S. Davidson, F. F. Lighthall, R. Waite, and B. Ruebush. *Anxiety in Elementary School Children.* New York: Wiley, 1960.

Shaffer, L. F., and E. J. Shoben, Jr. *The Psychology of Adjustment,* p. 427. Boston: Houghton Mifflin, 1956.

Smitter, F. C. *Experiences, Interests, and Needs of Eighth Grade Farm Children in California.* Sacramento: California State Department of Education, 1951.

Stanley, J. C. *Measurement in Today's Schools.* Englewood Cliffs: Prentice-Hall, 1965.

Steadman, E. R. "Fifteen Who Were Not Promoted," *Elementary School Journal,* 59 (1959), 271–6.

Torgerson, T. L., and G. S. Adams. *Measurement and Evaluation.* New York: Dryden, 1954.

Warner, W. L., M. Meeker, and D. Eels, "Social Status in Education," *Phi Delta Kappan,* 30 (1948), 113–9.

SUGGESTIONS FOR FURTHER READING

Crow, L., and A. Crow (eds.). *Mental Hygiene in the Classroom: A Book of Readings.* New York: Macmillan, 1963.
Part 9 discusses mental hygiene and discipline and features such writers as Crow and Crow, G. W. Denemark, Calvin Reed, Ralph Ojemann, and Frances Holliday, as well as Paul Anderson and Victoria Wagner. Part 3 discusses some of the dynamic forces in human behavior and includes studies and discussion of attitudes by Crow and Crow, Sister Josephina, and Dale Harris. Stress is discussed by E. Paul Torrance. Part 4 discusses frustration and defensive behavior. Part 5 includes articles on children in crisis by Warren Vaughan, Jr., on the culturally deprived child in school by M. Krugman, and on emotional problems of adolescents and children by W. G. Hollister and Jerry Kelley.

Holt, J. *How Children Fail.* New York: Pitman, 1965.
The reader is directed to this entire book, which is only 181 pages long. Based on a practicing teacher's observations and interpretations of classroom events, it shows in detail some of the stresses on children and effects on learning. It has fine illustrations of meaningful learning in mathematics using concrete aids and how such learning affects attitudes and motivations.

Sarason, S. B., et al. *Anxiety in Elementary School Children.* New York: Wiley, 1960.
This work discusses the assessment of findings on anxiety in children. Anxiety is seen to be of various kinds (see Chapter 7 of this volume), and implications for the study of anxiety and possible prevention or treatment are discussed.

10

STUDYING INDIVIDUAL CHILDREN

Recently the present writer interviewed a number of ninth-grade boys, and again it was apparent that important influences in pupil lives may or may not be known by their teachers. For example, Mark, a Jewish lad, was continually sad because all his relatives except his parents had perished under Hitler, and he envied boys who had grandparents, aunts and uncles, and cousins to visit and do things with. Frank was thrilled that he had been accepted for study at a school in Switzerland and eagerly spent his weekends brushing up on skiing. Jim was bothered at being "elbow high," for he received frequent black eyes while playing basketball with taller boys. George was planning on a career in psychology, motivated by experiences in managing a "day camp" the previous summer, where he had taken full responsibility for five smaller boys. Peter was an excellent cartoonist and had already sold to a boy's magazine. Several boys were "surfers" and pointed with pride to their badges of distinction—sun-bleached hair. But Leo, doing poorly in classes and feeling that he had no special talents, could look forward only to the time when he could drop out of school and get a job.

Knowing such things could help teachers in many ways.

Teachers agree that it is important to know as much as possible about the lives of their pupils; but, they argue, child study is time-consuming, and large classes make it almost impossible really to know all the pupils. Most teachers, however, already know a great deal about their pupils—without special study— and can interpret their behavior quite accurately. This information has not been painfully obtained, but has come about in the natural course of events of the school day. Children like to talk about themselves, and, especially in the lower grades, may gratuitously provide the teacher with information which their families would prefer to have concealed. In the upper grades and high school, students often have favorite teachers to whom they confide and from whom they ask advice—the teacher need do little more than make himself available. In addition, teachers learn much from reading themes, from tests, from classroom observation, and even from the school or city newspaper.

Yet it must be granted that there are many times when more extended study of pupils is required, especially when they are having problems with school relationships. In such instances the teacher really needs to make an extra effort to find information which will be useful, and this does take time and ability.

Further, it is becoming increasingly apparent to school psychologists and other specialists that the teacher is in a position to gain information about pupils not readily available to such specialists; therefore, when referrals are made, it is extremely valuable to the specialist to obtain what data he can from the teacher. Teachers are likely to be the most effective persons in dealing with (and living with) the problems of most pupils; the more information they can obtain, the more likely teachers are to do an effective piece of work with the children who have problems.

Although a teacher should not attempt to play the "amateur psychiatrist," he still may employ every means at his disposal to learn about the child's behavior as a basis for his efforts and those of specialists, should the latter become involved.

This chapter will consist of a résumé of teacher techniques for child study. These may be employed with successful as well as unsuccessful pupils. However, since child study in detail is time-consuming, we recognize that extensive study will probably be made only for those who present the greatest apparent problems.

Surface Impressions

In Chapter 8, we stressed the differences between the "causal approach" and the "surface approach" in teaching. There are a number of reasons why the surface approach is inadequate.

Children's behavior may be misinterpreted because the difficulties a child faces in overcoming problems may not be known; a "happy, well-adjusted" child may not in actuality be so happy and well-adjusted as he seems. We have referred previously to the fact that some high achievers are actually overachievers, anxious children who are attempting to compensate for personal or environmental problems by trying excessively hard to conform at school and please the teacher.

Another reason for misinterpreting children's behavior is that children can be chameleon-like in taking on the color of their environment. Small children, in particular, are likely to be situation dominated. J. Holt's remarks (Chapter 9) suggest why it may be. Children play roles appropriate to their perceptions of what is demanded of them and how they must measure up. Different contexts call upon them for different kinds of behavior.

Misunderstanding may come from inadvertently or uncritically accepting the opinions of others concerning some children. One cannot help but be influenced when another teacher warns him that "Peter steals," or if the cumulative record shows that Sarah lives in a culturally impoverished neighborhood. It is easy to forget that pupil behavior is a function of the interaction of many factors, and that one needs to be on guard against overemphasis of any facet of the child's character and history.

We need to keep in mind that the way a given situation appears to the teacher may be quite different from the way it is interpreted by the child. The ways a child thinks about himself and others has great influence upon his behavior; yet his impressions may be accurate—or inaccurate—just as those of others may be.

Still another source of misinterpretation is to fail to give the child credit for manipulating the environment. For example, one frequently hears that a given child is socially maladjusted because of a poor home situation. Yet it may well be that poor family relationships are the result, rather than the cause, of the child's poor social relationships. A teacher needs to ask what there is about such a child that causes others to react to him as they do. We need to ask about his behavior in terms of his personality dynamics, rather than to make assumptions which may or may not be true.

The teacher's first problem is to try to determine the *facts* of the child's behavior. He can then seek to interpret them and begin to check his hypotheses. But if he deals in general impressions, the level of his factual knowledge may be inadequate.

Specific Characteristics

STEREOTYPES

Enough has been said by others so that we need not belabor the point that teachers should respond to the specific characteristics of the individual child, rather than deal in stereotypes.

Stereotypes exist not only in regard to minority groups, sex roles, and the like, but are unfortunately sometimes utilized by the teacher in viewing children from the same family. For example, who has not heard such remarks as "All the Joneses are slow learners." "All the Smiths are unmotivated." "All the Browns are disciplinary problems."? One also stereotypes the individual child. Peter is "always slow to respond," but Mary is "always right on the ball." In one instance a student teacher told the writer: "Every time Arthur is called upon, he tries to get smart with me. What should I do about it?" It was suggested that she keep a careful log for a week, in order to determine the circumstances under which Arthur's misbehavior occurred. Later, bringing in the log, the young lady remarked ruefully, "I guess I was wrong about Arthur. I kept track all week long, and not once did he act wise. I must have judged him on the basis of one instance."

The same problem may be related to the child's environment. Thus the child who misbehaves under one teacher may be perfectly well-behaved under another. This is a fairly common finding by school psychologists and other specialists—the solution frequently is to move the child to another room. (Not every teacher can—or should be expected to—deal effectively with every child. Inability to work well with some children is not a failure on the teacher's part. Too many other factors enter into the situation to "blame" anyone.)

GENERALITIES

School records verify that most teachers' comments fail to be specific, even when instances of behavior are described in some detail. Such generalities are probably actually more informative concerning the teacher's impressions than concerning the actual behavior, although we do not discount the impressions of experienced, well-trained teachers. But let us illustrate with an example from a teacher's letter of referral for special study:

Amy seems entirely unmotivated. She doesn't get her assignments done on time, and usually they are pretty inadequate when they are turned in. She doesn't respond in class, rarely enters discussion, and never volunteers. When I call upon her she often says nothing. I think she is sullen. Lots of times she gets things wrong, even when I repeat the right answers several times. She may lack intelligence. In any case, she doesn't cooperate.

One could speculate about emotional problems, social problems, inadequate background, low intelligence, and a whole host of other factors. However, study of Amy revealed that she was partially deaf; her repeated efforts to obtain correct information usually did not result in better understanding, since the teacher usually just repeated what he had said before. Amy, therefore, finally became discouraged and ceased to try to learn from discussion or from the teacher's lecture.

The question arises: "Why was not the teacher informed that Amy was partially deaf? Furthermore, why did she not discover it for herself?" The answer lies in the fact that in ordinary interaction, such as at home, Amy could respond to a number of clues such as gestures, expressions, and knowledge of people's habitual behavior. Further, she could hear somewhat, in a small-group setting. But in a large group, and this is common with somewhat deaf people, she was less able to adapt to her hearing loss. In point of fact, Amy did not realize that she was hard of hearing, and simply felt that others did not speak clearly. Studies have shown that up to 10 per cent of the children in some schools have at least marginal loss of hearing. The teacher, not looking for this solution, frequently characterizes the partially deaf child as uncooperative, sullen, or "stupid."

Had the teacher carefully specified the conditions under which Amy did not seem to cooperate, she, herself, might have come to the conclusion that Amy did not hear well. Then Amy could have had an examination and medical help; she could have been moved to the front of the room, and other help given. Clues to difficulty in hearing include a strained position and facial expression when others are speaking, the lack of response to a softly worded question, the ability to respond well to the printed or written word, some difficulty in speaking appropriately (especially if vocalization is harsh or somewhat hard to listen to), constant reference to other children for assignments, and so on. Thus the mere act of trying to describe behavior as specifically as possible may lead to clearer understanding of its nature and cause.

Practice is the main thing that is required. *When* does Peter act "smart"? With *whom*? How *frequently*? In what *ways*? With what *effects*? And so on.

In the previous paragraphs, we cautioned teachers against forming premature conclusions about reasons for children's behavior. On the other hand, the teacher is usually faced with the need to act—there is classroom routine to carry on, work must be done, and discipline cannot be compromised. This dilemma is difficult to resolve satisfactorily. Teachers, being human, however, probably will do little harm if they base their actions on their experience in regard to behavior of children in general and most problem behavior specifically.

Essentially what we are trying to promote is not an unwillingness to act until "all of the facts are in" but a tentative attitude on the part of the teacher. Hypotheses for the child's behavior that reflect various possible explanations should be made. The teacher can use such hypotheses to provide focuses for study of the child; he can check the results of his own actions to see which, if any, of these hypotheses are valid. He can use such hypotheses to suggest further data to be gathered and to guide experimentation. There is thus a difference between jumping to conclusions and acting upon supposition, keeping "hands off" until a complete study has been made, and acting in a tentative problem-solving manner. The last, of course, is much preferable to the first two alternatives.

Criteria for the Study of the Child

ETHICAL CONSIDERATIONS

Ethical considerations are related to what information is sought, the sources employed, and the techniques used in obtaining data. Ethics are also involved in the ways such information is put to use.

There is an increasing hue and cry in the press (for example, Packard, 1964; Gross, 1962) and even hearings in Congress (Amrine, 1965; Vance, 1965; Clopton, *et al.*, 1965) to protect the privacy of the individual. This privacy should include that of the child and his parents. Teachers who make studies of children may run the risk of being accused of snooping or meddling with the lives of children and their families, even though such studies may be made with the best of intentions. Because such fears do exist, schools try to protect children and their families by limiting the kinds of information they collect and by safeguarding its usage. Some schools do not permit teachers access to certain pupil records; referrals to the psychologist, actions involving police intervention, personality test information, and sometimes even intelligence-test data may be withheld.

Those who believe in restrictions on data provided the teacher have a number of plausible arguments. It is said that some data are unreliable and that their use may do harm; thus certain personality tests have been attacked by some. It is also said that much such information cannot be understood by the teacher and that some of it is unnecessary prying. But the most telling criticism is sometimes made by teachers themselves, who worry lest they should be swayed by data others have collected. Some do not even wish to know anything about a child's ability, lest they stereotype him in their own minds.

It is this writer's contention that teachers are professionals and should be entitled to any information that will help them to do their work better. *As professionals, they should be ethical enough not to misuse information nor to divulge confidential data.* Furthermore, the professional teacher is in some ways like the physician who consults medical histories that may include lists of allergies and watches typical ways in which people react to illnesses; this study, in turn, helps him both to prevent and to understand certain problems. The professional teacher needs tools to work with, and one of these tools is some understanding of how the child has performed in the past so that he can sometimes prevent or alleviate certain problems. But *he should check the reports of others against his own impressions,* fully realizing that children change and that others may be inaccurate or mistaken. In a word, he collects what pertinent data he can but synthesizes it into a meaningful picture of the child tentatively and with due safeguards in his own thinking and dealing with the child.

What may be considered pertinent information may vary considerably with the situation. Unfortunately, as A. B. Abramovitz and E. Burnham (1959) have said, there is a tendency for some teachers to be too interested in the abnormal and in the psychological problems of children; their interests should more properly be in their pupils' functioning, scholastic progress, strengths, and normalities. We must agree that for the protection of a child referred to a specialist certain information must be interpreted to the teacher by that specialist. In some instances information might well be withheld entirely. There are ethical considerations concerning what information ought to be sought—or provided—since the child and his family must be protected. In other words, the teacher is entitled to any information that may help him in his efforts to aid the child; he is not, however, entitled to information which might be interesting, but not useful. The latter is especially true in regard to information which invades the privacy of the family.

HISTORICAL VERSUS CONTEMPORARY FACTORS IN BEHAVIOR

In working with children's problems, the question always arises as to where one should look in trying to ascertain the reasons for the child's behavior; once the reasons are understood, presumably the causes of the behavior might be dealt with, and desirable behavior instituted.

Now it is true that some of the reasons for a child's behavior may be rooted in the history of the child. His reactions to authority figures, for example, may represent a displacement or extension of his feelings toward his parents which were developed over a period of years. His apparent inability to concentrate on school tasks may be the culmination of a long series of experiences in which anxiety arose because of critical, punitive teachers.

But knowing the child's history may or may not help the teacher—or the psychologist. Some would argue that we are not usefully concerned with how maladaptive behavior begins, but rather, with finding what perpetuates it and the means we can employ to modify it. That is, in the case of reaction to authority, the fact that the child cannot react normally is of uppermost importance, rather than how he came to be that way.

We believe that it is necessary to delve into the history of the child only when his behavior cannot be understood in terms of current stimuli, responses, and reinforcements. Sometimes clues to the meaning of behavior can be gained by retracing some of the child's early experiences; however, in some instances it is a waste of time to explore the child's history, for the important factors in his behavior are clear enough in his current behavior. What one *should* be asking oneself is what stimuli now elicit inadequate behavior, what motives he reveals, what emotional reactions he is having, what reinforces his behavior, and how we can change it to make it more adaptive. For example, with a child who seems to fear tests, the teacher should be concerned with the *fear*. It makes little difference why he got that way. If he can be helped to be less afraid of tests, it is of small note that once he was afraid. Removing the aspects of test-taking that reinforce these fears could probably gradually extinguish these fears.

NEED TO DISCERN SPECIFIC BEHAVIOR

We have referred before to the need to see behavior in its specificity. Let us illustrate further what we mean. Consider that a child is crying and that when the teacher runs to help or comfort him, that he ceases to cry. When asked what the trouble was, the child says that he has stubbed his toe and that it hurts terribly. Now, on the face of it, it would seem that there is little here to discuss. A child has stubbed his toe; it hurts; the teacher comforts him; the child stops crying. However, a number of important considerations have been omitted. Here are some of them:

Did the child really cry because he stubbed his toe? Or did this merely act as an excuse to cry? Did he, in actuality, want the teacher's support and attention? In other words, can one take for granted that the child actually stated the real reason for crying?

Either hypothesis can be checked by noting not only his reactions to the behavior of the teacher, but when these reactions occurred. Thus if the child stopped crying immediately after the teacher came, it might be concluded that he really did hurt himself and that a little comforting was all that was wanted. But some children do not stop very promptly. Indeed, the attention of the teacher seems to prolong the weeping. In this case what he really wanted was attention, and, receiving it, was reinforced for crying. This surmise could be checked by seeing what would happen if the teacher, having once investigated and commiserated a little, refused to prolong the situation and left.

A different possibility exists if the child does not stop crying when the teacher comes and does not seem to want the teacher to comfort him. In this instance the hurt is apparently real, and the comforting does little to help. The teacher then might need to investigate the trauma more fully, in case the child has dislocated or broken a toe.

What we are saying is that it is not only the fact of an

incident, but the entire sequence of events which must be examined. When this is done, one can understand stimuli, responses, and reinforcements more clearly.

Another clue that would help the teacher to understand the incident just related is to recall the child's previous behavior in similar situations and a comparison of this child with other children in similar circumstances. If the child was a known attention-seeker, the teacher could wonder whether this was not simply another device to obtain attention, but if the child used no attention-seeking devices in other contexts, he could hypothesize that the hurt was real. Further, if other children of the age of this child cry when stubbing toes, his reaction would be valid—but in the case of an adolescent, on the other hand, humor, anger, or stoical silence, rather than weeping, should be his response.

Here is another example. In this situation, a school psychologist was testing a seventh-grade boy, quite routinely, to determine whether the boy should be placed in a class for the educable mentally retarded or whether he should remain in a regular class situation where he had not achieved very well. During the testing, the psychologist decided to break the ice by a few casual remarks and questions concerning the boy's interests, his dislikes in school, and so on. At this point the psychologist noticed that the youngster was writing on a piece of ordinary white bond paper, but that the writing was backward! The psychologist was intrigued by this, and he began to ask himself questions concerning the boy's perceptual responses and whether or not some such disorientation might not be the cause of his poor school achievement.

The psychologist asked the boy about his backward writing, but the boy only grinned and said, "I don't know." Being unable to gain anything more than a smile and a noncommittal remark, the psychologist subjected the youngster to an appropriate series of tests, only to find that there was nothing unusual about the boy except a borderline intelligence test score.

When the youth had left the testing situation the psychologist began to wonder. The boy had not appeared particularly upset by the questions concerning his backward writing—in fact, the opposite was quite the case. The boy seemed to enjoy the

TABLE 9. Ratings of 511 Teachers and 30 Mental Hygienists on Seriousness of Behavior Problems

Type of Problem	Teacher Score*	Clinician Score*	+ or —†
Heterosexual activity	17.3	9.9	—
Stealing	17.0	12.5	—
Masturbation	16.7	6.4	—
Obscene notes, talk	16.6	8.8	—
Untruthfulness	15.8	10.3	—
Truancy	15.6	10.3	—
Impertinence, defiance	15.0	7.1	—
Cruelty, bullying	14.8	13.5	
Cheating	14.7	10.3	—
Destroying school materials	14.3	5.1	—
Disobedience	14.1	6.5	—
Unreliableness	13.9	10.4	—
Temper tantrums	13.0	11.7	
Lack of interest in work	12.8	9.6	—
Profanity	12.3	2.9	—
Impudence, rudeness	12.2	7.6	—
Laziness	12.2	7.2	—
Smoking	12.0	2.3	—
Enuresis	11.8	9.2	
Nervousness	11.7	11.3	
Disorderliness in class	11.7	3.4	—
Unhappy, depressed	11.5	16.2	+
Easily discouraged	11.5	13.4	+
Selfishness	11.3	11.8	
Carelessness in work	11.3	7.1	—
Inattention	11.2	7.3	—
Quarrelsomeness	11.1	8.3	
Suggestible	11.0	13.3	
Resentfulness	10.8	14.1	+
Tardiness	10.5	5.6	—
Physical coward	10.4	12.0	
Stubbornness	10.3	10.9	
Domineering	10.3	13.0	+

° Extremely grave problem—rating = 20.5; considerable difficulty—rating = 12.5; slight problem—rating = 4.5.

† A + sign in the right column means that the clinician thought the item significantly more serious than did the teacher; a — sign indicates that teachers rated the item more serious than did clinicians.

SOURCE: Adapted from E. K. Wickman, *Children's Behavior and Teachers' Attitudes* (New York: The Commonwealth Fund, 1928), Table VIII, p. 243; Table X, pp. 246–7.

(TABLE 9 CONTINUED)

Type of Problem	Teacher Score	Clinician Score	+ or −
Slovenly in appearance	10.1	7.2	−
Sullenness	9.9	12.6	+
Fearfulness	9.7	14.0	+
Suspiciousness	9.1	16.4	+
Thoughtlessness	8.7	6.8	
Attracting attention	8.5	8.5	
Unsocialness	8.3	17.3	+
Dreaminess	8.3	11.3	+
Imaginative lying	8.1	7.5	
Interrupting	8.0	2.8	−
Inquisitiveness	8.0	5.3	
Overcritical of others	7.9	13.2	+
Tattling	7.5	8.8	
Whispering	7.5	0.8	−
Sensitiveness	7.0	13.1	+
Restlessness	6.9	6.4	
Shyness	5.4	12.5	+

questioning of the psychologist and smiled more or less openly during the process.

Knowing something about boys, the psychologist began to feel that he had been "had." He picked up the paper, examined the backward writing, and discovered to his dismay that the boy had simply been able to read the watermark on the paper. Since this was in script and the paper upside down, his efforts were merely those of copying the watermark and not of backward writing at all. And, like many boys, this lad had had his fun in fooling the psychologist.

Here, again, we have the problem of specificity. Had the psychologist examined the paper carefully at first and had he observed that the boy seemed to be copying, rather than writing, no doubt some of the interviewing and testing might have been eliminated.

TEACHERS' CAPABILITIES IN CHILD STUDY

Some years ago E. K. Wickman (1928) made a study that has since been replicated by others. He showed that teachers tend to recognize or detect problem behavior in children which is in a broad sense aggressive or hostile. He found that the teachers in his study were strongly concerned with behaviors related to sexual matters, with lying, bullying, stealing, and with impertinence or other forms of disobedience.

In contrast to beliefs of clinicians about the seriousness of various behaviors, however, teachers did not view shyness, sensitiveness, or overcriticalness as highly important. Teachers were not as concerned with the less obvious, withdrawing, kinds of behaviors, which nevertheless suggest poor mental health.

Teachers cannot be criticized for this view, for to them aggressive behavior is usually more a problem than is withdrawing behavior. The clinical belief is, however, that withdrawing behavior may be more serious than aggressive behavior, as the former represents a sort of giving up, a retreat from the situation, whereas aggressive behavior suggests that the child is fighting his problem, albeit improperly. Thus in working with withdrawing children it is necessary to find ways to help them regain enough confidence in themselves and others so that they will try to solve their problems, but in working with aggressive children, the motivation is already present and the essential problem is to redirect efforts in acceptable and useful ways.

Wickman's study has been criticized on various grounds, among them the fact that teachers and clinicians responded to somewhat different directions on the part of the researcher. Thus teachers were asked about problems that seemed serious to them, but clinicians were asked about seriousness of problems from a mental-health point of view. The main finding of interest here is that clinicians emphasized the seriousness of withdrawing behavior, but that teachers did not at that time consider such behavior important *to them,* or at least, not as important as aggressive behavior. Perhaps from the frame of reference of their jobs, they were right!

Later studies have suggested, however, that teachers fail to recognize many of the signs of poor mental health. There is hope for improvement, however, since E. C. Hunter's study (1957) showed that teachers were more aware of causal relationships in children's behavior than formerly, and that they were more aware of the significance of withdrawing behavior.

C. A. Ullmann (1957) and C. R. Rogers (1942), as well as others, have shown that teachers can learn to recognize children with problems, not only through observation of children's social behavior, but also through comparing children's abilities with their academic performance. The latter point needs some elaboration. E. M. Bower, *et al.* (1958), showed, as is frequently found, that on group intelligence tests disturbed children do less well than on individually administered tests, but that healthy children's scores correspond more closely from one test to another.

The disturbed child does not usually function at the full range of his abilities, and this shows up not only in intelligence tests but also in school achievement. Poor functioning is most frequently noticed in reading and arithmetic. Differences between the achievement of the disturbed child and others tend to increase with succeeding grade levels, especially in arithmetic. Thus children who fail to keep up with others of similar abilities should be studied. Teachers apparently do sense these relationships, for referrals to clinics by teachers contain a large number of children whose main problem seems to be poor scholastic achievement—at least insofar as the teacher is concerned.

The substance of the findings discussed here shows that there is no reason why teachers cannot locate children in need of further study and/or referral to specialists. Teachers need not fear that they are unqualified or that they will do damage or enter a domain in which they are not at home. So long as they deal with techniques in which they are trained, their value in locating children with problems and in obtaining useful data cannot be overestimated.

An Illustrative Study of a Child by a Teacher

To illustrate how teachers can gather important information concerning children we shall make use of an actual study done in the public schools. This study does not embody all the techniques teachers can use, nor does it represent perfection of method. However, this case gives an idea of the range of techniques available, and the wealth of data at the teacher's command.

The child whom we chose for our illustration is called "Jerry." He is a seven-year-old boy, in the second semester of first grade. His physical education teacher, a young lady, noticed him at the beginning of the school year and began to observe him carefully. Her reasons will become apparent as data are presented.

OBSERVATIONS

The following log illustrates a means of keeping objective observation records while not confusing data with hypotheses. Observations are usually recorded first, with comments (if desired) added after study of the factual data.

OBSERVATIONS	COMMENTS
Sept. 16. Jerry entered the gym at the tail end of the group. His head was hung low and he walked hesitantly. When I looked at him he shoved his fingers far into his mouth. This happened seven times in ten minutes. On three occasions he gagged.	This was Jerry's entrance to first grade physical education. Perhaps he was simply afraid of the new situation. Jerry had been in kindergarten. He seems very withdrawn. Is he self-conscious? When he put his hand into his mouth it seemed almost as if he wanted to swallow himself up. He is the oldest of six boys from an underprivileged home.
Sept. 17. Jerry's clothes are dirty, his hair uncombed, his hands and face grimy, and he smells of stale perspiration and urine. Jerry does not talk with the other children. He does not speak when other children are in the room. Sometimes he will say a few words when no other child is around. I have not heard him shout or laugh.	Why is Jerry withdrawing from group participation? Does he feel inferior? unaccepted by peers? Is Jerry neglected at home (cleanliness)? Does he feel at a disadvantage because of lower socioeconomic level of his home? Does he think other children reject him?

OBSERVATIONS

COMMENTS

Sept. 18. Jerry will not participate in any portion of gym class
on his own initiative. When
helped by the classroom teacher
or myself he will not put forth
strong efforts, but allows himself
to be led around the room and
through the motions.

Jerry does not appear to have
any physical defects. Does helping him make him feel more
secure and accepted? Or are we
reinforcing dependency? Does
helping him make him feel more
the center of attention, which he
dislikes? Is he demonstrating
negative attitudes towards school
(and authority) by refusal to
participate voluntarily?

Sept. 19. Jerry will not run, skip,
jump, or catch a ball. When we
have free play, Jerry sticks his
fingers in his mouth, drops his
head, and stays close to a corner,
wall, or chair.

When there is any "action" at
all, Jerry pulls into his shell for
protection. It is hard to know
whether he is afraid he cannot
do these things well, or whether
there is some other reason. I
have never seen him try things
on his own. Perhaps he has had
too many failures previously.

This teacher has already isolated some of Jerry's characteristics and has raised questions and suggested hypotheses for
further study. Note that these observations took place on four
successive days, at the beginning of the school year; the teacher
would continue to make observations, and at least "spot check"
throughout the year, in order to see any changes in Jerry's
behavior. When she raised questions concerning the nature of
Jerry's behavior, she would try to find ways to test her hypotheses. For example, she might try to place Jerry in small
groups with various children. She might extend the range of
activities, to see if there were any Jerry apparently liked and
was good at.

The key to obtaining useful information from observation of
pupils is that of making frequent, consistent attempts. Pupils
vary greatly in behavior from time to time, so that one-of-a-kind
observations are not usually useful. Pupils also change behavior
with the locale, suggesting the need to observe them in various

kinds of environments. (Yet chance observations cannot be rejected entirely, for significant events may occur but once, although the likelihood of observing such events is somewhat slim.)

Personal observations should be confirmed or negated by the observations of others, not only to check the consistency of the child's behavior, but to check the objectivity of one's own observations. Sometimes the observations may be summarized in "anecdotal records," although such summaries tend to represent interpretations rather than objective data. Nevertheless, they represent the conclusions of experienced personnel and should not be disregarded.

Jerry's gym teacher visited with others, and summarized their comments. Mrs. A., first-grade teacher, remarked: "Jerry is withdrawn, self-conscious, and inhibited. He will not respond orally before the group, although he will read with me alone, after school. Yesterday Jerry was asked to try to read some words which were on the chalk board. He hid his face in his knees and would not respond. The other children were quiet, but gave each other meaningful glances."

Mr. K., cafeteria supervisor, reported: "Jerry waited until all of the other children were served. He did not ask for his choices of food, but merely nodded when asked if he liked something. He ate quickly, by himself."

Miss M., art supervisor, stated: "When asked what colors he would like to use in order to make his school calendar, Jerry merely sucked his thumb and said nothing. I gave him a black, red, and yellow crayon, but he used only the black. His work was very messy."

Thus there is evidence that Jerry behaves similarly in various school situations. He is withdrawn from other children, although he will cooperate with adults when with them alone. There is not enough information available at this point to allow any conclusions as to why Jerry behaves this way, but several hypotheses could be made. It is clear that the gym teacher does not see Jerry differently than others see him.

Often simply noting everything that a child does for a few minutes will provide more clues to the meaning of his behavior, the quick surface impressions of a busy teacher. Jerry was studied carefully by his first-grade teacher for ten minutes. This is what she recorded:

Jerry sat down at his desk. He rummaged through it, lifting and dropping the lid four times. He took out a reading book and sat, chin in hands, for thirty seconds. He again rummaged through his desk. Found a pencil and went to the pencil sharpener. On the way he stopped to look at the turtle in the aquarium. He then stopped and asked me if it was all right to sharpen his pencil. He sharpened the pencil, returned to his seat, and sat down. He then tied his shoelaces. He untied them and retied them tighter. He opened his book and leafed through it. He turned to the page for today's lesson. Rubbed his eyes. Looked at the book for five minutes. Tapped his pencil on his desk, breaking the lead. Went back to pencil sharpener and resharpened pencil. I then called his reading group to the front of the room.

It is clear that Jerry is trying to escape from the study he should be doing, and has found a number of ways to waste time. He apparently has not found enjoyment or success in his studies. Other evidence already noted suggests that he does not wish to participate in any school experiences and does not do so voluntarily.

INFORMATION FROM PEERS

Children's opinions of one another may be of value; because they may know things about one another that adults do not know and because their reactions to one another represent a fact, their opinions are important. Things that happen on the way to school, in the washroom, or elsewhere can significantly affect peer opinions about a child.

Peer opinions are important since they may reinforce a child's negative feelings about himself, and his activities as a group member.

A number of sociometric devices may be employed in order to gain some idea of how children regard one another. (These devices can be made by the teacher or obtained commercially.) Jerry's first-grade teacher asked members of her class to list those with whom they would like to sit at the work table. She prepared a sociogram from the results. Data showed that

Mary was chosen fifteen times.	Mary chose eleven peers.
Peter was chosen eleven times.	Peter chose nine peers.
Harold was chosen ten times.	Harold chose ten peers.
Sue was chosen eight times.	Sue chose seven peers.
Jerry was chosen once.	Jerry chose no one at all.

In this class of twenty-eight pupils, the average number of times chosen was eight. It is apparent from these data that Jerry is not well accepted by the group and that he does not accept others.

Discussions of sociometric techniques are out of place here. The works of R. Cunningham (1951), N. E. Gronlund (1959), and the Los Angeles County Public Schools (1959) are illustrative of publications that can further the teacher's understanding of these techniques. One interesting device, especially usable with older pupils, is that of choosing actors for a "class play"; it is available only for research purposes at this time (Bower & Lambert, 1962).

INFORMATION FROM SELF-REPORTS

Self-report information may include data from informal or formal interviews, the reading of themes and other homework, examination of paintings and other art work, the use of questionnaires and checklists, and any other data furnished by the child himself. In seeking information of this kind, one hopes to learn how children perceive their environments, how they view themselves, and what they expect from the future. The data may not correspond well with objective "reality" and this is worth knowing. How the child accepts himself, to what goals he aspires, how he feels about others, his interests, his fears, and his frustrations are all important.

Jerry's teacher talked informally with him after school while helping him with his reading. Jerry apparently appreciated her interest in him, and began to tell her things about himself and his family life. For example, Jerry mentioned that he had "too many brothers and there wasn't enough toys and things to go around." Also, he wished that "Mom and Dad would quit fighting all the time." He liked to "go fishing with my Dad, but he doesn't take me very much." In the course of the conversation it became apparent that Jerry had been unfavorably compared to some of the other children in the family, and that he felt his mother paid more attention to them than to him. He felt out of place in school because he thought that other pupils did not like him, and because he "wasn't very smart."

Some clues to Jerry's behavior are evident. He feels inferior to other children, rejected, and insecure. He wishes for more family companionship and attention, especially from his father. His withdrawal at school is partly because he does not feel as confident as other children, and because he senses that most of them ignore or reject him. He offers no positive suggestions and seems to prefer to escape his problems rather than to seek a constructive solution to them.

Employment of interviews or other self-report devices as questionnaires depend for validity upon the willingness of the child to respond freely. No pressures may be used to get children to answer questions. When intimate questions are asked in interviews, children (or their parents) may resent them, so that it is better to stay away from sensitive areas, even though important information might be obtained. It is also important that the teacher be able to accept the revelations which may be made and not show shock or negative evaluation of the child.

In interviewing or "counseling" with a pupil, the pacing of questions should not proceed too rapidly or beyond the child's ability to verbalize his feelings. Unskilled persons, interviewing, may do too much talking, too much probing, or even "put words in the youngster's mouth." Care must be taken not to place the child on the defensive.

It may be argued that teachers should not seek information of this kind. Yet experience dictates that many older children would much prefer to talk to favorite teachers than to guidance counselors (primarily because they have had opportunities to know the teachers better and to identify with them); it is also true that younger children volunteer much information without request from the teacher. For example, in the writer's experience as a high-school band director, many youths discussed problems with him informally; a woman physical-education instructor was the confidante of several high-school girls; the industrial arts teacher was able to counsel successfully with several of his students; and a few home-room teachers were able to guide successfully some of their charges.

The examination of themes, paintings, poetry, craft projects, scrapbooks, and other productions may shed some light on feelings and attitudes. How revealing the free-choice theme may be is illustrated by the following work of a second-grade girl:

ONE NIGHT AT MY FRIENDS

One Saterday morning we got out of bed and had our brekfist. Then we got dressed. We played entill our frend called. She wanted us to come over and stay all night becuess she was lonesome. So we packed our Sutte cases. Her father piked us up and we went there. We had so much fun. Then her bruther Steven came home. We had Caserol for supper, was it ever good. After supper we got on our Good cloes and went to Church to see a play. Next Sunday it wood be Christmas day. The play we went to was our Savior Jesus Christ. It was a verey verey good play, it was. After we went to the play we went to get the Christmas tre. When we came home we decerated the tree. Was it fun. Diane slept in her bed and Terry and I slept on the Cowch. The cowch came out like a bed. In the morning we had brekfist and went home.

This is good, for a second-grade child. She gives evidence of being happy and having friends, religious experiences, and a sociable family life. She does not spell perfectly but has been taught (at Sunday school?) to spell "Christmas" and "Jesus Christ." The young lady has a good vocabulary and writes fluently. She sleeps away from home and takes her sister, Terry, along. Evidently the friend's parents are interested in children and she feels comfortable in their family. We would judge the subject to be secure, mentally healthy, socially adjusted, and bright.

INFORMATION FROM SCHOOL TESTS AND RECORDS

Tests of intelligence, interests, academic achievement, diagnostic tests of arithmetic or reading, aptitude, and prognosis are all employed in most schools. They are familiar to teachers so will not be treated here in any detail. However, two reminders will be offered as to their usage for child study in the present context:

VALIDITY OF RESULTS.   ▪   Aside from the validity of the test construction itself, there is the problem of whether the test validly represents the child's abilities. Any test is a test of performance, of course; the problem is whether the performance represented is an adequate sample of the child's *usual* functioning, and whether this, in turn, is somewhere near the limit of his capabilities.

For example, emotionally disturbed children may appear less intelligent than they actually are, since anxiety, fear of being tested, hostility (perhaps against the examiner), inability to concentrate because of tension, and other factors may affect their test scores. Children who suffer from cultural deprivation usually do less well on tests than their abilities would indicate, because of vocabulary and also conceptual experiences which are below those of other children. (The Head Start programs are aimed at this problem in part.) Children who have suffered poor physical health and extended absence from school, or who have frequently moved from school to school may look quite different on tests from those who have progressed normally in a stable setting. Sensory loss, especially in regard to hearing and vision, may affect what the child has gained from his life experiences, especially in regard to school work. Lack of motivation to achieve is another factor. All these factors add up to the child's failure to reflect his true ability (and accomplishment) on many of the standardized tests used by schools. If there is any reason to suspect such factors apply, the child should be tested individually, with as many oral and perhaps psychomotor opportunities to display aptitude or achievement as possible.

Some children appear anxious to complete the test, but do not seem to care whether they make high scores or not, so they skip items or give poor answers; such children, too, need individual testing, where they can be probed and encouraged to do better.

Finally, the remedial specialist or school psychologist is in a position to employ specialized tests to determine more accurately the nature of the child's abilities than can the teacher. These specialists can also isolate the child's precise learning problems, for example, inability to discriminate letters well, a lack of ability to discriminate spatial relationships, failure to associate stimuli and responses, and many other problems.

VALIDITY OF NORMS. ■ Standardized tests possess norms for aid in interpreting results. It must be remembered, however, that national norms may be at considerable variance from local norms, and that therefore the meaning of a test score will vary, depending on whether one is comparing a child with his immediate peers or with children from the national scene.

Psychological effects may differ, depending on the standard for comparison. How one views the child, how he views himself, and how other pupils view him may depend upon local norms. How he is guided educationally and vocationally may depend upon national norms.

For example, in a case known to the present writer, the parents were much concerned that their son, a high-school junior receiving a "C" average, might not be sufficiently bright to enter a "good" college. With such an academic average, was he underachieving, or was he simply average in intelligence?

Individual intelligence testing showed that the boy had an I.Q. of 120, quite enough for most college work. The "C" average was explainable, not as the result of lack of motivation and effort, but the result of his peers also having I.Q.s of 120 or more. Thus "average" for his school was far above "average" nationally, and in other schools his work would have merited grades of "A" or "B." Parental fears were allayed, the boy was given confidence in his own abilities and achievement, and pressures and anxieties were removed. Use of the academic average alone simply indicated problems which did not exist in the broader context, and had led to feelings and emotions which could have been disastrous.

Referring again to Jerry, our continuing subject, he was tested in the summer prior to entering first grade. An intelligence test and a reading readiness test were used. Later, in April of his first-grade year, he was tested with a standardized achievement test. The following data emerged:

MENTAL ABILITIES TEST

C.A. (chronological age), 5.9; M.A. (mental age), 6.1; I.Q., 105. Jerry is of normal intelligence.

READING READINESS TEST

Verbal Score—Age 6.6	Probably ready for reading.
Performance—Age 5.6	Probably not ready for reading.
Quantitative—Age 6.4	Probably ready for reading.

Jerry was considered probably ready for reading when begun in first grade but he might require extra help from the teacher.

The results of the standardized test of school achievement, compared with readiness tests, provide some idea of how well Jerry was progressing in comparison with abilities.

ACHIEVEMENT TEST

C.A.	Age 6.8
Reading	Grade 1.5
Arithmetic	Grade 1.4
Language	Grade 1.6

Achievement is less than expected; at the time of testing Jerry should have attained grade levels of 1.8 or 1.9.

At the end of first grade, Jerry's average school marks were:

Reading	C
Language arts	D
Spelling	C
Social studies	D
Mathematics	D
Physical education	D
Writing	C
Art	D
School citizenship	C
Days absent	8½

Jerry's marks are somewhat below what is indicated by the achievement test, on which he was also low; this suggests that the teachers felt that he was not making the proper efforts to achieve in school. This is confirmed by the remarks of the first-grade teacher, mentioned earlier. At the end of the school year, this teacher remarked that "Jerry is still withdrawn, self-conscious, inhibited, and would not respond orally before the group until second semester. He began to read to me alone, after school. But he still would not participate in gym. He has improved a little in social relationships."

HEALTH AND PHYSICAL ABILITY MEASUREMENTS

Jerry was examined by the school nurse and rated by his gym teacher. The latter noted that "Jerry's muscle tone is very undeveloped, and he is obese, weighing 62 pounds at 48½ inches tall. Teeth, eyes, and hearing are excellent."

One may suspect that the obesity may have prompted his unwillingness to participate in gym classes; it may also affect his acceptance of himself and even the attitude of his peers. It is doubtful, however, whether this alone would cause him to withdraw from active participation in gym and classroom activities. His lack of muscle tone suggests that he has not been active physically at home. Conditions outside the school have contributed to his school behavior; it is not only the school situation which causes him to withdraw.

With a little practice the teacher can learn to observe the physical attributes which suggest medical examination for the child. Symptoms of illness, gross physical defects, lack of energy, hearing or vision loss, speech impediments, and lack of coordination are easily noticed. The teacher should know whether examination has been made and treatment instituted, and whether the child requires special consideration in the classroom.

Health histories—obtained by the school physician, nurse, or even the teacher—may help to suggest any special treatments or privileges that should be instituted. For example, Jerry's health history showed that he is a bed wetter; he suffers severe, frequent head colds; he lacks physical endurance; and he sometimes loses bladder control in school. Such symptoms may be causally related to emotional problems or vice versa. In any case, Jerry should be given frequent bathroom privileges, he should be carefully observed for symptoms of colds, and he should be helped to develop physical endurance and strength.

INFORMATION FROM OTHER SOURCES

Information obtained from referral sources will be discussed later in this chapter. Here we shall discuss working with parents as a source of data which may help the teacher further understand a child and learn to help him in a school setting.

In Jerry's case, a visiting teacher went to his home and talked with his parents. The following information was relayed to the school:

Jerry is receiving little training in social interaction, so should be helped, especially, at school. He lacks suitable adult identifying figures, and the teacher may be able to have Jerry identify with her and to model suitable behavior for him.

Jerry seems insecure. He is under pressures of several kinds, and receives inconsistent reinforcement concerning his failure to participate in class. (He is alternatively bribed by his grandmother to participate and threatened when he does not.) His problems essentially stem from his home background. Too much should not be expected of him at this time. Effort should be expended to provide him with general cultural experiences, plus practice in talking, communicating in other ways, and in social interaction.

Little change is to be expected in his out-of-school life. The school must try to provide compensating experiences; these may extend even to teaching eating habits and cleanliness.

Interpretation of Data

BRINGING INFORMATION TOGETHER

A child-study report (see Appendix D) is valuable for several reasons:

It helps the teacher to understand the child, since all information is tabulated, correlations can be seen, confirmations and inconsistencies are apparent, and hypotheses may be drawn.

It provides material for others who work with the child: other teachers, guidance workers, school social workers, and psychologists.

It provides material for discussion with parents.

It can be followed up and the child's progress or lack of progress noted.

It serves to indicate something of the number and kinds of problems children in the school may have. When a number of reports on different children are brought together, needs for changes in school programs or facilities may be recognized. For example, if a number of children are from underprivileged homes, as was Jerry, it might be necessary to augment the school lunch program. Perhaps the medical facilities should be extended. Parent education, modification of the gym program, and other changes might be indicated.

It alerts the teacher to the variety of reasons contributing to misbehavior or problems of learning or mental health and helps the teacher apply the causal approach.

This holistic attack on child study not only considers the various factors which might influence the child, but their interrelationships are remarked. This is in contrast to the more atomistic approach where the same kinds of assessments may be made, but are not brought together in any systematic way. Frequently in many schools a great deal of data are available concerning pupils, but they are rarely studied or attempts made to correlate them. This being the case, the teacher or specialist is working much more in the dark than need be.

In developing a child-study report, the following questions should be considered:

1. What is known about the child himself?
2. What is known about the child's home and school environment?
3. What are the child's apparent problems?
4. What hypotheses may be formed about causes and ways to remediate them?
5. What other information may be needed?
6. What tentative conclusions may be drawn?
7. What may be attempted in helping the child?

Care must be taken to distinguish between fact and surmise, hypothesis and conclusion. Whenever a finding is in doubt or when information is lacking, study should be continued until clarity is obtained on such points.

INFORMATION ABOUT JERRY

Physical Health and Appearance. Jerry is in good general physical health, although he has frequent colds and is somewhat lacking in strength and endurance. He is short for his age and somewhat obese (nurse, visiting teacher, school records). Jerry has undeveloped muscle tone, but his hearing, vision, and teeth are excellent (gym teacher, nurse). Jerry's eating habits are poor (cafeteria supervisor, visiting teacher). He has had no accidents of consequence (visiting teacher, parents). His bed-wetting is considered due to emotional causes (gym teacher, visiting teacher).

Emotional Health and Social Adjustment. Jerry is self-conscious and withdrawn (gym teacher's log, anecdotal record, interview). He does not speak in class and will not participate in school activities (log, anecdotal record, cumulative record). He does not feel accepted by other pupils or by adults, quite rightfully feeling this way (sociogram, log, anecdotal record, interview, visiting teacher). He does not appear to accept others (interview, sociogram). Jerry lacks self-esteem (log, anecdotal record, cumulative record, interview). He lacks friends (cafeteria supervisor, visiting teacher, sociogram, teachers' remarks). He shows signs of tension and anxiety (gym teacher, interview, visiting teacher).

Family Conditions. Jerry is the oldest in a family of six boys (gym teacher). He is from an underprivileged family (visiting teacher). The father is admired by Jerry, but pays the boy little attention (interview). The grandmother is an influence, but alternately threatens and bribes the boy, and may be compounding his problems (visiting teacher). Jerry feels neglected and is jealous of his brothers (interview).

INTERPRETING MATERIAL ON JERRY

A number of hypotheses concerning the nature of Jerry's problems may be formed.

1. Jerry feels rejected, is rejected, and in turn rejects others. His social development is therefore inadequate and his mental health has suffered.

2. Jerry lacks self-confidence and self-esteem. He therefore lacks motivation to achieve and employs defenses of a withdrawing nature.

3. He is threatened by social situations and classroom interaction. He therefore fails to participate in school activities. This is reinforced by peer treatment of him.

4. Family relationships have caused emotional signs such as bed-wetting, frequent colds, and withdrawing behavior. In view

of the parental situation, it is not surprising that Jerry has suffered; very possibly his brothers will also show emotional signs.

5. Jerry's school environment demands competition on physical, social, and academic levels. He does not feel able to compete with his peers; in actuality, he is inferior physically and has a poor cultural background, and lacks required study skills.

6. Jerry's appearance, withdrawing behavior, and lack of participation cause him to drop increasingly behind the others in most areas.

Other hypotheses are possible, of course, and those listed need to be further checked out. It seems necessary for psychological examination to be made of Jerry by a specialist, and if hypotheses are born out, treatment will be required on a number of fronts (including home, grandmother, health, peer attitude, educational remediation, and probably some individual counseling) .

REMEDIAL TREATMENT FOR JERRY

In the case of Jerry there were two important results from the study begun by the gym teacher. First, all teachers understood Jerry better and were able to initiate efforts in their classes to help him. Second, Jerry was referred to a child-study clinic for further evaluation. This referral, in turn, reinforced the school's efforts to help the boy, and resulted in home counseling, which also was of benefit.

The child-study clinic consisted of a team of workers which included psychologists, a psychiatrist, and social workers. Study led to the belief that Jerry's main problem was his deep-seated feeling of inferiority due to neglect at home by the mother, and failure of the father to fully accept his son.

It was decided that because of his feeling of rejection and inferiority, teachers should not try to force Jerry to talk in class, but to let him move at his own speed into group participation. Continued encouragement and individual remedial instruction in academic and physical education classes were recommended. Jerry was not to be allowed to "just sit in class," but attention was not to be called to his behavior through comments, and he was not to be subjected to strong pressures to achieve. Friendly support from the teacher, together with reinforcement of any efforts that Jerry might make to help himself, was recommended as a course of action.

At the same time, it was realized that, if left to participate only when he felt like it, Jerry might never join in group activities, for such was his pattern. His assignments were thus manipulated so that work was on his level and he would be helped to know success; his strong points would be taken advantage of, rather than attention being given so strongly to his weak points. After gaining a degree of confidence in his ability to achieve, Jerry would be encouraged to enter group activities by assuming a somewhat passive role at first, with more active participation to come later.

His physical-health and endurance problems would be subjected to individual exercises and advice from the gym teacher, and ways would be found to help Jerry gain a more adequate diet at school. Attempts to work with the home were deemed likely to be fruitless, in view of the mother's attitude and the relatively off-hand behavior of the father. An attempt was made to counsel the mother, however, to see what could be gained in improving Jerry's home life.

Psychotherapy was not considered feasible or necessary at that point, for Jerry had demonstrated some progress, slow though it might be.

Attempts were also to be made to help Jerry's peers accept him; one way was to have Jerry act as a helper to the class in certain ways, and another was to place Jerry at the table with the child who had said he would like Jerry to sit with him.

Further study of Jerry was to be made by the school from time to time, with a second referral to the clinic if necessary.

Although Jerry's problems were not primarily of school origin and although little could be done to alleviate the home situation, it was believed that the school could help Jerry to help himself. In cases like that of Jerry, schools can try to help pupils learn to withstand the stresses in their lives. Schools can provide satisfaction of motives for acceptance and self-esteem, they may provide models for behavior, and they may provide satisfaction of the motive to achieve. In substance, the school cannot solve a child's problems, but suitable study and remedial efforts within the traditional sphere of influence of the school can both improve scholastic achievement and do much for the outlook and behavior of the child.

□

REFERENCES

Abramovitz, A. B., and E. Burnham. "Exploring Potentials for Mental Health in the Classroom," *Mental Hygiene,* 43 (1959), 253–9.

Amrine, M. "The 1965 Congressional Inquiry into Testing: A Commentary," *American Psychologist,* 20 (1965), 859–71.

Bower, E. M., P. J. Tashnovian, and C. A. Larson. *A Process for Early Identification of Emotionally Disturbed Children.* Sacramento: California State Department of Education, 1958.

Bower, E. M., and N. Lambert. *A Process for In-School Screening of Children with Emotional Handicaps.* Sacramento: California State Department of Education, 1962. Distributed for research purposes by Educational Testing Service, Princeton and Los Angeles.

Clopton, W., S. Shriver, M. H. Freedman, Senator S. J. Ervin, Jr., Representative C. E. Gallagher, and J. W. Macy, Jr. Invited Comment, *American Psychologist,* 20 (1965), 875–84.

Cunningham, R. *Understanding Group Behavior of Boys and Girls.* New York: Columbia University Teachers College, 1951.

Gronlund, N. E. *Sociometry in the Classroom.* New York: Harper, 1959.

Gross, M. L. *The Brain Watchers.* New York: Random House, 1962.

Hunter, E. C. "Changes in Teachers' Attitudes Toward Children's Behavior Over the Last Thirty Years," *Mental Hygiene,* 41 (1957), 3–11.

Los Angeles County Public Schools. *Guiding Today's Children,* Part I. Los Angeles: California Test Bureau, 1959.

Packard, V. *The Naked Society.* New York: McKay, 1964.

Rogers, C. R. "The Criteria Used in a Study of Mental Health Problems," *Educational Research Bulletin,* 21 (1942), 29–40.

Ullmann, C. A. *Identification of Maladjusted Children.* Washington, D.C.: U.S. Department of Health, Education and Welfare, 1957.

Vance, F. L. "Work of the APA Committee on Psychological Assessment in Relation to Public Concern About Testing," *American Psychologist,* 20 (1965), 873–4.

Wickman, E. K. *Children's Behavior and Teachers' Attitudes.* New York: Commonwealth Fund, 1928.

SUGGESTIONS FOR FURTHER READING

Gronlund, N. E. *Sociometry in the Classroom.* New York: Harper, 1959.
This book amplifies techniques mentioned in this chapter; it is usable for elementary-school teachers, in particular, who are interested in techniques and interpretation of sociometry.

Los Angeles County Schools. *Guiding Today's Children,* Part I. Los Angeles: California Test Bureau, 1959.
Here is an excellent discussion of studying and interpreting results of data on children. Practical in orientation, it is written for teachers and guidance personnel.

WORKING WITH
INDIVIDUAL PUPILS—
LEARNING PRINCIPLES

The following illustration, again a report by a student-teacher, is a good introduction to this chapter. We think the application of learning principles will seem obvious:

Don is almost five years old and is like most of the other boys in kindergarten, except that he is constantly seeking attention. For example, when the teacher is seated on a chair in front of the class Don runs to sit in front of her, and holds on to her leg. If the class is asked to sit and wait for the teacher because she is busy at her desk, Don runs to the desk and will not sit until told to do so—at least two or three times. He just grins when the teacher tells him at first and does not move until she actually yells at him.

Once when the class was making jello, each child had a chance to stir it. After being told specifically to hang on to the spoon, he just let go of it and let it drop into the bowl and sink into the jello. On another occasion, the class was making construction paper figures. Each child was told to take one piece of paper and make one figure. Don took five pieces of paper and made five figures.

I feel that in Don's case, the teacher's responses should be considered important, for she seems to reinforce everything that Don is doing to seek attention.

For example, in the case of the jello, the girls were supposed to go to the activity room but the boys were to remain seated, except for Mark, who was to carry equipment for the teacher. But Don immediately ran to help, and she gave him something to carry. While doing "jumping jacks" some of the boys had difficulty co-ordinating their movements. Don was one of them, so the teacher went to help him, but gave no help to the others. Sometimes when the group is sitting together, Don moves away and sits under a table. When the teacher notices him she yells at him to get out. He refuses, and she goes to pull him out while the class laughs and giggles.

I think it can be seen that Don's attention-seeking activities are resulting in the teacher attending to him, and thus are being rein-forced.

We shall return to Don later, after some discussion of learn-ing principles which can be employed to control behavior. The questions we shall keep in mind are: How can Don's behavior be extinguished? Should it be inhibited? What alternative ways might we choose, so that the outcomes would be most desirable?

This chapter is concerned primarily with the remedial efforts of the teacher, with or without help from a specialist. We shall consider the role of the teacher in fostering appropriate motives and responses and in helping the child to extinguish those undesirable to society and those producing problems for the child (Reger, 1965). Unclear perceptions thus need to be clarified; the child must be helped to face reality; motives must be examined; defenses must be dealt with; appropriate models must be provided; and reinforcement principles must be ap-plied to shape acceptable behavior. The teacher can be an identifying figure, supportive and understanding, as well as a reinforcer of responses. He can help the child to improve social relationships, gain competency over his tasks, and develop de-sirable expectations concerning himself and his efforts to solve problems.

Assessment and Remediation

Chapter 10 dealt with the study of the child, interpretation of data on him, forming hypotheses about him, and the need to validate these hypotheses. These attempts to understand the child's behavior may be termed assessment or evaluation. (Although children with problems make up the bulk of those professionally evaluated, it might be wise to study competent children to learn why competency develops, rather than to concern ourselves so entirely with maladaptive behavior.)

Assessment is of little value unless it leads to definite recommendations for remediation. Further, recommendations are of little value when framed in generalities; they must lead to specific actions on the part of the teacher or others trying to help the child.

It must not be thought that a nice "clean" assessment of problems, coupled with specific recommendations, necessarily leads to improved behavior on the part of the child. Remediation is essentially a problem-solving process, and, like all problem-solving processes, must be tentative and experimental until ultimate solution is attained. Thus hypotheses concerning a child's behavior may lead to remedial actions, but these, in turn, may suggest the need for more data, for altered hypotheses, or for alteration of remedial tactics. Essentially one works back and forth from assessment to remediation, noting carefully any altered responses on the part of the child. One gains a lead to the child's behavior, tries something, but, if it does not work, alters one's tactics, assuming that they have had time enough to be successful if they are going to be.

There are two main methods in remediation, based on different conceptions of the nature of personality. One position consists of dealing with a person's motives, perceptions, and attitudes. This position emphasizes the belief that such variables determine the choices one makes, hence his behavior. The freedom of the individual, his self-determination, and his choices among possible behaviors are stressed.

From this point of view, because a variety of behaviors can come about from a given motive, changing the actions themselves is not particularly helpful; the underlying motives must be altered. Thus if a child dislikes another child, he can be prevented from hitting the other, but unless the dislike is dealt with it will be shown in some other way or at some other time. Self theorists and psychoanalysts attempt to help their clients understand the meanings of their problem behaviors, so that they can deal with the presumed conflicts, frustrations, and anxieties that motivate them. They feel that, when motives, attitudes, or perceptions are changed, behavior too will change.

Chapter 12 examines the self and perceptual and attitudinal variables. But this chapter stresses a more behavioristic approach. We shall be concerned here with changing behavior itself. By reinforcing appropriate actions and by negatively reinforcing or extinguishing inappropriate behavior, teachers may reduce or do away with problems. As the pupil is living a more acceptable and efficient existence, he receives more reinforcements, and his feelings and attitudes are in turn likely to become more positive. This approach considers the behavior itself the main problem. The angry child already mentioned will be prevented from expressing his anger and having it reinforced. When it is not reinforced, it will be extinguished, and more appropriate behavior will be elicited. It is not necessary, from this position, to assume that other "symptoms" will result.

Essentially this process is a shaping process, frequently employed experimentally (for example, see Staats & Staats, 1963; Ferster & Skinner, 1957) but more recently by therapists (see Franks, 1964; Wolpe, et al., 1964).

We shall consider briefly one other aspect of the relationships among motives, perceptions, and behavior. One is used to thinking that his attitudes and values give direction to behavior. Such may not always be the case, however; at least sometimes it is found that attitudes change concomitantly with behavior, or even as the result of behavioral change. Sometimes one is forced or inveigled into acts which are dissonant with his attitudes (Festinger, 1964). In such instances, his attitudes may change in a direction in accordance with his actual behavior. Whether such change comes about as a means of reducing dissonance (or conflict) between act and attitude, or as a defense, or for some other reason, studies have shown that this does occur. For example, even when a person's attitude is against racial discrimination, he may, because of outside pressures, be unable to live in certain areas or sell his home to certain people. As a result, he may become somewhat prejudiced himself. K. Lewin (1953) was able to get housewives to cook certain cuts of meat that they normally disdained, primarily on the basis of aiding the war effort. One outcome was that they began to change their attitudes about such cuts of meat to where they found them "tasty," "economical," or otherwise desirable. W. J. McGuire (1966) cites amusing studies in which students were paid money to lie to other students, saying that they were enjoying what were really extremely boring tasks; in time, such students were found actually to assume attitudes much like those they were trying to purvey to their peers.

In substance, reinforcement theorists pay relatively less attention to internal variables and more to manipulating environmental reinforcers. But the manipulation of reinforcers must be carefully made so that the desired behaviors result, without bad side effects, and this demands a high degree of precision in stating conditions under which reinforcement principles will be employed. Failure to do so, as we shall see, may result in intensifying inappropriate behavior or failure to learn new and appropriate acts.

General Factors Required for Behavior Change

UNDERSTANDING THE CHANGE NEEDED

Arthur Staats and W. H. Butterfield (1965) have experimented with the use of concrete reinforcement (reward) in the improvement of children's learning. They feel that social reinforcement, such as teachers' approval, must be learned in early childhood; failure to see such approval as a reinforcement results in many school learning situations failing to provide reinforcement so that the child does not learn well. Accordingly, tokens, which could be accumulated and used to purchase candy, toys, or even a bicycle, were employed in laboratory situations to try to reinforce learning behavior.

One study by Staats used four-year-old children who were taught to read, using reinforcement versus no reinforcement. When reinforced, the children's attention was good, they worked hard and learned rapidly; when no reinforcement was provided, they fooled around and learned relatively little. The attention span of a four-year-old is said to be only about five minutes, but Staats was able to hold the attention of his reinforced children for as long as forty minutes.

He also worked with a juvenile delinquent who lived in a detention home, was a continual behavior problem in school, and had never passed a course in his life. After eight and one-half years of schooling, this boy's reading level was that of second grade. A probation officer employed the reinforcement techniques Staats suggested, and after four months of training, the reading achievement had increased to the 4.3-grade level. The boy passed all his courses in school for the first time, and his misbehaviors in school decreased to zero. During the duration of the experiment, the boy had earned tokens valued at $20.31.

As was stressed in Chapter 10, one cannot deal in generalities if he expects to achieve and measure behavior change. There are two immediate requirements for remediation: understanding the changes in behavior required and understanding the factors maintaining present behavior.

To understand the nature of the changes needed, one first must specify the present behavior of the child. To do so requires knowing the stimuli that are eliciting the behavior, the nature of the behavior itself, and behavior which would be preferred.

Referring back to Staats' work, to help the children with reading it was first necessary to determine their current behavior. This pattern included lack of attention, fooling around, and inability to read words or to concentrate. The stimuli—words printed in books—were clear enough. So were the desired responses, namely, attention, discriminating words, pronouncing words, and understanding their meaning. In this instance it was not necessary for Staats to try to remove or extinguish present reponses; when appropriate responses were elicited and rewarded, inappropriate behavior was dropped by his pupils.

In other instances it might be necessary to reduce inappropriate behavior before desired behavior could be instituted. For example, we might refer to the case of teaching a child who is afraid of the water to swim. It is unlikely that he can be taught to swim until his fears have been reduced or entirely extinguished. (The old practice of throwing a nonswimmer into the water succeeded in most cases in teaching fear of the water, rather than swimming.) The behavior present is thus a manifestation of fear and must be removed. The desired behavior is learning to swim, and it must be instituted.

The argument may be advanced that, when one learns to swim, his fear of the water is reduced; why not start immediately teaching him to swim? This method does work, in some instances, but it depends on the degree of fear present. Highly fearful people are likely to be unable to make adaptive responses and cannot concentrate on swimming techniques; furthermore, high anxiety tends to produce inefficient behavior, as we have seen in previous chapters. Should the fear be controllable by the learner, however, as with mild anxiety, it could motivate him to learn to swim. When specifying present behavior, one thus needs to describe, not only the nature of the behavior, but also its degree.

Let us take one other example. In Chapter 10 we referred to a child who cried when he stubbed his toe and speculated about whether he was simply showing that he was hurt, whether he was seeking attention, or whether he had other motives and emotions. One needs to specify the present behavior as one understands it. What is desirable behavior when hurt? Perhaps the child should bear his pain stoically. Perhaps he should learn to laugh at small hurts. Perhaps his crying is of no concern—his reaction is natural for his age, and he will one day outgrow it. But if he is seeking attention, what behavior should be changed or instituted? Probably several changes are desirable; among them the child should learn to seek attention in acceptable ways, and he should learn to develop feelings of self-confidence, better social relations, and so on. Diagnosis is thus helpful in specifying present behavior. In deciding what behavior to institute, however, one must depend on his value systems.

It is important—indeed, essential—that teachers be highly sensitive to the behavior they wish to reinforce, either negatively or positively. Failure to be clear on this point can result in harm or at least in unadaptive behavior. For example, we have talked about teachers' placing too much emphasis on children's getting correct answers to problems. Although accuracy is desirable, a

teacher may inadvertently reinforce anxiety, conforming behavior, or dependency. In Chapter 4 we discussed discipline,
noting that one could negatively reinforce problem behavior
and also that use of frequent aversive stimuli might cause
children to dislike school, school subjects, or the teacher. Extreme cases can result in strongly reactive behavior, as well as
causing children to reject school mores and values.

UNDERSTANDING FACTORS MAINTAINING PRESENT BEHAVIOR

Behavior does not continue unless it is reinforced in some
way. That is, there must be something accruing to the child, or
he will substitute new behavior for the present action. One
needs to ask oneself what the child gains from his actions.
Unless more powerful reinforcers are found, he will tend not to
change.

For example, some children clown in class. The teacher
usually scolds, punishes, or removes the child from class. Frequently the child is counseled, and it often seems odd that,
when he realizes that his clowning will get him into trouble
with the teacher and may cause him to fail his course, he still
continues. Although it seems self-defeating, he continues his
course of action.

What is missing, of course, is the teacher's realization that the
child is gaining something from the clowning that he does not
get from paying attention and cooperating in class. The chances
are that he is getting attention and even admiration from some
of his peers, he is building some self-esteem, and he is getting
out of studying. In addition, he is manipulating the teacher.
These results are powerful reinforcers for his behavior. But, as
with Staats' work with the delinquent, when the teacher is able
to muster more powerful reinforcers for cooperation and study,
even the class clown may change to a good student.

Similarly, teachers are sometimes more highly supportive of
children who are hostile or aggressive than they are of others,
feeling that such children lack affection and that the teacher's
evidence of friendship will cause the child to be less hostile. Yet
a teacher may inadvertently be reinforcing such hostile behavior, since the child is gaining attention and support, which

can outweigh any guilt feelings he may have, or any punishment he receives for misbehavior.

One other point: The effects of previous learning, and constant elicitation of the same responses, make older, well-learned responses most likely to be dominant in the response hierarchy. As any teacher is aware, it is thus far easier to teach adequate behavior in the first place than to attempt to change inadequate behavior. However, the previous learning is not all-powerful in determining behavior, and if motives, reinforcements, perceptions, and other factors in behavior can be altered, new learning will take place.

OPPORTUNITY TO MANIPULATE THE ENVIRONMENT

As we are considering here primarily the effects of environmental stimuli and reinforcements we must remember that recommended methods will be ineffective unless there is indeed ability to manipulate the child's environment. (Because parents are so able to closely govern the environment of the small child it is not surprising that early family influences are the most important on the child's life.)

The important factor in molding a child's behavior is that of making his environmental experiences as consistent as possible, from place to place and from time to time. Maintaining this consistency is not much of a problem in the elementary school, since children tend to be grouped in self-contained classrooms, and the teacher need only be consistent in the ways he reinforces behavior. It is a much greater problem in junior- and senior-high-school levels, since each pupil may have several teachers, who may not always agree on what changes are desirable and who may not be consistent among themselves in reinforcing such behavior.

To illustrate, let us consider such trivial behavior as that of permitting or not permitting gum-chewing in class. If some teachers permit it and others do not, the child must learn under which conditions he may or may not chew gum. This is not particularly difficult for him to learn. What happens, however, is that with alternatively negative and positive reinforcement, the pleasure of gum-chewing may become the over-riding factor and it will continue in all classes. If all teachers frowned upon this practice, we might expect the habit to be weakened or broken.

Now to consider a more important kind of behavior, one which has mental health connotations, let us look briefly at attention seeking, as when a child speaks without permission, makes "smart" remarks, or otherwise bothers the teacher and his peers. If he is allowed to get away with this behavior in some situations and is punished in others, the inconsistency of reinforcement will do little to modify his behavior. Or, consider the effects when one teacher is strongly punitive to a child and another teacher is supportive. The child will not only react with different behavior in respect to teachers, but also his identification with adults and their values may be confused or conflicting.

Problems also arise in regard to the child's out-of-school environment. Not only the home, but the peer group, provides reinforcements for behavior. The problem is greater at the teen-age level than in elementary school, for adolescents are much more mobile and self-sufficient than children. To foster consistent reinforcements, it is desirable to confer with parents and to develop peer attitudes in line with school values, whenever possible.

The teacher is beset with the practical school problem of managing thirty or more children. This means that the extent to which the stimuli and reinforcements for a given child can be altered is limited. Here again, however, if the teacher is able to keep in mind what behaviors he wishes to reduce and what ones he hopes to foster, many opportunities can be found in any classroom to individualize treatment of the children.

Teachers sometimes feel that children ought to be expected to conform to classroom norms of behavior and should not expect individual treatment. They also feel that children resent special treatment of one another, and may be jealous, feel rejected, or otherwise have undesirable attitudes about such teacher behavior. These arguments have some merit, but the writer believes they are based on a misconception of what is meant by individualizing treatment. Our position is not that some children ought to be punished, others ignored, and others reinforced for *similar* behavior, but rather, that the teacher should suit *all* of his activities to his understanding of the meaning of the child's behavior. For example, one pupil may burst out with a remark in class. Perhaps he simply lacks impulse control, and the teacher can "shush" him with a remark and a smile. Another child, coming forth with a remark, might be deliberately baiting the teacher, and in this instance an admonishment of stronger note might be required. Some children are too forward in pushing their ideas, and teachers try to get them to be considerate and listen to the ideas of others; equally, some children never volunteer an opinion, and the teacher needs to draw them out. The teacher's approach must vary for these kinds of children, yet no one would consider that such individualization is inappropriate.

One other point must be made. Changing behavior takes time. Teachers sometimes say that they have tried "such and such" with a given child, and it "didn't work." True, the teacher may have been using inappropriate methods. However, it may also be true that the teacher is seeking too big a change too quickly.

Psychologists refer to "shaping" behavior, and to the methods of "successive approximation." To illustrate, we refer to a film by B. F. Skinner, *Learning and Behavior,* in which he shows how he can train a pigeon to turn in a circle, a behavior foreign to pigeons. Skinner has the pigeon hungry enough so that it wants to eat—that is, there must be a reinforcer that can be used, in this case, food. He then watches for the pigeon to make part of a turn, and then reinforces the pigeon with food. At the next trial, he waits until the pigeon turns a little bit further, before reinforcing it. In this way, waiting each time until more of a turn has been made, Skinner can eventually get the pigeon to make complete turns for him.

We can do the same thing with children. The reader may wish to refer back to Chapter 10, to some of the data about Jerry, who refused to participate in gym class. It was thought probable that Jerry did not like to participate because he was obese, somewhat lacking in muscle tone, felt badly about not having clean clothes, and felt somewhat rejected by other pupils. The teacher, in this case, had a number of techniques at her disposal. First she could remove some of the obviously negatively reinforcing aspects of the situation—she could try to see to it that Jerry's clothes, hair, and cleanliness didn't stand in the way of his relations with other pupils. This would necessitate conferences with the mother, and perhaps the teacher would sometimes need to send Jerry to the washroom to clean up before school. The teacher then could begin to shape Jerry's participation in gym gradually. She would (and did) work with him individually, and reinforce him for going through the motions with her. She could then encourage him to go through some of the familiar activities by himself, praising him when he did so. The next step would be to allow him to have experiences with small groups of others, carefully chosen so that he would not show up to disadvantage. Finally, Jerry might be encouraged to participate with the entire group. Teacher time is, of course, a problem in this case. However, schools are beginning to appreciate the need for teachers' helpers to provide such individualized instruction.

Reducing Inadequate Behavior

DISCRIMINATION

Sometimes inadequate emotions and overt behavior come about because the pupil fails to discriminate between different situations, or between changed conditions and the original state of affairs. For example, people are not all alike, therefore the young child may be disappointed if he expects his age mates to react similarly to each other regarding his behavior. Small children frequently react to their teachers just as they do toward their parents, and problems may result, for the roles played by teachers are not the same as those of parents.

The child's behavior may be inappropriate in other ways. Situations that formerly provoked anxiety need not do so when the child is older. When smaller, he may have been made anxious by pets or other animals; now that he is older he need not fear puppies or kittens. Perhaps he was criticized strongly by a previous teacher for poor work, but he can be shown that the present teacher has a more helpful attitude. Perhaps he was once laughed at for a poor recitation in class; it can be shown that in *this* class pupils try to be helpful to each other.

The child must also learn to discriminate between symbols

and actual phenomena. Words become objects of emotional re-action and are reacted to just as the child may have reacted to the situations that gave these words their initial meaning. For example, "school," "teacher," "arithmetic," and "reading" all convey feelings to the child, just as do "dentist" or "squad car" to some adults. If certain classroom situations invoke thoughts of unpleasant experiences, the child may react emotionally whenever these situations are symbolized by words.

Symbols, especially words, however, may not be adequate conveyors of reality. Although they are useful ways to short-cut problem-solving activities, symbols frequently provide errone-ous emotional connotations. One reason is that feelings about symbols may have been developed before the child had a clear concept of the phenomena they represent. Equally, the phe-nomena themselves may have changed. Furthermore, the child may overgeneralize or stereotype, without noting that one teacher is not like another, one mother is not like another, and so on. The point is that words are not things, although they are often reacted to as if they were. Such discrimination has to be learned.

Children sometimes have thoughts that are distasteful to them and cause them to feel guilty, anxious, or fearful. Sex, dislike for parents, or temptation to steal can cause emotional reactions in children; they may react to the thoughts as if they were actually carrying them out. It is sometimes useful to show children the difference between thoughts and actions. To illus-trate, a teacher might find occasion to comment, "You said you wanted to push Sally, but you didn't really do it, did you?" Or: "Pete, you say you dislike school as much as you do, but all day you seemed to have a good time. I don't think you really dislike school as much as you do the *thought* of school, do you?" Or: "All of us get angry sometimes, but so long as we don't take out our feelings on people, no harm is done."

Again, children may not be aware of how their own behavior affects others. Jerry, in our illustration, had to be helped to see how his own withdrawing behavior, his lack of cleanliness, and his refusal to talk induced others to ignore or reject him. This ability to discriminate between cause and effect, the relation-ship between self and others, and the real feelings of others may have to be taught.

The need to discriminate among people and situations, between fantasy and reality, and in other ways may thus be an important first step in reducing undesirable behavior. To be helpful, teachers need first to learn how children perceive the situations in question; they can then help the child to perceive them more adequately, with resulting modification of feelings and behaviors. (Similarly, children need to learn how situations *are* alike, so that appropriate behavior will generalize.)

NEGATIVE REINFORCEMENT

We referred to negative reinforcement in Chapter 5 when we discussed school discipline. Negative reinforcement is the provision of painful or unpleasant consequences to responses. As we earlier remarked, negative reinforcement can cause behavior to be inhibited; however, it may not cause the desire to behave in such ways to be inhibited. The result may be that when the negative reinforcement is not present, the behavior may be reinstated.

Nevertheless, it is sometimes necessary to punish. Certain behaviors can be ended by negatively reinforcing them in consistent, prompt ways; harshness or severity is not required, consistency of reinforcement being more important. Let us consider the case of parking one's automobile in a no-parking zone. If one is consistently tagged by the police, eventually he will give up this behavior. The parking fines need not be large. On the other hand, if most of the time he gets away with illegal parking, a few fines will not cause this behavior to cease.

Similarly, in the classroom, children can learn to cease undesirable activities if they are consistently admonished or punished; but if we sometimes ignore such behavior, laugh at it, or seem to condone it, we will tend to lack control.

EXTINCTION

When an activity is not met with reinforcement, the activity tends to cease. Most people lose their fears of lightning, of snakes, or of spiders, which they may have imitated from others as small children, simply because they never are hit by lightning or bitten by snakes or spiders. However, for extinction to occur, the behavior must be elicited. If not elicited, the lack of reinforcement cannot be effective; previous learning will continue. Thus to remove fears of lightning, one must have safe experiences with lightning; similarly to remove fears of snakes or spiders, one must have experiences with them—sometimes through the means of a biology class. The writer remembers an instance where most of the pupils in a biology class showed some antipathy for snakes but in course of study began gradually to handle them. Eventually even the girls were enjoying picking them up and enjoying their "clean, cool feel."

Teachers may be familiar with "negative practice," or practicing errors until the errors are dropped. For example, when one makes a consistent error in typing, he may extinguish the tendency to make that error by practicing the error, prior to practicing the correct response. Piano teachers frequently use this technique also.

This kind of extinguishing has been amusingly employed by one teacher in regard to two children who habitually made faces at each other. She let them sit face-to-face and told them to make faces at each other; at first this was great fun, but as time went on it became an effort. In this instance only one "cure" was required.

In the matter of aggressive behavior, if a child's hostile actions do not bring him what he wants, the behavior will eventually be dropped. Children who have tantrums can thus be taught not to act in this way by removing them from the presence of others and by not allowing them to gain their desires. Attention seekers, disciplinary problems, and others can be made to study by themselves; they thus fail to gain the reinforcements of peer attention or admiration, and their behavior should be extinguished. At first, however, when behavior meets frustration, the child intensifies his efforts to gain reinforcement. Care must be taken not to allow intensified efforts to be reinforced, as parents sometimes do by "giving in" to the child when he has a violent temper tantrum or screams loudly enough.

In the case of Don (p. 317), who exhibited extreme attention-seeking behavior, the following technique was tried by the student teacher:

I decided to see whether I could stop Don's attention-seeking behavior by ignoring him. On the first day of my teaching, Don acted up as usual, hanging on to my leg, talking out of turn, and so forth. I ignored this until he got to be really bad. Then I took him aside and said that as long as he continued to act up I would not consider him a part of the class and would not even recognize that he was there. He followed me around, and I pretended that he wasn't there. He continued to act up that day, and I continued to ignore him.

The next day he did not do as many things out of line. Once when he acted up during a lesson, I waited until the lesson was over, took him aside, and reminded him again of what I was doing and why I was doing it. One day while the class was putting on a dramatization, I told the class that those talking out of turn or trying to get ahead of someone so that they could act first would lose their turns. Eventually Don did both. When he did, I said, "Someone has just lost his turn," and nothing more. When it came to the end, Don wanted his turn. I took him aside while the class was doing something else and again explained why he got no turn and why he would not continue to get any if he kept on acting the way he did. I thus took away not only his uncalled-for chances for attention, but his regular chances in the curriculum pattern when he disturbed the class.

He is becoming progressively less of a problem for me, although his attention-seeking behavior has not entirely ceased. However, I feel that this is a successful way to deal with Don, for the cooperating teacher still treats him in her usual way, always giving him attention, and he continues to consistently act up for her.

COUNTERCONDITIONING

"Counterconditioning" refers to changing the emotional tone associated with an event from negative to positive or vice versa—by manipulating the nature of the reinforcements to responses. For example, as J. Holt showed in Chapter 9, many children are fearful of making mistakes. They have been criticized, feel threatened, and are anxious; therefore they resort to many artifices and devices in order to be "right" or at least to appear "right" in the classroom.

Making mistakes, however, is simply consonant with trying to learn something new. One does not make mistakes if he always sticks to tried and true patterns of behavior. If teachers would encourage pupils to try to learn something new, rather than to continually emphasize "correctness," taking risks might become fun, and true learning could increase. Teachers should treat children's mistakes simply as clues to problem solving; children should be positively reinforced for constructive efforts, even if the answers obtained are incorrect. Thus defensive activities would tend to be reduced, allowing for instituting more desirable behavior.

Introducing Adequate Behavior

One of the problems of negative reinforcement or punishment is that while it can cause inappropriate behavior to be inhibited, it does not necessarily ensure that desirable behavior will be instituted. The child may, or may not, know what behavior is desirable; he may, or may not, institute desirable behavior, even when he understands what is wanted.

In introducing adequate behavior there are essentially two problems: the first is that of eliciting the behavior so that it can be reinforced; the second is that of reinforcing such behavior adequately. The teacher therefore is faced with a decision—he can either wait (and hope) for adequate behavior to occur and then reinforce it, or, he can attempt to instigate the adequate behavior and reinforce it when it appears. For classroom efficiency and economy of time, the latter method is usually employed.

SYMBOLIC ACTIVITY—URGING, EXPLAINING, ADVISING

Teachers, parents, and others make frequent use of verbal persuasion, exhortation, or suggestion.

Such methods are of value in introducing behavior when the child is not clear what behaviors are desired; indeed, this process is what teaching frequently is. Thus one helps children to learn courtesy by urging politeness and explaining how others feel and react, he helps children learn to control emotional expressions, or he helps children to discriminate between moral values. In general, children recognize the reasons for following the advice of parents and teachers, and their socioemotional development proceeds quite normally.

Such methods are also useful in other ways. They can help a fearful or anxious child to overcome his aversive tendencies enough to at least attempt tentatively to reach his goals. Through the use of reassurance, encouragement, and verbal reinforcement, the child may be helped to perform acts which are threatening to him, and he may be induced by admonishment or warning not to employ defenses or to withdraw. The teacher can also help the child to understand more clearly the results of various choices of behavior.

Sometimes, however, verbal suggestion or persuasion does not achieve desired results, behavior does not change, and desired acts are not instituted. One frequent problem with the use of suggestion is that the advice is phrased negatively; in this way the child is told what not to do, and negative emotions are thus induced, with aversive feelings and behavior resulting. Constructive suggestions may not be forthcoming. This is a problem with verbal censure or castigation. Another stumbling block occurs when the child learns to ignore suggestions of others because they have been so frequently forthcoming that they have aroused defenses. Thus he may not listen to them, or may seem to acquiesce, yet fail to follow through on suggestions. Other reasons for the failure of persuasion may be that other motives are competing with the child's desires to please the teacher, or perhaps the child had tried to follow the suggestions but failed to attain any satisfaction.

To illustrate:

George D., a junior high-school boy, finally "got the word" about school achievement. Capable of high quality work, George had "goofed along" and had made little real effort. One day the school guidance counselor tested several of the students, and, finding that George had a very high intelligence quotient, discussed with him the advantages of working hard and doing one's best. He pointed out the educational and vocational opportunities that would be lost if George did not improve, and suggested that George would find much satisfaction along with material advantage in achieving highly.

It didn't quite work out that way, however. George made quite a point at home of working at his homework, but George's father, inconsiderately, simply chose to tell George that "that was what he should have been doing all along"; he referred to George's wasted time and was happy that George was "finally going to take advice."

George's peers were somewhat disappointed that he no longer

had so much time for sports or play and took the trouble to deride him as a "grind," a teacher's pet, and a person who had been brainwashed.

Teachers also did not seem to notice any difference in George's behavior or in the results of his work, and his report-card grades remained the same.

George is now somewhat bitter, and, when anyone urges him to work harder, George takes it with a grain of salt.

Of course, one should be reinforced by his own feelings of satisfaction; yet when positive behavior is not reinforced by society (which may well be the case, for society and everyday events cannot well be predicted or controlled), he may not continue efforts to act as suggested. Definite provisions for reinforcement must be made if suggestions are to be accepted by others (Lindsley, 1963).

MODELING

Children learn much from example, especially the examples of parents and teachers. Imitation comes about primarily when the child identifies with the adult (or other person), but he does not usually model after someone whom he dislikes.

Examples for imitation come from many sources. Among them are actual people, of course, but also characters in films, books, or television. Probably the most difficult task is to teach the child which examples should be imitated, and the success of this process depends on the child's identifying with the teacher. This identification, in turn, depends on the teacher supplying positive reinforcements whenever possible. Thus in the classroom the teacher may wish to make such remarks as, "Peter didn't really feel like finishing his homework, but he did, and it is a good job," or, "Mary certainly is considerate of others, isn't she?"

Children tend to imitate behavior that seems to them successful. Thus whether a given behavior is imitated depends partly on how the model is reinforced. For example, if the teacher is urging children to be hard working like himself, it must be apparent that he himself is gaining from hard work. If the teacher wants children to imitate courteous people, courtesy must be rewarded in front of the children. Sometimes a positive reference to desirable acts is enough, as just illustrated; on the other hand, sometimes concrete reinforcements such as special privileges may indicate the usefulness of imitating such behavior.

REINFORCING ALTERNATIVE RESPONSES TO INADEQUATE BEHAVIOR

Dependence may be considered an illustration of inadequate behavior; independence and initiative would be far more desirable. Let us examine the case of Laura:

Laura was usually found in the classroom with her hand raised for help with her seatwork assignment. When the teacher appeared, Laura made little effort to help herself, and the teacher found himself doing Laura's work for her.

Not only was Laura dependent at school, but she was also heard to say about the home, "I can't do this." She was not trying to get out of doing things, for her dependence showed itself frequently in regard to things she really wanted to do. For example, Laura wanted to learn to ride her bicycle but was afraid to make the attempt without the help of an adult.

The teacher determined to help Laura become more self-sufficient. The first step consisted of removing the reinforcements that fostered dependence; for example, when Laura raised a hand for help, the teacher always asked to see what efforts Laura had made on her own. If little evidence of effort was shown, the teacher remarked that he would return when Laura had something to show him.

Equally, whenever Laura showed at least the beginnings of initiative, the teacher found ways to praise her. Emphasis on getting the work correct was removed; penalty for failure was reduced; and Laura received credit for desirable efforts, whether those efforts were successful or not. The pleasures of thinking and acting for oneself were stressed. Laura was encouraged to take pride in doing her own work—then when she was successful she could be proud of doing it all by herself.

Both at home and at school Laura was given opportunities to make choices, but, when she had chosen, she was required to complete whatever she had started. At first she chose easy tasks; gradually, however, she moved toward more complex tasks and found considerable satisfaction in being able to do them for herself.

Examples of reinforcing alternative responses are numerous in the classroom; the wonder is that so many teachers negatively reinforce inadequate behavior without sufficiently pointing out and reinforcing adequate behavior in its place.

Take, for example, the instance of a child who daydreams in class. The teacher is likely to tell him to pay attention, but may do little about helping him learn to attend and reinforcing him for doing so. Much can be done, however. The teacher can actively involve the child in a discussion of the class work; he can work with the child individually, showing him how to study and find satisfaction in his work; he can comment to the child about how attentive he has been, when such is the case; and he can involve the child in group work. Other ideas will occur to experienced teachers; the essential point is that a teacher can pick and choose among the behaviors he wants to reinforce, so that those responses tend to become dominant and inadequate responses tend to be dropped.

At this point a few reminders of factors related to the use of reinforcement in shaping behavior may be useful. The following points should be considered.

KINDS OF REINFORCEMENT

Not everyone responds to the same possible reinforcers; that is, what may reinforce one person may not reinforce another. One's motives, previous experiences, perceptions, and other individual factors help to determine what will be reinforcing in a given instance and to account for differences among people and among one individual's reactions at different times.

Teachers appeal to inner reinforcers when they relate the child's behavior to his own internalized attitudes and values, when they appeal to his conscience, or when they ask him to imagine how others feel about his behavior. The particular self-attitudes and goals of the child should not be forgotten; if they are different from those the teacher expects, what may logically seem reinforcing may not be so at all.

Social reinforcers have already been discussed at some length and will be only briefly mentioned here. It is important for teachers to know whom the child's models and identifying figures may be and whether or not they include the teachers themselves. They also have to learn which particular kind of social reinforcement the child prefers (some children may be embarrassed, for example, at too enthusiastic or open praise from the teacher).

Concrete reinforcement deserves a little lengthier discussion at this point. Its value has frequently been overlooked or derided as bribery. Some educators have argued that concrete reinforcement (sometimes termed "incentives") is not desirable as it is not related directly to the school task itself. The child then may not learn to find satisfaction and continuing motivation in the work he is doing but may consider it merely a means to achieve some desired reinforcement.

Yet concrete reinforcement may produce desired behavior when other reinforcers do not seem to have much effect. They may be a means of getting the child to do a lesson that he is otherwise unwilling to do; once embarked upon study, he may find other reinforcers as he pursues his tasks. The incentives used in school may supplement other reinforcements and are not necessarily "bad" in themselves. It is primarily when children work for material rewards alone and resort to superficial study, cheating, undesirable competition, or other undesirable behavior that incentives can justly be criticized. The teacher should remember that he himself works for the concrete reinforcement of money. Although he may find other rewards in his teaching, if the money were seriously inadequate, he probably would change jobs.

C. W. Slack (1960) wanted to modify socially undesirable attitudes of delinquents. He promised to pay money to delinquent youths if they would talk into a tape recorder for an hour at a time. He stated that he did not care what they said, as long as they talked.

At first, some boys were suspicious. They did, however, come to Slack's office, and talked into the recorder; they were paid, as promised. Some were late or truant, but, by paying more money for promptness, Slack began to get them to appear regularly and on time.

As it happened, after a time the youths began to run out of nonthreatening or banal things to talk about, and they usually began to discuss their own feelings and attitudes and those of their peers. Some eventually were able to drop suspicion and to discuss their own problems to the point at which they could think through them. Some ended by asking workers for advice. The result was improved social behavior for a number of these youths. Concrete reinforcement was thus a starting point for shaping behavior; eventually the boys came to find value in social reinforcement and reinforcement in their own systems of values.

GRADUAL SHAPING OF BEHAVIOR

Shaping of behavior, too, has already been discussed. Emphasis will be placed here on the general finding that teachers may sometimes be too impatient in expecting improved behavior from children and, as a result, may change their methods too quickly. Particularly in regard to attitudes, long-standing emotional reactions to certain people or other stimuli, and self-perceptions, the teacher is prone to worry about the small or unnoticeable improvement his actions may have brought forth; he then discounts his efforts and tries something else.

It is also true that teachers may fail to reinforce small changes in desired directions. Yet it is clear that, if a child begins to move toward desired goals, it is important to reinforce such change, not only to keep it coming, but also to confirm the child's awareness that his behavior changes are in the correct direction.

Guidance counselors are frequently disturbed by the fact that they can sense attitudinal changes in children referred to them by teachers but that teachers are not always satisfied with the progress that is made. Counselors then remark that "It took this youngster fifteen years to get the way he is, but I am supposed to remake him in a couple of short counseling sessions." This problem suggests that the teacher not only should appreciate *any* useful changes that are begun but also should foster them by adding reinforcements to those of the counselor.

It should also be noted that any sudden changes in behavior, attitudes, or self-perceptions should be partially suspect. Healthy personalities change slowly; it is primarily trauma that makes for sudden change, although there have been dramatic instances in history when ne'er-do-wells have been "converted" quickly by religious leaders or others. On the other hand, the story of Helen Keller is more typical; it took her teacher-companion a long time to help Miss Keller overcome her temper tantrums and to make positive progress toward her remarkable socialized behavior.

Finally, children sometimes regress to previous undesirable behavior, because of habit, competing reinforcements, or even the desire to test others and see how much the behavior to which they have been urged is really prized. Such regressions should not be regarded as indicators of incorrect teaching techniques; rather, they should suggest a careful look at what is being reinforced—and renewed (and improved) efforts.

IMMEDIACY OF REINFORCEMENT

Work with the Job Corps and other agencies dealing with underprivileged children and youth has shown the necessity for immediate reinforcement if progress is to be made. In the school setting children are frequently asked to take on faith the value of working hard at school tasks. Goals are long-term, achievement of such goals is remote, and the reinforcement or payoff is phrased in such terms as "When you are an adult, you'll be glad you learned good English" and "How do you expect to get into college if you don't cultivate good study habits now?" As a result, many children are not motivated to study. Reinforcement is too distant.

Underprivileged youth, in particular, does not accept long-term goals and rewards. Too frequently these children become school dropouts and have rarely received any reinforcements of consequence for their school efforts. Their histories are full of discouragement, frustration, and dislike of school.

Accordingly, agencies dealing with these youths set up short lessons (one or two days in length) rather than long units. Upon completion of each lesson, points are awarded. Completion of several units is noted with a certificate. The youth can be continuously aware of what he has accomplished and can take pride in such progress. He is reinforced frequently and immediately, rather than only at certain times (when report cards come out, in the typical school program). Furthermore, points earned contribute to leaves, raises in pay, and other incentives.

Teachers are also urged to remark immediately on any progress such youths have made. Although these programs do not succeed with all young men, they work with many; as, almost by definition, more typical school programs have been unsuccessful with such youths, it is gratifying to notice the success that the new programs have achieved with many of them.

□

REFERENCES

Ferster, C. W., and B. F. Skinner. *Schedules of Reinforcement.* New York: Appleton, 1957.

Festinger, L. *Conflict, Decision, and Dissonance.* Stanford: Stanford University Press, 1964.

Franks, C. W. (ed.). *Conditioning Techniques in Clinical Practice and Research.* New York: Springer, 1964.

Lewin, K. "Studies in Group Decision," in D. Cartwright and A. Zander. *Group Dynamics.* Evanston: Row, Peterson, 1953, pp. 287–801.

Lindsley, O. R. "Free-Operant Conditioning, Persuasion, and Psychotherapy," University of California at Los Angeles, 1963 (Mimeographed).

McGuire, W. J. "Attitudes and Opinions," *Annual Review of Psychology,* 17 (1966), 475–514.

Reger, R. "On Psychiatry in the Schools," *Journal of School Psychology,* 4 (1965), 45–51.

Skinner, B. F. *Learning and Behavior.* Carousel Films, 1959.

Slack, C. W. "Experimenter–Subject Psychotherapy: A New Method of Introducing Intensive Office Treatment for Unreachable Cases," *Mental Hygiene,* 44 (1960), 238–56.

Staats, A. W., and C. K. Staats. *Complex Human Behavior.* New York: Holt, Rinehart, Winston, 1963.

Staats, A. W., and W. H. Butterfield. "Treatment of Nonreading in a Culturally Deprived Juvenile Delinquent: An Application of Reinforcement Principles," *Child Development,* 36 (1965), 925–42.

Wolpe, J., A. Salter, and L. J. Reyna (eds.). *The Conditioning Therapies.* New York: Holt, Rinehart, Winston, 1964.

SUGGESTIONS FOR FURTHER READING

Bandura, A., and R. H. Walters. *Social Learning and Personality Development.* New York: Holt, Rinehart, Winston, 1963.
The entire book exposes a social learning theory, and teachers will find the principles discussed in this chapter treated to scientific laboratory examination. The book is difficult, however, although short and highly readable. It is more valuable for basic theory than for applications.

Staats, A. W., and C. K. Staats. *Complex Human Behavior.* New York: Holt, Rinehart, Winston, 1963.
Chapter 11 in particular discusses behavior problems and treatment and is useful in extending the ideas in this chapter.

WORKING WITH INDIVIDUAL PUPILS— THE SELF

If you were Mary's ninth-grade teacher, you would have been concerned, as she was, to read the following short essay:

M E

I think I'm not very good looking and not so smart. I try to stay out of trouble, but it finds me. I am in it all the time. I would like to be a person who can be good and stay out of trouble and not hurt others. I think others think I'm a dope. They don't like the way I dress and how I act. It's so hard for me to be what they want me to be.

I would love to have a pretty little house. The house we live in is not like the other houses. It looks so old and is shaped like a barn. I wish I would look real pretty. The others in my room have real pretty hair and I don't. I'm not very happy.

Here is a statement of how Mary feels about herself and her situation. It is clear that she is not pleased with herself, nor with her relations to others. She evaluates herself negatively, and explains this on the basis that others think ill of her.

Such views of oneself are not desirable—one could say they are unhealthy—at least they have led to Mary's getting into difficulties and feeling guilty about it.

Many therapists and most school guidance counselors would feel that the way to improve Mary's behavior is to help Mary view herself in a more positive light. She must learn to accept conditions in her life which she cannot control, and she must try to accept others. If her attitudes could be changed, her behavior should also change—for the better. Counselors might talk with Mary, to try to get her to understand more clearly what she is really like and how others perceive her, to help her accept herself and her situation in life, and to learn to adjust better socially. Prominent among those who foster this point of view are C. R. Rogers (1951) and A. W. Combs and D. Snygg (1959), whose works are listed in the Suggestions for Further Reading at the end of this chapter.

Notice particularly the difference in emphasis between this chapter and Chapter 11. Here we are working with some personality variables which affect how stimuli are perceived, what stimuli are attended to, which responses are elicited, and what reinforcements are sought. The variables in question—views of self and others, values, and attitudes, for example—provide for somewhat generalized outlooks on life. This is in contrast to the previous discussion, centered primarily on the modification of specific behavior.

The Self

With human beings, as with other living organisms, stimuli come to have meanings. These meanings will vary, however, depending upon the context in which the stimuli are perceived; for this reason, behavior varies also. For example, when one touches a hot stove, his response to the stimulus of heat and sensation of pain is to withdraw the finger immediately. But, if the source of heat is a barbecue grill that is about to topple over on one's child, the withdrawing response will be inhibited, and the pain will be endured until the grill can be stabilized. In essence, the stimulus has taken on a different meaning, and responses have altered accordingly. One's emotions, his value system, attitudes, and motives have intervened to alter the meaning of the stimulus of the hot grill and the behavior that is elicited.

The "self" has been defined as an organized set of psychological processes that govern behavior (Hall & Lindzey, 1957). The organized total of the variables mentioned, plus such others as learned perceptions and certain generalized behavior (like problem-solving processes), can thus be construed as making up the "self." Because the self is relatively stable, organized, and structured, one is not at the complete mercy of the immediate environment. One can select among stimuli and interpret them partly as outgrowths of continuing attitudes; one's behavior is thus governed by these processes, as well as by factors in the immediate environment itself.

The self is largely the product of learning. Because it does affect behavior in general, rather than simply in specific situations, if aspects of the self can be modified, behavior can be affected in a wide variety of situations.

We are still discussing learning principles; the main difference between this chapter and Chapter 11 is that now we are stressing the modifications of motives, attitudes, perceptions of self and others, and values, rather than specific overt or emotional responses. We are discussing factors that partially govern these responses, rather than the responses themselves. (These factors, of course, are subject to learning principles, for they are types of responses too.)

The Self-Concept

The self-concept or perceived self is simply the summation of the ways one evaluates his own characteristics and behaviors. In a sense, it represents one's expectations as they refer to his characteristic behaviors and abilities. It need not always be clearly formulated. The insecure child probably does not reason to himself that he is insecure, but he behaves as if he expects others to reject him. The child who lacks self-confidence may not say to himself that he is inadequate, but he behaves as if he expects to fail at tasks which are set for him. Thus the self-concept affects behavior since it affects the ways one expects his actions to be reinforced. It embodies both cognitive and affective components. If the self-concept, which is learned, is modified, behavior, in turn, should be modified.

The self-concept is individual to the person. This being the case, it is extremely difficult, if not impossible, to understand the acts of another without having some idea of what his behavior means *to him*. The observer who does not take into account his subject's point of view is likely to be wrong in interpreting what he is observing.

How one interprets a situation will determine what he expects from a given behavior in that situation. His desire for certain reinforcements determines to some extent what he pays attention to and what he disregards. His attitudes and values help to determine whether he considers his behavior successful or not, and are related to what he may learn from a given sequence of events.

Thus in essence each one of us lives in a world of his own making. Reality is therefore subjective insofar as any one person is concerned; what he *believes* to be true *is* true insofar as determining his actions is concerned, whether "objective" observers would agree or not. To the extent that people can communicate with each other and really assess their individual points of view, they are more able to understand, hence predict and control, behavior.

The above does not imply that one should not be concerned with norms or with a typical child's behavior, since this is valuable in comparing the individual with his group, but one must recognize the limitations in trying to predict individual acts from average behavior. To enjoy greater success in dealing with others, one must understand how they construe the situations they find themselves in.

The self-concept is an aspect of personality teachers and others who work with children should understand.

DIMENSIONS OF THE SELF-CONCEPT

R. C. Wylie (1961) suggests that the self-concept is better thought of as differentiated, rather than as general. That is, the child does not have "over-all" opinions or expectations of himself which affect all of his behavior, but rather, he has essentially a series of self-concepts as an achiever, a peer, an athlete, and so on. To the extent that one's various self-evaluations are consistent with and reinforce each other, the self-concept may be considered somewhat general; to the extent that one may evaluate himself highly in one area and lower in another, the several dimensions must be assessed individually.

From the point of view of the child's mental health, three characteristics of the self-concept must be considered. We shall list them here, but elaborate later; they apply to all aspects of self-evaluations that should interest the teacher.

REALISM OF THE SELF-CONCEPT. ▪ To what extent would others agree that Mary is accurate in her description of herself and how others feel about her? If unrealistic, maybe attempts should be made to help her view herself and her situation more accurately.

ACCEPTANCE OF SELF. ▪ To what extent does Mary feel favorably or unfavorably about herself? When one has a preponderance of negative self-attitudes, his behaviors, in turn, are usually quite unadaptive or inefficient.

To illustrate, there is a vicious cycle in behavior as related to acceptance of self. The person who generally feels inadequate enters into situations rather fearfully. Because of his anxieties, his behavior may be inept. In turn, he fails to achieve his goals successfully, and the resulting negative reinforcement causes the acceptance of self to become even lower. There are ways to deal with this cycle, which we shall discuss in this chapter.

STABILITY OF THE SELF-CONCEPT. ▪ Attitudes, as a rule, do not change rapidly, and since the self-concept is essentially a system of attitudes toward oneself, frequent or wide changes in the self-concept cannot be expected in the healthy individual. Inconsistency in the self-concept over time suggests confusion and possibly the effects of trauma. One would wish to investigate the life of a child having this pattern, to see why he does.

In effect, then, it's important to know how the child views himself in areas related to personal and social adjustment, and whether such self-evaluations are realistic, stable, and reasonably accepting. Should they not be, such attitudes should be changed. This process involves more than counseling the child; it involves changing the pattern of his reinforcements.

ASSESSMENT OF THE SELF-CONCEPT

Wylie (1961) provides an extended critique of research on the self-concept, and points out many of the problems in assessing the self-concept. An extended commentary on methods of assessment is beyond the scope of this book, but we shall briefly mention some of the cautions to be employed.

Specialists and researchers have employed a number of tests or questionnaires for assessing children's self-concepts, and sometimes these have been tried by teachers. In most instances, however, teachers will be given the results of such tests by guidance counselors, rather than be expected to give and interpret them themselves.

One of the problems with tests or questionnaires is that the child may know and give the socially correct answer to questions, which may not be the accurate answer in his case. For example, if a child is given choices such as the following, it would not be difficult to know which answer would be most desirable, and to portray himself accordingly:

Question: My relationships with other boys and girls are generally
   a. very adequate.
   b. so-so.
   c. usually quite poor.

Question: I feel that I am
   a. very popular with my peers.
   b. about as popular as most.
   c. rather unpopular.
   d. disliked.

The child may withhold some of his feelings, or he may be unable to express how he feels. The items may not seem to fit, they may be variously interpreted, or the child may not know the answer, never having thought about the question being asked. There are additional problems built into such devices, such as the limited range of questions, forced comparisons that may not be valid, and others. These statements are not meant to throw cold water on the use of self-concept inventories *per se*, but, rather, to suggest the need for sophisticated interpretation of results and application of findings with due caution.

Other devices employed by experts include projective techniques, Q-sorts, and rather comprehensive interviews.

For the teacher, such findings should be backed by observation and experience with the child. Observation may include attempts to answer such questions as:

Does the child generally act self-confidently?

Does he approach others with apparent expectations of being accepted?

Does he present the results of his efforts with an air of expecting positive—or negative—evaluation by the teacher?

In comparing the results of observation with those of questionnaires or interviews, one is more able to come to some conclusion concerning the child's self-expectations than through the use of any method alone, although correlation of data obtained will not be strong.

The illustration of Mary, at the beginning of the chapter, suggests that themes or other free expressions of the child can be helpful; confidences given the teacher may provide clues; and information from parents or other teachers may be useful. In essence, the techniques presented in Chapter 10 may help the teacher understand how the child views himself and his relationship to the environment.

Some writers have examined the inter-relationships of self-acceptance, acceptance of others, and acceptance by others. One may gain clues to the child's social orientations and their relationship to his self-attitudes by observing him with this relationship in mind. For example, A. H. Maslow (1954) has suggested that self-esteem, coupled with a feeling of acceptance by others, may promote the tendency to be helpful and kindly. Because the child feels positively toward himself and thinks others evaluate him highly, he need not be defensive and is free to accept others. Persons with high self-esteem but who feel that they are not appreciated may react with hostility and resentment (as is possible in some children of certain minority groups). Those with low self-esteem but who feel accepted by others may be grateful and docile or dependent. Those with neither high self-esteem nor feeling of acceptance by others may be discouraged and self-abasing.

Although it is likely that people who feel accepted by others probably react by accepting others in turn, this is not necessarily always the case. W. F. Fey (1957), for example, states that those who accept themselves and also accept others are likely to show personal responsibility and to assert self-determination (that is, are not easily led or bossed around). But those low in acceptance of self and high in acceptance of others will cooperate, as followers, but shun leadership; those low in acceptance of self and of others may be distrustful; and those acceptant of self but not of others may act as though they feel they are popular, but in reality will not be.

In keeping with what we might expect from feelings of self-worth, B. Chodorkoff and L. Lepine (1955) show that persons low in self-esteem tend to be situation-dominated rather than independent and self-directive.

One can sometimes, therefore, gain an idea of the general level of self-esteem of the child and his feelings of acceptance or rejection by others, by noticing his social interaction. The isolated child probably does not feel accepted. The dependent child may need more self-confidence. Hypotheses such as these may be made, but it is necessary to seek additional confirmation, since these formulations are general and since situational variables are important factors in behavior.

DEVELOPMENT OF THE SELF-CONCEPT

The self-concept develops slowly over the years—generalizations come about as the result of repeated environmental re-inforcements. Once developed, it changes slowly, but change does occur. Appropriate re-evaluations of oneself are healthy signs.

PARENTAL INFLUENCES. ■ Development of the healthy self-concept comes with success in dealing with the environment and in receiving appropriate reinforcements. The ultimate or pervasive motive, according to Combs and Snygg (1959) is that of feeling adequate; this belief is echoed by R. W. White (1959), who stresses the "competency motive." The small child who easily learns to walk, talk, and to satisfy his parents in various ways, is thus likely to feel more comfortable about himself and to receive more reinforcements; he therefore has a "healthier" self-concept than does one who frequently feels rejected or faces frustration.

The social environment, because it defines roles, is probably more important to the formation of the self-concept than is the nonsocial environment. In the early years the reactions of parents are most important, and, because the mother tends to spend more time with the child than does the father, her personality and behavior are of crucial importance during the most formative years. In most homes the baby is fondled and petted, and his parents quickly respond to his needs. They show delight when he smiles or coos and give him much evidence that he is desired. When he has many such experiences, his perceived self reflects feelings of security and self-esteem. If he is ignored, nagged, and apparently unable to satisfy his parents or if he encounters inconsistency in their treatment of him, he may feel inadequate, blameworthy, and insecure.

At this point it should be noted that the child's perceptions are important in determining how he will react to the re-inforcements that parents provide him—that is, what he regards as reinforcements and what evaluations he believes parents are making of him. For example, demanding parents may seem never to be satisfied and may be perceived as devaluing the child, whereas in reality they may simply be trying to help him put forth his best efforts.

On the whole, a child's level of self-regard is associated with parents' reported regard for him (Wylie, 1961). Parents may, however, have conflicting views of the child or differ from each other in their evaluation of him. In this case, the child is more likely to exhibit maladjustment. Because one cannot take for granted that the child's perceptions of his parents' feelings about him are accurate, one must consult with parents when the child does not have desirable feelings about himself. (It is also for these reasons that teachers should not infer anything about parents on the basis of children's comments. Today, people are somewhat prone to blame parents when a child is maladjusted, yet parents may not be the real problems. This stereotype must be resisted.)

When the child enters school, other influences on self-evalu-ation intervene. He is forced to rethink the utility of his behavior and to re-evaluate himself, for in the eyes of teacher and peers he may not be evaluated in the same ways that his parents evaluated him. His role within the family ("our son," "our baby") may have been cause for acceptance within the home but has little influence at school. Much of what may have been forgiven at home will not be overlooked at school; demands may be placed on him that are not present in home surroundings. At school he must demonstrate his worth, and starting school is stressful for some children.

It should be noted that children's attitudes toward parents and others may be displaced *to* teachers. Anticipations of evaluations by parents may affect ways children expect to be evaluated *by* teachers. A problem is to help children learn to discriminate between such attitudes and evaluations. For example:

Peter J., a fourth grader, felt that the world would be a better place if there were no women. Why not, as he is in a foster home, the fifth in a series of trials, in which he has had conflict with his foster mother every time?

One reason for such conflicts is the fairly frequent visits his real mother makes to the foster homes. She carries on, to Peter J., saying: "They are all so mean to me, and now they are trying to get my other two children away. And your foster mother isn't doing right by you. If they'd let me, I'd take you home and take good care of you."

The foster mothers have been unanimous in saying that such visits have harmed their relationships with Peter J. Their explanations to him that his own mother did not take care of her children and that that is why he is living elsewhere simply turn resentment against them. Three foster mothers gave up. The fourth was almost "as bad" as Peter's own mother in neglecting him. The fifth is being as accepting as possible but may not take the pressure for long.

Peter J.'s parental conflicts are reflected at school. He resents women teachers, dislikes the older girls, and refuses to visit the lady counselor. If Peter J. were placed with male teachers or allowed to talk with a male counselor, he might be helped. But because he feels that women do not accept him, his reactions are those of frustration, feelings of inadequacy, and—most important—hostility. It is not surprising that conflicting feedback from his mother and his foster mothers have caused him to be confused about his acceptance by others, especially women.

INFLUENCE OF PEERS. ▪ As the child matures toward preadolescence and adolescence, the reinforcements from the peer group may influence him more than those from parents or other adults. The inconsistencies, moodiness, and rebellion of some adolescents result from a conflict of values (hence evaluations of self) between adults and peers, home and school, or between the youth's internalized values and the expectations of the peer culture.

Friends are chosen for many reasons, such as common interests, similar talents, propinquity of homes or placement in school classes, or for other reasons. The self-attitudes are influenced by the opinions of others, even though these opinions may initially be resisted. It has been found that one's friends influence one's self-concept more than acquaintances; friendship choices are important, therefore, since they strongly influence one's evaluations of himself.

Conversely, an individual's evaluation of his friends depends partly on his own value system, and he tends to endow (in his own mind) his friends with acceptable personality characteristics, whether or not more objective observers would agree. People tend to describe others whom they like least as less similar to themselves than those whom they like best, although this description of similarity may be partly determined by one's degree of self-esteem; that is, those who have high self-esteem may tend to devalue disliked acquaintances (Lundy, et al., 1955).

Thus one seems to choose his friends partly because they are favorable to him, and he endows his friends with characteristics he finds acceptable to himself. Yet his need for acceptance by his friends makes him more vulnerable to their criticism. Friendship choices of high-school students and their evaluations of each other show that those who suffer greatest lack of morale when criticized by others also show low self-acceptance. Those successful in relations with others tend to fewer negative self-attitudes.

It seems clear, too, that when some students are not accepted by the more desirable peers, they will tend to congregate in a subsociety of their own, in which mutual reinforcement and acceptance can be found. Minority groups are formed for the purpose of such mutual support, and may be extremely stable. In turn, values common to such a group are fostered, and, because of feelings of rejection by the larger society, a lack of identification with the larger society and its values may result. This tends to occur, even though the values held by the group may initially be at odds with those of some of the members.

One cannot work successfully with such children unless he accepts them and in turn is able to win a measure of acceptance by them. The teacher must find values in such children and reinforce their feelings of self-worth. For children who are isolated from the larger peer group, achieve poorly, or react by causing disciplinary problems, enhancing their feelings of acceptance and self-worth can help them reidentify with more desirable social values and institute behaviors which society will reinforce.

For example:

The physics room at A. High School was adjacent to a store- and workroom in which the laboratory apparatus was kept and experiments were prepared. When Mr. Jones began his fall classes as a teacher new to the system, he was warned by his department head as follows:

"Don't let such kids as Bob K., Leonard R., or Johnny J. ever get into your workroom. They'll steal you blind. They are the nucleus of a small gang who have caused no end of troubles around here. Most of the teachers can't stand them."

But Bob K., Leonard R., and Johnny J. asked Mr. Jones whether they could not study in the workroom, since they always seemed to get in trouble in the study hall. Thinking it over, Mr. Jones decided to take a chance.

"Fellows, if you study in here, there are two things I want you to agree to. First, you realize that I'm responsible for all of this equipment and what goes on; if I allow you to be in here, don't let me down by being noisy, breaking things, and so on. Secondly, I'll have to have a reason for getting you out of study hall. Will you agree to helping me set up the experiments, and to help repair some of the apparatus if it gets broken?"

The boys agreed. And, as it happened, the experiment worked. They began to find some interest in school, and enjoyed working with the physics apparatus. True to their agreement not to let Mr. Jones down, they caused no trouble. Furthermore, informal contacts with Mr. Jones resulted in friendships, and informal counseling. This help, in turn, was reflected in improved behavior in other classes.

In this instance, Bob and Leonard became students at a non-degree-granting school of "engineering" and Johnny became an electronics technician in the armed forces. While it is true that all such teacher efforts do not work out as well as this, it is also true that students frequently respond to positive evaluations by their teachers and to appeals to their higher values more than one would think; it is well worth the attempt, we believe.

SUCCESS AND FAILURE. ■ L. Diller (1954) found that subjects who were exposed to failure on tasks did not openly admit that their self-attitudes had deteriorated, but that he could find evidence that their inner feelings or expectations had become less positive. After a success experience he found that both admitted and inferred attitudes toward the self were improved.

Findings such as this are related to one's own values and attitudes, which provide for inner or self-reinforcements. As one matures, he develops expectations for himself which essentially become standards; he evaluates his behavior as successful or not, in terms of such standards. Should he frequently fail to meet these standards, his self-attitudes are likely to deteriorate. Anxiety and feelings of guilt and inadequacy may result. These reactions are sometimes noted in university students who have been popular, high achievers, or otherwise successful in public schools in their home communities, but who, when faced with competition in a selected university student body, find themselves less successful than they had hoped. Such students show a variety of behaviors; some seek counseling, others drop out of the university, and still others engage in immature or deviant behavior. Such unfortunate reactions are one reason, of course, why we should help students become clearly aware of their abilities and aid them in developing realistic self-expectations.

PHYSIQUE. ■ Body image has been extensively studied, as have the effects of physical disabilities and chronic ill health on mental health and achievement. The field of rehabilitation counseling takes cognizance of the difficulties faced by persons who are physically inadequate and the related mental-health factors.

Physical characteristics affect the self-concept, especially during developmental years, even for healthy children. For example, findings show that, during preadolescence, boys who are much less physically mature than others tend to feelings of inadequacy (Smith & Lebo, 1956) and late-maturing boys may feel rejected and act aggressively (Jones & Mussen, 1956). The early maturer tends to be self-confident and has high goals, but the late maturer tends to be dependent upon others and seeks their support.

Part of this is due, of course, to the image of athletic prowess fostered by society in regard to boys (and to the image of beauty, for girls).

The teacher should look carefully at every child physically far from the norm for signs of lack of self-esteem, feelings of rejection, or other indications of negative self-attitude.

INTELLIGENCE AND ACHIEVEMENT. ■ Bright children tend to have high self-esteem and to be more realistic about themselves than dull children, partly because they tend to have more positive reinforcements, and partly because of their intelligence and self-insight. However, relationships are not simple. J. C. Bledsoe and K. C. Garrison (1962) found that in fourth and sixth grades, children of high self-esteem were immature for their ages and might be conceited, overconfident, and not as well received by adults as others. Low self-concept children had more modesty, humility, and were more self-effacing. Extremely high self-concepts might be indicative of sociopathic behavior, but extremely low self-concepts might indicate a tendency to neurotic behavior; for essentially normal children there was less predictive relationship between self-concept and mental health.

Academic achievement and intelligence, in this study, were significantly related to the ideal self for girls, and girls were found more self-confident than boys at the fourth- and sixth-grade levels. Girls had been exposed to women teachers more than boys had to men teachers, hence had more opportunity to learn and to view themselves in the feminine role. (On the other hand, as we previously have remarked, school may simply provide girls with more positive reinforcements than it does for boys, at least at the elementary level.)

In summation, there are a number of influences upon the developing system of self-attitudes of a child. Among them are parental reinforcements, peer reinforcements, successes and failures, intelligence, and even one's physical characteristics. Some influences can be modified or counteracted, and some may require that the child re-evaluate himself in accordance with reality, learning to accept his limitations without self-devaluation.

We will consider some of the relationships of self-attitudes to mental health and then can discuss how undesirable attitudes may be attacked.

Self-Concept and Mental Health

We earlier remarked that three important dimensions of the self-concept are degree of self-acceptance, reality of self-concept, and stability of self-concept. They are related to adjustment, but, because adjustment has been found to be difficult to define (Chapter 1), the relationships are not always comparable among the various studies that will be mentioned.

Wylie (1961) believes that those who employ self-concept points of view in counseling or therapy seek the following changes:

The self-concept becomes more realistic, if therapy is successful.
There is increased congruence between self and ideal self if this congruence has been very low.
There is slightly decreased self-ideal self congruence, if the congruence was unwarrantedly high.
There is increased acceptance of one's limitations as well as of one's assets.
There is increased realism in the ideal self.
There is increased consistency among various aspects of the self-concept and of the ideal self.

Let us first concern ourselves with the concept of congruence of self and ideal self, essentially one's self-acceptance or self-esteem. The person who lacks a certain degree of congruence between self and ideal self is motivated toward self-improvement, and this motivation is healthy. If there is too great a discrepancy between his ideals and his opinions of himself, however, there may be considerable guilt, anxiety, defensiveness, or other symptoms of maladjustment (Bruce, 1958; Lip-sitt, 1958).

T. E. Hanlon (1954) suggests that those who do not have reasonable congruence tend toward withdrawing behavior, which may be neurotic; J. Block and H. Thomas (1955) found people with low congruence to be confused, too introspective, and unrealistic and contradictory in their aspirations. Block and Thomas felt that people with medium congruence were reasonable in self-appraisals, could accept ambivalence in their feelings toward others, and were comfortable in interpersonal relationships. Those with high congruence, however, seemed to require acceptance and popularity with peers but seemed also to control their own expressiveness and popularity. They wished, they said, to be less sentimental, less jealous, and more self-dependent. Again, people with medium degrees of self-satisfaction appear most mentally healthy and adjusted.

As congruence of self and ideal self is essentially a measure of self-acceptance, we are saying that children should be self-acceptant but not complacent.

Relationships between adjustment and self–ideal self are not linear—that is, more "sickness" does not necessarily make for a lower degree of self-acceptance. Wylie (1961) and B. R. McCandless (1961) discuss this point. Whereas healthy people are reasonably self-accepting, people with neurotic behavior are likely to be quite unaccepting; but people showing psychotic behavior may either be self-accepting or not. The last, who are out of touch with reality, may highly overestimate their qualities.

Stability of the self-concept is related to mental health in that, if the concept changes too markedly or too rapidly, a lack of personality integration may be suspected. Under normal circumstances, the self resists change. When events seem to call for re-evaluation of oneself, as when one meets such serious failures as the loss of his job, he reinterprets the situation in ways that do not threaten concept of self or suggest need for change. He is thus likely to blame others, to rationalize, to minimize the importance of failure, or to find other ways to defend the concept of self that he has developed. Similarly, though less happily, the concept of self as inadequate or unworthy seems hard to change, and the treatment of people with deep feelings of guilt or inferiority is also very difficult.

If resistance to change is too complete, the self-concept may not be in accord with reality. Essentially, the normal, healthy personality is able to accept new evaluations, and the concept of self will change accordingly but rather slowly; those whose self-concepts fluctuate widely or those whose self-concepts change completely appear to be those in poorest mental health.

The dimension of realism of the self-concept has already been touched on. Essentially, the healthiest person is he who evaluates his abilities and behavior in accordance with others' evaluations. This congruence does not always occur, however. Sometimes ignorance or lack of experience, inconsistent evaluations by others, lack of intelligence, or other problems prevent a realistic self-appraisal. In such cases, there may be little difficulty in helping the subject to become more realistic. An unrealistic self-concept may, however, come about through defensive behaviors. Some persons cannot admit their shortcomings, even to themselves; they indulge in fantasy, denial of reality, or other mechanisms which permit them to reduce feelings of threat, but which prevent them from realistic self-evaluations. Others cannot admit their strong points, and become depressed, suffer from feelings of guilt, or have other problems of adjustment. In either case, realism of self-evaluations should lead to more realistic levels of aspiration, better social interaction, and improved chances of reinforcements from others and from attaining one's own goals.

Changing Self-Attitudes

THE TEACHER–PUPIL RELATIONSHIP

Rogers uses the term "helping relationship" (1958) to define desirable teacher attitudes and behaviors. He applies the term to parent and child, counselor and client, and (in most circumstances) teacher and pupil.

He suggests an "acceptant-democratic" attitude. Thus the teacher must be able to accept the child, even though he cannot accept the child's behavior. The child must be respected as a person and valued as a human being with potential for the future, even though he is smaller, less mature, and less well-educated than the teacher. The teacher therefore does not focus his efforts on dominating the child, for he recognizes the child's right to be "what he is." Rather, the teacher tries to orient the child's *actions* toward successful achievement and adjustment. Rogers also stresses the need of the counselor or the teacher to understand what others' behavior means *to them*.

In furthering the desired relationship the child should be allowed to make his own decisions wherever possible. In carrying out this idea, the child will be observed to make certain mistakes. When this happens, unless there is danger to the child or to others, he should be allowed to suffer the consequences of his actions.

The helping relationship depends upon the real, rather than the expressed, feelings of the teacher. Rogers feels that the teacher should be *congruent,* which means that he should be able to express his real feelings. The advantage of congruence is that the child can perceive the teacher as honest and trustworthy, rather than as a person who is hiding something from him.

The helping teacher also should refrain from involving himself emotionally in the child's problems. He should permit the child to be an individual, hence possibly different from the way the teacher might wish him to be. The helping teacher is nonthreatening, although he may seek to change the child's behaviors. He does not devalue the child as a person. He is not prejudiced by the child's past or present, but can view the child as he may be in the future.

In brief, he respects the child's autonomy and tries to help him solve his own problems in his own ways.

OUR ROLE AS ADULTS

The important role adults play in the development of children's feelings demands that we have a clear conception of the kinds of feelings that are healthy, constructive, "good," and those that are unhealthy, destructive, "bad." Our adult role also requires an awareness on our part of what we can do to help children acquire constructive, healthy feelings, and what we should not do to spare them feelings that are unhealthy, destructive.

In brief, our role requires us to AVOID doing anything that will make a child feel*

> *inferior, petty, mean*
> *confused, bewildered, fearful*
> *ashamed of his family, or social status, or anything about himself*

Our role requires us to AVOID doing anything to make a child feel

> *that adults are unreasonable, impossible to please*
> *that nobody cares, nobody understands him, there is nobody to help him when he needs it*
> *that life is burdensome, uncertain*
> *that he is a failure*
> *that we expect too much from him*
> *that he is unimportant, in the way*
> *that new experiences are risky, frightening, to be avoided*
> *that people do not like him*

To this end, it's important that we AVOID

> *laughing at a child or belittling him*
> *teasing, threatening, frightening him*
> *using shame or sarcasm*
> *pointing out the child's shortcomings or comparing him unfavorably with others*
> *setting goals beyond his capacity for attainment*

And that we DO all the things that help a child feel

> *that he is an important and worthwhile person*
> *that people accept him, and that he is one of the group*
> *that people are essentially pleasant*
> *that he can cope with most situations that are likely to occur*
> *that life is good and it is good to be alive*

SELF-ATTITUDES RESISTANT TO CHANGE

Children may have negative or unrealistic ideas about themselves, and we may wish to change such self-attitudes. As we

---

* SOURCE: Nina Ridenour, *Building Self-Confidence in Children*, p. 47. Copyright © 1954 Science Research Associates, Inc. Reprinted by permission of the publisher.

have seen, however, the self-concept develops gradually and comes about from many experiences. It is not easily changed; when it does change, it does so slowly, especially if the person has a number of defenses that help him to limp through life in a perhaps uncomfortable, but bearable, way; to change one's views of himself might require that he face his own inadequacies, which could be more threatening than staying the way he is. It is easy to understand that one might refuse to face his inadequacies, especially if he is low in self-acceptance.

It is also true, however, that children who are discouraged, lack self-acceptance, and feel inferior may refuse to recognize their *good* points. Mary, for example, seems to feel that she is "all bad," yet she is not.

In addition to the defenses one erects around his self-concept, resistance to change may be aroused by the ineptness of people trying to help. Sometimes one can move too quickly, and the conflict between the child's present perceptions and those one is trying to inculcate is too great. Quick change brings confusion and may be threatening. Most people cannot accept a quick revaluation of themselves.

Here is a case in point:

A small boy was considered a nuisance by his parents and teachers. He continually sought attention, was a bully, and showed small regard for the truth. As do many such children, this boy put on a front of unconcern and bravado. Underneath, however, he felt insecure. His delinquent behavior was essentially defensive.

One teacher, feeling that this might be the case, attempted to build the boy's self-esteem by playing up some of his good qualities. At first she met only surprise from the boy, who had had few pleasant comments from others. Later she met suspicion and resentment, and the boy's behavior intensified, for he believed the teacher was trying to "get around him." He also doubted the sincerity of the teacher, as he himself felt some guilt and undervalued his own worth.

Sometimes children test the sincerity of the teacher by continuing or even intensifying their poor conduct. Once they trust the teacher, they can begin to change. In this case, however, the teacher was disappointed that her kindly efforts were spurned. She came to the conclusion that her appraisal of the boy was wrong and resorted to threats and punishment to make him behave. This switch, of course, resulted in further resentment on the child's part, with consequent increased poor behavior. In addition, his feeling of rejection and his lack of trust of adults were intensified.

If the self-concept is to change, change must be pictured as an opportunity to enhance oneself. Many children cannot admit, even to themselves, that change is desirable, for this admission would imply that they are inadequate, which would be too threatening to them, particularly if they are insecure.

Consider how some children are bluntly told that their attitudes must change or they will be failed, sent to the principal, dropped from school, or referred to the psychologist. Such children usually become more defensive. Yet when they are placed in nonthreatening environments, they can begin to admit their shortcomings and learn to understand the meanings of their behavior. Such reactions illustrate negative reinforcement and aversive behavior, discussed in Chapter 11. Psychotherapy usually depends on the creation of a permissive, nonthreatening atmosphere; in such an environment people can begin to discuss their problems, for they do not feel that they will be negatively evaluated, a further threat to their self-esteem.

The teacher is not a therapist. Yet he often counsels children informally. If he can present the child with the understanding that he is trying to help, rather than to govern, and if he can show the child that he recognizes the child's good qualities, he is more apt to achieve desirable results. (The teacher, however, by virtue of his role, must evaluate and control. To that extent, he cannot help being somewhat threatening. For serious problems the school psychologist or guidance counselor should be involved; these people have no disciplinary functions and can keep the child's confidences; they are therefore less threatening to him.)

IMPROVING SELF-UNDERSTANDING

Self-understanding can be improved in two general ways. We can foster the "causal approach," as described in Chapter 8, and we can present the child with objective evidence of his own characteristics. We shall deal briefly with these methods, beginning with the latter.

Some children simply have misconceptions concerning their own characteristics and the ways they appear to others. These misconceptions may come about because of misinterpretations of others' reactions to them or because they have aroused negative reactions from others. Sometimes they overgeneralize and fail to discriminate clearly between their desirable and undesirable characteristics.

Mary, for example, thinks that others do not like her. She has had some negative experiences with others, both at home and at school, and it is not surprising that she feels rejected. She also has guilt feelings about her conduct and as a result does not see how others could possibly like her—after all, she doesn't really like herself.

Mary's teacher employed sociometric techniques with her class. She asked the students whom they would like to work with on a class project, and it was found that four girls mentioned Mary as one of their choices. The teacher proceeded to inform Mary of this fact; furthermore, she saw to it that Mary was placed with these girls. Their genuine friendliness provided positive reinforcements for Mary, who began to see herself as at least somewhat likable and in turn extended friendship and cooperation to the others.

It has been found (Ringness, 1965) that bright junior high-school boys are not always clear about their intellectual assets and liabilities. In this particular study, few boys had had differential test results explained to them. They were not clear about their abilities or their ability patterns. Some highly gifted boys thought of themselves as only somewhat superior; some low-achieving bright boys thought of themselves as "stupid." Not only had those boys never been given feedback concerning their potentials, but they had also never been asked to do any self-analysis of their apparent abilities and interests. It would seem that one function of testing and of guidance would be to provide feedback to the boys and their families, rather than simply to their teachers.

One improves self-understanding through "causal" tactics also. That is, one can ask children to examine their motives. the stimuli to which they respond, the nature of their responses, and the reinforcements that typically follow certain behaviors. Here is an example:

One fourth-grade boy was highly competitive academically. He and two or three other pupils normally stood at the top of the class in practically all academic areas. When this child managed to be "best in the class," he bragged incessantly. He showed others his report card and told them how excellent he was. It wasn't long before he began to be highly unpopular with the other students.

The teacher handled the problem in an informal after-school session with the boy. She mentioned to him that maybe he had felt that he wasn't getting along quite as well as he would like with some of the other children, for he seemed not to play with them at recess anymore. Did he feel that way too? "Well, yes," was the answer. The other boys seemed to think that he was trying to be superior; at least that's what they told him. He wasn't, and he didn't see why they should say such things. The teacher wondered whether his competitiveness and the way he acted when he was top of the class could have anything to do with it. Did the boy remember what he had done when the report cards came out? Well— he had shown them around and maybe pointed out how good his was. It *was* good, and he was proud. But he didn't intend to be "superior."

Why might he have done this? Could he see how it affected the others? Weren't some of them good at things—maybe not in studies, but in sports or things? Did they try to be superior? Why might one need to show how good he was?

This sort of analysis continued, and the boy began to see that he was trying to compensate for feeling inferior in playground activities. He was not good at ball playing, and was unable to keep up at other play activities. He was probably trying to make up for this lack through his studies. The eventual understanding arrived at was that he could do his best in studies, and others would recognize his abilities; however, he would do better not to brag or show off. A more constructive effort would be to try to improve in sports and to be helpful to other students if they wanted his legitimate assistance in school tasks.

IMPROVING SELF-ACCEPTANCE

From a mental-health point of view, one of the most important changes in self-perception is to learn to accept oneself and to live with one's limitations if they cannot be overcome. There are two general ways in which children can be helped to self-acceptance. The first is to provide them with acceptance from others, so that they receive essential positive reinforcements; as the concept of self is largely built from the reinforcements given by others, anything that shows children that they are valued is useful. The second method is to work with any disabilities that the child may have and to capitalize upon his assets, so that he can obtain more environmental and inner reinforcements.

Intervention can be employed to help ensure more successful experiences. For example, the following techniques have been known to "work" in the case of some pupils.

DEVELOPMENT OF SPECIAL ABILITIES TO GAIN RECOGNITION FROM OTHERS. ▪ For example, a child known to the writer was re-tiring. He took little part in group play and did not defend himself in controversies. It happened that one day another child fought with him and knocked him down. When this defeat became known at home, the father decided to try to teach the child something about boxing. Eventually the child became somewhat habituated to being hit and to hitting others, and developed considerable skill. The time came when he "took on" the school bully and defeated him. From that point on, a general feeling of confidence seemed to be generated in the boy; in addition, he received considerable recognition and accep-tance from his peers.

Some children have other abilities that can be developed. For example, talent in art can be utilized in many ways, including the school newspaper or yearbook, murals for classroom walls, staging for class plays, and so on. Even when talent is not present, some recognition can be promoted by teaching certain children to run the movie projector or public address system, developing them as specialists in laboratory apparatus, and so on.

HELPING THE SUBJECT TO HELP OTHERS. ▪ This method acts in two ways; the student receives some positive feedback for his efforts, and he also feels better about himself for having been helpful. Many opportunities can be found for letting a child help the teacher or his peers. (In one high-school setting a very troublesome boy was encouraged to become quite socially ad-justed by working in the school library.) Some children can help others at seat work, being carpenter for the school play, running the tape recorder for the debate contest, and so on.

TEMPORARY OR PERMANENT CHANGE OF ENVIRONMENT. ■ On occasion there simply is no opportunity for positive reinforcement because of prevailing attitudes of teacher or peers. For example, a girl was returned to her own high school after having spent nearly a year in the state reform school. Neither teacher nor other students were able to accept her, although the state school had considered her rehabilitated and she herself wanted to erase the bad impressions people had of her. It was necessary for the welfare authorities to transfer her to a private institution that specialized in providing an education and a home-like atmosphere for girls like herself. Eventually she was graduated from high school, went to another state, and obtained a job among people not so familiar with her past.

All teachers do not like all children. All children do not like all teachers. When there is a definite personality clash, change might well be instituted. Other appropriate changes might be made when a child must be retained in grade; he might even profit from special classes for retarded or emotionally disturbed children.

PROVISION OF EXTRA SUPPORT AND REINFORCEMENT. ■ When one has formed a self-concept low in self-esteem, he tends to interpret the remarks, glances, and movements of others as confirmation that he is unacceptable. Often such interpretations are not realistic.

Following is an example:

One small girl was overly supervised during early childhood. The mother nagged her, circumscribed her play, warned her of constant danger, and showed alarm when the child followed normal impulses to explore her world. When the child got dirty, as children do, she was immediately bathed and her clothes changed. The child was taught that children should be seen and not heard and was given lengthy instructions in party manners. She was urged to be polite, to do her homework perfectly, to avoid games with noisy, boisterous children, and to pay careful attention to grown-ups. Nothing the child ever did was so right or so good that it could not be improved.

As a result the child tended to withdraw and was consequently ignored by the other children. She was obsessed with the need to do everything absolutely right and would pester the teacher for precise directions and careful evaluation of her work. When given a choice of assignments or play activities, the little girl would vacillate, frequently making remarks like "Oh, I don't know" or "Well, I'm thinking" or "I'm not sure."

The teacher took great pains to help the child learn to relax and to overcome her extreme insecurity when things did not go exactly right. She was allowed to play in the sandbox, to paint, and to manage the dolls during her free time. When the girl got paint on her apron, the teacher laughed lightly. When she made a mistake in her reading lesson, the matter was smiled away. The teacher also consulted the parents to see whether or not they could take some of the pressure off the child.

In helping this child accept the reality of her own very considerable ability, it was first necessary to show her that others did not evaluate her in the same ways as did her parents. It was pointed out that others made mistakes. Others got dirty. It was all right to be noisy at the proper time. And her reading and other work were going very well, in spite of not being perfect.

As the child watched the others, she began timidly to loosen up; she made her first efforts at mingling with them in activities. Finding that she was accepted, she began to act more as a first grader normally does but kept an eye on the teacher to see how she was being evaluated. All went better until one day the mother visited the classroom, whereupon the child "froze up" and acted as before. Luckily the mother could see the results of her handling of the child and made an effort to be less critical. The child began to glory in new-found freedom. At first she even went slightly overboard for a time, but eventually she settled down to being a typical child for her years.

People need concrete evidence that they are liked, that they are successful, and that feelings of low self-esteem are not justified. A simple pat on the back or superficial praise is not enough. Reinforcement must be provided when justified, but false praise should not be given.

CHANGING THE CHILD'S BEHAVIOR. ▪ Sometimes a student receives little positive reinforcement because he is genuinely not acceptable to others because of his own behavior or appearance. In such instances, it is quite obviously necessary to attempt to change the child himself. For example, in Chapter 4 we discussed the need for teachers to *tell* children when their behavior displeased the teacher. Sometimes this behavior comes about because children genuinely do not know how they affect others and sometimes because they need reminders.

There are many ways that a teacher can improve children's acceptability to others. For example, he can sometimes help the child to become more physically attractive. Some children do not bathe frequently, do not change clothes as often as they should, and do not keep groomed in other ways. Perhaps the child can be educated to cleanliness—we know of one teacher who actually took a child to the showers once a week.

A teacher can help the child to make outgoing efforts. For example, pairing children for drill, for recess games like ping-pong, for getting the milk, or for seat projects can be a start. When sociometric tests show a given child to be an isolate, he can be paired with stars, who are frequently outgoing and with whom the child may identify. (On the other hand, sometimes stars will ignore the isolate, and it may be wiser to place him with another isolate or less outgoing child. Experience must be the dictator.)

Specific training in human relationships may help. Some children simply do not know how to approach others. One first-grade teacher devised the following procedures for teaching children to be considerate of others:

1. Signals were worked out, so that anyone who displeased another by interrupting, poking, talking, or in other ways could be warned. For example, if Jerry talked to Joan and she did not want her task interrupted, Joan might hold up a hand.
2. "We may sit by our special friends if." "If" was followed by variety of things like being quiet and not bothering others. Our teachers say this method was especially valuable with children who were too aggressive in personal contacts.
3. Role playing was tried. The teacher invited children to act out how they felt when others approached them in certain ways and to show how they preferred things to go. For example, when Gerald wanted to play during recess with the only truck in the room, he grabbed it away from little Joanna. Noticing this act, the teacher asked two other children to act out the little hap-

pening and was amused to see the signs of disgust the "acting Joanna" employed. A repeat, with proper behavior, followed, as did a short discussion. Afterward, Gerald usually asked permission to play with toys that others might be using.

4. Discussion in anticipation of specific situations may have value. Before a class party, as on Valentine's Day, many kinds of behavior were discussed by the elementary-school children this teacher worked with. They were thus prepared for certain events and how to act.

5. Individual counseling was used. "Would *you* like somebody who always cries if he can't have his own way?" "How would *you* feel about somebody who was always pushing?"

6. Stories were used to illustrate good behavior. One teacher read the story of the *Smallest Boy in the Class* (Beim, 1949). In this story the smallest boy acted bigger than any of the larger children when he shared his lunch with a classmate (see Chapter 8).

A Further Report on Mary

Mary's teacher talked with Mary, after reading her theme (at the beginning of the chapter). She discovered that Mary worries because others know that she is from an impoverished family. She believes that others are unfair and mean because they don't seem to like her, and she thinks that others are not interested in her problems. She has a hard time studying and thinks that she is not as bright as her classmates. She is unhappy that she must give up things for others in her family and that she cannot do many of the things she would like, partly because she lacks spending money.

Mary is not allowed to attend boy-girl social activities. She believes that too many people tell her what to do, and she therefore likes to do things "old-fashioned" people tell her are wrong.

In school, Mary finds it hard to get acquainted. She feels unnoticed, does not think her few friends are "the right kind," and she is disappointed that she is not invited to parties. Mary would rather stay away from social gatherings and is lonesome even with others around. She feels that she has made mistakes others won't forget, and that she has more problems than most.

Her head often aches, her eyes smart, and she has frequent nightmares. Her muscles sometimes twitch; she is restless, often tired, and finds it hard to pay attention. She forgets easily.

When we evaluate these data we begin to feel that her problems are correlated. Mary's physical symptoms are probably at least partly psychosomatic, although she should have a physical examination to make certain that she is not suffering from neural, glandular, or other physical illness. Mary's self-concept and feeling of acceptance by others are essentially negative.

Yet Mary is not realistic. In sociograms it was found that four pupils chose her as the person they would like for a friend; on the whole, she seemed accepted by the class. Her insecurity with her peers is the result of faulty self-perception, and the teacher has taken opportunities to show Mary that in reality her classmates accept her more than she believes. Mary was requested to help on several committees, and has begun to be a little less self-conscious and insecure.

□

REFERENCES

Beim, J. *The Smallest Boy in the Class.* New York: Morrow, 1949.

Bledsoe, J. C., and K. C. Garrison. *The Self Concepts of Elementary School Children in Relation to Their Academic Achievement, Interests, and Manifest Anxiety* (Cooperative Research Project 1008). Athens: University of Georgia, 1962.

Block, J., and H. Thomas. "Is Satisfaction with Self a Measure of Adjustment?" *Journal of Abnormal and Social Psychology,* 51 (1955), 254–9.

Bruce, P. "Relationship of Self-Acceptance to Other Variables With Sixth Grade Children Oriented in Self Understanding," *Journal of Educational Psychology,* 49 (1958), 229–37.

Chodorkoff, B., and L. Lepine. "Goal Setting Behavior and Expressed Feelings of Adequacy; and the Correspondence Between the Perceived and Ideal Self," *Journal of Clinical Psychology,* 11 (1955), 395–7.

Combs, A. W., and D. Snygg. *Individual Behavior.* (Rev. ed.) New York: Harper, 1959.

Diller, L. "Conscious and Unconscious Self-Attitudes after Success and Failure," *Journal of Personality,* 23 (1954), 1–12.

Fey, W. F. "Correlates of Certain Subjective Attitudes Toward Self and Others," *Journal of Clinical Psychology,* 13 (1957), 44–9.

Hall, C. S., and G. Lindzey. *Theories of Personality.* New York: Wiley, 1957.

Hanlon, T. E., P. R. Hofstaetter, and J. P. O'Connor. "Congruence of Self and Ideal Self in Relation to Personality Adjustment," *Journal of Consulting Psychology,* 18 (1954) , 215–8.

Jones, M. C., and P. H. Mussen. "Self-Conceptions, Motivations, and Interpersonal Attitudes of Late and Early Maturing Boys," *Child Development,* 28 (1956) , 243–6.

Lipsitt, L. P. "A Self-Concept Scale for Children and its Relationships to the Children's Form of the Manifest Anxiety Scale," *Child Development,* 29 (1958) , 463–71.

Lundy, R., W. Katkovsky, R. Cromwell, and D. Shoemaker. "Self Acceptability and Descriptions of Sociometric Choices," *Journal of Abnormal and Social Psychology,* 51 (1955) , 260–2.

McCandless, B. R. *Children and Adolescents,* pp. 187 ff. New York: Holt, Rinehart, Winston, 1961.

Maslow, A. H. *Motivation and Personality.* New York: Harper, 1954.

Ringness, T. A. *Non-Intellective Variables Related to Academic Achievement of Bright Junior High School Boys* (Cooperative Research Project S–035) . Madison: University of Wisconsin, 1965.

Rogers, C. R. "Characteristics of a Helping Relationship," *Personnel and Guidance Journal,* 37 (1958) , 6–15.

———. *Client-Centered Therapy.* Boston: Houghton Mifflin, 1951.

Smith, W., and D. Lebo. "Some Changing Aspects of the Self-Concept of Pubescent Males," *Journal of Genetic Psychology,* 88 (1956) , 61–5.

White, R. W. "Motivation Reconsidered: The Concept of Competence," *Psychological Review,* 66 (1959) , 297–333.

Wylie, R. C. *The Self Concept.* Lincoln: University of Nebraska Press, 1961.

SUGGESTIONS FOR FURTHER READING

Combs, A. W., and D. Snygg. *Individual Behavior.* (Rev. ed.) New York: Harper, 1959.
An excellent exposé of the phenomenological version of "self theory." Especially the first thirteen chapters and Chapter 19 discuss the theory itself and applications to treatment. It is interesting reading and makes a good case for the theory.

Staats, A. W., and C. K. Staats. *Complex Human Behavior.* New York: Holt, Rinehart, Winston, 1963.
Chapter 6 in particular discusses the self and other personality-theory concepts; the book is related to behavioristic psychology.

Wylie, R. C. *The Self Concept.* Lincoln: University of Nebraska Press, 1961.
This book is an excellent critique of concepts, methodology, and findings about the self-concept to 1960, with suggestions for the direction of further study—somewhat technical.

WORKING
WITH PARENTS

Chuck was in fourth grade, but he certainly was a problem to his teacher. He constantly demanded her attention and refused to work by himself. He was hyperactive and rarely settled down to concentrate on anything for very long. Chuck failed to play with his classmates, although they sometimes asked him to join them. His comment was merely that "they bored him."

If Chuck could get anyone to do things for him, he would usually try to do so. His conversation was adult for his age, and he brought forth ideas that seemed unusually mature for a fourth grader. Oddly, however, his ideas didn't always coordinate, as if he wasn't certain of their implications.

Chuck was informal, rather than respectful. He often spoke to the teacher in a manner more customarily reserved for peers. He sometimes seemed hurt when the teacher tried to get him to stop bothering her and to join his peers in some project. Once he wondered whether or not she liked him anymore.

A visit to Chuck's home clarified the behavior considerably. Chuck was an only child, a late arrival in his parents' lives. His father was frequently away on trips, leaving Chuck and his mother by themselves in their large, comfortable home. But, being somewhat new to the community and being a person who was quite retiring, Chuck's mother had made almost no friends and leaned on the boy for companionship. She treated him as a peer, talked "grown-up" language to him, and accepted his demands for attention. They played all sorts of games together, and she catered to Chuck's every whim.

Small wonder, then, that Chuck was bored with his peers—he was used to an adult to play with—one who would try hard to find new ways to amuse him. Why would he want to work at school when things had been made easy for him at home? It was easy to see why he continually demanded attention and why he was confused and hurt when it was not supplied.

A succession of conferences with the family and with Chuck resulted in different parental behavior at home and in Chuck's gaining a better idea of the differences between home and school. Chuck is now beginning to work independently—and even to enjoy his new friends among the pupils.

This anecdote is a true one from the files of a teacher in California. It is a simplified illustration of a school problem that has its origins in the home. Luckily, it was quite easily solved.

There are a number of values in school contacts with parents, not only in those between teacher and home, but also those between counselors, social workers, school psychologists, and nurses and the home. We shall list some possible benefits shortly.

Relationships Between the Child's Life at Home and at School

Following are some typical relationships between a child's home and school life:

1. The child may find success, security, and actualization at both home and school. His total environment is therefore conducive to good mental health.
2. He may lack positive reinforcement both at home and at school. A vicious cycle of poor home and school influences thus operates to prevent healthy development. His behavior reflects the results of the total environment through poor achievement, behavior problems, or emotional disturbances.

3. The child may be well accepted, secure, and happy at home but may fail to find satisfactions at school. He may reject the values and mores of teachers and peers and lack motivation for academic achievement. He may drop out of school early, play truant, or become a discipline problem. (Such results are more frequent among children from minority groups or from certain lower socioeconomic-class conditions.)

4. He may find school meaningful and satisfying, but conditions at home may be poor. In this instance, his school behavior cannot help but reflect home conditions, although he is not reacting against the school itself (such as the boy who hit his teacher, see Chapter 11).

Most children have reasonably good relationships at home and at school. Yet even so, there are problems that all children must meet in growing up, and cooperative and mutually reinforcing home and school efforts can be useful.

UNDERSTANDING THE CHILD'S BEHAVIOR

As we know, children vary their behavior from situation to situation. The child who is cooperative and helpful at school may be more of a problem at home and vice versa. It is not that there is inconsistency in children's behavior or that there is no stability to their personalities, but simply that they have learned to discriminate among various situations—and the reinforcements offered may be varied from home to school.

When the child's actions in various environments are known, his behavior is more clearly understood. It is useful for teachers to gain experience with children in such informal situations as on playgrounds, in club activities, and even in stores or about the neighborhood. Equally, parents should understand how their children behave in the classroom. Both parents and teachers can contribute much to the joint understanding of the child, as we shall discuss more fully later.

CONSISTENCY OF REINFORCEMENTS

The school cannot "do it all." Although the child is in school for perhaps 1,100 hours a year, it is true that he is elsewhere for much of the time, and especially the small child will be found in or about the home. When parents ignore a given kind of behavior that the school is trying to curb or when the school attempts to foster values that the home does not espouse, there is less likelihood that the child will learn what the teacher would hope for. If home and school can agree on desirable behaviors for the child, there will be less chance of one counteracting the other.

The consistency with which a child is treated should help him achieve a better contact with and understanding of reality, and a personal stability and impulse control he might not otherwise gain so completely. Confusion of efforts may lead to conflict and frustration, and even to anxiety and defensive behavior.

On the other hand, school is not home and home is not school. It is just as important to discuss legitimate differences between expectations and methods of dealing with the child as to be concerned about where they should coincide.

Family Influences on the Child

IMPORTANCE OF FAMILY RELATIONSHIPS

The position we have taken is that behavior is largely influenced by learning, and that learning is primarily (at least at first) governed by environmental reinforcements. The home is obviously of prime importance in determining the child's overt behavior, emotional reactions, perceptions, attitudes, and values. Although personality is modifiable at all ages, the earliest influences exert prior claim in determining the child's general outlook and expectations, hence give direction to the ways he will approach the school.

Tendencies to certain behavior patterns develop at an early age and persist unless some influence intervenes. A child who is dominated by his parents may thus find giving in to others a more workable way of life than continual struggle and rebellion. Although he may not attain autonomy and self-actualization by such responses, he may suffer less anxiety. In time he may become psychologically unable to defend his rights and opinions.

A child who is too protected may become unusually fearful of danger. A child who is rejected or frequently negatively reinforced may feel that, if he were only more adequate, his parents would show him more love. He may thus become overly sensitive to the ways others evaluate him and may carry feelings of inferiority and even guilt throughout his life, unless help is given. Children who feel secure and who are given evidence of affection and children who are treated with respect for their worth as human beings tend throughout their lives to have self-esteem, confidence, and feelings of being acceptable to others. Childhood learning thus predisposes one to good or poor adjustment or mental health.

Equally, the child learns many kinds of coping behavior at home. J. H. S. Bossard (1954) suggests that the family provides the child with basic opportunities for receiving affection; developing individual abilities, self-esteem, ability to live with others, attitudes, and basic tools (like talking, dressing, and concepts of the world) ; and a chance to learn acceptable living habits.

School, as the child's "second home," bears the same burdens of influence on the child. Children approach teachers as they approach their parents, and frequently teachers have similarly powerful influence (especially with the young child) .

THE ADEQUATE HOME

Bossard and E. S. Boll, in an earlier work (1943) , found that the ideal family provided emotional security and feelings of worth, of belonging, and of being wanted. When the child is genuinely loved and respected in his home, he has more opportunities for independence and responsibility and is encouraged to make his own plans and choices whenever feasible. Enough privacy is supplied so that the child can develop autonomy. For example, he is allowed possessions he can dispose of as he sees fit, for they are entirely his own.

R. Dreikurs, *et al.* (1959) , make much of the need for the child to be treated as equal to adults in human rights. This approach requires respect for the child's emotions and allows him to express his views; if they are inappropriate, they are dealt with in a manner that does not shame him or make him feel inferior. Although the child may be young, he should be treated as a full-fledged member of the family. Love and respect are not synonymous, for some varieties of love smother the child or overindulge him, providing parents with satisfactions for their motives but doing harm to the child's self-respect and independence.

To help the child learn to accept responsibility, a parent must plan carefully. Parents may underestimate the child's stage of development and his need for independence and may be too restrictive for his fullest growth. Yet one cannot force mature behavior, and in his striving for emancipation the child needs the security and support of controls provided by parents. Parents should therefore watch for the child's attempts to gain independence and to accept responsibility and let him try his own ideas out on levels suited to his age. His successes are evidence of maturation and learning; his unsuccessful efforts are evidence that he is not yet ready to cope with problems on that level. Teachers, as well as parents, may employ the same approach. They will find that, because children differ in development, what responsibilities one child can accept may be too much for another. Efforts can be tentatively made to allow children to accept responsibility and make choices, but care must be taken not to permit them to get into too deep water.

SOME INADEQUACIES IN FAMILY LIVING

A number of patterns of family living have been studied to learn their effects on the child. For example, P. M. Symonds (1949), in early studies, looked at dominance-submission and acceptance-rejection dimensions in home relationships.

Some families were considered by Symonds to be overacceptant of the child. The parents might be overindulgent to the child, causing him to be "spoiled" and demanding, or they might be overprotective and restrictive, causing him to be timid and fearful. When overindulged, the child learns unrealistic expectations about his own importance and regards the parents almost as servants who will cater to him (see Chuck's case at the beginning of the chapter). Such parents may spend much time with the child and seldom refuse his demands for toys, money, or special privileges. They defend him against foes. He learns to dominate situations by being aggressive, throwing temper tantrums, and by "being difficult." He does not learn to accept responsibility or to consider others; consequently he has problems at school.

The overly protected child may be anxious about school, because he is fearful and school is a new and untried environment. He may withdraw, since he has not learned to handle social situations by himself and expects help and protection from others which he does not receive. (One form of "school phobia" is a result of overprotection. It is thought related to the emotional characteristics of the mother. She cannot bear to deprive herself of her child, hence communicates her anxieties to the child in subtle ways, for example, "Now don't be afraid, Peter. Mother will not be far away." Such a mother, fearful of losing her child, tends to overprotect him and sensitize him to the "dangers" of the environment and to restrict his normal activities.)

Underacceptant families also exist. The child may be ignored or even rejected. Parents may overemphasize his shortcomings, punish him severely, criticize him harshly, or even try to frighten him. They may leave him alone a great deal and may compare him unfavorably to siblings or peers. Such children may be the picture of insecurity, and spend much effort in attention seeking, striving for some evidence of affection from parents, teachers, or classmates. They may later cease trying to win affection and become jealous, hyperactive, hostile, or delinquent. Dreikurs (1957), in a provocative book, has shown how a progression of deteriorating behaviors may result if the situation is not relieved.

The dominating parent tends to produce a child who is more conforming than does the submissive parent. Such a child tends to make better impressions on others. He adjusts better in school and conforms more to group practices. He has been taught to obey and may be a "model child." Yet he may be overly submissive and unable to defend himself. He may have difficulty in making decisions. He may also be shy, retiring, or self-conscious. His parents expect too much from him and tend to restrict his activities.

Submissive parents give in because they do not have the necessary confidence in dealing with their children, and tend to yield whenever parent-child conflict ensues. This may be because of basic insecurity the parents have had all of their lives;

neurotic behavior results in difficulty in bringing up healthy children. It is also possible that such submissiveness can come about from misinterpretations of books on child rearing. Although modern psychology does not promote a submissive approach (or *per*missive, in the extreme sense) nor is it desirous to allow the child to rule the home, some parents are afraid of stunting their child's growth in independence by overcontrolling him; hence they go too far in the other direction. Such parents have essentially abdicated their responsibility to teach the child acceptable behavior. Their children tend to be disorderly and to lack discipline. They may defy authority and act unmanageably. (However, they do tend to have self-confidence and to express themselves effectively.)

Such other writers as J. Kagan and H. S. Moss (1961) have agreed with Symonds (1949) on dimensions of love versus hostility and autonomy versus control as being important in the child's development. It must be recognized, however, that interrelationships are complex. Some rejecting parents may be also indulgent, as a result of feelings of guilt and a desire to compensate; such parents may provide the child with material possessions, but fail to take a real interest in him. Some rejecting parents are submissive and prefer to see as little of their children as possible. Submissive parents may complicate matters by inconsistency; in desperation they become harsh with the child, but then feel remorse and become unduly indulgent. They vacillate, which confuses the child. Other problems occur when one parent is acceptant and the other is rejecting, or when one is dominant and the other is submissive.

Much research has tended to point up the influence of the mother in fostering the child's behavior pattern; this is thought to be because he spends more time with his mother in early childhood. However, the father also plays an important role, and his absence from the family or his unwillingness to take an active part in child rearing may cause many problems. Complete families have not been studied very frequently, but those studies that have been made suggest that frequent constellations of family life for disturbed children are

1. both parents inconsistent, impulsively acting out their emotions, and arbitrary in their handling of the child;

2. a self-preoccupied, rather weak father and an aggressive, also self-preoccupied, but strong mother; and
3. "average" mothers (i.e., not different as a group from the mothers of nonproblem children) and arbitrary, demanding, and restrictive fathers. (McCandless, 1961, p. 114)

As R. F. Peck (1958) has indicated, the child seems most able to cope with life when his family life is characterized by stability, consistency, warmth, and mutual trust between the parents and between parents and child. He prefers to see a lenient, democratic family atmosphere, with regular and consistent family life.

RELATED HOME CONDITIONS

BROKEN HOMES. ■ Homes may be disrupted in a number of ways. Death of one or both parents, absence of a parent because of business or military obligations, divorce, protracted illness—all produce incomplete families. The child who loses a parent experiences emotional crises tending to result in marked feelings of insecurity, especially for the early school-age child who has previously had the security of both parents. Loss removes the advantages of having both parents as models and having different kinds of reinforcements that can be supplied. If the child loses the parent with whom he most identifies or whom he uses as a model, problems relating to sex-role identification, attitudes, and values may result.

Studies of children from broken homes (Russell, 1957; Torrance, 1945) show that they tend to experience more scholastic retardation *or* overachievement; more behavioral, social, emotional, and physical health problems; and more serious maladjustment than do children from complete homes. Those from families with separations or divorces seem to have more problems than those whose parents are dead; included are greater tendencies to anger and self-centeredness, less sensitivity to social approval, less social control, and more depression. Lying, stealing, and other forms of disobedience are more common. There is a possibility that the conflict and emotional upheaval leading to divorce is more influential in determining such reactions than the fact of divorce itself. Parents who are unable to resolve their differences may use the children as pawns against each other. The parents are not usually displayed in an appealing light, and even the parent with whom the child most identifies may lose status in his eyes.

R. V. Burton and J. W. M. Whiting (1961) have considered what happens to boys when raised totally by their mothers. Cross-sex identification, i. e., the identification of the boy with his mother, is thought to raise problems in his assumption of the male role. There is some evidence that boys raised without fathers tend to be somewhat infantile and dependent; they defend themselves against femininity by either rebellion or by exaggerating their "masculine" behavior. J. McCord, *et al.* (1962), however, feel that the anxiety, delinquency, and other manifest problems are due less to the absence of the father than to the general instability of broken homes. They tend to support the notion that parental characteristics, rather than presence or absence *per se,* are determining factors of most importance.

ROLE IDENTIFICATION. ▪ There is frequently a need for boys to have a stronger, male identifying figure than is provided by some fathers. F. N. Cox (1962) found that the development of positive social relations is related to a positive attitude toward the parent of the same sex as the child.

A. Bandura and R. H. Walters (1959) noted that, in a study of aggressive boys, there was considerably less identification with, and more hostility toward, fathers than with nonaggressive boys; fathers were unlikely to serve as important models for the former. They further suggest that fathers of aggressive boys tend to spend less time with them in early childhood in affectional interaction, display a lack of warmth for them, are more hostile, rejecting, and punitive. The boys, in turn, are more critical and disparaging of their fathers. If the father can accept the boy, reward him with affection and approval, he should identify with his father.

N. Bayley and E. S. Schaefer (1963) show that in early childhood boys tend to do well if their mothers are loving, but it is necessary to grant boys autonomy at adolescence.

In general, studies show that girls have fewer identification problems, since they continue to identify with their mothers;

they are not required to make the shift from mother-orientation to father-orientation that boys must make. It is therefore not surprising that boys overtly show more behavior problems, especially those of an aggressive nature, reflecting rebellion, lack of socialization, sex-role confusion, or overcompensation in the male role. Boys are referred to school psychologists nearly four times as frequently as girls, partly because teachers cannot tolerate their aggressive acts, but partly because there are more problems for them in our matriarchal schools (at least at the elementary-school level).

The child's position in the family, the number of his siblings and their interrelationships, the presence of others in the home, neighborhood peer relationships, and other related factors all interact to make the child what he is when he enters school. Sometimes it is possible to modify some of these factors; for example, fathers can sometimes be helped to find mutual activities with their sons (as in the Y.M.C.A. Indian Guides program). P.T.A. seminars and lectures can sometimes help parents to understand their children and to learn some principles of child rearing more successfully. Individual conferences with parents can sometimes help clarify problems and lacks in the child's home or school life that can be compensated for or improved by home-school efforts.

Home-School Conferences

BASIC ASSUMPTIONS

Our point of view makes several assumptions about home-school relationships. They include:

Parents have a right to know how their children are achieving (and behaving) in school. Emotional and social adjustment, interests, abilities, and attitudes studied by the school should be reported. The school has the responsibility not only to report marks and grades but also to supply other information in which parents may be interested.

Schools have a right to know factors in the child's home life that may account for or help to explain his behavior in school. For example, school values may vary from those of the home.

Perhaps the parents place pressures on the child to achieve more highly than he is capable of doing; perhaps he is being forced to compete with siblings of greater ability. The methods of exerting discipline may vary between home and school. Such information can aid school personnel to understand the child.

(We recognize the legitimacy of privacy for home and school; prying should not be attempted. It is our position that parents and school usually wish to exchange information about the child for the good of the child. If adequate safeguards are provided, invasion of privacy should not exist.)

Many parents are fully capable of observing and interpreting the child to the school. Although professional jargon may not be understood by some parents, most are reasonably skilled in understanding human nature. Their long acquaintance with the child in a variety of situations can be valuable in interpreting him to teachers.

Parents are capable of understanding professional concepts and of applying them in working at home with the child. When school objectives are understood and accepted, parents can frequently supplement the work of the teacher. For example, a parent may have the impression that teachers prefer him not to help the child with reading, and in some instances they don't. Yet many children learn to read even before entering first grade because they are interested enough to ask questions of parents or siblings, particularly when parents sit down and read to the children. So, although parents should not put pressure on the child to learn to read, there seems no good reason why they should not help and encourage him when appropriate occasions arise. This encouragement may increase his motivation as well as his ability to read. Schools might do better to discuss how parents can be helpful, rather than to resist parental efforts.

Parents are capable of helping their children in many areas in which the school is interested but may lack facilities. For example, some parents are highly competent in mathematics, science, shop, sports, music, and so on. The writer was once a junior high-school science teacher and found that one of the boys had a more extensively equipped laboratory in his home basement than was possessed by the school, which was not surprising, as his father was a research specialist for a major manufacturing company and both he and the boy participated in experiments as a mutual hobby.

Mutual respect and cooperation can usually be fostered between home and school. When such cooperation cannot be achieved, however, perhaps other community agencies can be helpful to the school. For example, rehabilitation counselors can supplement the work of such school specialists as counselors and psychologists. When lack of cooperation is noted, it is wise to check with such agencies. Frequently uncooperative homes have been receiving special assistance from welfare agencies or other community groups (Elmott, 1960).

PLANNING FOR CONFERENCES

Purposes for teacher-parent conferences (or conferences between guidance personnel and parents) may be formulated by either party but should be jointly understood. Among the many possible purposes of such conferences are

1. to acquaint parents with information about the child in school;
2. to obtain from parents information about the child at home;
3. to gain rapport with parents, preparatory to initiating cooperative efforts;
4. to exchange suggestions for helping the child with problems of learning, social behavior, or health;
5. to evaluate jointly information received from various sources (for example, child-study devices);
6. to hypothesize reasons for the child's behavior and problems;
7. to consider the child's progress and to suggest modifications in previous plans for helping him;
8. to agree upon specific responsibilities of home and school in helping the child.

Similar goals are suggested by J. W. Loughary (1961) and T. A. Brodie (1958), who discuss conferences between parents and school counselors that may amplify, reinforce, or complement conferences between teachers and parents. As will be discussed in more detail in a later chapter, coordinated efforts of the entire "school team" are desirable. Loughary's objectives are as follows:

1. to provide parents with achievement and aptitude data on the child;
2. to help parents make educational plans for the child;
3. to help parents understand their child's abilities and potentials;
4. to help parents understand their child and accept his environmental variables, including the parents themselves;
5. to help parents whose children have specific behavior problems.

Brodie adds:

1. to establish a good working relationship between home and school with a view to mutually stimulating the student's academic achievement and social adjustment;
2. to improve public relations: to create a favorable community attitude toward the school and its policies;
3. to give parents a diagnostic view of the child's achievement, specialized aptitudes, and general academic characteristics, as measured by standardized tests and through classroom observation—and to some degree to analyze the educational and vocational implications of these data.

Parent conferences may thus involve teacher, parents, counselor, and even the child. Many purposes may be served, and conferences therefore require careful planning. When conferences fail to produce satisfactory progress, it is usually because parents and teachers are confused about why the conference is being held, which sometimes happens when conferences are set up according to formal calendars; they become requirements without real or specific motivation or meaning.

In planning conferences some schools ask parents in advance for the kinds of information sought by the school. For example, the Long Beach, California, Public Schools' *Handbook for Parent Conferences* (1955) suggests the following kinds of information that might be sought:

HOW THE CHILD FEELS ABOUT SCHOOL

what he likes best
what he dislikes
whether he likes to attend

HOW THE CHILD SPENDS HIS SPARE TIME OUTSIDE OF SCHOOL

with friends
with hobbies
with home responsibilities

WHAT PARTICULAR PROBLEMS THE CHILD MIGHT HAVE

with friends
with health
with fears
with strong feelings

WHAT TALENTS, INTERESTS, AND HOBBIES THE CHILD MIGHT HAVE

in drawing, music, writing, dancing, etc.
in cowboys, magic, space travel, science, etc.
in collecting, modeling, nature study, sports, etc.

WHAT ATTITUDES THE CHILD HAS IN THE HOME

toward brothers or sisters
toward parental suggestions
toward home responsibilities

WHAT RECENT CHANGES THE PARENTS HAVE NOTICED IN THE CHILD

the way he works
the way he plays
the way he relates himself to other people

WHAT SPECIAL HELP THE CHILD MIGHT NEED

in the school
in the home

Others (Georgiady & Romano, 1962; Peters & Farwell, 1959) have prepared checklists for parents so that they can inform the school of areas they wish to discuss. Checklists allow parents and teachers to be prepared for discussion, and they provide take-off points for discussion, but they are not intended to be all-inclusive or exclusive about information to be shared about the child.

IMPROVING COMMUNICATION WITH PARENTS

SETTING THE STAGE. ▪ Unless rapport is gained, little real communication results from people simply talking with one another. Setting the stage is important in fostering initial favorable attitudes toward the conference.

People communicate best when they feel comfortable in their surroundings. There is an immediate need for privacy because little can be comfortably brought out for discussion when others are present, when it is noisy in the conference room, when there are interruptions, or when it is evident to others what is taking place. Access to an office is desirable; the classroom is appropriate only when it is certain that others will not intrude.

An atmosphere of informality and of social equality between teacher and parents is helpful. The teacher should not barricade himself behind his desk but should sit informally with parents. Comfortable chairs are helpful; coffee is usually welcome; and, if smoking is permitted, it may help to relieve initial tensions.

Materials essential to the discussion should be at hand, for example, samples of the child's work, his cumulative record, test results, and recorded observations.

Notes should be taken concerning the conference, especially when agreements about future procedures have been reached. Parents should receive copies.

How much "small talk" should take place is a matter of judgment, but the conference should be steered toward "business" as soon as rapport seems established. The time of both parties is valuable.

SENSITIVITY TO FEELINGS. ▪ Some of the most important communication between people comes about through the ways they express their feelings. What is said in conference may not be as important as what is felt and how these feelings are expressed. Equally, what is *not* said may be as important as what *is* said.

Clinicians use the term *clinical sensitivity* to describe the ability to understand how people feel as well as what they think and say. Clinicians are given training in learning how to interpret the ways people feel and express emotion. The term "empathy" is sometimes used in this regard and implies the ability to understand the emotions of others necessarily sharing in them.

Development of sensitivity to feelings is important to the teacher in his dealings with adults as well as with children. No one can tell another person how to become sensitive, but practice in trying to understand others can help. For example, when a mother says, "I try too hard with Mary, but I love her to death even though she is failing in school," the teacher might ask himself if this indicates that: the mother is disappointed in the girl, resents her failings, and is frustrated; the mother is excusing herself for her part in Mary's failures; the mother is bidding for sympathy, covering up rejection of the child; or she is implying something else.

Sometimes one may ask for clarification of how the other person feels, rather than what he thinks. For example, it is quite appropriate to ask a parent, "How did you feel about Johnny's hitting the other child?" or, "Were you happy with Susie's report card?" The teacher, of course, will not try to probe in the same way as the psychologist, but nevertheless needs to cultivate the ability to be sensitive to communication by feelings as well as by what is verbally expressed and inherent in the language content.

One more suggestion may be offered. The teacher can be on the lookout for *expressive behavior* of the parent. The parent may show muscular tenseness, twitch, demonstrate a tic, twist the hands, or have other nervous mannerisms. At such points it should be apparent that this is a sensitive aspect of the parent's feelings about the child or himself, and tact or even change of subject should be employed. Nonetheless, such areas may need further exploration and might be approached obliquely.

The teacher needs also to be alert to his own feelings and attitudes and how these may affect the conference. If he should dislike a parent or the child or if his mood should shift, he should think through how he feels, why he feels that way, and how his feelings may affect the interaction and any judgments that might be made. Frequently one can tell from his own reactions something about the other person's feelings. For example, if the conferee is becoming angry, his anger may be reflected by the teacher, although the teacher may not be entirely aware of how his own feelings came about.

Sometimes teachers visit the homes of pupils, particularly if parents seem unwilling or unable to attend conferences at school. Here is an example:

Miss Every, fourth-grade teacher at Sunnydale School, finally determined to visit Mrs. Leon, mother of "Missy."

Accordingly, Miss Every asked Missy to inquire of her mother when it would be agreeable for Miss Every to call. Missy shilleyed and shalleyed but finally "allowed" that it would be "O.K. if you come out after school on Wednesday. Can you give me a ride, and I'll show you where we live because otherwise you maybe couldn't find it?" Miss Every agreed.

The Leons lived in an outlying area in a far-from-sumptuous home. The farmyard was unkempt, the house could have stood a coat of paint, and the general air was that of shiftlessness and poverty. Miss Every regretted her decision to call, not because she was afraid of dirt or lack of neatness but because she did not want to embarrass Mrs. Leon, who might be expected to resent callers from what she could perceive as a higher station in life. Missy ran on ahead, however, and Miss Every walked up to the stoop.

The door opened, and a large woman, neat and clean, carrying a baby in her arms, smiled hugely. "Come in Miss Every, come in, come in." The interior of the home, though bare, was well kept and not in keeping with the exterior of the establishment. Immediately Mrs. Leon offered the baby to Miss Every to hold and stepped into the kitchen to fetch coffee and newly made doughnuts. A lively conversation ensued, in which Miss Every was made to feel at home, and in which she hastily revised earlier opinions about Missy's home life. She heard about the other eight children of the family, the ill health of Mr. Leon, the helpfulness of the neighbors, and how well Missy pitched in.

The only sad note of the "conference" occurred as Miss Every was leaving. "Good-bye, Miss Every," said Mrs. Leon. "It was d. . . . white of you to call. Nobody from school has ever been here before; and—you can see why—I can't ever leave the place what with nine kids and a sick man, and all. Except for the neighbors, I haven't been anywhere or seen anyone in over three months.

But now, maybe, when Jim gets better, I can come to see you at school. You're my friend, now."

SOME BARRIERS TO HOME-SCHOOL COOPERATION

If one were to visit the teachers' lounge during a free period he might hear such comments as:

"What can you expect from Merry S.? After all, her mother is never at home. She is out bridge-playing all day long—they even have games in the morning now, or so I hear. If the mother would stay home and take care of those kids, the children would do better at school, but she expects *us* to bring up her children for her."

Or: "I'm going to get another Jones this fall. There isn't one of them that can read at grade level. And the mother! Sometimes I'm sure she is mentally retarded. The father flits from job to job, and he practically lives in that tavern. These Joneses always make for trouble and I think they shouldn't be in school at all. But I suppose I'll suffer through another one, as usual."

But if one could listen in on home conversations, he might hear the other side of these stories. For example, Mrs. S., Merry's mother, thinks: "Look at Merry's teacher. She expects high standards from the kids but she won't give them any real help. Only yesterday Merry stopped in for some special help after school and the teacher was 'too busy.' The faculty had a meeting, she said. Seems to me they meet most of the time. Anyway, she doesn't understand children. How could she, not having any of her own?"

Mrs. Jones is frustrated too. "It's hard to help the kids with their schooling when they won't even try. If their father were able to hold a job and took some hand in disciplining them, it might help. But he doesn't believe in education—didn't have any himself, and he thinks *he's* doing okay. But if the teacher would only tell me what to do, I might at least get little Joey through high school. He's the brightest one in the family anyway."

Although everyone knows better, we all *do* indulge in stereotypes and base some of our opinions on hearsay. When one views the teacher as he is portrayed in comic books or other public media, he appears to be

unfair in grading,
unable to understand children,
personally unattractive,
mousy and unaggressive,
unable to discipline properly,
inclined to complain,
highly unrealistic,
entirely theoretical and impractical.

But some teachers are

overpaid for little work,
snobbish and superior-acting,
too demanding,
too intellectual.

And, if one listens to teacher stereotypes about parents, he may discover that parents are

disinterested in school,
out to make trouble,
biased in favor of their children,
inclined to blame the teacher for all problems,
culturally impoverished,
unwilling to help the child,
unable to control the child.

Admittedly these comments are exaggerated, and of course they do not hold universally. Yet there is enough truth in the stereotypes presented to suggest that barriers to communication may exist.

DEALING WITH BARRIERS TO COMMUNICATION

If communication barriers exist, they may prevent efforts at home-school cooperation from succeeding. Unless these barriers are lowered, it is unlikely that honest cooperative efforts will result. Because everyone tends to view situations from his own frame of reference he may not be sensitive to the situation as viewed by others. In this section, we shall consider some fairly typical feelings of parents and suggest possible procedures for the teacher to overcome them. The teacher may thus be better prepared for reactions he may meet when trying to work with some parents.

Most child-guidance clinics will not attempt therapy with a child unless they can also work with the parents. The attitudes and feelings of parents are so pervasive in the child's life that, unless they can learn better how to understand his problems, work with the child himself is not likely to be successful. The teacher, although not a therapist, can learn to understand parents' feelings toward the school and toward the child. He cannot help parents to work through their feelings in the same way as does the clinician, but he can at least show them alternate ways of thinking about the child and his problems.

PARENTS' DEFENSIVENESS ABOUT THE CHILD. ▪ Defensiveness is likely to be present if parents have had complaints about the child's deportment, achievement, or social adjustment. Some parents push the child for his future good, demanding too much from him and reliving their own lives through his or attaining their aspirations through his successes. In such instances their defensive attitudes are based on unrealistic aspirations. Other parents are overly protective and see criticism of the child as a threat to themselves. They may accept the child's version of what has happened at school as correct without considering his defensive maneuvers. In this way they resort to denial of reality, a form of escape. Other reasons for defensiveness can readily be hypothesized.

If the child's behavior suggests that the parents are not doing an adequate job of child rearing, they may be threatened, hostile, and full of excuses. The teacher can help reduce emotional tensions by helping the parents understand that their child *is* accepted, although his school work may be poor, he is a disciplinary problem, or he is not as bright as some of his classmates. If the teacher appears to accept the child, parents can be more hopeful of success in dealing with his problems and can thus admit the existence of such problems and their fears about him. It is threat-reducing to treat the problems in a professional, encouraging way, rather than by seeming to be punitive of the child's deficiencies. Fixing blame does no good when parents are threatened. A wise teacher points up the strengths as well as the weaknesses of the child and discusses him as a person who has problems to be met. The teacher points to progress where he can and emphasizes the child's efforts to improve. He also points out the values of individual differences and does not insinuate that the child should be more "like the others."

Parents who are defensive about their child may not fully accept him, for some of their expectations for him have not been realized. They may therefore feel that he has let them down. Perhaps they can be helped to be less rejecting and more understanding and learn to relax their tensions about him. For example, some parents are "college conscious" and find it difficult to accept the fact that their son probably will not be accepted at a "better" college or university because of poor marks or lack of intellectual ability. Yet a healthy personality, good character, and carefully cultivated skills may be far more valuable than academic success and a college degree. Among the ways of relieving tensions of this sort are to suggest that the boy may find himself more readily in a smaller college, in industry, or in the business world. Questions may arise as to whether or not the boy really wants to face college competition and enter into professional life. Many successful farmers, actors, salesmen, and others would be out of place at college, yet contribute well to society and live happy and useful lives.

This sort of acceptance is not easy for parents to achieve, especially if the child is seriously handicapped in some way, that is, if he is blind, deaf, mentally retarded, a cerebral palsy victim, or seriously disturbed. They may need the help of family service agencies or psychological counseling from a private source. If parents cannot resolve their own problems, they will only compound those of the child. Group therapy has been tried by some clinics with excellent results, and if parents are seen by the teacher as serious threats to the child's efforts to improve, it may be possible to find a way to suggest to them how other parents have benefited from "educational sessions" or "specialized counseling."

The teacher must keep one caution in mind: He must not be

a Pollyanna and lead parents into false hopes. It is better for them to face up honestly to the strengths and weaknesses of the child when they are discovered, and although attention is directed to the child's efforts to improve, his weaknesses must not be minimized.

PARENTS' DEFENSIVENESS ABOUT THEMSELVES. ■ This situation arises when they feel guilty because the child is frequently in trouble for disciplinary reasons, when it is apparent that he is not able to get along with others well, or when he is loafing, tardy, truant, or otherwise irresponsible and uncontrolled. Sometimes parents expect too much of the child, but, equally, they may expect too much of themselves, forgetting other factors in the child's life.

If it appears certain that the parents have been at fault in their handling of the child, the teacher might ask if they have any worries over the child's rate of progress. This approach implies that the parents are aware that all is not well, and that they are duly concerned over the child's problems. The way is thus cleared for a discussion of suitable methods which might help solve the problems. For example, when ten-year-old Peter has been caught smoking on the school grounds, the teacher might gain better results by asking how Peter's father feels about smoking, whether this is a problem at home, and what he suggests the school and parents together might do about the situation.

All parents do not have guilt feelings about handling their children. Some are simply defensive because they feel inferior to the teacher. Perhaps they lack education, have a low economic status, feel that they are members of a minority group which is not accepted, or have other misgivings about their success in life. In such instances it is safer to ignore these factors entirely and to treat such parents with the same respect and attention accorded to other parents. Sound reasoning, and excellent attitudes toward children exist in all walks of life, and parents should not be prejudged by grammar or appearance. The teacher should not call attention to possible shortcomings by vocally "explaining them away," or by protesting his acceptance of parental virtues, or by expressing false admiration or sympathy.

PARENTS' IGNORANCE OF THE CHILD'S PROBLEMS. ▪ It is quite possible that some parents are ignorant of the problems the child faces at school, since not only may the child act quite differently at home, but he may be capable of misrepresenting his successes (or failures) to his parents. This is frequently true of children who are achieving poorly. They deny failure, rationalize poor marks, or even alter or intercept report cards.

When the child's parents are unaware that problems exist, or they are not clear as to the extent or true nature of the problems, they must be carefully oriented before useful discussion can follow. As few parents can be objective about their children, especially when shocked by sudden disclosures of inadequacies, care must be used in presenting data.

PARENTS' NEED FOR HELP. ▪ Discussion sometimes discloses that parents are aware of problems their child may have, yet feel at a loss to help him. Perhaps they have tried a number of methods, with little success. Sometimes they are afraid to admit failure and are unable to ask for help. In such cases they may minimize the problem, disclaim responsibility and ability to assist, or employ other defenses.

The teacher may suggest that he, too, needs help in understanding the child. He may introduce suggestions tactfully, and his willingness to "work on the problem together" with parents may help build a feeling of mutual support.

Obviously the teacher may be as much at a loss as the parents. In such instances he may wish to seek the assistance of such experts as guidance personnel, school psychologist, or social worker. The atmosphere of "I'm not sure either, but let's see whether we can't work together on this" is healthy and reassuring. Exhortation and advice are likely to prove barriers to fruitful communication.

PARENTS' FALSE SENSE THAT PROBLEMS ARE UNDER CONTROL. ▪ They may believe that the child's problems are gradually being solved and that no further help or discussion is needed. This belief may be quite honest and based upon fact. Some parents may actually be providing the child special assistance of which the teacher is unaware. Other parents may feel that the child could suffer from more rigorous efforts to help him. A few parents may lack confidence in the teacher's ability to assist.

POSSIBILITIES OF FAMILY TROUBLE. ▪ Some homes are undergoing crises, like financial difficulties, alcoholism, or divorce. When the problem becomes evident, it is necessary to act carefully to avoid invasion of privacy or to avoid taking sides. The teacher may accept information offered by the parents, keeping in mind that he is hearing only a one-sided interpretation of the situation. He may not offer sympathy or suggestions in regard to such family problems but can, of course, suggest family counseling. *Attention must be focused on the problems of the child and what conditions may be changed to relieve them.*

A CASE OF FAMILY FINANCIAL PROBLEMS

Karl lived on a farm back in the hills. He was frequently truant from school but usually had an excuse, signed by his mother, saying that he had a headache or was coming down with a cold. When he *was* in school, he was sleepy most of the time and, on one or two occasions, actually fell asleep in study hall. His grades were failing, and Karl was referred to the guidance counselor.

The counselor found out little from Karl, who was defensive. He would "try to keep awake and to be at school more." He hoped his headaches would cease and that he wouldn't catch so many colds. But Karl's record didn't improve, and the counselor decided to visit his home.

Rapport with Karl's mother was not easy to gain; she was defensive about Karl and felt that the school gave him too much work to do and too little help. She was sorry he had been absent so often but didn't know what could be done about it. But, as the counselor exhibited friendly concern, Karl's mother began to let out the real truth.

Karl's father was chronically ailing, and Karl was needed to do the chores on the farm and sometimes to help out in the fields or in other ways, which was really why he was sometimes absent. The farm was not making much money, and Karl had a job that paid a little, which helped out some. The family was independent and did not believe in seeking welfare payments.

Actually, it developed, Karl would arise at five o'clock in the morning, do the farm chores, catch the school bus at seven, and remain in school until three-thirty, when he would bus home. He would do the evening chores by himself, eat, then bicycle the three miles back to town, where he set pins at the bowling alley until eleven at night. Karl would then bicycle back home, to repeat the whole process the next school day. Small wonder that he was tired all of the time; it was amazing that he held up as well as he did.

The counselor tried to help. He obtained a job for Karl in the school cafeteria, which provided a free lunch and some pay, almost as much as he earned at the bowling alley. Karl was then to quit his pin-setting job. The counselor also was able to show the family that there was an advantage in accepting government farm subsidies, rather than being independent at Karl's expense. In time, Karl's tiredness disappeared, and his school work improved. Karl's mother, too, was happy that the counselor had helped solve their problems.

PROBLEMS WITH THE SCHOOL. ▪ Sometimes the child's problems are caused or augmented by teachers or other school staff (including the teacher sponsoring the conference). Just as parents may feel guilt and show defensiveness or hostility, so may teachers. Some may be punitive, suspicious, or overcritical. Others may show little understanding of child development.

If the parents have negative attitudes toward the school because of previous experiences, ways must be found to foster better rapport. Parents may be quite justified in their feelings about the school, but, on the other hand, they may have misinterpreted certain remarks or occurrences. They may also fail to discriminate between teachers, and between other school conditions.

In any case, school staff cannot ethically "mix in" where colleagues are involved. One can suggest a parent conference with teachers who may be involved, or a visit to the school principal, but he cannot ethically discuss fellow staff members with parents. If, however, the present teacher is reasonably willing to listen to problems and to consider parents' ideas, much can be done to foster mutual good will.

The above remarks have been mainly concerned with parental feelings and attitudes, seemingly neglecting those of the teachers. As this book is written for teachers, the intent is to suggest meaningful ways in which the teacher may approach a conference. However, these same points apply equally well to the teacher. Alerted to problems in human relations, he will be on guard lest he, himself, contribute barriers to effective communication. Like the therapist, he should be aware of his own biases, prejudices, and customary reactions. He may quite validly indicate his feelings to the parents, for he has the same right to express them as any other human being, but he must take care that they do not throw a false light on the problems of the child nor interfere with effective parent-teacher communication.

J. W. M. Rothney (1958) suggests some problems inherent in parent-counselor conferences which also exist in parent-teacher conferences. For example, conferences may be difficult because suggestions made by counselors (teachers) may be taken by parents literally as recommendations. T. A. Brodie (1958), in a similar vein, finds that parents may take the counselor as authority, and an ill-considered remark could conceivably traumatize anxious or suggestible parents. Interview data may be looked upon as a "verdict," and parents may expect the counselor to provide a directive judgment from "irrefutable test evidence." The teacher may also run into similar problems and must be careful not to commit himself or parents to action without sufficient evidence; and, when commitments are made, he must make certain that they are regarded as tentative testing of hypotheses. He must also make sure parents do not "use" him to support their own ideas, especially in regard to their efforts to coerce the child. The hidden meanings in communication must thus be considered, as well as what is openly voiced.

AGREEING ON ACTION

Once problems have been stated, information shared, and hypotheses on the child's problems have been presented, it is necessary to suggest and agree on action to help him. If action cannot be agreed on, perhaps further study of the problem is indicated. Agreements must represent both what the teacher and parents believe they can reasonably accomplish and what they sincerely wish to accomplish. Undue optimism or pessimism should be avoided. It has been shown (Rosenthal, 1964) that, in therapy, patients tend to improve or not in line with the expectations of the therapist. That is, their expectations seem to influence the way they proceed with patients and thus indirectly affect recovery. The phenomenon of the *self-fulfilling prophecy* is involved. Equally, the teacher or parent who is not truly convinced that help can be given to the child is not likely truly to help the child.

Action on many fronts is usually called for. The parents may agree to supervise study hours for the child and the teacher to provide special help when needed. The parents may attempt to help the child feel more self-confident through interaction with him at home, and the teacher may try to do the same thing at school. Perhaps referral to specialists is indicated and it should be agreed on how and by whom such referral should be initiated.

Complete change should not be expected immediately. Too harsh or too extensive change in methods or environment can be harmful to the child. The most important problems should be attacked first, and the others held for future consideration. Decisions to act should be aimed at specific problems, rather than those which remain broad and ill-defined. Time should be allowed for tactics to bear fruit. Provisions should be made for follow-up and for future conferences when needed. Parents and teachers must recognize that their hypotheses and plans for action may be erroneous, hence must be considered tentative at best. Further study and planning should be accepted as a probable necessity.

INVOLVING THE CHILD

When working with the home we need to consider not only the parents, but the child himself (Rothney, 1958). He may feel that he is in the midst of a conspiracy directed against him, or he may feel like a helpless pawn while discussions about him continue. He may resent parent-teacher conferences; he may attempt to play parents against the teacher, or vice versa. He may feel that he is not being given a sufficient voice in plans for him and that he is not being respected as a person.

The child has a right to be heard. *When* this opportunity should be afforded depends upon the situation, but he probably should not be invited to make suggestions or asked to accept responsibilities until parents and teachers have ample opportunity to attempt to understand his problems and come to some agreement. Then he should be invited to comment.

Frequently, the child may prefer to talk to a guidance worker or someone other than parent or teacher, for he may believe that either or both are to blame for many of his difficulties and that if he were to defend this point of view he might lose their good will. He may be quite correct, especially if they are punitive rather than understanding.

Some schools have instituted the "three-way conference," in which, after parents and teacher have conferred, the child is asked to state his views and to make suggestions. This technique has seemed particularly useful with older children and adolescents, although the use of such a device should be determined by the nature of the problem and the judgments of parents and teacher.

In any case, however, if best results are to be obtained, the child must provide a measure of cooperation. He should probably be a party to any definite agreements directly involving his behavior. For example, if he is a low achiever and his ability is not in question, he should be asked to help analyze his problems and suggest methods of self-improvement. He should be required to accept responsibility for his own behavior. He should not depend on others to do his work for him, nor should he allow others to make decisions for him that he can make himself.

Manipulation of the child's environment may not help him to improve unless at least partial cooperation can be obtained from him. One can attempt reinforcements, both positive and negative, and one can attempt to elicit desired behavior by reasoning and exhortation. Reinforcements, however, function only in terms of the child's own frame of reference; his perceptions and expectations are important. Unless convinced that he will benefit from cooperation, he may work against parents and teacher, with further frustration to child and adults alike.

EVALUATION, FOLLOW-UP, INVOLVING OTHERS

The question arises of how valuable parent-teacher conferences really are. One study (Juneau, Wisconsin, Common School, 1959) found that 82 per cent of the parents involved felt that their conferences fully informed them concerning their child's progress; 74 per cent felt that their questions were successfully answered; 57 per cent felt that their understanding of the school's goals was improved; but only 47 per cent were able to work out a joint home-school plan to help the child. Sixty-five per cent felt that they had increased their understanding of the report card, but only 36 per cent felt that the preconference suggestion sheet of possible discussion topics truly served its purpose. A majority of parents, 89 per cent, felt free to call teachers to arrange for future conferences. Most parents discussed their conferences with husbands or wives if both partners had not been present; furthermore, most discussed the conferences with their children.

We believe that records should be kept of the discussion at each conference, of problems, hypotheses, and steps agreed upon. Parents and teacher should receive copies. If plans for helping a child are forthcoming, future conferences should be scheduled to see how those plans have been carried out and how the child has progressed. Such follow-up conferences also provide means for checking hypotheses, trying new tactics, and further developing home-school relations.

Finally, although the emphasis in this chapter has been on conferences about children with problems, we do not believe that such limitations should be placed on home-school cooperative effort. Problem prevention may be fostered; children may be helped to develop unusual talents; and other values attend such conferences. Although time for conferences may be limited, we argue that whenever they seem likely to bear fruit, regardless of the children involved, they should be instituted.

The question may be whether or not routine conferences are desirable, as when teachers report achievements of pupils on specified days at the end of marking periods. The writer is ambivalent concerning this practice. Too frequently teachers are pressed for time, and there is always a problem of scheduling. Sometimes parents require more time to talk with the teacher than is available. In other instances, such conferences become primarily matters of public relations.

Our contention is that achievement reports are probably best handled through report cards or letters, unless something requires special explanation or discussion. On the other hand, it is highly desirable that parents and teachers meet sometimes during the school year; perhaps an open house or other similar technique can be the answer. Parents should be encouraged to visit the teacher when they have questions, and there may sometimes be special pupil programs or other events to which parents can be invited without disrupting classroom proceedings.

In any event, to provide teachers with ample opportunity for conferences with parents, released time should be provided. Some schools are able to provide such extra time by use of team-teaching, student-teachers, helpers, or by combining classes for films or other special large-group projects.

□

REFERENCES

Bandura, A., and R. H. Walters. *Adolescent Aggression*, pp. 310–1. New York: Ronald, 1959.

Bayley, N., and E. S. Schaefer. "Maternal Behavior and Personality Development: Data from the Berkeley Growth Study," in R. E. Grinder. *Studies in Adolescence*, pp. 141–51. New York: Macmillan, 1963.

Bossard, J. H. S. *The Sociology of Child Development*. New York: Harper, 1954.

Bossard, J. H. S., and E. S. Boll. *Family Situations*. Philadelphia: University of Pennsylvania Press, 1943.

Brodie, T. A., Jr. "Some Administrative Considerations Relating to Parent-Teacher Conference Planning," *National Association of Secondary School Principals Bulletin*, 42 (1958), 73–9.

Burton, R. V., and J. W. M. Whiting. "The Absent Father and Cross-Sex Identity," *Merrill-Palmer Quarterly*, 7 (1961), 85–95.

Cox, F. N. "An Assessment of Children's Attitudes Toward Parent Figures," *Child Development*, 33 (1962), 821–30.

Dreikurs, R. *Psychology in the Classroom*. New York: Harper, 1957.

Dreikurs, R., R. Corsini, R. Lowe, and M. Sonstegard. *Adlerian Family Counseling*. Eugene: University of Oregon Press, 1959.

Elmott, C. D. *Children With Problems* (Supplementary Report 1, Special Guidance Project, Children from Multi-Problem Families). Santa Barbara: Santa Barbara City Schools, 1960.

Georgiady, N. P., and L. Romano. "Guide Your Parent-Teacher Conferences to Success," *Wisconsin Journal of Education*, 49 (1962), 5–6.

Juneau, Wisconsin, Common School. *Evaluation of Parent-Teacher Conferences*. Juneau: Unpublished study, 1959.

Kagan, J., and H. S. Moss. "Personality and Social Development: Family and Peer Influences," *Review of Educational Research*, 31 (1961), 463–74.

Long Beach, California, Public Schools. *Handbook for Parent Conferences*, 1955.

Loughary, J. W. *Counseling in Secondary Schools.* New York: Harper, 1961.

McCandless, B. R. *Children and Adolescents,* p. 114. New York: Holt, Rinehart, Winston, 1961.

McCord, J., W. McCord, and E. Thurber. "Some Effects of Paternal Absence on Male Children," *Journal of Abnormal and Social Psychology,* 44 (1962), 361–9.

Peck, R. F. "Family Patterns Correlated with Adolescent Personality Structure," *Journal of Abnormal and Social Psychology,* 47 (1958), 347–50.

Peters, H. J., and G. F. Farwell. *Guidance: A Developmental Approach.* Chicago: Rand McNally, 1959.

Rosenthal, R. "Experimenter Outcome-Orientation and the Results of the Psychological Experiment," *Psychological Bulletin,* 61 (1964), 405–12.

Rothney, J. W. M. *Guidance Practices and Results.* New York: Harper, 1958.

Russell, I. L. "Behavior Problems of Children from Broken and Intact Homes," *Journal of Educational Sociology,* 31 (1957), 124–30.

Symonds, P. M. *The Dynamics of Parent-Child Relationships.* New York: Columbia University Teachers College, 1949.

Torrance, P. "The Influence of the Broken Home on Adolescent Adjustments," *Journal of Educational Psychology,* 18 (1945), 359–64.

SUGGESTIONS FOR FURTHER READING

National Education Association. *Conference Time for Teachers and Parents.* Washington, D.C.: National Education Association, 1961.
Further suggestions on parent-teacher conferences and how they may be handled are presented here.

Seidman, J. M. *Educating for Mental Health: A Book of Readings,* pp. 3–43. New York: Crowell, 1963.
H. H. Anderson, G. L. Anderson, I. H. Cohen, and F. D. Nutt offer articles comparing the image of the teacher by adolescent children in four countries.

14

RECOGNIZING
AND REFERRING
SPECIAL CASES

Sometimes a teacher will see that some children need more specialized study and assistance than he can provide. In such instances he is likely to refer them to a guidance worker, psychologist, or clinic; studies show that most referrals of children to specialized resources are initiated by the classroom teacher. The "whens" and "hows" of such referrals are the subject of this chapter.

It is our contention that many children who should be referred to specialists never receive such help. One reason is that all too frequently there is a shortage of resources to which the child can be referred (and the shortage appears to be continuing). A second reason is that the teacher—quite rightfully—hesitates to arrange for intervention in the life of the child and his parents. One reason for this hesitation is that anything done for or to the child which does not routinely happen to all children may produce all sorts of fears in the child and his parents; there may be stigma associated with special study of the child; and there may be resentments with which to contend. Further, many teachers may wonder if they are not "oversold" on psychology or psychiatry, and thus too quick to make judgments about pupils; they wonder if they may not tend to make mountains out of molehills, and be unduly concerned.

As a result many children who might be quite easily helped during the early stages of their problems do not receive the benefits of expert study; nothing helpful happens until matters have progressed so far that the child's behavior becomes a serious problem in the classroom. This may be too late for the kinds of help that could have been offered earlier, and damage to the child may ensue which could have been avoided. Probably more is lost by failure to refer children when the teacher is unable to understand their behaviors and cope with them, than by unnecessary referral which clogs referral sources and may disrupt the lives of families.

Needs for Referral

Not all disturbed children "climb the walls" or "hang from the chandeliers." It is often surprising to teachers who visit a residential treatment center that many of the patients seem more "normal" than some of the pupils they have had in their classes. Indeed this is often the case and for two main reasons: First, some children in the classroom who require specialized help may have been overlooked, as their behavior is explained away as the results of cultural differences or simply as disciplinary problems; second, some children may have been referred, and recommendations have been made that these children are better off in the regular classrooms than in residential centers. Some children in any school may be receiving outpatient care from a psychiatrist or psychologist, and teachers are not always privy to such arrangements.

We believe that all children who cause unusual problems in school should have expert study. There are a number of reasons for this recommendation.

Some children cannot profit from school. Certain children cannot profit from school, or they disrupt school to the point where others cannot profit. They may be dangers to themselves or to others. Whether or not a given child is in this category can be determined only by a qualified professional mental-health worker. For example, one third-grade teacher known to the writer was forced to work with a child who seemed, to her, severely mentally retarded. For three years the child had been passed along from grade to grade as a "late-maturer," becoming frustrated at her inability to achieve success in academic learning. The teacher noted that she showed a tendency to hit and bite other children; sometimes she screamed and yelled; she destroyed her work; the others were somewhat afraid of her. The child refused to stay in her seat, and was prone to bothering others. The teacher felt strongly enough about the problems thus created that she obtained referral to a psychologist. It was found, as the reader will suspect, that this small girl was not only severely mentally retarded, but also highly disturbed emotionally. Treatment at a residential center was sought, and the child began to show less disturbing behavior.

On the other hand, some teachers may be a bit too prone to think some children do not belong in their classrooms. This is especially true if the child is actually somewhat emotionally disturbed. However, when such children have been evaluated and recommendations have been made to the teacher for working with them, the fears and irritations of most teachers can be allayed. We shall say more later, but at this point we wish to emphasize that school is the most beneficial environment for most "problem children" and that the teacher is a useful remedial resource. Most disturbed children can be annoying—few, however, are sources of danger or cannot be adequately handled.

Early diagnosis may aid therapy. If children who need treatment are recognized early enough, prompt treatment may rehabilitate, alleviate, or at least prevent further damage. The concept of preventive psychiatry (Caplan, 1962; Allinsmith & Goethals, 1962) embodies primary prevention, by which one tries to manipulate the environment to eliminate poor mental health; secondary prevention, by which rehabilitation is provided; and tertiary prevention, by which, although damage to the child cannot be alleviated, further damage is at least prevented.

The child and adolescent population in residential treatment centers is frequently larger than one might expect. Many of the patients have not had early diagnostic referrals, and their problems have not been treated until their adjustment has become so poor that residential treatment is necessary. Yet for many such children there is a history of deviant behavior going back to early school years. In addition to prolonging a child's suffering, such failure to diagnose early is economically wasteful; treatment at initial stages of maladjustment is frequently less time-consuming and demands less extensive interference in the life of the child than in later stages.

Teachers, especially in the primary grades, are sometimes more tolerant of inappropriate behavior than they ought to be, and many times they excuse it on the grounds of the child's immaturity. Their attitudes may reflect inadequate knowledge of the developmental characteristics of children, insufficient understanding of healthy individual differences, and lack of information on symptoms of poor mental health. Teachers should become more sophisticated in these areas. Children and adolescents who become disturbed rarely become so suddenly; more usually, the development of poor mental health is gradual and occurs over a period of time, so that the alert teacher looks not only at present behavior, but at trends in the child's habitual ways of acting.

There is some danger of compounding problems. Teachers are usually quite understanding of children, so that the chances of damaging a child psychologically are relatively slight. Yet there have been instances where pressure to learn has been placed on children with perceptual handicaps or brain injury; where some have been harshly disciplined, yet were too disturbed to control their behaviors; or where withdrawing, depressed, or hostile children have been managed in ways which compounded their problems. There is less risk of such happenings when teachers recognize their own limitations in understanding children and request expert study for those they cannot seem to handle in the usual ways.

Seeking Appropriate Kinds of Referral and Remediation

The kinds of problems exhibited by the child may be clues to the kinds of referral sources which should be sought. Not all children with problems require psychological evaluation; some can be helped by guidance workers, remedial specialists, or others. It is true that many children have related multiple problems. On the other hand, the primary symptoms are usually a good clue as to who should see the child first.

HANDICAPS

Handicaps consist of many kinds, of course, but as we use the term, they are organic or physiological in nature. Insofar as mental health is concerned, handicaps are a concern in several ways. For example, the person with a sensory, motor, or orthopedic handicap may be frustrated by his inability to cope with his environment. He may be sensitive to the reactions of others about him. He may have a negative "body image." He may have been taught to be dependent, or to expect special consideration from others. Children who have had long illnesses, or who are unable to compete with other children in playtime activities, are often demanding, irritable, depressed, or otherwise have some symptoms of poor mental health. The handicapped also include mentally retarded, at both the educable and trainable levels. Such children, especially if brain-injured, may show emotional problems.

The teacher who has a handicapped child in her room is aided considerably if she is given full information concerning the nature of the handicap and the child's optimal manner of functioning. Remedial suggestions may also be provided. Sometimes special facilities are provided for the deaf or partially deaf child or the blind or partially blind child, and so on. Involved in working with these children are such experts as rehabilitation counselors, physical and speech therapists, teachers of the deaf and of the mentally retarded, and reading specialists.

Ordinarily children who are handicapped have been carefully evaluated before placement in the classroom. However, this is not always the case, and there may be children who have not been evaluated and who are hard of hearing, with visual defects, minimally brain-injured, perceptually handicapped, or, as in the illustration, mentally retarded. Under circumstances where such problems are suspected, medical sources are indicated as the beginning referral agency.

Sometimes questions are raised as to whether handicapped children are "better off" in the regular classroom or whether they should not be placed in "special rooms." Such questions are not easy to answer, and answers must rest on careful consideration of the individual case. In general, if the child can remain in the regular room without too much stress or frustration, he is better off to be there. A number of arguments for this position can be advanced. First, he is thus encouraged to learn to deal constructively with his handicap; most of his life he will not be in a sheltered position and must learn to live a satisfactory life in a "normal" setting. He is helped to face reality; he does not lose opportunities to learn that are afforded by the regular classroom; he can be helped to learn by listening to, working with, or associating with healthy children; and he is not encouraged to magnify his handicap. Further, as in the case of educable mentally retarded and some forms of emotionally disturbed who are placed in special rooms, there is a problem in re-entry to the "normal" world when the help in a special room has been exhausted. This is particularly true in the case of mentally retarded children for whom there are no special school facilities at the secondary school age level. There are also the problems of proliferating special rooms *ad infinitum,* obtaining properly trained teachers, and encouraging teachers to want all deviant children removed from their classes.

On the other hand, it is quite obvious that special education is not only desirable but necessary for a portion of the child population. Great strides in working with the perceptually handicapped, children with cerebral palsy, the deaf, and other handicapped children have been made. Special equipment may be provided, as when children with heart defects are enabled to have supportive furniture or when hydrotherapy is provided children with muscular problems. The deaf can be aided in lipreading and in other forms of communication through special methods such as are used in the John Tracy Clinic of Los Angeles. Trained teachers who have small classes can thus individualize instruction and accomplish a great deal. For example, in rooms for the emotionally disturbed practices can be followed that are unsuitable in the regular room; one can vary task requirements, change time intervals, and so on.

Some children, particularly some disturbed boys and girls, cannot tolerate pressures of a room full of peers, or regular classes (although sometimes they can do so for brief periods of time and may be placed in regular rooms for part of the day). Also, the effects of having such children in the room may be detrimental to the other children and the teacher, so that special rooms should be provided.

In substance, then, we urge that regular teachers be given consultant help and that they accept handicapped children in their rooms when the children may benefit and when other children and the teachers are not placed under too much pressure by their presence; but, when such placement is not feasible and special requirements suggest the desirability of special placement, referral for decision should be made promptly.

EMOTIONAL DISTURBANCE

We have already discussed problems in defining emotional disturbance or poor mental health and have given attention to things the teacher might do to help children whose emotional lives are problems to themselves or others. Obviously, however, there may be instances in which the teacher is unable to understand or deal with the problems, as in the case of severe maladjustment. In such instances the school psychologist, psychiatrist, or other mental-health specialist should be consulted. An illustration, the "case" of Emil, as described by one of his parents, follows:

A CHILD WHO REQUIRES IMMEDIATE
REFERRAL

Emil will deliberately do things which we disapprove of. He goes to the city dump, in spite of our punishing him, admits having been there, and seems to show no guilt or remorse. He seems deliberately to defy us and seems to want to be punished.

At school he has been kept late for arriving late for class, in spite of having been sent from home earlier than usual. He does not restrain his impulses, and will suddenly make loud noises during class; even when warned to be quiet, he distracts his peers. When on one occasion he was sent from the room, his teacher asked why he did not stop making noises when she asked him to; he replied that "something inside me just told me to make noises, and I couldn't stop."

He keeps putting his papers on the floor, in spite of being urged by the teacher to keep them in his desk; he frequently does naughty things in this manner and is often negativistic. In winter, he takes off his mittens, cap, and jacket; in warm weather, he wants to wear boots and extra clothing. If crossed, he displays a temper tantrum.

He cannot sit still, and at times he will scream and run about the house rapidly, and never stops until someone stops him. He seems to fear nothing and climbs tall trees, leaves his parents in large department stores, tries to pet strange animals on the street— or even gets close to the cages at the zoo.

Emil shows little emotion. He doesn't like to be kissed, held, or read to. He pushes his parents away and is indifferent to his brothers and sisters. He doesn't cry and tries to be a "tough guy." Punishment does not help—even spanking.

Lately Emil has become unclean insofar as toilet training is concerned. Although the doctor can find no physical cause, he is incontinent. He is wet many times and sometimes even worse. Although he was completely trained at the age of three, he now doesn't seem to care. We have tried everything we know; we know it isn't physical, since he has had a careful medical examination. Now we are seeking psychological evaluation.

EDUCATIONAL DEFICIENCY

Educational deficiency is simply failure to achieve in school at a level commensurate with that of other children of the same age and similar mental abilities. Children with educational deficiencies are not necessarily "underachievers" but may simply have received early training—in facts, skills, study methods, and so on—that was inadequate. There are various causes: absence from school for extended periods of time, changes from one school system to another with consequent missing of sequential material, lack of motivation at one time or another, immaturity when beginning school, inadequate teaching, and many others.

Children who show no other problems than that of poor learning can be helped by remedial instruction. Ordinarily the teacher can ascertain specific problem areas, although specialists in remediation may be required to aid in setting up special programs, employing reading pacers, or other specialized techniques.

CULTURAL DEFICIENCY

Children from culturally deprived homes differ widely, yet there are certain problems common to many of them. A language deficiency is one such problem: inadequate vocabulary, lack of practice in communicating via symbols (that is, oral and written words), lack of experiences to build concepts, lack of expectation of academic success, and inadequate academic motivation.

Such children are at a disadvantage in first grade, and their cultural lag tends to continue and frequently to increase throughout the school years. Many are not promoted to certain grades; dropping out of school at the minimum legal age limit is quite frequent. Because of the attitudes of these children and their parents—and because of the attitudes of other children, parents, and teachers toward them—these children are frequently truant, tardy, disciplinary problems, and frequently convinced that school offers little or nothing to them.

Many cities are beginning programs to bring these deprived children's verbal and conceptual experiences more into line with those of children from more privileged homes. At this writing, Head Start and other programs seem to be concentrating on preschool experiences as means of "heading off" some of the problems, although the lasting effects of such programs are questionable and other supplementary methods may be required.

Culturally disadvantaged children probably should be assessed by school psychologists or other specialists, so that their specific needs can be determined and proper programming established.

MANIFOLD HANDICAPS

For some children many problems coexist in their lives and reinforce one another. These children need help of many kinds. For example, in one study, some fourth-grade children who were mentally retarded (Ringness, 1959) were evaluated, then individually taught arithmetic; it was found that these children were not only retarded but that they frequently also came from underprivileged homes, were somewhat emotionally disturbed, and were frequently physically handicapped.

Although a child may be referred to a psychologist, clinic, or other source for a given reason, in the course of assessment other problems may be found.

G. M. Gilbert (1957) studied the reasons for referral of children to metropolitan child-guidance centers. He found that 45 per cent of the referrals were for academic problems, that is, impaired capacity to learn; 27 per cent for suspected mental retardation; 30 per cent for aggressive or antisocial behavior; 22 per cent for passive withdrawn behavior; 23 per cent for emotional instability and anxiety symptoms; 14 per cent for hyperactivity and motor symptoms; 6 per cent for toilet training problems; 2.5 per cent for sexual problems; and 14 per cent for miscellaneous problems (Gilbert's terminology). These figures add up to more than 100 per cent because some subjects showed multiple problems.

C. R. Rogers (1942a), in an early study, found that one child in four had a serious reading deficiency, usually correlated with emotional problems; one in six was maladjusted according to the personality tests he employed; one in eight showed observable evidence of poor mental health; and nearly one-third showed some degree of poor adjustment. C. A. Ullmann (1957) found 8 per cent of his subjects to be severely maladjusted. N. Clancy and F. Smitter (1953) found 11 per cent of their school population to be emotionally disturbed, with an increase to 35 per cent in school districts where there were special classes for the mentally retarded. All in all, these trends continue to be borne out in the experience of clinics and school psychologists. In effect, probably 10 per cent of the pupil population have serious problems of one form or another, and they are often multiple problems. Teachers should be alert, then, to the nature of available referral sources and the means of instituting such referrals.

Principles for Referral

ETHICS OF REFERRAL

T. Szasz (1965) has seriously questioned many referral policies and, indeed, believes that schools permit mental-health specialists to intervene in children's lives too often. He has wondered whether or not some school personnel do not use the possibility of referral to a psychiatrist or psychologist as a threat to keep children in line, and whether or not many times the child's human rights are invaded by the use of psychological means to change his behavior. He suggests that psychiatric help should be separate from the schools and should be undergone voluntarily, if such help seems necessary. In effect, he emphasizes the point that children (and adults) should have a certain freedom of choice about their own behavior and characteristics. If they do not conform to society's demands, they should be treated as disciplinary or academic problems but not as personality or "mental health" problems. We saw in Chapter 1 that Szasz disagrees completely with the concept of mental health and prefers to think in terms of conformity to the value judgments of the individual versus society.

Others (for example, Ausubel, 1900) take issue with Szasz and find an analogy between physical and mental health.

Regardless of one's position in this controversy, however, it is clear that some students are not capable of profiting from school without some form of intervention in the form of evaluation and possible remedial tactics. In addition, they pose problems for school personnel that make it necessary to compare the benefits to the larger society with the rights of the individual. Although it may be most desirable that the child or the family initiate efforts to obtain specialized help, it is not always possible. The school may have to call attention to such needs and unfortunately may sometimes have to exert pressure for the good of the child *and of the school.*

As children are not always in a position to understand the consequences of their behavior, they should not necessarily be allowed complete freedom to be as they may wish to be. That is, a child may prefer not to engage in social interaction with other children, yet his preferences may lead him into considerable conflict with society as well as failing to provide him with happiness, self-esteem, and success. Such a child requires help, even though he may not recognize this need himself.

An important point, however, is that one must exert caution in intervening in the lives of children and their parents. A teacher should closely examine his value judgments and the means by which he decides that a child should be referred. He should consult parents when making referrals. Such referrals should be made only when experience dictates that the child, the classroom, and the home may profit from them. In some instances, the teacher may be able to handle the child's problems himself. In other instances, referral to specialists in fields other than psychology may be the answer. It is our hope that this chapter may somewhat clarify the issues involved.

EXPECTATIONS FROM REFERRAL

One should not expect miracles from specialists. Although psychologists, psychiatrists, remedial specialists, and others have tools and knowledge that enable them to work with children in ways not possible for the teacher, they cannot be expected to solve long-standing problems overnight, nor can they always help the child when the total environment is not conducive to his mental health. Furthermore, it should be recognized, some children are so damaged that they cannot be completely rehabilitated; in such instances one must work within the framework of their limitations.

Among the benefits that the school may gain from referral of the child to specialists are the following:

1. The child will be carefully evaluated to probe the nature of his problems, their possible causes, indicated treatments, and the degree of progress expected. How these findings are interpreted to the school depends upon the professional judgment of such specialists; ethical and practical problems are involved.
2. Some insight into the dynamics of the child's behavior may be provided for the teacher. For example, his defenses, his feelings about himself and others, his reinforcements, his emotional states may be discussed.
3. Because the teacher is considered a prime remedial source, many specialists will consult *with* him (as opposed to recommending *to* him) about ways to help the child. Both specific and general suggestions will be provided.
4. The teacher may receive support for his views of the child. Many teachers feel inadequate when unable to cope with some children's behavior and have some fear lest they compound the child's problems. Support from the consultative resource can be beneficial.

5. Special provisions may be obtained for the child who requires them.
6. Follow-up will be instituted, to initiate any change in procedures that may be called for.
7. The child may improve in behavior as the result of referral. Improvement will probably be gradual, if it occurs.

Note that the teacher is considered a colleague of the psychologist or other specialist. The teacher should be able to translate the findings of the specialist into the classroom setting; he should be able to provide the specialist with information (see Chapter 10) ; and, equally, he should be able to explain what can or cannot be accomplished in the classroom setting. The teacher has considerable control over the child's life; he has rapport; he has contact with the home; and he is equipped in no small part for remedial activity. Furthermore, as most children remain in the classroom, the teacher must make many decisions about the referred child as opposed to the classroom group; however, it should be noted that the group itself may be helpful if certain circumstances permit.

There is no magic, even for the skilled clinician, that enables one to make a quick, easy, and accurate assessment of the problems of children. Although specialists may have had years of training and experience in assessing mental health or other problems, they dislike to offer interpretations about a child's behavior without the most complete evidence possible. They prefer to suggest hypotheses for continuing study, rather than to evaluate on the basis of insufficient evidence; it is not that referral sources are indefinite or indecisive, but that, except for extreme cases, evaluation is seldom quick or easy.

KNOWING WHEN TO REFER

GENERAL PRINCIPLES. ■ Even the healthiest child may do some odd things at times, but if data are carefully collected and studied the teacher is not likely to delude himself into seeing serious problems where they do not exist. Evidence may be added and evaluated by others, so that the weight of cumulative experience with the child may supplement the conclusions of the individual teacher.

Behavior should always be considered in relation to its context, its apparent aims, its reinforcement, its repetitive nature, its adaptive or unadaptive character, and its progression toward the healthy or the unhealthy. Sometimes behavior that seems quite abnormal is found to be reasonable when the total situation is known. Here is an example:

One well-behaved child came to school so dirty and unkempt that other children refused to sit beside him. The teacher tried the usual remedies: She tried to educate the boy to cleanliness, saw to it that he washed at school, and on one occasion even took him home with her and "did his laundry." All efforts failed to improve on his cleanliness, suggesting to the teacher a lack of pride, inability to consider others, and perhaps other motivational or emotional lacks.

A visit to the home was enlightening. Mother proved to be an "intellectual" who was above the mundane things in life and refused to make any effort to keep her son clean. In a word, Mother was a "beatnik"; she believed that other things in life were more important than cleanliness. She refused to train her son in such health habits as regular hours for sleep, balanced meals, attention to illness, and exercise. The house was messy; Mother was untidy. There were no soap or clean towels in the bathroom and no clean clothes in the boy's closet. Obviously, attention was required for the mother, rather than solely for the boy. His home examples, early training, and indeed his value system were not conducive to cleanliness at home *or* at school.

In this instance, pressure was put on the mother not to neglect the child; in such cases it is sometimes necessary to involve welfare or social workers. But here the school itself may be able to confer with the parents and obtain good results (see Chapter 13 on cooperation between school and home). The school also worked with the boy himself, to try to induce him to take responsibility for his own health habits, and gradual progress resulted.

Behavior must also be interpreted according to the expected maturity of the child. If his peers have moved past a given stage of behavior (such as the restlessness of many six-year-olds or the self-consciousness of many adolescents), the subject should also progress within a reasonable span of time. If he does not or if he begins to behave in ways more suitable to younger children (as in wanting to play with much younger children), he is worthy of concern. Sometimes children prefer to play with the opposite sex, as when elementary schoolboys prefer the company of girls. Depending on the reactions of the peers, as well as on the child himself, this tendency may be cause for further study.

The suddenness of behavior changes is important. The healthy personality tends to change slowly. If a child's behavior fluctuates markedly and rapidly, it is more worthy of attention than if change occurs over a period of weeks or months.

BEHAVIORAL SIGNALS SUGGESTING STUDY OR REFERRAL. ■ The "sign approach" to diagnosis is not considered entirely adequate, for as we suggested, normal children sometimes show bizarre behavior and maladjusted children are frequently overlooked because they show no strangeness. It is also worthy of reminder that behavior may be caused by a complex of internal and environmental variables, so that behavior *per se* does not always indicate a problem or lack of problems. However, there are some signals which do suggest the need for further study of the child, as we shall briefly indicate.

In examining "signals" one must not only consider the presence or absence of such behavior, but note the intensity, frequency, pervasiveness in respect to the environment, and the showy or bizarre characteristics of the behavior. Relatively mild signals tending to result in future disability may be signals for referral; however, highly intense, dangerous forms of activity always indicate the need for *immediate* study by a specialist. For example, when a child talks to himself constantly, this may be merely a habit which should be investigated. On the other hand, reference to suicide should cause immediate action to take place.

One needs also to look for what is "not there." Healthy children are curious, interested in others, like to relate to others. They are energetic, like to play, and are quite competitive. They usually have many interests, are capable of giving and receiving friendship, and are sympathetic to others and to animals. Children who fail to show such characteristics may be maladjusted in some ways.

Most teachers feel that they know quite well which children in their classes should be referred for further evaluation. However, the following suggestions may point up forgotten areas and lend support to teacher opinions. It is somewhat risky to try to categorize behaviors which suggest maladjustment; however, for purposes of focusing the teacher's observation of the child, we shall mention some physical, social, emotional, and intellectual behaviors which may suggest the need for special study and referral:

PHYSICAL SIGNALS. ▪ There are many obvious physical symptoms which suggest the possibility of emotional problems. For example, children who are very poorly coordinated or lack control of their limbs, who are subject to much twitching, who have tics, who carry their limbs in unusual postures, or who seem to show compulsive movements should be studied. Children who are hyperactive or unduly lethargic should receive inquiry. Vomiting, eneuresis, frequent headaches, panting, and other possibly psychosomatic characteristics should be medically studied; they may be organic, resulting from real physical disability, or primarily emotional in nature. Recent loss in strength and previously good coordination, convulsions, frequent fainting, constant or recurrent trembling—all suggest the need for study. We have already touched upon handicaps and their possible emotional connotations; we might also mention obesity, constant illness, and asthma or other allergic or psychosomatic problems. It goes without saying that such children should have competent medical examination; in many instances this will have already taken place, and the teacher needs only to be familiar with the problem as it relates to classroom procedures.

SOCIAL SIGNALS. ▪ Social signals refer to the child's interaction with others as opposed to emotional signals which may be manifest when the child is alone. Disturbed social relationships should always be a cause for concern. In general, the child who is a problem to others is a child who has problems. Constant demonstrations of dependency, feelings of inferiority, excessive shyness, self-consciousness, withdrawing behavior, and inability to stand up to others may suggest possible depression, guilt, insecurity, or anxiety. Aggressive, hostile behavior is equally suspect. Attempts to engage others in deviant behavior, especially bizarre or highly unusual behavior, may suggest that help is needed. Attention-seeking, extreme boldness or chance-taking to impress others, constant reference to sex (more than seems usual in children), delinquency, truancy, lack of interest in others suggest need for study. (Frequent truancy is often the first overt sign the teacher sees in children who later become delinquent.) Reference to E. K. Wickman's list (Chapter 10) will suggest other signs; children who withdraw from others or who act against others are children with problems.

EMOTIONAL SIGNALS. ▪ Excessive use of defense mechanisms such as daydreaming, regression to behavior characteristic of much younger children, unusually affectionate behavior in regard to possessions such as pets, books, or toys, and unwillingness to participate in normal school activities may be signs of serious withdrawal. Habitual defiance, sullenness, rebelliousness, frequent fighting, and "chip-on-the-shoulder" attitude also suggest emotional (and social) problems.

Unusual sensitiveness, distrust, cruelty, morbidity, moodiness, lack of emotional control, suspiciousness, delusions, compulsive actions, and inconsistent behavior are all signals that help is needed. It should be borne in mind that some of these characteristics are governed by the actions of others. However, if the child is indiscriminately suspicious of everyone, or moody without apparent cause, etc., the problem is more likely to be within the child than environmentally determined.

INTELLECTUAL SIGNALS. ▪ Any child who has great difficulty in remembering, who frequently learns concepts incorrectly, who cannot concentrate, who makes bizarre statements, who has highly peculiar interests, or who achieves far below expectation should be studied by the teacher or a specialist. Organic factors like brain injury, deafness, neural impairment, or poor eyesight may be the reason. Cultural factors may enter in. Children with such characteristics *may* have emotional problems, however. This possibility should not be overlooked.

Psychologists and others recognize that it is difficult to distinguish between normal behavior and behavior suggestive of poor mental health without considering the total effective functioning of the individual. A lack of competence in one area may not be significant if the over-all behavior contributes to successful living. C. L. Kline (1953) is concerned with what he calls *"excess* shyness," *"marked* dependency needs," and the like, as all of us show such behavior at times. Such qualifying adjectives do present problems, for they presume that the teacher can distinguish what is excessive and what is not. Yet the teacher does have two criteria for making such judgments: He can compare his subject with others in the class and with others of similar background characteristics, and he can compare the pupil as he is today with the way he was previously. In addition, most experienced teachers have "built-in" norms for the behavior of children in the age group with which they are working.

STUDIES OF TEACHER RECOGNITION OF SERIOUS CASES

Rogers, whose early study (1942b) we have mentioned, employed an index for recognizing maladjusted children, in which some of the criteria related to information at hand in the school (1942a). As in other studies that we shall briefly discuss, multiple diagnostic techniques were employed. Rogers' indexes were as follows:

Chronological misfit (age differs from median of classroom group by more than one year).

Intellectual misfit (mental age is more than one year below or two years above the median for the classroom).

Academic misfit (reading achievement is more than one year below or two years above the median for the classroom).

Reading disability (reading age is more than one year below mental age).

School failure (is repeating grade or half-grade).

Truant (truant during term studied).

Personality problem (score of more than 150 on a specially prepared teacher-rating scale).

Maladjusted (score of more than 40 on the Loofbourow Personal Index for pupils in grade six or of less than 96 on the California Personality Test for pupils in grades four and six; such cases scored below the thirty-fifth percentile).

Sociometric indication (one-seventh or more of subject's classmates wrote in his name on one or more significant items of the "guess who" game in the primary grades).

Observer ratings of maladjustment as moderate or serious, used in place of "guess who" games in some primary grades.

Rogers considered a child maladjusted if he reflected four or more of these indexes. Such a child frequently had a history of unhappiness and unfortunate life circumstances.

(Note that the term "maladjustment" was used. This term suggests that children so labeled did not fit well in the groups in which they were located. As we examine the indexes, it is evident that, on some of them, a child might not be the "problem" so much as the fact that he was miscast in his school role. For such children a change in grouping might be of significant help.)

There is also a cultural bias in the indexes. It was found that more children from underprivileged homes were seriously maladjusted than were children from favored environments. It is not certain that children living in underprivileged areas are not rated low by teachers because of behavior resulting from cultural mores, that tests do not discriminate in favor of children from privileged environments, that children in underprivileged areas do not come from less adequate families, or that other factors are not operating.

C. A. Ullmann (1957) also attempted to categorize children as well adjusted or not, and he employed opinions of teachers as well as mental hygienists. In a pilot study of twenty-two mental-health specialists and fifty teachers, he employed a rating scale of 195 items. Teachers were asked to rate one "poorly adjusted child" and one "well-adjusted child" against the scale. The mental hygienists were asked to rate the items as indicative or not of good adjustment.

Items in Ullmann's study on which teacher-clinician judgment converged:

ITEMS CONSIDERED MOST INDICATIVE OF MALADJUSTMENT

Other children regard this child as a pest.
The child cannot be depended upon to complete a job.
It is hard for him to keep his mind on what goes on in class.
The child is continually on the defensive.
The child has trouble getting along with others.
Others cannot work with him.
The child is quarrelsome.
He is easily irritated, flustered, or upset.
The child rubs others the wrong way.
The child always seems stirred up.
He is always thinking up alibis.
He is easily confused.

He lacks confidence in himself.

The child is resentful.

He cannot make up his mind until it is too late.

ITEMS CONSIDERED MOST INDICATIVE OF GOOD ADJUSTMENT

The child takes an active part in school activities.

He is alert, interested.

He pitches in when things are to be done.

Others come to him for help.

He is popular with all his classmates.

The child gets along well in school activities.

He participates actively in school functions.

The child is happy and easy to get along with.

He finishes well whatever he undertakes.

He completes work which he has been given whether someone checks on him or not, even when much effort is involved.

The child carries through an undertaking about as well as others his age.

He can be depended upon by an adult leader of a group to do his share.

He is considerate of others.

The child is popular, has many friends.

He associates himself with many group endeavors.

Other children are eager to be near him or on his side.

He accepts suggestions.

He makes sensible, practical plans.

A typical child for his years.

He considers the welfare of his class, team, club, or school, as well as his own personal interests.

The child helps others who are having difficulty.

The child is self-confident.

He figures things out for himself. (Ullmann, 1957, p. 15)

Teachers rated most comfortably those items that came closest to their day-to-day experiences with children: work habits. Teachers also quite plainly believed that politeness and obedience were characteristics of good adjustment, whereas clinicians quite plainly believed that the significance of such items was at least equivocal. Teacher ratings of adjustment were in closer agreement with sociometric ratings than with scores on personality tests (which agreed well with each other). It is therefore clear that different pictures of adjustment are obtained from teacher and pupil raters than from the children themselves in tests.

The California State Department of Education (Bower, *et al.*, 1958) also made a study of the ability of teachers to detect maladjusted children in the middle grades who were thought to be "emotionally disturbed." Classes in which one or more of these children were enrolled were studied, but the teachers were not informed of the reasons their classes were selected.

The teachers gathered data. Included were group intelligence-test scores; scores on reading and arithmetic achievement tests; scores on a personality inventory; a projective sociogram; figures on school absences for a four-month period; age-grade relationships; data on the socioeconomic status of the families of the subjects and other children; and teacher ratings of children on physical status and adjustment.

Analysis of data showed that, on group intelligence tests, the scores of the emotionally disturbed child tended to be below the scores of other children in the class but that, on individually administered I.Q. tests, they were equal to those of the rest of the class. The difference between individual and group intelligence-test scores was statistically significant, suggesting that, when the scores on two such tests differ widely, there is need for further study.

It was further shown that differences in achievement between the disturbed child and others in his class tended to increase with succeeding grade levels, such differences being greater in arithmetic than in reading achievement.

Personality-test data were essentially a measure of similarity between perceived self and ideal self. It was found that disturbed boys showed greater dissatisfaction with self than did other boys. Disturbed girls, however, did not report as much discrepancy between self and ideal self; they did express greater dissatisfaction with parent-child relations than did the boys.

The sociometric device employed was entitled "A Class Play." Children were asked to choose themselves or others for the roles in an imaginary play. It was found that the emotionally disturbed children were selected most often for negative roles (for example, "someone who is often mean and gets into fights a great deal" or "someone who is always getting angry about little things"). They were picked less often than others for favorable roles.

Students who were frequently truant generally had school difficulties. Children from lower socioeconomic-class homes were more likely to have overt or "acting out" symptoms, but those from favored neighborhoods tended to internalize their problems.

Teacher ratings of emotional judgment were found to be valuable, providing the teacher had insight into child development, was motivated to make judgments, was in reasonably good mental health himself, and had insight into his own strong and weak points and biases.

In the studies we have mentioned it is seen that various sources of evidence about the mental health of the child tend to supplement and confirm each other. Many such sources are available to the teacher (see Chapter 10) and guide him in knowing whether to seek referral for the child to clinical experts.

School Resources in Referral

REFERRAL PROCEDURES

In referring a child, the teacher needs first to determine how far he will push his request. As we have repeatedly suggested, in most instances the study of the child by the teacher is very important—data can permit others to consider with the teacher whether referral is indicated, and the data can be of help to the referral agency. Obviously, however, if alarming symptoms are found, action should be instituted without delay.

Schools usually have carefully defined policies for referral with channels of authority and procedures delineated. There are sound reasons for this policy. First, coordinated efforts cannot be brought to bear if various staff operate without communication and if suitable records are not kept. (Teachers are frequently surprised to learn how much clinical agencies may already know about a given child who is being referred.) If several teachers and specialists work with a child, coordination of efforts is not only desirable but essential.

Second, authority rests with the school administrator. Because he must accept responsibility for what happens to children in his school, he must be given the prerogative for deciding what steps will be taken.

Third, legal and ethical aspects of referral must be considered, as discussed at the beginning of this chapter. A child should be exposed to special attention only with concurrence of parents and school staff. The fact that a child is singled out for *any* special attention can be threatening to him; he should receive such attention only when all concerned are convinced that more will be gained than lost by intervention. Some parents are threatened by clinical study of the child. They worry about stigmatization of child and family, that their own deficiencies will be held up to view, that the teacher is prejudiced against their child, or that his problems are teacher-induced. Consultation with parents is also necessary because the child may already be under study or treatment without the school's knowledge. (In situations in which parents fail to recognize the need for treatment of the child, it is the prerogative of the board of education, in most school systems, to decide. If the problems of the child warrant—as when he is dangerous to himself or others or if he is obviously neglected or cannot learn within the school context—legal steps can be taken to remove him from the school program. Such action introduces welfare departments and possible court intervention and is reluctantly undertaken by school authorities; however, sometimes for the good of the child or the school it must be done.)

SCHOOL PERSONNEL

School systems vary widely in regard to specialized personnel. Some metropolitan systems have child-guidance clinics attached to the central staff or coordinated closely but under the auspices of some other city agency. Other communities have limited resources and must use part-time guidance workers. A few have no school resource personnel at all and must depend on private sources or state agencies for assistance with emotional problems of children. Although the training and functions of referral personnel within the schools vary widely, it may be helpful to distinguish some of the various specialists frequently found in the schools.

THE SCHOOL PSYCHOLOGIST. ▪ The profession of school psychology is relatively new, and at the present time there are far too few school psychologists being trained to meet the demand. The requirements among state certifying bodies vary somewhat (Camp, 1960), but a considerable degree of uniformity is being lent to training programs through efforts of the School Psychology Division (Division #16) of the American Psychological Association (Gray, 1963a) and other professional groups.

S. W. Gray (1963b) has shown how functions of the school psychologist vary with the school and the community. R. E. Valett (1963) and F. Mullen (1958) have described the work of the psychologist in some detail, but the following functions seem most common:

diagnosis of problems of individual children;

counseling with parents and teachers;

referral for therapy or other treatment;

advising the school on mental-health conditions;

providing in-service training and consultation to school personnel;

keeping appropriate records and interpreting them to others as desired;

overseeing the work of trainees and others with less background or experience who work clinically with children;

performing appropriate research.

Training required of school psychologists has tended to emphasize both a strong background in teaching and other aspects of education and in clinical techniques and practices. The school psychologist has been more oriented toward psychological assessment than toward remediation, and his function as a *school* worker (as opposed to a therapist in individual counseling) has been emphasized.

The school psychologist may be certified at various levels of training and experience. He may, at the first level, be primarily a psychometrician or a specialist in intelligence and personality testing. His work then consists primarily of screening children for various special classrooms (retarded, emotionally disturbed, neurologically impaired, slow learners, remedial, gifted) and of diagnostic study of individual children who may need referral to other resources for treatment. His training consists in learning how to use intelligence, personality, and achievement measures in a sophisticated manner. He holds at least a master's degree.

At a higher level, the school psychologist may have two, three, or more years of graduate work specialized in his area; optimum training is thought to require the Ph.D. degree. The more qualified psychologists have had both practical experience in a psychoeducational clinic of the training institution where they learn their techniques and practice them under immediate supervision, and an internship in a public-school setting where they can polish their techniques under supervision in a more realistic "practical" setting. A psychologist trained at this level is acquainted with advanced techniques of personality assessment and may also be equipped for play therapy or individual clinical counseling. He is also able to read and perform research adequately.

Teachers with little grounding in clinical areas are flatteringly prone to treat the specialist with respect and awe. He is sometimes almost mystically regarded, as one with techniques for understanding children not possessed by teachers. On the other hand, some psychologists (perhaps rightfully) have been regarded as unrealistic and impractical, and far-removed from the problems of the child as manifest in the classroom setting. What, then, are the tools the well-qualified school psychologist may possess?

As in any other profession, it is the training, experience, and abilities of the person, himself, that are important, rather than the devices he employs. That is, the tests and other techniques the psychologist uses are only valuable insofar as their results are interpreted by a clinician who is skilled in understanding children and capable of tying together information from a variety of sources. The skilled psychologist is knowledgeable about learning, development, personality, and adjustment, and is sophisticated about measurement. He has a frame of reference built from work with a wide variety of normal children as well as those with problems. He has seen the results of his diagnoses carried into remedial practices, and has developed a sensitivity to clues which might escape a person less trained in this area.

The school psychologist employs achievement tests, just as does the teacher, but is primarily interested in how the child's achievement (or lack of achievement) may be related to other variables in his personality and background. He looks at the child as an individual and a member of the family group, class-room group, and normative age group.

The typical school psychologist is trained in administering the various types of intelligence tests, both group and individual, and in many kinds of diagnostic tests to help him understand the child's personality, specific deficits, and manner of functioning. He is also equipped to study learning problems and to make recommendations based on his findings.

It must be emphasized, however, that there is no "magic" in these techniques and that results of psychological evaluation must be interpreted in the light of other information about the child that may be available. The real competence of the psychologist is in his ability to determine what data are required and to interrelate them meaningfully.

Psychologists are emphasizing more and more an approach to remediation based on learning theory (Lindsley, 1964). They spend time not only in testing children but also in talking with teachers and observing classrooms. They are then more able to help the teacher devise what are essentially "programmed" situations for helping the child, using techniques similar to those mentioned in Chapter 11: reinforcement, deconditioning or counterconditioning, and inhibition.

A. Bandura (1961), T. Ayllon and J. Michael (1959), and others have successfully employed techniques based on learning theory in hospital settings, and interest in application to the school setting is increasing. In the event that research continues to show gains in this frame of reference, there will be much less emphasis on the causes of the child's behavior in an historical sense and more on present factors maintaining it. Even serious problems may be attacked through reinforcement principles; studies range from A. J. Yates' work with tics, in which he employed extinction (1958), through the work of J. Wolpe

(1958), who among other things was able to reduce anxiety through relaxation and reinforcement procedures.

There are problems in school psychology as a profession. For example, schools have not yet learned how to use the psychologist's limited time to best advantage. S. W. Gray (1963) has also shown that unfortunately, as more psychological services become available, the greater the demand for them seems to be. The case load of a school psychologist varies with his duties but is commonly believed not to include more than 300 cases a year. For this reason, his work must be supplemented by that of many other workers and especially by the classroom teacher to the best of his training and ability.

GUIDANCE AND COUNSELING WORKERS. ■ The area of guidance and counseling is defined somewhat differently by its practitioners. Some define "guidance" as the total aspect of working with the child in providing assistance with educational, vocational, and personal problems or plans; and "counseling" as a subcategory in which personal relationships between counselor and counselee deal with primarily personal problems. On the other hand, "guidance" may refer to the information-providing, exploratory activities by which either individual children or groups of children learn about schools, curricula, and college and vocational opportunities, whereas "counseling" may refer to the personal relationship aimed at solving problems of personal or social adjustment. In any case, guidance and counseling workers tend to deal with all these functions, their emphasis depending upon their training and their schools' needs and philosophies.

The emerging concept of the school guidance worker as a member of the pupil personnel team is that he is less closely related to teachers and administration than formerly and is receiving more extensive training in psychology, so that he is becoming more like the school psychologist in training and function (Reed & Stefflre, 1963). This point of view is not accepted by all, for some believe that the guidance worker's function cannot be divorced from close contact with the continuing school situation. E. Landy and E. Scanlon (1962) suggest that the guidance program and therapy provided for disturbed children should be collaborative and supplementary, each furnishing a kind of help that the other does not. The child would then receive both educational and clinical aid and counseling. As with school psychology, there are unresolved issues in roles and functions; it must be kept in mind, however, that one difference between the school psychologist and the guidance and counseling worker is that the latter offers many services to children without "problems," who are functioning well in school and community. Most recently, counselors have been moving into elementary schools, where their functions more clearly supplement those of clinical workers.

In the total school picture, the guidance worker is the liaison among the various teachers who deal with a particular problem child, the parents, and the child himself. He can provide continuity of diagnosis and remediation over the entire period of the child's school life. He is therefore usually the first professional resource consulted at the secondary-school level and frequently performs a similar function in the elementary school.

Guidance and counseling workers are certified differently by the various state departments of public instruction (Camp, 1960). In general they have teaching licenses based upon four-year college degrees plus one or two years of specialized graduate work. In the graduate program, they not only learn counseling techniques but are also given extensive training in theory of personality, adjustment, learning, and measurement, along with practice or internship in guidance and counseling.

Although they do not usually possess the proficiency in psychological diagnosis attained by the psychologist, they receive some training in this area. Those working toward the doctorate frequently take work in school psychology as their minor area, and many who are not pursuing the degree also take courses in that area; the result is that school guidance and counseling workers are becoming much more sophisticated psychologically than was formerly the case.

The guidance worker possesses skill in the use and interpretation of various standardized tests of ability, achievement, and aptitude. He may be the person in the school who does the group testing, tabulation of results, and interpretation of findings. He may also employ such individual tests as those for assessing mechanical aptitude, clerical aptitude, and the like. If he has had psychometric training, he may also be qualified in the use of individual intelligence tests and perhaps of various instruments for assessing personality and adjustment.

One of the guidance worker's main tools is the interview. He may consult with teachers, parents, or pupils for the purpose of identifying problems, obtaining information, interpreting findings, and making plans for remediation. He may consult with individual children or with groups on educational and vocational plans; he may provide information, or he may simply assess students' interests, plans, and programs.

As a counselor, he also employs the interview extensively. He does not engage in "therapy" as such but prefers to refer serious problems to specialists. He does, however, deal with personal problems that are not indicative of extremely serious disturbances, primarily through interpersonal relationships that he establishes with individual students.

Guidance workers are in contact with the home and with community agencies that can help children with special needs. Their relationships with children are such that they can frequently help them through problems by manipulating the school setting, and they have influence in such areas as class placement, class load, and administrative matters related to children's well-being.

The guidance worker can help the teacher in several ways (Minneapolis Public Schools, 1948) :

1. He can help the teacher to know individual pupils better by giving them reasons for pupil behavior.
2. He can help the teacher to interpret and use results of standardized tests.
3. He can help the teacher plan group discussions and other activities for orientation, self-appraisal, and life adjustment of pupils.
4. He can help teachers advise pupils who come to them for aid.
5. He can assist the teacher in helping pupils get changes in program where needed.

THE SCHOOL SOCIAL WORKER. ▪ The school social worker deals with children as members of families. He visits homes and observes living conditions. He consults with parents and with community agencies and tries to see to it that the child has opportunities for good mental health to the extent that the social environment can be managed. Unfortunately, the work of the school social worker has sometimes included checking on truancy and frequently dealing with delinquent behavior of children, which makes it difficult to maintain the kinds of relationships desired.

The school social worker is usually required to have a master's degree in his specialty, which takes about two years of graduate study. Many social workers qualify as *psychiatric social workers* and, because of their special training, may employ certain kinds of therapeutic techniques. Because they work with the schools, it is useful for them to have training and understanding of the curriculum and the teaching-learning process.

Essentially the social worker deals with people through the interview process. As with school psychologists and guidance and counseling workers, the school social worker's value lies primarily in his training and experience, as well as in his own personal qualities.

Some school systems, for example, the one in Santa Barbara, California, have studied the use of social workers in relation to less serious needs than those for which they are ordinarily employed. The results have been encouraging, for it has been demonstrated that there is a more favorable climate for success when referral to the social worker takes place before problems become serious; and less contact with clinical workers may therefore be needed.

The school social worker is still relatively rare, except in metropolitan areas, yet his contributions are extremely valuable, and, if a team approach to the problems of the child is envisaged, he is essential. Not only can he gather information that other workers may not be able to gather, but his ability to work with parents as well as with children is required in many cases for successful treatment of the child.

OTHER SCHOOL SPECIALISTS. ▪ Many special workers, like speech therapists, remedial teachers, school nurses, consulting physicians, psychiatrists, and psychologists, may be available for referral within the school context.

The concept of "staffing" a child who has problems suggests that the various specialists who have seen the child should be brought together to discuss his problems; the broader the scope of data collection, diagnosis, and therapy, the more likely are the results to be favorable. A child with serious problems may thus be seen by a team of specialists, plus the teachers, and in a group meeting on the child's problems there may be the teacher, principal, psychologist, school nurse, speech therapist, and others, working together for the benefits to be derived from group deliberation and proposed treatment on a "total" basis.

Community Resources for Referral

Many communities maintain child-guidance clinics, the staffs of which include psychiatrists, psychologists, and social workers. Referrals to such clinics may come from physicians, courts, parents, or schools. Because many sparsely populated areas cannot afford clinics in each small town, there is a trend toward having a clinical staff attached to the office of the county superintendent of schools or to a county welfare agency. The clinic staff may travel to outlying areas, or the child in need may be transported to the centrally housed clinic. Joint efforts by two or more counties or other governmental bodies are not uncommon.

In many states the departments of education provide for psychological examination of certain children, especially those who are handicapped. The child may be referred for evaluation by his school, and a traveling psychologist, physician, or other specialist visits the child. Frequently such study determines whether the child will be placed in a residential center for the mentally retarded or emotionally disturbed, in a special classroom within the school, or in a regular class. State facilities sponsor and supervise school programs in special education. Except for screening or other evaluative service, however, they usually cannot offer individual services.

State welfare departments, especially those of the youth authority, are also involved in examination of children. They may be concerned when a child or his family becomes dependent, when the child is neglected, when need for foster-home placement arises, or when the child is involved in delinquent or criminal acts.

Many colleges and universities maintain special child-study centers (speech and hearing, psychoeducation, remedial reading, neuropsychiatric institutes, and others). They are justified on the basis of training interns in these specialties and for permitting research. Children receive study and sometimes treatment in return for volunteering as subjects for the training and research needed. Many hospitals also work with children who are orthopedically handicapped, blind, suffering from cerebral palsy, organically or mentally retarded, and so on.

Private Resources for Referral

Physicians, welfare agencies, psychologists, and other specialists are usually aware of the private resources located near the school. Private practice in psychiatry, psychology, and other specialties should be considered a resource whenever the family can be induced to make use of such services and when the fees normally charged can be paid by the parents or with assistance from some charitable organization without undue hardship. Suggestions on how such help may be obtained should come from physicians, psychiatrists, psychologists, or others who are in positions to know the training and reputations of private practitioners. Such recommendations are important, for some clinicians seem more successful with children, others with adults, some with special kinds of cases, and so on.

Aid for children can frequently be obtained if the family is unable to foot necessary bills for diagnosis or therapy. Such groups as the Catholic Social Welfare Bureau, Children's Service Society, Jewish Family and Children's Service, Lutheran Welfare Society, and the St. Vincent de Paul Society, to name but a few, may aid in obtaining help for children. The local ministry can put parents in touch with such groups and suggest the kinds of aid they extend. Many communities have such specialized groups as the Society for Brain Injured Children, Council on Alcoholism, Mental Health Association, and others that can provide information to parents and that can sometimes provide certain therapeutic services, either directly or indirectly through financial assistance. Local social workers have access to information about such agencies and can frequently make contacts for families.

At this point the reader may raise the question of who should seek out such resources and how school contact with such resources should be made. It is clear that teachers themselves should not have to make such efforts; as previously mentioned, there should be (and usually is) a channel for referral, beginning with the teacher and extending through the administrative structure of the school. The primary reason for listing resources is to suggest to interested school personnel that some referral sources may be overlooked. A second purpose is to acquaint the teacher and other school personnel with the types of services frequently available and to suggest that outcomes from referral will therefore be expected to vary.

Teachers sometimes find that, when children are referred, waiting lists of agencies are so long that the children's problems (and the teachers') become greatly intensified before anything is done. This criticism may be valid in some situations. The teacher can and should, however, keep the administration aware of the progress of the child; the administration, in turn, may seek other than the usual resources, particularly in rapidly deteriorating situations.

□

REFERENCES

Allinsmith, W., and G. W. Goethals. *The Role of the Schools in Mental Health*. New York: Basic Books, 1962.

Ausubel, D. P. "Personality Disorder Is Disease," *American Psychologist*, 16 (1961), 69–74.

Ayllon, T., and J. Michael. "The Psychiatric Nurse as a Behavioral Engineer," *Journal of the Experimental Analysis of Behavior*, 2 (1959), 323–34.

Bandura, A. "Psychotherapy as a Learning Process," *Psychological Bulletin*, 58 (1961), 143–59.

Bower, E. M., P. J. Tashnovian, and C. A. Larson. *A Process for Early Identification of Emotionally Disturbed Children*. Sacramento: California Department of Education, 1958.

Camp, D. *Guidance Workers Certification Requirements* (Office of Education Bulletin 14, OE–25005–A). (Rev. ed.) Washington, D.C.: U.S. Department of Health, Education and Welfare, 1960.

Caplan, G. (ed.). *Prevention of Mental Disorders in Children*. New York: Basic Books, 1962.

Clancy, N., and F. Smitter. "A Study of Emotionally Disturbed Children in Santa Barbara County Schools," *California Journal of Educational Research*, 4 (1953), 209–18.

Gilbert, G. M. "A Survey of 'Referral Problems' in Metropolitan Child Guidance Centers," *Journal of Clinical Psychology*, 13 (1957), 37–42.

Gray, S. W. (ed.). "The Internship in School Psychology," in *Proceedings of the Peabody Conference*. Nashville: George Peabody College for Teachers, 1963a.

———. *The Psychologist in the Schools*. New York: Holt, Rinehart, Winston, 1963b.

Kline, C. L. "Recognizing Emotional Problems in Adolescent Girls," *Wisconsin Medical Journal*, 52 (1953), 482–6.

Landy, E., and E. Scanlon. "Relationship Between School Guidance and Psychotherapy for Adolescents," *American Journal of Orthopsychiatry*, 32 (1962), 682–90.

Lindsley, O. R. *Operant Conditioning and School Psychology*. Paper presented at Institute for School Psychologists, University of Wisconsin, Madison, July 10, 1964.

Minneapolis Public Schools Division of Secondary Education. *Helping Adolescents Grow Up*. Minneapolis: Minneapolis Public Schools, 1948.

Mullen, F. (ed.). *The Psychologist on the School Staff. Report of the Committee on Reconsideration of the Functions of the School Psychologist, American Psychological Association*, 1958.

Reed, H. J., and B. Stefflre. "Elementary and Secondary Program," *Review of Educational Research*, 33 (1963), 152–62.

Ringness, T. A. *Emotional Reactions to Learning Situations as Related to the Learning Efficiency of Mentally Retarded Children* (Cooperative Research Project SAE 6434). Madison: University of Wisconsin, 1959.

Rogers, C. R. "The Criteria Used in a Study of Mental Health Problems," *Educational Research Bulletin*, 21 (1942), 29–40.

———. "Mental Health Findings in Three Elementary Schools," *Educational Research Bulletin*, 21 (1942), 69–79.

Szasz, T. Paper presented at conference on Moral Dilemmas in Schooling, *Mental Health Services in the School: A Critical Review of the Principles and Practices of School Psychiatry*. Childhood Education Center, Madison, Wisconsin, May 14, 1965.

Ullmann, C. A. *Identification of Maladjusted Children* (Public Health Monograph No. 7). Washington, D.C.: U.S. Department of Health, Education and Welfare, 1957.

Valett, R. E. *The Practice of School Psychology*. New York: Wiley, 1963.

Wolpe, J. *Psychotherapy by Reciprocal Inhibition*. Stanford: Stanford University Press, 1958.

Yates, A. J. "The Application of Learning Theory to Treatment of Tics," *Journal of Abnormal and Social Psychology*, 56 (1958), 175–82.

SUGGESTIONS FOR FURTHER READING

Buhler, C., F. Smitter, and S. Richardson. *Childhood Problems and the Teacher*, Part III, "The Psychologists's Collaboration with the School." New York: Holt, Rinehart, Winston, 1952.
This book is an early, but useful, discussion of the topic.

Krugman, M. (ed.). *Orthopsychiatry and the School*, Part 3, "The Predictive Value of Teachers' Referrals." New York: American Orthopsychiatric Association, 1958.

15

SCHOOL AND COMMUNITY MENTAL-HEALTH PROGRAMS

For maximum progress in pupil mental health, a definite integrated approach must be made by the schools. That is, although it is highly desirable for any given teacher, counselor, or other school person to practice mental-hygiene principles, significant progress will be most likely when all who deal with a given pupil are coordinating their efforts and are oriented in the same direction.

We have emphasized that there are mental-health factors to be considered in the child himself, his home and family, the teacher, and almost every aspect of the curriculum. We have suggested that there are many school roles related to mental health, such as teaching coping skills, preparing children for adequate social relationships, recognizing and referring children with problems, remediation when possible, and refraining from placing undue stresses on children. Any program for mental health must recognize all these facets, even if it does not directly deal with all of them.

This chapter treats developing school mental-health programs and how they relate to the immediate community and the broader state and national context.

School Mental-Health Programs

INITIATING PROGRAMS

Mental-health programs come about in a number of ways, but common to all is that small groups of people have become aware of the need for such programs and have taken steps to raise interest in the schools and to arouse action. Such groups may consist of parents, teachers, counselors, administrators, or combinations of them.

Most successful programs are not formally instituted at first. They rarely can be functional when imposed on a school faculty by administrators. When formal programs are initiated as something that "good schools should have" or because they would "make good in-service training projects for the year," they tend to be artificial and contrived. It is when school problems—discipline, learning, curriculum, and the like—are studied, that mental-health needs are recognized and programs of value can be initiated. One cannot legislate "mental health."

We do not mean that sometimes stimulation cannot come legitimately from outside sources. A parent may become concerned about what is happening to his children in school and approach teachers or even a P.T.A. to see what can be done. A teacher may attend a summer class and learn something of the possibilities of mental-health practices—for example, relationships between good mental health and learning, human relationships, and relationships between discipline and mental health—and wish to see such practices and principles tried in his school. State supervisors or school evaluation teams may point out needs. School-instituted studies may show something of the extent of failures, dropouts, disciplinary problems, and referrals to clinics and may point the way to further study of mental-health relationships. Administrators may also recognize needs and attempt to interest staff, but a genuine commitment must be encouraged so that the staff does not simply "go through the motions" to please the administrators.

We shall illustrate with some issues raised by participants at a short institute on school administration and mental health, showing the kinds of questions and comments that can lead to study and programs:

We have a strong concern for mental health of teachers. Several staff members annually have personal problems (which reduce their ability to function well).

We have a need for liaison service (on our staff).

We are worried about detection of early symptoms and pressures.

How can teachers be helped to deal with both personal as well as academic problems? [This administrator believes that good work by teachers will benefit both the personal and academic growth of children.]

How about in-service and preservice education of teachers?

How can we relate research findings to learning of boys and girls?

How can teachers be helped to work with children who have problems which should not be referred?

What effect do teacher expectations have on children?

What can we do in the classroom to give all children greater feelings of well-being?

How far can the school go after one identifies special needs of children?

How can a school build better rapport between the school and the home? (Proceedings of the Wisconsin Institute, 1962, pp. 38, 39)

All in all, sixty-four issues and problems were raised and discussed at this institute. Speakers, workshops with consultants, and other resources were available to help these administrators build mental-health programs in their home schools and communities.

Similar question raising may be accomplished in the confines of a school system. Once an airing of problems and issues has taken place, there are numerous ways to start. In developing programs, the following steps seem imperative, although they need not be undertaken in the prescribed order:

1. Considerable information on mental-health principles and how they relate to the work of the schools is needed. These data can be gained from reading, discussion, lectures, workshops, in-service study groups, consultants, and others.
2. There must be clear ideas of the needs for the schools involved. Studies must be made. This requirement is not for "research" so much as for identification and ranking of problems and clarification of their nature.

3. There must be ideas of what can reasonably be undertaken, resources available, and staff possibilities. Many programs "start small," with attention to one or two mental-health concerns.

4. Machinery must be devised so that action can be taken. For example, sometimes teachers are sent to special workshops in mental health at school expense. They then return to take initiative in communicating their knowledge to their respective staffs. If a study group is to be formed, released time may be needed. Finances must be arranged; materials and other resources must be provided.

5. Principles must be applied. Teachers must be free to use their understandings without fear of criticism. They must be encouraged to use mental-health practices by administrators and consultative personnel. Interpretation of these practices to the community and its acceptance of them must be sought.

6. Evaluation of results must be made and modifications of the program introduced if necessary.

SOME KINDS OF MODIFICATIONS

As we have discussed in this book, teachers must work with both children who are healthy and those who have problems. To illustrate the modifications in school programs and additional facilities that might be provided for children with problems, we refer to some of the work of E. Bower (1962).

Bower first discusses children with transient problems that are the result of normal crises. For children such as these, the total (regular) school program may be sufficient. However, as children's problems become more serious, other measures may be needed. Thus for children who show early signs of emotional distress, screening and mental-health consultation may also be needed. A specialist should probably evaluate such children and consult with the teacher and/or other school personnel.

A third level of seriousness is that of children with marked and recurrent emotional difficulties of mild but annoying intensity. These children may require screening, mental-health consultation, and also remedial instruction, special placement, or a child-care program. Such children cannot be expected to benefit from the school program without these added facilities—if indeed they are retained at all. The fourth level, that of children with marked and recurrent emotional difficulties of moderate intensity, may call for case-centered collaboration (clinical teamwork) and involve play activity (or therapy), parent group counseling, and, depending upon the subjects, adolescent group work.

Borderline psychotic or severely neurotic children may require special teachers, special day schools, home instruction, or other special treatment. Severely disturbed psychotic children require residential schools, special day schools, or home instruction.

It is doubtful that *all* these provisions could (or should) be maintained by any school system. Rather, they represent a constellation of the efforts of schools, mental-health clinics, and even possibly some state agencies; but, in order to provide for *all* pupils, a program must embody some integrated schema.

W. G. Hollister, on the other hand, writes of preventive and positive aspects of mental-health procedures. Concerning himself with the concept of "strens," Hollister says:

What is a "stren"? It is an experience in an individual's life that builds strength into his personality. Notice that the term is defined in the subjective sense—in terms of the impact of the experience on the individual.

Why do we need such a term? We need it as a conceptual tool, as a collective noun to help us focus more of our efforts on the challenge of building strength into children, rather than devoting the major part of our time to repairing the impact of traumas and maldevelopment. (Hollister, 1964, p. 31)

Hollister is addressing himself primarily to school psychologists and describes interventions that they might make into the typical program, in order to provide strens for children. Applying Hollister's concept, N. M. Lambert (1964) discusses some interventions that prevent poor mental health by modifying or eliminating stresses, by isolating vulnerable children from excessive stress, or by intercepting problems at an early stage to prevent further deterioration. Miss Lambert also takes note of interventions that both prevent trouble and build resistance to it by increasing psychological safety, reinforcing personality strengths, developing motivation, educating for expected behavior (anticipatory guidance, corrective learning experience), and bringing about group interaction.

For example, in regard to activities for children subject to or threatened by stress that can be modified or eliminated, Miss Lambert mentions shortening the school day to a period of time in which the child can function fairly well; placing the child in a smaller classroom group either within the class or in another class; lowering, modifying, or changing curricular demands; and having conferences with parents to help them understand the effects of excess pressure on the child. Or, in trying to reinforce personality strengths, intervention might take the form of finding a new activity for a child, challenging enough that his success in it will help him feel his own ego strengths; planning failure and success in supportive situations; and finding ways to let an insecure child know that he can trust you. (Because she is referring to intervention through recommendations from the school psychologist to the teacher, the examples shown above refer to children who have been seen by the psychologist, hence may be presumed to have problems. The concept of "strens" and many of Miss Lambert's recommendations, however, apply just as well to healthy children.)

The school mental-health program should embody the school goals mentioned in Chapter 1; when these goals cannot all be immediately included, it should be clearly recognized that, as the program matures, attention will be directed to areas that are lacking.

SOME FACTORS TO CONSIDER

Financial resources are required for such programs. Specialized personnel, reduction of teacher load, time for attendance at in-service or other training functions, special materials, space, and other requirements demand money. Fortunately, many Federal, state, and foundation sources exist for obtaining such funds. The Federal government, through the U.S. Department of Health, Education and Welfare, provides school systems with money for projects of many kinds. The state department of public instruction or any college or university can supply information about the programs available. Perhaps the Elementary-Secondary Education Act of 1965 is more widespread in supporting school efforts than are some of the more research-oriented programs. Resources like the National Institute of

Mental Health, the Children's Bureau, and programs in anti-poverty and urban development should not be overlooked, however.

For full-fledged mental-health programs, specialized personnel are required (see Chapter 14). There is a current shortage of such personnel, and it threatens to continue. One means of dealing with this shortage is to employ consultative mental-health personnel on a part-time basis. For example, employees of hospitals and residential treatment centers, as well as private practitioners, may make their services available. A longer-term practice is to subsidize certain school personnel while they undertake training in counseling, school psychology, school social work, and other specialties.

RESEARCH AND FOLLOW-UP

The term "research" sometimes frightens people not familiar with statistical techniques, instruments for personality evaluation, and the like. As the term is employed here, however, it refers both to status studies, in which the aim is to discover the needs of the school and pupils, and to studies to develop and assess experimental programs. Luckily in most school systems there are people becoming much more used to research than school personnel used to be; field research is becoming a function of the grammar and high school, rather than being confined to a college or university setting. In addition, many colleges and universities are willing—even eager—to collaborate with schools in research on new ideas. Faculties of such institutions are frequently able to act as consultants to school systems.

A REPRESENTATIVE PROJECT

To illustrate one kind of project in which several schools are collaborating with university staff members, here is a proposal forwarded for funding by twenty-two school districts in a cooperative educational service agency area in Wisconsin. These schools were sadly lacking in psychological services, and a university faculty member was asked to suggest some means of providing such services.

The recommendation, in substance, was that mental-health provisions ought to stress early intervention, in regard to children with learning problems, as we suggested in Chapter 14. Accordingly, a team consisting of a school psychologist, social worker, and remedial specialist were to be employed to evaluate a number of first-grade children referred by their teachers on the basis of social and/or learning problems.

To test whether the team's recommendations would be useful, half of the children evaluated would act as a control group, and no treatment would be extended; a future re-evaluation of all of the referred children could determine whether those who were "treated" had improved more than those who were not.

The team was to act remedially in two ways: the social worker would consult children's families when required; and the psychologist and remedial specialist were to work with each child's classroom teacher, to determine how that teacher might better work remedially with the child.

It is hoped this project—now getting underway—will fulfill a number of objectives:

to sensitize teachers to the special needs of any children in their classes, and to help them seek referrals when they felt these were indicated;

to provide assessment techniques in order to discover the requirements, problems, and background of children who had problems;

to institute early intervention, thus hopefully finding relatively short treatment spans, heading off more serious future problems;

to help the teacher learn to help these children, as well as to gain understandings which would help all children;

to assist families in dealing more successfully with their children;

to help the schools coordinate more usefully with families;

to research effectiveness of such procedures;

to study how children who were untreated might change;

to (hopefully) develop additional techniques of assessment and remediation;

to provide training for psychologists and social workers at the intern level and in-service training for teachers.

Programs of which the writer is aware are currently dealing with the values of teacher helpers, concrete reinforcement, preschool education for the culturally deprived, methods of working with the perceptually handicapped (and brain-injured), individualized reading, and programmed instruction (as a remedial device).

The reader will undoubtedly know of programs in his own community or nearby aimed at improving instruction. Whether such programs are positive or negative influences for mental health would have to be considered.

There are a number of kinds of study that need to be made but either have not been made or have been made only infrequently. For example, in the proposal described above, it is quite possible that the remedial tactics might be successful in regard to most children. However, few schools have instituted long-term follow-up studies. It is entirely possible that the children helped might later "relapse" into a problem state because of continuing home or school problems. The effectiveness of remedial efforts must be studied partly on the basis of such long-term practices.

Another kind of study with mental-health implications—infrequently made, if ever—is that concerning why some children improve in certain areas, apparently without treatment. Again, why do some children *not* have problems? What is it that makes healthy children healthy—in spite of poor environmental circumstances in some cases? We fail to study our healthy children as adequately as we study those with problems.

EVALUATING SCHOOL MENTAL-HEALTH PROGRAMS

As with evaluating teaching, evaluating the success of school mental-health programs is difficult. It is frequently hard to ascribe cause-and-effect relationships to given programs when changes in individual pupils or in groups of pupils are noted. It is also difficult to assess affective variables, and they are the variables most central to the study of mental health. A number of broad guidelines can, however, be established and a number of quite objective assessments made.

The criteria for success of a mental-health program are not merely the number of services provided or actions taken but their success or failure. Provision of a counselor does not necessarily mean that counseling will be effective, nor does teaching mental-health principles to teachers mean that they will be put into practice. Accordingly, in evaluating a program, it is the condition of the pupils and staff that is important, rather than the provisions made.

We shall begin by suggesting some of the broad criteria that others have listed. H. L. Shibler (1955), for example, believes that the following questions should be asked:

1. Is there awareness of need of additional social services on the part of the general public?
2. Is there adequate financial support of local and state programs?
3. Is there public support through private and voluntary organizations' services—forums, churches, local mental-health societies, state mental-health agencies, etc.?
4. Is there awareness of need on the part of the faculties of the school system?
5. Is there adequate training of the school staff?
6. Are there available adequate services of expert consultants and psychologists, psychiatrists, psychiatric social workers, visiting teachers, guidance clinics, and institutional facilities?
7. Is there an observable change in the behavior of the student body?
8. Are there curricular changes that better meet individual and group needs?
9. Is there a comprehensive program that is broad enough in prevention and treatment of mental illness to meet the varying needs of the school and community?
10. Is there an observable improvement in the working conditions for teachers and is the environment for students conducive to good mental health?
11. Is the mental-health program having a noticeable effect on the community in general?
12. Are there provisions for a program of continuous evaluation of the mental-health program? (Shibler, 1955, pp. 2–4)

Shibler thus believes that, unless the school program is having a noticeable effect in the community and is enlisting support on a broad basis, it may not be entirely adequate. This point of view suggests that the schools alone can do relatively little if there are community situations working against them. A total community approach is thus preferred.

An interesting series of questions to be asked about the mental-health program in the schools was developed by the Committee on Education Practices of the National Council of Independent Schools (1952). A faculty meeting devoted to discussion of the school situation as reflected in answers to these questions can provide significant information about the success of current mental-health provisions. A later discussion, when compared with the original, can show whether or not improvement is taking place. *The Committee stresses that this technique is not a comprehensive survey instrument or test but is rather a series of "loaded" questions about the application of mental-hygiene concepts in the school.*

In substance, the Committee's questions are as follows:

PROGRAM

1. What kind of respect is accorded the learning that comes by way of such activities as fine arts, rhythms, dancing, music, drama, physical education, industrial arts? Are these activities respected? Are they reserved only for those with special talents? How much time is given to them? When in the school day? Are results of arts and shop work shown in the school plant?
2. How important in the school life are student councils and committees, discussion groups, student religious activities, community work, or "work time"? Clubs?
3. The chance to express oneself creatively—whether in arts or in other activities—enables young people to rid themselves of stresses and strains, to grapple with problems, and to express strong feelings in a way that is acceptable and health giving. Is this understood and used to advantage?
4. Are these activities related to academic work and to each other— to what are they relevant?
5. Is the mastery of tools of learning treated so that these tools become elements of security in a child's life?
6. In the various studies is "meaning" or significance an objective— for example, the applicability of current issues outside the school? Does such work help the student to understand and face his changing world?

GUIDANCE

1. Is there is adviser to whom each child can turn?
2. Is such adviser a counselor who sits less as judge and disciplinary agent and more as the person to whom the boy or girl can talk?

3. Is there a pooling of insights by the adults who deal with each child to the point of a shared approach?
4. Are environmental factors studied and interpreted?
5. Is the testing system used as one kind of evidence rather than a categorizer of children, a measure of teaching, or an end in itself?
6. Is there true regard for all kinds of gifts and degrees of success— for the achievements of those who are limited in academic, creative, or athletic ability as well as those gifted in these ways?
7. Is the marking and report system a teacher's or parent's weapon, or is it a medium of learning and teaching and guidance?
8. Is there capable guidance (consultant help) of staff members in the understanding of young people?
9. What is the relationship between the school and available psychologists and psychiatrists?

ATMOSPHERE

1. Do children have a sense of belonging, each one to something in which he is a responsible participant?
2. Does the school belong to the students in the sense that they know its activities would not go on unless individuals and groups played their part?
3. Is there a good understanding of the relative part to be played at different ages and stages by student initiative and teacher direction?
4. Do teachers learn as they teach?
5. Is there such genuineness in all relationships that both acceptance and constructive criticism of others and of oneself are possible and natural?

APPROACHES

1. Children only learn deeply and fully that which they are ready to accept. Is what is expected from and presented to a child based on knowledge of his readiness and ability?
2. Is sufficient leeway allowed both within the classroom and without for pupils to make mistakes? Room for mistakes permits experiments in learning and for some errors which promote the student's knowledge of himself.
3. Are there goals and standards definite enough to provide a good degree of security for pupils?
4. Does the school unfold a life sufficiently vital to contain, for the pupil, a vision of full and satisfying years ahead, a life which affords ample scope for his next years *as he sees them?*

5. Is there contemplation of the needs of both boys and girls and of the meaning of the sexes to each other?
6. Is there a common understanding through actual school experience of such phases of life as: independence, freedom, interdependence, responsibility, discipline, structure, and self-discipline?
7. Does the school aid parents? Is there a natural, honest, and constructive cooperation between home and school?
8. Is the recognition of spiritual values a significant force in the life of the school?

Because pupil mental health is difficult to single out as a variable in pupil behavior and other factors must always be considered, any evaluation of mental-health practices must always be tentative, in one sense of the word. Community culture, including attitudes and values, the physical and social environment, and past experience all contribute to behavior and may partially obscure findings. However, when emphasis is given to the *quality* or *meaning* of behavior, rather than to its objective or surface manifestations, many kinds of pupil acts can be indicative of the state of pupil mental health.

For example, one can study the pupil dropout rate, and find ways to assess the reasons. Although dropping out of school may tell more about the family or the community than about the school, nevertheless, school dropouts are usually youngsters who fail to find school living a way to satisfy their needs; many lack a feeling of identification with the school, a feeling of belonging, and a feeling of worthwhile achievement.

Equally, one might look at the absentee list, the truancies, and the tardiness reports, to see the kinds of reasons given and how they may relate to pupil personality adjustment.

One may assess achievement, and if a large number of underachievers are found, this may act as a signal for further study of school teaching practices.

One may consider the disciplinary situation, both in terms of number of offenses, their nature, and the kinds of pupils involved.

One may study carefully the cases of pupils referred to guidance and counseling personnel or to the school psychologist. Study of these can sometimes lead to weak points in the school program.

One may note how students respond to school activities to which they are invited on a voluntary basis, compared to how they respond to those they are required to attend. What does such participation tell about school morale, needs, and values?

It is also useful to ask teachers about the morale and mental health of their pupils. Being in company with children all day long provides them with ample opportunity to make judgments, even if the child-study techniques mentioned in Chapter 10 are not employed.

Community Mental-Health Programs

Community mental-health programs are as diverse in kind and extent as are school programs. Attempts, fostered by local health agencies, by mental-health associations, or even by state boards of health, education, or welfare, may be made to integrate the possible resources of the entire community. Action may be taken on the following fronts, with the schools as an integral part of the program:

1. Prevention of poor mental health

   provision of adequate living conditions for all families;

   removal of deleterious influences, such as slums, hangouts for criminals and delinquents, stoppage of drug peddling, and the like;

   parent education for child rearing;

   provision of adequate recreational facilities such as clubs, parks, ball diamonds, crafts;

   enforcement of civil rights codes;

   provision of adequate facilities for the aging, including recreational and inspirational;

   providing for adequate physical health through public health measures and facilities such as adequate water supplies, food inspection, etc.;

   adequate medical facilities, including hospitals.

2. Provision of referral agencies

   private practitioners in psychology and psychiatry;

   child guidance clinics; mental health clinics;

social welfare agencies; family service agencies;

mental health facilities in hospitals and residential treatment centers;

provision for public assistance when needed and finances do not permit self-supporting treatment;

centers for treatment of alcoholics; associations for alcoholic assistance.

3. Educational assistance

mental health study groups, as in churches, P.T.A.'s, teacher groups, service clubs;

provision of literature on mental health;

publicizing mental health needs;

adult education; family welfare education; child-rearing education; as in vocational or adult classes, college extension classes, or informal institutes.

4. Surveys of needs

consultant services, provided by money from municipal sources, grants, and funds;

citizen surveys, undertaken locally, with local talent primarily; school surveys.

5. Provision of adequate school facilities

normal children;

children with special needs.

6. Coordination of services

mental health associations;

municipal bodies;

coordination with state and federal agencies;

coordination of private efforts, efforts of churches, service clubs, and others.

Many studies and articles have suggested how various communities have initiated and conducted such activities. For example, M. M. Lawrence, *et al.* (1962), showed how school and community mental-health services could be initiated; A. D. Buchmueller (1958) showed a county program; R. Robinson, *et al.* (1960), discussed existing community mental-health research in some detail. References to these and other related studies can be found in a review by R. L. Cutler, *et al.* (1962), which also refers to certain continuing school practices that seem to have merit.

Limitations of School Mental-Health Practices

A number of studies have suggested that school attention to mental-health needs, especially the drafting of teachers as part of the mental-health "team" is useful; among them are those of E. L. Phillips (1957), V. S. Bernard (1958), A. B. Abramovitz and E. Burnham (1959), B. Biber (1961), Cutler (1961), and R. M. Brandt and H. V. Perkins (1958). There is thus ample evidence that attention to the things suggested in this book is valuable, not only for the mental health of pupils (and teacher), but also for teaching and learning efficiency, control of discipline, and other related school problems.

But we shall not argue that magical changes will take place in the lives of all; it would be a mistake to oversell mental-health ideas as a panacea for all school problems. There are many school and teaching problems not directly related to mental health; among them are problems of school finance, adequate staffing, the building program, determining adequate curricula, and others that either extend beyond consideration of mental health *per se* or are only indirectly related to mental-health considerations. Furthermore, for reasons of staffing, finance, and community attitude, it is sometimes difficult to put into practice some of the suggestions that we have made.

One of the problems of school workers is that of the sheer numbers of people who are in poor mental health and the numbers who are mentally ill. It has been suggested that as many as 10 to 20 per cent of all school pupils are not making adequate adjustments to life, either personally or socially, and that these children should definitely be seen by counselors, psychologists, or psychiatrists for diagnosis and recommendations. The teacher must work within his prescribed role, with groups of children, so that attention to the deviant children who need special help is not always possible. There are occasions when the needs of the majority must be weighed against those of the few, and when lack of time or other resources may prevent the teacher from being as helpful to those few as he would like to be. As a result, many children with whom more time should be spent in individual study and remediation will be handled on the basis of expediency. Even more serious, there are not enough diagnosticians, therapists, or treatment centers for those with serious problems.

Because of sheer force of numbers of problems, it may thus be necessary to try to "hold the line," rather than to make the kinds of progress we should desire. That is, it may be necessary to help some children remain in the present state of health they are in, rather than to do the kinds of diagnostic and remedial things which would be more desirable.

Another limitation is the lack of knowledge in the field of mental health, as well as the resulting lack of knowledge of classroom teachers. Theories of personality, tactics of diagnosis and therapy, and the efficacy of therapeutic efforts remain issues in mental-health professions.

Prescribed roles of teachers also limit functioning as mental-health workers. Not only are teachers not clinicians, but they should not be. Thus every child should not be treated as a potential "case"; this is not a viewpoint we wish to encourage. Every discipline problem is not the result of poor mental health, nor is every instance of poor learning. Even the most healthy children are sometimes hard to live with; normal children are not all sugar and spice, and they have problems too.

Teachers cannot neglect their subject matter responsibilities, and must spend hours preparing, teaching, and testing the results of learning activities. Some mental-health concepts can be at variance with the typical school situation; for example, permissiveness, *sometimes* valuable in therapy, has little place in school. It is also difficult for the teacher to be at once in command and at the same time a trusted confidante of each child; he must discipline, and this may interfere with counseling. He must evaluate, and this may lead to a pupil failing a course. The teacher cannot be all things to all people, and must avoid undertaking conflicting roles when possible.

Many problems are somewhat remote from school control. Thus our rapidly changing society may counteract the help a teacher or even a full school mental-health program can give.

For example, many children come from migratory families and are little influenced by schools. Others move frequently because of the father's job demands. Such movements place strains on many children, especially at adolescence.

National security and its implications for service in the armed forces is a real worry to young people. There has been a change in attitude toward early sex relationships, early marriage, going to college, and the seriousness with which some young people attack their studies. Many believe they should enjoy life at the present, for there may be no future. Others resent the fact that college or vocational plans may be interrupted by war or by military service. Girls want to marry while they can, and sometimes pressure boys into marriage before the latter are ready. Coupled with this is an insecurity due to loss of prestige and world position of our country as a whole. The international unrest, racial and ideological problems, and lack of feeling of national security contribute.

Mass media of communication must also share some blame for undesirable attitudes and emotional tensions of young people. With a major share of most popular television programs either escapist (comedians, westerns, hillbilly programs) or dealing with crimes, and with movies dealing extensively with horror and sex, we may expect some problems to result. Such media seem more realistic and thrilling than what the school portrays, and studies have shown that the average student may spend as much as twenty-five hours per week in front of the television set, but thirty or less hours at school.

Values of American society today are confusing to many. Newspapers show that some persons of presumed high repute have cheated on income tax, defrauded the government, or have otherwise cut corners; children may be expected to wonder about the differences between what school (and parents) try to teach them and what they read. Even omitting consideration of such moral transgressors, today's values are confusing. Sometimes emphasis is given to the need for better diplomats and improved knowledge of societies and teach consideration for all mankind; on the other hand Americans tend to admire the aggressive, "self-made" man who may often be highly selfish, ruthless, and, although legally correct, morally indefensible.

Another limitation exists in that where family problems are

severe, as is the case with most children who have serious problems, what can be done by the school may be more than offset by what goes on at home. In fact, the conflicts in standards between home and school may sometimes worsen the mental health of the child.

Finally, we must again refer to many unsolved problems in mental health. Diagnostic instruments are not perfect and one cannot always be certain what is causing behavior. One cannot always tell the inter-relationship of organic and psychological factors which may be causing poor mental health. It is not known how to deal with some kinds of poor mental health; of the kinds that can be helped, there is no assurance of how permanent the improvement will be. Much more must be known about the nature, cause, and remediation of mental-health problems; how attitudes are fostered; and how emotions may be brought under control. The complexity of personality stands in the way. The affective area, with which we have been most concerned in this book, is not yet entirely understood although knowledge is vast and is growing.

Conclusion

This text has been based on a number of postulates. It has been written for teachers, rather than for clinicians; yet the belief has been held that in the aggregate, teachers may have more to do with children's mental health than clinicians do because they are in contact with more children for a longer period of time. It is based on the belief that most pupils are reasonably healthy, but that all have problems, and that in most school situations the potential for good mental health can be increased. When this is done, not only may children's mental health improve, but learning efficiency may likewise improve for many. Further, children in good mental health are much more likely to make functional use of what they have learned in school, than if they are anxious, in conflict or under tension.

However the teacher works and whatever beliefs the teacher holds, he does work with human personalities. He is an influence, for better or worse. It has been our thesis that when the teacher performs his usual tasks, but thinks diagnostically and has mental-health concepts in mind, his work with children will be more efficient, happy, and satisfying.

☐

REFERENCES

Abramovitz, A. B., and E. Burnham. "Exploring Potentials for Mental Health in the Classroom," *Mental Hygiene,* 43 (1959), 253–9.

Bernard, V. S. "Teacher Education in Mental Health—from the Point of View of the Psychiatrist," in M. Krugman (ed.). *Orthopsychiatry and the School,* pp. 184–203. New York: American Orthopsychiatric Association, 1958.

Biber, B. "Integration of Mental Health Principles in the School Setting," in G. Caplan (ed.). *Prevention of Mental Disorders in Children,* pp. 205–17. New York: Basic Books, 1961.

Bower, E. "The Epidemiology of Emotional Handicap and Psychoeducational Processes," *Proceedings of Wisconsin Institute on School Administration and Mental Health,* Addenda B, Annex III. Madison: State Superintendent of Public Instruction, 1962.

Brandt, R. M., and H. V. Perkins. "Teachers Change as They Study Children," *Childhood Education,* 34 (1958), 218–20.

Buchmueller, A. D. "A Health Department School District Mental Health Program," in M. Krugman (ed.). *Orthopsychiatry and the School,* pp. 141–8. New York: American Orthopsychiatric Association, 1958.

Committee on Education Practices. *Some Inquiries Helpful in Appraising Mental Health in a School.* Boston: National Council of Independent Schools, 1952.

Cutler, R. L. "Research Evaluation of a School Mental Health Program," *American Journal of Orthopsychiatry,* 31 (1961), 339–46.

Cutler, R. L., P. E. Spieth, and M. R. Wilkinson. "School and Community Mental Health Programs," *Review of Educational Research,* 32 (1962), 476–83.

Hollister, W. G. "The Concept of 'Strens' in Preventive Interventions and Ego-Strength Building in the Schools," in N. M. Lambert, *et al.* (eds.). *The Protection and Promotion of Mental Health in the Schools,* pp. 30–5. Bethesda: U.S. Department of Health, Education and Welfare, 1964.

Lambert, N. M. "Applications of the Taxonomy of Strens in Specific School Situations," in N. M. Lambert, *et al.* (eds.). *The Protection and Promotion of Mental Health in the Schools,* pp. 36–42. Bethesda: U.S. Department of Health, Education and Welfare, 1964.

Lawrence, M. M., I. J. Spanier, and M. W. Dubowy. "An Analysis of the Work of the School Mental Health Unit of a Community Health Board," *American Journal of Orthopsychiatry,* 32 (1962), 99–108.

Phillips, E. L. "The Use of the Teacher as an Adjunct Therapist in Child Guidance," *Psychiatry,* 20 (1957), 407–10.

Proceedings of the Wisconsin Institute on School Administration and Mental Health, Addenda B, Annex III. Madison: State Superintendent of Public Instruction, 1962.

Robinson, R., D. F. DeMarche, and M. R. Wagle. *Community Resources in Mental Health.* New York: Basic Books, 1960.

Shibler, H. L. "Evaluation of a Mental-Health Program," in N. B. Henry (ed.). *Mental Health in Modern Education,* pp. 271–304. Chicago: University of Chicago Press, 1955.

SUGGESTIONS FOR FURTHER READING

Krugman, M. (ed.). *Orthopsychiatry and the School.* New York: American Orthopsychiatric Association, 1958.
This entire book is devoted to practices and methodology regarding children with problems.

Robinson, R., D. F. DeMarche, and M. R. Wagle. *Community Resources in Mental Health.* New York: Basic Books, 1960.
This book is valuable for perspective and ideas and supports many of our points more completely.

□

APPENDIX A

PUPIL-TEACHER RAPPORT SCALE

Board of Education of the City of New York
Bureau of Educational Research
Division of Tests and Measurements

TEACHER . . . . . .   CLASS OR GRADE . . . .   SCHOOL . . . .
OBSERVER . . . . .   PERIOD OF OBSERVATION . . . . .   DATE . . . . . .
SUBJECT OR ACTIVITY OBSERVED . . . .
TYPE OF ACTIVITY OR INSTRUCTION . . . .
STRUCTURE OF GROUP FOR TEACHING . . . .

RATINGS

1st   *2nd*   *3rd*

Pupil-Teacher Interaction Pattern

1. Teacher peripheral (teacher in hands
   off, *laissez-faire* role) . . . .
2. Teacher-centered (attention to
   teacher, e.g., lecture, reading) . . . .
3. Teacher-pupil reciprocal (50%
   teacher—50% pupil interaction) . . . .

SOURCE: J. Wayne Wrightstone, "Pupil-Teacher Rapport Scale" in J. Seidman, *Readings in Educational Psychology* (Boston: Houghton Mifflin, 1955) , pp. 105–6. Reprinted by permission of the Board of Education of the City of New York.

4. Teacher as equal person (teacher as
1 in group of 10, 20, 30, etc.) ....

Degree of Social Interaction

1. No interaction (e.g., listening to
lecture, silent seat work) ....
2. Infrequent interaction (occasional
conferences with teacher, etc.) ....
3. Interaction (natural pupil interaction
in semi-free situations) ....
4. Frequent interaction (e.g., inter-
change in a free situation) ....
5. Maximal interaction (e.g., conference
in subgroups, etc.) ....

Quality of Social Interaction

1. Aggressive (verbal or physical of
pupils, one against others) ....
2. Competitive (individual vs. individual
or vs. group) ....
3. Toleration (lack of warmth, coolness
toward each other) ....
4. Friendly—Cooperative (willingness to
cooperate, share ideas, etc.) ....
5. Warm personal (extreme warmth and
insight into each other) ....

Interest

1. Lack of interest (day dreaming,
wandering attention) ....
2. Boredom (yawns, whispers, looking around) ....
3. Mild lack of interest (polite behavior,
forced attention) ....
4. Mild interest (relaxed attention, but
attend to task) ....
5. Attentive interest (enters into tasks
with energy and spirit) ....

Enjoyment

1. No enjoyment (matter-of-fact, signs
   of aversion) ....
2. Little enjoyment (signs of
   weak enjoyment) ....
3. Fair enjoyment (some signs of
   pleasure, little joy) ....
4. Mild enjoyment (pleasure is restrained,
   somewhat active) ....
5. Extreme enjoyment (zest or relish for
   an activity) ....

Role Structure

1. Clear pupil role (operation of activity
   is smooth, effective) ....
2. Uncertain pupil role (some confusion
   is present in role) ....
3. Confused pupil role (activity dis-
   jointed, air of confusion) ....

Emotion of Leader

1. Aggressive (openly hostile—sarcastic,
   etc., toward pupils) ....
2. Irritable (tone or irritability in dealing
   with pupils) ....
3. Toleration (teacher is straining to
   keep from irritability) ....
4. Pleasant-reserved (friendly and reserved
   with depth of contact) ....
5. Warm and sympathetic (sympathetic,
   "good fellow" relations) ....

Teacher Orders or Suggestions

1. Mandatory (peremptory orders, to
   be obeyed at once) ....
2. Compliance expected (compliance
   in important matters) ....

3. Avoids coercion (mainly uses non-
   coercive suggestions) . . . .
4. Optional (commands used in
   emergencies only) . . . .

Physical Tension of Group

1. Restless (tension as exhibited in nervous
   habits) ; Keyed-up (extreme restless-
   ness—tense expressions) . . . .
2. Mildly relaxed (slight atmosphere
   of tension) . . . .
3. Median relaxation (some normal signs
   of tension) . . . .
4. Very relaxed (physically and psychologi-
   cally taking it easy) . . . .

Emotion of Pupil Group

1. Strained, fearful (element of fear
   of teacher) ; Irritable, dislike
   (symptoms of irritability and dislike) ;
   Hostile (aggression) . . . .
2. Businesslike, non-expressive (respectful,
   little or no expression) . . . .
3. Pleasant, respectful (pleasant and respectful
   toward teacher) . . . .
4. Friendly, spontaneous (teacher is
   spontaneous—one of group) . . . .
5. Confiding, intimate (close attach-
   ment approaching admiration) . . . .

□

APPENDIX B

MODIFICATION OF BALES'
INTERACTION PROCESS ANALYSIS
FOR TEACHERS

Categories used in observation:

A.	*Positive reactions*	1	Shows solidarity, raises others' status, gives help, reward
		2	Shows tension release, jokes, laughs, shows satisfaction
		3	Agrees, shows passive acceptance, understands, concurs, complies
B.	*Attempted answers*	4	Gives suggestion, direction, implying autonomy for other
		5	Gives opinion, evaluation, analysis, expresses feeling, wish
		6	Gives orientation, information, repeats, clarifies, confirms
C.	*Questions*	7	Asks for orientation, information, repetition, confirmation

SOURCE: Adapted from R. F. Bales, *Interaction Process Analysis* (Cambridge, Mass.: Addison-Wesley, 1950), p. 59.

	8	Asks for opinion, evaluation, analysis, expression of feeling
	9	Asks for suggestions, direction, possible ways of actions
D. *Negative reactions*	10	Disagrees, shows passive rejection, formality, withholds help
	11	Shows tension, asks for help, withdraws out of field
	12	Shows antagonism, deflates others' status, defends or asserts self

After learning code so that it can be used without hesitation, someone sits in the back of the room and employs it on a teacher-pupil interaction graph, during periods of class discussion. A chart, with names of pupils somewhat as follows, may be devised:

Teacher   C–7   B–6   C–8   B–4
                   \   /   \   /   \   /   \
Mary S.   D–11   D–12
                                              \   /
Joe J.   A–1   A–3
                                                                \
Harold K.   A–2

Peter V.

Jeanne L.

   Etc.

As this chart was marked, what opinion do you get about the discussion? Was it teacher- or pupil-dominated? What is Mary S. like today? Joe J.? Are all participating?

□

APPENDIX C

DIMENSIONS
OF TEACHER LEADERSHIP

How would *your* pupils answer the following questions? The first seven items indicate the extent to which the teacher is seen by pupils as task oriented. The next nine questions deal with the dimension of authoritarianism; the final eleven items deal with the expressive dimension.

Task Dimension of the Teacher's Classroom Behavior

Are you given new work in arithmetic before you are able to get the right answers to the old work?

I am not given new kinds of arithmetic until I can do the old kind correctly.

I am sometimes given new kinds of arithmetic before I can do the old kind.

I am almost always given a new kind of arithmetic before I can do the old kind.

Does the teacher see to it that you complete all of the written assignments or not?

Makes sure we complete practically all written assignments.

Sometimes makes sure we complete written assignments.

Hardly ever makes sure we complete written assignments.

SOURCE: C. W. Gordon and L. M. Adler, *Dimensions of Teacher Leadership in Classroom Social Systems* (Final Report, Cooperative Research Project 1084) (Los Angeles: University of California, 1963) , pp. 117–25.

Does this teacher go over a day's work with you again before going on to the next lesson, or do you go on without reviewing?

Reviews every lesson (either at the end or the beginning) .
Reviews most lessons.
Reviews some lessons but not regularly.
Hardly ever reviews lessons.

What does this teacher most often do when he is teaching the class something new and the pupils don't understand?

Tries to explain it again another way.
Gives the same explanation over again.
Moves on to something else even though we don't understand.

How often are you required to show the teacher (by writing or telling the answer to a question or a problem) that you understand what is being taught?

Several times every day.
Once every day.
Almost every day.
Several times a week.
Never.

When you have learned a certain kind of arithmetic, do you use it over again during the year or stop using it after you have taken up a different kind of problem?

Keep using a kind of arithmetic over and over again.
Keep using a kind of arithmetic sometimes after we have taken up a new kind.
Hardly ever use an old kind of arithmetic after we take up a new kind.

How are your papers usually corrected?

I don't know, papers aren't returned.
A grade or comment for the whole paper is given but all mistakes are not marked.
All mistakes are marked.
All mistakes are marked and we are shown how the work is wrong.

Authority Dimension of the Teacher's Classroom Behavior

Do pupils have to get permission to leave their seats in this class or not?

> We can never leave our seats without getting permission.
>
> We can leave our seats without permission if we follow certain rules.
>
> We can leave our seats without getting permission almost any time.

How much instruction does the teacher give a social studies committee?

> We never have social studies committees.
>
> The teacher tells the committee exactly *what* to do and *how* to do it.
>
> The teacher tells the committee *what* to do, but lets it decide *how* to do it.
>
> The teacher leaves almost everything up to the committee.

When the class starts a new social studies unit, who plans how you will do the work?

> We do it the way the teacher plans it.
>
> The teacher and the pupils plan it together.
>
> The teacher expects the pupils to work out a plan, but he gives advice if we ask him.
>
> The plan is entirely up to the pupils.

When the teacher has made up his mind about something, has he ever changed it when the pupils objected?

> Hardly ever.
>
> A few times when the pupils had good reasons.
>
> Quite often, whether the pupils had good reason or not.
>
> Practically every time anyone objected.

What does the teacher do when he and the pupils disagree about some idea in social studies?

> Doesn't encourage pupils to express opinions.
>
> Lets pupils express their opinions but only sees his side.
>
> Lets pupils express their opinions and we look at both sides.

When the teacher asks pupils to do something they do not want to do, does he or does he not explain why they have to do it?

He almost always explains why.
He sometimes explains why.
He hardly ever explains why.

How often would you say this teacher has changed assignments this year because the pupils objected to them?

Hardly ever.
A few times when the pupils had good reasons.
Quite often, whether the pupils had good reasons or not.
Practically every time anyone objected.

After you *know what* you are going to do in this class, who usually decides *how* you are going to do it?

The teacher decides and tells us.
The teacher listens to our ideas about it, but he decides.
The teacher talks it over with us, and helps us decide.
The teacher lets us decide.

How many committees have you been on this year in this class?

None.
One or two.
Three.
Four.
Five or more.

Expressive Dimension of the Teacher's Classroom Behavior

Does this teacher show that he wants to make the work interesting for the pupils or does he not?

Almost always interesting.
Sometimes interesting.
Not very interesting.
Practically never interesting.

Does the teacher ask you questions in a way which makes you nervous and uncomfortable about answering them, or does he ask you questions in a kind way?

　Just about always kind.
　Often kind, but occasionally makes me uncomfortable.
　Often makes me feel nervous and uncomfortable, but not always.
　Just about always makes me nervous and uncomfortable.

Does this teacher show that he dislikes pupils in the class or not?

　Shows dislike for none of the pupils.
　Shows dislike for a few pupils.
　Shows dislike for some pupils.
　Shows dislike for most pupils.
　Shows dislike for everyone in the class.

Does this teacher try to make the class enjoyable for the pupils or not?

　Almost always tries to make the class enjoyable.
　Sometimes tries to make the class enjoyable.
　Practically never tries to make the class enjoyable.

Does this teacher show that he likes pupils in this class or not?

　Shows he likes all pupils.
　Shows he likes most pupils.
　Shows he likes some pupils.
　Shows he likes just a few pupils.
　Shows liking for none of the pupils.

Is this teacher usually fair or usually unfair when he decides things about pupils?

　He is always fair.
　He is usually fair.
　He is fair to most pupils; a few are treated better; a few are treated worse.
　He is unfair to most pupils.

Does this teacher help you with the work or let you get it for yourself?

> I hardly get any help.
>
> I get some help but not as much as I need.
>
> I get all the help I need.

Does the teacher make sure you learn the facts or is he more interested in how pupils feel about things?

> Shows little or no concern about the facts or how we feel.
>
> Just makes sure we learn the facts.
>
> Makes sure we learn the facts but is sometimes interested in our feelings.
>
> More interested in our feelings than in our learning the facts.

Does this teacher show that he will help you with school work and also help you with anything else you would like to talk to him about?

> Neither with school work nor anything else.
>
> Without school work but nothing else.
>
> More with school work than other things.
>
> About the same with school work and other things.
>
> More with other things than school work.

Does this teacher give you credit for how well you do on your papers and tests or does he give you credit for trying and showing improvement?

> Only for how well I do on papers and tests.
>
> For how well I do on papers and tests and for trying and showing improvement.
>
> For trying and improving whether I do well on papers and tests or not.

In this class are you supposed to use the teacher's ideas, the ideas in the book, or your own ideas?

> We are supposed to use our own ideas *more than* the teacher's or those in the books.
>
> We are supposed to use the teacher's ideas, the ideas in the books, and our own ideas.
>
> We are only supposed to use the teacher's ideas and the ideas in the books.

□

APPENDIX D

1. *Introductory information*

   Child's name   Age
   Address   Reason for study
   Parents' names   Person making study
   Sex   Date

2. *Physical status*

   Medical report
   Description of child by teacher; any symptoms
   School health and attendance record
   Information from family
   Other information (child, school nurse, and so forth)

3. *Intellectual abilities and cultural background*

   Standardized ability test scores
   Abilities noted by teacher
   Special talents, hobbies, interests, background (for example,
     art, music, mechanics, drama, speech, travel)

4. *Academic and school-related achievement*

Cumulative record data
Present school marks
Standardized achievement-test results
Teacher remarks
Extraclass activities, honors, awards, projects, clubs
Job opportunities and experiences, community activities
(paper route, 4-H Club, Little League, church, Scouts,
and so forth)

5. *Social adjustment*

Relations with family, peers, teachers, siblings
Sociometric data
Parent conferences, remarks of school personnel
Positive character attributes, disciplinary record

6. *Other information*

School psychologist's report (pertinent information only)
Social worker's report (pertinent information only)
Other data (for example, remedial help, speech therapy)

7. *Interpretation*

Summary of data
Hypotheses
Tentative conclusions
Recommendations

8. *Follow-up information*

Techniques tried
Results, changes in behavior, adjustment, and so forth
Recommendations for future treatment

□

APPENDIX E

GUIDING PRINCIPLES
ON EMOTIONAL
AND MENTAL HEALTH

In the succeeding statements some principles are suggested in the following areas: physical environment, school personnel, school curriculum, educational methods and practices, and home, school and community relationships. In addition a number of questions are listed for your consideration with the specific objective of helping you to determine what would be involved in making practical application of these principles. You may be able to raise other questions in relation to your local situation.

I. Area of Physical Environment

PRINCIPLES

The physical environment of the school affects the physical and emotional comfort and well-being of the children and the school personnel. This influences how well the school attains its varied and broad objectives.

SOURCE: *Suggested Guiding Principles on Emotional and Mental Health in the School* (Madison: Wisconsin State School Health Council, 1956).

QUESTIONS

1. What can your school do to see that buildings and grounds contribute to physical and emotional comfort, safety and well-being of all of the children and school personnel?
2. What persons in your school and the community could best be involved in making an inventory of buildings and grounds so that proper account can be taken of such aspects as safety, comfort, aesthetics, flexibility, etc.?
3. What ways are there to determine how the teachers, the pupils, the parents, and the community feel about the existing conditions of the school physical environment? In what ways can they jointly secure improvement based on their feelings?

II. *Area of School Personnel*

PRINCIPLES

All school personnel (administrators, supervisors, teachers, custodians, cooks, lunch room managers, bus drivers) have a vital influence on the attainment of the broad and varied objectives of both education and health. Such personnel contribute best to these objectives when the following is true:

School personnel have a sound knowledge of growing and developing human beings, their behavior, and their ways of learning. This would, of course, include the ability of such personnel to apply the same understanding to themselves.

Teachers have had adequate training in subject matter and the skills involved in teaching.

The school administration understands how to encourage and guide teachers to grow personally, professionally, and socially in order that their increased skills and satisfactions may be reflected in the quality of their teaching.

The school board and the community provide an atmosphere in which the teachers and administrators are enabled to function at their best. This atmosphere would involve practical policies built around understanding and respect for the needs of school personnel as individuals.

QUESTIONS

1. What are some of the ways in which teachers as well as other professional and non-professional personnel can be helped to increase their knowledge and understanding of child growth and development?
2. What criteria can the administrator use in selecting well qualified and well adjusted school personnel especially in light of current personnel shortages?
3. How can the school program be adjusted to meet the needs of teachers which influence the learning and adjustment of children? How can these needs be defined by the school administrator?

III. *Area of School Curriculum*

It is generally acknowledged that the school curriculum consists of all the learning experiences the pupil has under school auspices. This would include not only the more organized aspects of classroom learning but also the informal learning which goes on both in the classroom and elsewhere in the school and through which boys and girls gain experience, learn important attitudes, social skills and ways of behaving.

PRINCIPLES

A curriculum which will insure the maximum effective learning and adjustment of all pupils would be based on the following principles:

Every subject matter area including the co-curricular program and all experiences in the school day is significant and can be used to contribute to improved personnel attitudes and group relationships.

The curriculum should be set up in recognition of the fact that the child learns as a "total" or "whole" person.

There must be recognition that no two children or their needs are alike: thus these individual differences determine the flexibility of the curriculum, the variability of content of curriculum and the adaptability of standards and achievement goals.

While being careful to take into account these individual differences, it is at the same time vital to base the curriculum on the known facts about developmental characteristics of age maturity or grade groups.

The curriculum should be built on the concept that education is life and, therefore, the content of the curriculum will be realistically geared to the interests and to the varying needs of children today, as well as with a view to preparations for the future. This would include not only basic skills but their appropriate integration in vocational, recreational, family, and community life education.

QUESTIONS

1. In what ways do the various subject matter areas and co-curricular activities in your school curriculum contribute to individual and group adjustment of pupils?
2. Does an evaluation of your curriculum give evidence that it takes into account the concept that the child learns as a "whole" person? What are the indicators that any given part of the curriculum is not geared to this concept?
3. What provision does your curriculum make for a child with special needs as:

   a. The gifted child?
   b. The slow learner?
   c. The child with physical or sensory defects?
   d. The emotionally unadjusted?
   e. Special academic disabilities?

4. How can these curricula be set up so that these children with special needs are not set apart and unduly stigmatized?
5. Is the curriculum geared to the known facts of child development at the different ages or grade levels?

For example:

    a. Is reading instruction initiated at the appropriate point in terms of known facts about the requisite maturations of children who are ready for reading?

    b. Is there planned progression in the physical education program taking into consideration such factors as age, sex, physical condition, ability, and interest?

    c. Is the program of competitive interscholastic sports introduced at an age level that is appropriate in terms of the child's maturation?

    d. Is there a planned progression in the presentation of family life education and preparation for marriage, from kindergarten through 12th grade based on the stages of maturation of pupils?

6. Has the curriculum taken into consideration all facets of life preparation, such as family living, preparation for citizenship, work experience, vocational choice and college preparation?

7. Does the curriculum give continuous opportunity to relate all knowledge to an understanding of *self* and other people? Do you have a course or unit of study explicitly relating to self-understanding and providing opportunities for free group discussion?

8. Does the curriculum enable the child to learn by doing?

9. What are the effects of non-participation or of restricted participation in co-curricular activities? What are the effects of excessive participation in co-curricular programs?

IV. Area of Educational Methods, Practices and Policies

Educational concepts relating to the child's emotional health become effective to the extent that educational methods, practices and policies are in harmony with these concepts. Such methods, practices and policies encompass more than classroom techniques. They also include broader aspects of school program planning and policies such as: staff development, grading and promotional policies, pupil groupings, teacher loads, supervisory methods and practices, and extended school services.

PRINCIPLES

The educational methods, practices and policies of a school should derive from the most authoritative facts about child development and the nature of the teaching-learning process. Since much of current educational methods and practices originated before this relatively new knowledge about child development was readily available to educators, most schools are confronted with the need for making some basic modifications. These modifications cannot be brought about without acquisition of this knowledge by all school staff through a planned program of in-service training and other forms of staff development.

In order to be most effective, the methods of teaching these concepts of child development and the teaching-learning process must in themselves illustrate sound concepts of the teaching-learning process in practice. The classroom teacher must then, in turn, have the opportunity to try out and to experience the application of these theories and teaching methods in her own classroom, and must be helped to be secure in her right to experiment.

Democratic methods in supervisory and administrative relationships are essential in putting into practice these concepts of emotional health and child development.

Experimentation and adaptation of school program, methods and policies implies that there must be adequate communication, understanding and support from the school board, parents and citizens of the community.

QUESTIONS

1. How can your school establish a program or in-service training to promote better understanding of emotional health? In what ways can your school administrators and school board promote such programs? In what ways can the normal resistance to new ideas be met?
2. Where and how may resource materials relating to child development be obtained? How can your school staff screen

the mass of materials available to select that which is sound and most suitable for your needs? How can you make such a professional library available and promote its effective use by all staff?

3. What role should parents and students play in determining school practices and policies?

4. In what aspects of school practice and policy is there likely to be sharp conflict between principles of child development and practical considerations? To what extent are these practical considerations modifiable? Can carefully considered experimentation contribute to a solution of the problem posed by such conflict?

5. How can each individual on the school staff evaluate his own relationship with supervisors and with persons supervised in terms of accepted principles of democratic practices in supervisor-supervisee relationships?

6. How can the varying points of view of educators, parents and pupils as to grading and promotional policies be resolved in light of sound principles of child development and emotional health?

7. What are the implications of your current school practices in pupil grouping for the emotional health of pupils?

8. What are the criteria for determining what constitutes a suitable teaching load in terms of:

   a. Grade level?
   b. The given teacher?
   c. Size and make-up of the class?
   d. Special assignments and responsibilities given to the teacher?

9. Are reading education methods in your school uniformly consistent with accepted principles of child development? How early can reading disabilities be detected? By what methods? What programs can be instituted to prevent progressively more serious adjustment difficulties growing out of a reading difficulty?

10. In what ways could extended school services contribute to promotion of emotional health of children? Recreational programs after school hours? School camping? Twelve

months employment of certain school staff for individual and group child study and service?

V. Area of School, Home, Church and Community Relationships

PRINCIPLES

The home, school, church, and community are all members of the team concerned with the child's life adjustment and experience. This team must provide at least the essentials of the child's needs for food, shelter and clothing, physical protection, affection, emotional security, spiritual guidance and stimulating growth experience.

Each of these (home, school, church, community) has a specialized responsibility for meeting these basic needs of children. It is vital that there be good communication and mutual understanding among these four because of possible overlapping, gaps or omissions and the fact that all influence the same child.

The school is in an advantageous position to detect these situations where children may require help that will prevent difficulties, or require special services that will ameliorate more serious problems. The school can do this because of its daily contact with pupils over a period of years, because of its personnel, professionally trained in the understanding of children's needs, and because teachers have the opportunity to observe all children. With this knowledge the school should accept responsibility for bringing together the home and the appropriate community social service in order to provide in a coordinated way for the children's needs. While most school teachers are alert to needs of children in their classroom, they may need help in carrying out their strategic responsibilities.

QUESTIONS

1. How can the school, the home, the church, and the community acquire a common body of knowledge and understanding about emotional health and child development? How can they share in the planning and conducting of child-study programs? How can they apply such understanding in

planning a harmonious program of experiences for the child in all his activities and living in his home, school, church, and community?

2. How can home, school, and community work together to make the initial transition from home to school a more positive experience for all children?

3. Can parents and other persons outside the school be drawn into some direct educational activities in the school? How can school personnel be drawn directly into appropriate programs for children outside the school?

4. How are responsibilities for individual and group guidance and counseling in your school shared by teachers, administrators, supervisors, and special services personnel? What is expected of the home-room program? How is it geared into the total guidance services program of your school?

5. What portion of the teacher's workday is reserved for pupil counseling, guidance, and for parent-teacher conferences? What portion of principal or supervisor's time for this purpose? How can teacher loads and schedules be arranged to allow more time for guidance and counseling?

6. On what aspects of the guidance and counseling program do teachers feel that they need help? How could such help be provided?

7. In light of the school's strategic opportunities to further prevention through early detection of problems, the following questions will suggest ways in which the school may carry out this function in conjunction with the home and the community, and help define the particular role of special services in this relationship:

   a. What is the function of a psychologist in the school setting? A social worker? A psychiatrist? If such special services are not available in your school, can they be obtained as needed from other local community agencies? From colleges or universities? From state agencies?

   b. How does your school do early case finding to identify those children with problems of adjustment requiring special help? At what grade level can such early identification be most helpful to the child? Are teacher observations alone enough to do an effective job of early identification? What systematic methods of screening are available to help the teacher?

c. Once identified, how and to whom are children with incipient adjustment problems referred for special help which may be needed?

d. How do your county child welfare worker, juvenile probation officer, county officer, county welfare department, juvenile court and law enforcement agencies serve the needs of children which may be discovered by the school? How could they serve these needs more effectively? What is the function of a school social worker in relation to these community services?

e. If there is a child guidance clinic in your community, how are referrals made by your school? How are teachers involved in treatment and follow-up? If no guidance clinic service is available, is such service needed in your community? How can it be provided? What is the function of a school social worker in relation to a community child guidance clinic?

f. If resources for special help are not available in the school or in the community, what can teachers do to try to provide the help needed for the child? What volunteer resources for help are available in the community?

g. How can your school most effectively involve parents in the school-home-community relationship? Are teachers or other school personnel given released time from regular classroom or administrative duties for parent-teacher conferences? How can parents participate in planning for most effective use and scheduling of parent-teacher conferences? How does a school social worker participate in school-home relationships? In the absence of a school social worker, how can the school teacher learn about home conditions of children in her classroom?

8. In what ways can the insights gained from the study of special problems of children be used jointly by school, church, home, and community to the advantage of all children?

Index

Abelson, R., 116
Abramovitz, A. B., 4, 14n., 15, 292, 453
Abramowitz, J., 154, 155
absentee rate, 25
acceleration, 263
achievement
  and curricular measures, 146–9
  and grouping policy, 256–8
  high, 97, 133–4, 144–5
  and identification of student, 153
  implications of, 144–5
  low, 97, 134, 144–57 passim
  and mental health, 131–57
  and motivation, 176–8
  over-, 25, 134–6
  and personality, 138–45
  prediction of, 132–8
  and self-attitudes, 355–6
  and socioeconomic status, 176–7
  and stress, 269–70
  see also underachievement
achievement orientation, 76, 77
Adams, G. S., 261
adequacy, feeling of, 281–2
adjustment and stress, 270–1
Adler, L. M., 81, 465n.
Ager, E., 104
aggressive behavior, 109–10, 165, 209
  dealing with, 122–3
  group hostility and, 125–7
  and sex-role confusion, 381, 382

agriculture as subject, 239
Allen, G. M., 123
Allinsmith, W., 22n., 406
Allport, Gordon W., 11, 12, 13, 19
Alpert, R., 265
Alves, G. J., 142
ambivalence, 201
American Psychological Association, 427
Amidon, E. J., 71–3
Amrine, M., 291
Anderson, R. C., 69–71
anxiety, 99, 100, 187, 189, 192, 195–7, 219–20, 254–5
  and changing behavior, 322–4
  conflict, frustration, and, 198–9
  dealing with, 217–9
  definition of, 197–8
  and failure, 354
  results of, 203–7
Ashby, N., 276
assessment
  and remediation, 318–21
  of self-concept, 346–9
Atkinson, J. W., 177
attention seeking, 317–8, 331–2
Ausubel, D. P., 414
autism, 208
autonomic nervous system, 188
autonomy, 11, 359, 375, 381
Ayllon, T., 429

Baer, D. M., 118
Bales, R. F., 90, 463n.
Bandura, A., 103, 111, 186, 381, 429
Banham-Bridges, K. M., 191
Barr, A. S., 33–4
Barron, F., 244–5
Bass, B. M., 74, 84
Bayley, M., 153
Bayley, N., 381
becoming, concept of, 13, 19
behavior, pupil
    adequate, introducing, 333–41
    change in, 321–8
    family influences on, 375–82
    goal-directed, 197
    historical versus contemporary fac-
        tors in, 293–4
    inadequate, reduction of, 328–33
    motivation and, 160–3
    and remediation, 317–41 passim
    and self-concept, 342–70 passim
    "shaping," 327, 339–40
    specific, need to discern, 294–7, 322,
        374
    see also pupils
behavioristic approach, 320
Beim, J., 369
Bell, M., 257
Bernard, V. S., 51, 453
Biber, Barbara, 11–2, 51, 225, 453
biological drives, 168–9, 170
Blackboard Jungle, The, 107
Bledsoe, J. C., 139, 355
Block, J., 357
Blommers, P., 260–1
Bloom, B. S., 245, 261
"body image," 354–5, 408
Boll, E. S., 376
Bosdell, B. J., 150–1
Bossard, J. H. S., 270, 376
Bower, E. M., 299, 304, 424, 441
Bowman, B. H., 139, 141
Boyd, G. R., 139
brain injury, 407, 408
Brandt, R. M., 453
Brodie, T. A., 384–5, 398
Broen, W., 206
broken-home conditions, 380–1
Bronfenbrenner, U., 270
Brookover, W. B., 142, 269
Bruce, P., 357
Buchmueller, A. D., 452
Burnham, E., 4, 292, 453
Burton, R. V., 381
Butterfield, W. H., 321

California Psychological Inventory
    test, 140
California State Department of Edu-
    cation, 424
Camp, D., 427, 431
Cannon, W. B., 188
Caplan, G., 406
Carter, R. S., 144
Catholic Social Welfare Bureau, 435
Cattell, R. B., 37
"causal" approach, 240–2, 363
children
    creative, 244–5
    family influences on, 375–82
    and home-school relations, 373–5
    as individuals, 285–370 passim
    see also pupils
Children and Adolescents, 268
Children's Bureau, 444
child study
    criteria for, 291–9
    illustration of, 299–316
    and individual child, 285–370
    interpretation of data in, 311–6
    and remedial treatment, 314–41
    report on, 471–2
    and self theory, 342–70
    teacher capabilities in, 296–9
Chodorkoff, B., 349
Christensen, C. M., 75
CIBA Pharmaceutical Company, 9
Clancy, N., 413
classroom
    control of, 94–128
    emotions in, 191–2
    morale of, 63–91 passim, 95–6
    social climate of, 89–90
    see also control, classroom
"clinical sensitivity," 387–8
Clopton, W. S., 291
Coffield, W. H., 260–1
Cogan, M. L., 75
Coleman, J. C., 277–9
Combs, A. W., 15, 19, 343, 349
communication, 270
    in groups, 86
    nonverbal, 40–1
    teacher-pupil, 39–42
communication skills, 235–8
communities
    mental-health programs in, 451–3
    and school, home, church relations,
        480–2
compensation, definition of, 210
"competency motive," 349

conditioning, 111–20 *passim*
  counter-, 332–3
  of emotions, 189–91
conflict, 195
  anxiety, frustration, and, 198–9
  approach-avoidant, 201–2
  dealing with, 215–7
  definition of, 197
  double-approach, 201, 215–6
  results of, 201–3
conforming pupil personality, 79
conformity, 20, 21, 99, 100, 164
"congruence" (Rogers), 41–2, 359
control, classroom
  and learning theory, 111–4
  methods of, 98–101, 114–28 *passim*
  and pupil personality, 96–101, 108–10
  and reasons for misbehavior, 101–11
  and teacher personality, 110–1
Co-operative Program, 155
Council on Alcoholism, 435
counseling techniques, 150–1, 430–2
counseling workers, 430–2
counterconditioning, 332–3
course content
  and mental health, 222–49 *passim*
  need for improvement of, 226–7
Cox, F. N., 381
Crandall, V. J., 175
creativity
  in children, 244–5
  definition of, 243–4
  fostering of, 245–7
Crescimbeni, J., 47
crime, incidence of, 94
criminologists, 230
cultural deprivation, 155, 307, 412
cultural norms, 9–10, 246
Cunningham, R., 304
curricula
  and achievement, 146–9
  and mental health, 222–49 *passim*
    475–7
  and stress, 254–67
Cutler, R. L., 453

D'Andrade, R. G., 177
defense mechanisms, 195, 202, 203, 207–
  13, 318; *see also specific defenses*
deficiencies
  cultural, 412
  educational, 411
delinquency, 4, 94, 322
departmentalization, 146

diagnosis, 406–7
  by school psychologists, 427–30
  signals used in, 418–21
Diller, L., 354
Dimond, S. W., 262
discipline, school, 94–128 *passim; see
  also* control, classroom
discrimination in pupil behavior, 328–
  30
displacement, 165, 203
  definition of, 210
"disturbed" children in special classes,
  259–60
Dittmann, A. T., 41
Dollard, J., 103
Doris, J., 207
Dreikurs, Rudolph, 17, 108–9, 110, 111,
  118, 376, 378
Drews, E., 143, 256–7
drives, 168–9, 170
dropout problem, 153–6, 450

Eber, H. W., 37
Edison, Thomas, 15
Edwards, A. L., 30
Edwards Personal Preference Schedule,
  30
ego strength, 99
Einstein, Albert, 15, 19
Ekstrom, R. B., 257
elementary-level teaching, 230–1
Elementary–Secondary Education Acts,
  267, 443
Elmott, C. D., 384
emotional adjustment and achievement, 139–40
emotional disturbance, 410–1; *see also*
  mental health
emotions
  in the classroom, 191–2
  conditioning of, 189–91
  dealing with, 277–81
  motivation and, 160–92 *passim*
  role of, 187–90
"empathy," 388
environment, 171
  change of, 366
  child's ability to manipulate, 325–8
  mastery of, 11
  physical, 473–4
escapism, 208
Esteem for the Least Preferred Co-
  Worker (LPC), 73–4
ethics of child study, 291–4

evaluative practices, 263–4
  in marking and grading, 18
  and testing problems, 264–5
extinction, 330–2, 429
extracurricular activities, 240
extroverts, 98

failure and self-attitude, 354
families
  overacceptant, 377–8
  underacceptant, 378
  see also parents
fantasy, 208
  definition of, 211
Farquhar, W. W., 139
Farwell, G. F., 386
fear, 255–6, 330–1; see also anxiety
fearful teacher personality, 78–9
Feldhusen, J. F., 104
Ferster, C. W., 320
Festinger, L., 320
Fey, W. F., 349
Fiedler, F. E., 73–4
fine arts as subject, 232–4
Flanders, N. A., 71–3, 83
Frankel, E., 139
Franks, C. W., 320
Franseth, J., 258
French, W., 22
Freud, Sigmund, 101–2, 174, 211, 215
Friedenberg, E. A., 121
frustration, 195–7, 219–20
  anxiety, conflict, and, 198–9
  dealing with, 213–5
  definition of, 197
  results of, 199–201
frustration tolerance, teaching of, 126–
  7, 213–5
Frymier, J. R., 271

Ganzer, V., 207
Gardner, J. E., 25
Garrison, K. C., 139, 355
Georgiady, N. P., 386
Gewirtz, J. L., 118
Gilbert, G. M., 413
Gilmore, L., 248
Goertzel, M., 14n.
Goertzel, V., 14n.
Goethals, G. W., 22n., 406
Goodstein, L. D., 139
Gordon, C. W., 81, 465n.
Gottlieb, D., 269
Gough, H. C., 30
Graff, F. A., 141

Gray, S. W., 22, 427, 430
"Great Society," 267
Gronlund, N. E., 304
Gross, M. L., 291
group
  activities of, 247–8
  assessing morale of, 89–91
  characteristics of, 73–4
  face-to-face, 84
  hostility of, 125–7
  improving morale of, 84–91
  and leadership modes, 73–4
  needs of, 85–7
  and negative influences, 87–9
grouping policies, 18, 21
  and achievement, 256–8
  "homogeneous," 256–8
  and personality variables, 258–9
  recommended, 259–60
guidance workers, 430–2
Guilford, J. P., 245, 247
guilt, 99, 100, 191, 202

Haber, R., 265
Haines, A. C., 51
Hall, C. S., 344
handicaps, 407, 408–13 passim
Hanlon, T. E., 357
Hatfield, A. B., 51
Havemann, Ernest, 13
Hawkins, A. S., 242
"Hawthorne effect," 153
Head Start programs, 267, 270, 307, 412
Health, Education and Welfare, U.S.
  Department of, 443
health, emotional (or "mental"), see
  mental health
health, physical, 6, 8–9, 310, 312–3
  and self-attitude, 354–5
Heil, L. M., 77–81
Hicks, F. R., 42
Higher Horizons Program, 155
Hoffman, M. L., 99
Hollister, W. G., 442
Holt, J., 254–5, 279, 282, 287, 332
home economics as subject, 239
home-school conferences
  and agreement on action, 398–9
  assumptions of, 382–4
  and barriers to cooperation, 390–1
  evaluation of, 400–2
  and involving child, 399–400
  and parent-teacher communication,
    387–90, 391–8
  planning for, 384–7
  see also parents

homework, 275–6
Horowitz, F., 207
Horwitz, M., 125, 126
hostility, 348
  group, 125–7
Hoyt, D. P., 139
Hull, C. L., 203
Hunnicutt, C. W., 98
Hunter, E. C., 298

identification, 103–4, 115, 131, 335–6
  cross-sex, 381
  definition of, 209
  role, 381–2
Impellizzeri, I. H., 153
in-groups, 271
in-service education, 53–7
insulation, definition of, 211
intelligence and self-attitudes, 355–6
intelligence test, 132
Interaction Process Analysis (Bales),
  90, 463–4
interviews, 432
introjection, definition of, 209
introverts, 98–9

Jacubzak, L., 116
Jahoda, Marie, 11
Jewish Family and Children's Service,
  435
Jones, M. C., 355
Juneau, Wisconsin, Common School,
  400

Kagan, J., 379
Kahl, J. A., 176
Kaluger, G., 259
Kaplan, L., 42, 270
Kearney, N. C., 22
Keller, Helen, 339–40
Keys, N., 206
Klausmeier, H. J., 248
Kline, C. L., 420
Kolb, D. A., 176
Krugman, M., 153

Lambert, N. M., 442–3
Landy, E., 430
Larson, E. A., 30, 51
Lawrence, M. M., 452
Lazarus, R. S., 22
learning activities and mental health,
  240–9

learning theory (and principles), 111–
  4, 429–30
  and individual pupils, 317–41
Lebo, D., 355
Lepine, L., 349
Lesser, G., 116
"level of aspiration" (LOA), 174–6, 177
Lewin, K., 82, 85, 320–1
Lighthall, F. F., 207
Lindsey, M., 50
Lindsley, O. R., 335, 429
Lindzey, G., 344
Lippitt, Ronald O., 71n., 82
Lipsitt, L. P., 357
Long Beach, California, Public Schools'
  Handbook for Parent Conferences,
  385
Loughary, J. W., 384–5
Lovaas, O. I., 237
lower class, 268–70
Lundy, R., 352
Lutheran Welfare Society, 435

McCandless, B., 268–9, 357, 380
McClelland, D. C., 176, 177, 178
McCord, J., 381
McCuen, J. T., 146
McGuire, W. J., 321
McKenney, J. W., 245
Mahone, C. H., 178
"maladjustment," 196–7, 350, 421–2
Mammarella, R. J., 47
Manifest Anxiety Scale, 205
marking and grading practices, 18, 265–
  7
Martin, R., 259
masculinity, 381
Maslow, Abraham H., 16, 19–21, 63,
  170–1, 245, 348
mass media, 455
mathematics as subject, 238
Matthews, R. A., 43
measurement, 263
Medley, D. M., 75
Meeks, A. R., 151
Menninger, K. A., 13, 14
Menninger, W. C., 46
Mental Abilities Test, 308–10
mental health
  and classroom control, 94–128
  and course content, 222–49
  and cultural norms, 9–10
  definitions of, 7–10
  as educational concern, 3–7, 23–5
  and emotions, 160–92 passim
  and extracurricular activities, 240

mental health (*cont.*)
  guiding principles on, 473–82
  and individual pupil, 285–370
  and motives, 163–8
  and needs of children, 15–21
  versus physical health, 8–9
  poor, causes of, 46–50
  poor, incidence of, 6–7, 42
  poor, symptoms of, 42–6
  and referrals, 404–36
  and school achievement, 131–57
  school goals and, 22–3
  school roles in, 22–7
  and self-concept, 356–8
  of teacher, 38–60 *passim*
  teacher roles and, 26–7
  and teaching method, 222–49
mental-health agencies, 24
Mental Health Association, 435
mental-health programs, 438
  community, 451–3
  school, 439–51
Michael, J., 429
middle class, 268, 270
Miller, N. E., 103, 197, 201, 202
Minneapolis Public Schools, 432
minority groups, 226, 352
Mitchell, J. V., 36–7
Mitzel, H. E., 75
models (and modeling), 103–4, 131, 318, 335–6
  sex role, 273
morale, classroom, 63–91 *passim*
  and discipline, 95–6
Morgan, H. W., 141
Morrow, W., 143
Moss, H. S., 379
motives (and motivation)
  achievement, 141, 176–8
  affiliation, 141
  and behavior, 160–3
  conflicting, 165–8
  and emotion, 160–92
  and group morale, 85
  growth-directed versus maintenance-directed, 170–2
  healthy versus unhealthy, 163–5
  as a hierarchy, 170–2
  nature of, 168–74
  of pupils, 16–21, 120–1, 160–92, 318
  and school practices, 174–87
  of teachers, 36, 48–9
  and teacher traits, 178–81
  unclear, 165
  see also needs, children's; needs, group; needs, teachers'
Mullen, F., 427

Murray, H. A., 15, 30
music as subject, 239
Mussen, P. H., 355
Muuss, R. E., 225, 240

National Association for Mental Health, 6, 7, 12, 248
National Council of Independent Schools, 448–50
National Education Association, 55, 274
National Institute of Mental Health, 7, 443–4
needs, children's, 15, 63
  affectional, 17–8
  effects of not satisfying, 18–9
  growth-directed, 19–21
  maintenance-directed, 16–9
  physiological, 16
  safety, 17
  status, 18
needs, group, 85–7
needs, teachers', 58
Neill, A. S., 67–8
neurosis, 4, 189, 355, 357, 442
"neurotic" anxiety, 198; *see also* anxiety
nonconformity, 101
"normality," concept of, 10–1
Norman, W. T., 139

Ojemann, R. H., 225, 226, 229–30, 240, 242
O'Malley, K. E., 42
Operation Return, 155
opposing (type) pupil personality, 79
Otto, H. J., 256
overachievement, 25, 134–6; *see also* achievement

Packard, V., 291
Page, E. B., 184
paranoia, 8
parents, 24, 99–100, 104, 417
  capabilities of, 383
  communication with, 387–90, 391–8
  conferences with, 382–402
  defensiveness of, 392–4
  domination of, 99, 378, 379
  expressive behavior of, 388
  and pupil achievement, 149–50
  and self-concept of child, 349–51
  submissive, 378–9
  working with, 372–402
parent study groups, 149

Parker, C., 257
Peck, R. F., 380
peers
  information from, 303–4
  and self-concept, development of, 351–4, 365
  and stress, 271–3
  subject's helpfulness to, 365–6
perceptions, pupil
  changes in, 242–3
  unclear, 318
Perkins, H. V., 453
permissiveness, 454
personality
  and achievement, 138–45
  "adequate," 30
  development of, 13
  and grouping policies, 258–9
  integration of, 11
  interaction of, 77–84
  pupil, 79–81, 96–101, 108–10, 342–70
  and remediation, 319–21, 326–7
  and school discipline, 96–101
  teacher, 30–8 passim, 75–84 passim
"personality" as peer norm, 18
personality studies, 30–3, 424
  and teacher behavior, 33–8
Peters, H. J., 386
Philips, B., 206
Phillips, E. L., 453
physical ability, 310
physique and self-attitude, 354–5
Pierce, J. V., 139, 141
pleasure principle, 102
prevention areas, 5, 406
  and aggressive behavior, 123–5
  primary versus secondary, 22n.–23n.
principals and teacher supervision, 55–7
projection, definition of, 209
promotional policies
  and acceleration, 263
  and retention in grade, 260–3
psychiatry, preventive, 406
psychoanalysis, 165, 207, 212, 319
psychologists, school, 427–30
psychopathology, 4
psychosis, 4, 357, 442
psychosomatic illness, 4, 192, 202, 370
punishment, 118–9
pupil orientation, 67, 76
pupils
  achievement of, 131–57 passim
  changes in perceptions of, 242–3
  creativity of, 243–7
  emotions of, 160–92 passim
  fear in, 255–6

pupils (cont.)
  generalities about, 289–91, 322
  home life of, 373–82
  and learning principles, 317–41
  misbehavior of, reasons for, 101–11
  motives of, 16–21, 120–1, 160–92
  needs of, 16–21
  personality types among, 79–81, 96–101
  and self-concept, 342–70
  socioeconomic status of, 77, 88–9, 153, 176–7
  as stereotypes, 288–9
  and teacher personality, 75–7, 111
  see also behavior, pupil; children; teacher-pupil relations
Pupil-Teacher Rapport Scale, 89–90, 459–62

Quiet One, The, 107

Rachman, S., 116, 119
rationalization, 174, 203
  definition of, 209–10
reaction formation, definition of, 210–1
records, school, 306–8
Reed, H. J., 430
Reese, H., 206
referral, 404–5
  appropriate kinds of, 407–13
  needs for, 405–7
  principles for, 413–25
  private resources for, 435–6
  school resources in, 425–35
referral signals
  behavioral, 418–9
  emotional, 420
  intellectual, 420–1
  physical, 419
  social, 419–20
Reger, R., 318
regression, 340
  definition of, 211
reinforcement, social
  and conflict, 197
  consistency of, 374–5
  definition of, 114
  efficacy of, 115–8
  and extinction, 330–2
  immediacy of, 340–1
  kinds of, 337–9
  in learning theory, 111–4
  and motivation, 169–72
  negative, 118–9, 172, 185–7, 330, 333
  positive, 172, 184–5

reinforcement, social *(cont.)*
  and remediation, 318–41 *passim*
  and self-acceptance, 366–7
  verbal, 333–5
remedial instruction, 151–3, 262
remediation, remedial treatment, 314–6
  and assessment, 318–21
  and learning principles, 317–41
  and referrals, 404–36
Replogle, V. L., 54–5
repression, definition of, 211–2
research, 444–6
retention in grade, 260–3
Rich, J. M., 270
Ridenour, Nina, 360n.
Ringness, T. A., 30, 39, 47, 51, 77, 96, 97, 139, 140, 141, 142, 166, 177, 276, 363, 412
Robinson, R., 452
Rogers, Carl R., 13, 41–2, 68, 237, 299, 343, 358–9, 413, 421
role demands, conflicting, 106–7
Romano, L., 386
Roosevelt, Eleanor, 15, 19
Rosen, B. C., 177
Rosenthal, R., 398
Rothney, J. W. M., 398, 399
Rowland, L. W., 43
Russell, I. L., 380
Rust, R. M., 141
Ryan, F. J., 141
Ryans, David, 34–6

St. Vincent de Paul Society, 435
Sarason, I., 265
Sarason, S. B., 206, 207
Scanlon, E., 430
Schaefer, E. S., 381
schizophrenia, 8, 208
schools
  achievement in, 131–57
  advantages of, 23–5
  conditions in, 107–8
  discipline in, 94–128 *passim*
  versus home life, 373–5
  mental-health goals of, 22–3
  mental-health practices of, 453–6
  and mental-health principles, 473–82
  mental-health programs of, 439–51
  mental-health roles of, 22–7
  referral resources of, 425–35
  stress in, 252–82
school tests in child study, 306–10
School to Employment Program, 155

Schramm, W., 236
Schubert, D. G., 25
science as subject, 238
Sears, P. S., 174, 177
secondary-level teaching, 37, 231–2
security, 141–3
self-acceptance, 346
  improvement of, 364–9
self-actualization, 11, 47, 63, 114, 245
  in group activity, 248
  and student needs, 19–21
self-attitudes, 337
  and achievement, 355–6
  causing changes in, 358–69
  and success and failure, 354–5
self-concept, 344–5, 369–70
  assessment of, 346–9
  and changing the self-attitude, 358–69
  development of, 349–56
  dimensions of, 345–6
  realism of, 346, 358
  stability of, 346
self-control, 126–7
self-controlled teacher, 78, 79, 80
self-esteem, 141–3, 208, 348–70
self-fulfilling prophecy, 24
self-report information, 304–6
self-restraint, 124–5
self theory, 212, 319–20, 342–70
self-understanding, 362–4
sex role, 381–2
  and stress, 273–5
Shaffer, G. W., 22
Shaffer, L. F., 270
Shaw, M. C., 142, 146
Shibler, H. L., 447
Shipley, J. T., 42–3
Shoben, E. J., 270
Sixteen PF (Personality Factor) test, 36–7
Skinner, B. F., 68, 126–7, 215, 320, 327
Slack, C. W., 338
Smith, M. Brewster, 11, 12
Smith, W., 355
Smitter, F. C., 269, 413
Snider, B. C. F., 242
Snygg, D., 15, 19, 343, 349
social class and stress, 267–71
socialization, pupil, 101–6
  and achievement, 140–1
  and conditioning, 114–20 *passim*
social sciences, 229–30
  secondary-level, 231–2
social workers, school, 432–3
Society for Brain Injured Children, 435

socioeconomic status (SES), 77, 88–9, 153
   and achievement, 176–7
   and stress, 267–71
sociopaths, 355
special classes, 259–60
"special rooms," 409
Spence, K. W., 205
Spinoza, B., 19
Staats, A. W., 20n., 320, 321–2, 324
Staats, C. K., 20n., 320
"staffing," 433–4
Stagner, R., 41
Stanley, J. C., 264
Steadman, E. R., 262
Stefflre, B., 430
stereotypes, 288–9
Stern, H. G., 151
Stiles, F. S., 225
stimulus-response, 111–4, 189–90, 322
Stirling, N., 248
Stratemeyer, F. B., 50
stress, psychological
   ability to handle, 277–82
   and academic pressure, 275–7
   and curricular conditions, 254–67
   and peer-group acceptance, 271–3
   and sex role, 273–5
   and social classes, 267–71
   sources of, 252–82 passim
stress tolerance, 277–82 passim
striving pupil personality, 79
students, see pupils
student-teachers
   and classroom interaction, 63–6
   vocational attitudes of, 47–9
study skills, 151–2
stuttering, 205
sublimation, definition of, 210
success and self-attitude, 354
"successive approximation," 327
superstitious ritual, 203
suppression, 211
surface approach, 240–1
   and individual child, 287–8
symbolic activity, 333–5
Symonds, P. M., 46–7, 377, 379
Szasz, Thomas, 8–9, 413–4

tasks, school, 181–3
Taxonomy of Educational Objectives, 261
Taylor, R. G., 139, 141, 142
teacher leadership
   and classroom morale, 63–91

teacher leadership (cont.)
   dimensions of, 81–2, 465–70
   poor, 87–8
   style of, 67–74
teacher-parent relations, 372–402
teacher-pupil relations
   as child-leader relationship, 71–3
   and classroom control, 111
   communication in, 39–42
   and congruence, 359
   personality interaction in, 77–84
   and teacher personality, 75–7, 178–81
teacher roles, 26–7
teachers
   in child study, capability of, 297–9
   congruence of, 359
   diagnosis by, 406–7, 418–25
   elementary, 37
   and individual child, 285–316
   mental health of, 38–60 passim
   as models, 40
   motivational orientations of, 36, 48–9
   and personality studies, 30–8 passim, 75–84 passim, 111–2
   personal life of, 58–60
   as persons, 29–60
   professional aid requested by, 54–5
   professionality of, 34
   pupil-centered, 67–8
   referrals by, 421–5
   secondary, 37
   selection and training of, 50–3
   and "struggle for power," 109, 111
   supervision of, 55–7
   working conditions of, 57–8
teaching
   as career, attitudes toward, 47–9
   causal verses surface approach to, 240–2
   "democratic," 67–71
   functional, 226–9
   method of, and mental health, 222–49 passim
teaching behavior
   "authoritarian" versus "democratic," 68–71
   authority dimension of, 81, 467–8
   expressive, 40–2, 81–2, 468–70
   mental health and, 38–42
   task dimension of, 81, 465–6
   and understanding of others, 38–9
Teahan, J., 143
terminology, 7–11
test anxiety, 198, 264–5, 282
Test Anxiety Scale for Children, 265
testing conditions, 264

tests, school
  in child study, 306–10, 424
  evaluative, 263–5
  norms of, 308
Thematic Apperception Test, 30–2
therapy and early diagnosis, 406–7
Thomas, H., 357
Thompson, G. G., 98
Thompson, M. L., 51
Thorndike, R. L., 132, 143
Thurston, J. R., 104
Todd, F. J., 141
Topp, R. F., 46
Torgeson, T. L., 261
Torrance, E. P., 243–4, 246
Torrance, P., 380
Tracy, John, Clinic of Los Angeles, 409
treatment centers, residential, 405, 406–
  7
turbulent teacher personality, 78, 79

Ullman, C. A., 299, 413, 422–3
underachievement, 25, 136–8
  dealing with, 145–57
  teacher's attitude toward, 156–7
  see also achievement
undoing, definition of, 210

Valett, R. E., 427
values, value systems, 338
  of American society, 455
  lower-class, 269
  middle-class, 268
  peer, 173, 352

Vance, F. L., 291
vandalism, 94
Vanishing Adolescent, The, 121
verbal ability, 154, 205
"vocational" courses, 154

Walden Two, 68, 126
Wallen, N. E., 75–6, 77
Walsh, A. M., 142
Walters, B. C., 381
Walters, R. H., 103, 111, 116, 186
Warner, W. L., 270
wavering pupil personality, 79
Wegrocki, H. J., 10
White, Ralph K., 71n., 82
White, R. W., 349
Whiteside, G., 206
Whiting, J. W. M., 381
Wickman, E. K., 297–8, 420
Wilhelms, F. T., 50
Wilson, R., 143
Wirt, R., 206
WISC intelligence test, 147
Withall, J., 90
Wodtke, K. H., 75–6, 77
Wolpe, J., 320, 429–30
Worcester, D. A., 33
Wrightstone, J. W., 89, 459n.
Wylie, R. C., 345–6, 350, 356, 357

Yates, A. J., 429

Zelen, S. L., 225